SHAKESPEARE SURVEY

ADVISORY BOARD

SHAKESPEARE SURVEY

AN ANNUAL SURVEY OF

SHAKESPEARE STUDIES AND PRODUCTION

44

EDITED BY

STANLEY WELLS

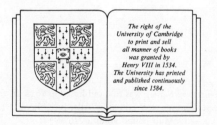

The right of the
University of Cambridge
to print and sell
all manner of books
was granted by
Henry VIII in 1534.
The University has printed
and published continuously
since 1584.

CAMBRIDGE UNIVERSITY PRESS

CAMBRIDGE

NEW YORK   PORT CHESTER   MELBOURNE   SYDNEY

Published by the Press Syndicate of the University of Cambridge
The Pitt Building, Trumpington Street, Cambridge CB2 1RP
40 West 20th Street, New York, NY 10011, USA
10 Stamford Road, Oakleigh, Melbourne 3166, Australia

© Cambridge University Press 1992

First published 1992

Printed in Great Britain at the University Press, Cambridge

A cataloguing in publication record for this book is available from the British Library

Library of Congress catalogue card number: 49–1639

ISBN 0 521 41356 7 hardback

Shakespeare Survey was first published in 1948. Its first
eighteen volumes were edited by Allardyce Nicoll. Kenneth
Muir edited volumes 19 to 33.

CE

EDITOR'S NOTE

Volume 45 of *Shakespeare Survey*, which will be at press by the time this volume appears, will focus on '*Hamlet* and its Afterlife'. Volume 46 will have as its theme 'Shakespeare and Sexuality', and will include papers from the 1991 International Shakespeare Conference. Volume 47 will concentrate on 'Playing Places for Shakespeare'.

Submissions should be addressed to the Editor at The Shakespeare Institute, Church Street, Stratford-upon-Avon, Warwickshire CV37 6HP, to arrive at the latest by 1 September 1992 for Volume 46. Pressures on space are heavy; many articles are considered before the deadline, so those that arrive earlier stand a better chance of acceptance. Please either enclose return postage (overseas, in International Reply coupons) or send a copy you do not wish to have returned. A style sheet is available on request. All articles submitted are read by the Editor and at least one member of the Editorial Board, whose indispensable assistance the Editor gratefully acknowledges.

Unless otherwise indicated, Shakespeare quotations and references are keyed to the modern-spelling Complete Oxford Shakespeare (1986).

In attempting to survey the ever-increasing bulk of Shakespeare publications our reviewers inevitably have to exercise some selection. Review copies of books should be addressed to the Editor, as above. We are pleased to receive offprints of articles which help to draw our reviewers' attention to relevant material.

Richard Hillman's university was, regrettably, misidentified in the List of Contributors in *Shakespeare Survey 43*; he teaches at York University, North York, Ontario, Canada.

S.W.W.

CONTRIBUTORS

CATHERINE BELSEY, *University of Wales College of Cardiff*
PHILIPPA BERRY, *King's College, Cambridge*
JOHN RUSSELL BROWN, *University of Michigan*
WILLIAM C. CARROLL, *Boston University*
JOHN DRAKAKIS, *University of Stirling*
RICHARD DUTTON, *Lancaster University*
BALZ ENGLER, *University of Basel*
DOMINIQUE GOY-BLANQUET, *University of Amiens*
MARGOT HEINEMANN, *New Hall, Cambridge*
PETER HOLLAND, *Trinity Hall, Cambridge*
T. H. HOWARD-HILL, *University of South Carolina*
ROSLYN L. KNUTSON, *University of Arkansas at Little Rock*
TOM MCALINDON, *University of Hull*
MAURICE POPE, *Oxford*
NIKY RATHBONE, *Birmingham Shakespeare Library*
PIERRE SAHEL, *University of Aix-en-Provence*
R. S. WHITE, *University of Western Australia*
BLAIR WORDEN, *St Edmund Hall, Oxford*
H. R. WOUDHUYSEN, *University College, London*

CONTENTS

ILLUSTRATIONS

SHAKESPEARE AND POLITICS

BLAIR WORDEN

I

There has not been an age so sympathetic as the present to the study of the political content and the political context of Shakespeare's plays. Politics are now everywhere in literary criticism. In Shakespeare's time men followed Aristotle and applied the language of what we regard as private ethics to the conduct of public life: today's critics, when they give currency to a term such as 'sexual politics', extend the language of public life to private ethics. Even if we restrict ourselves, as I shall, to a more traditional definition of politics, we notice the transformation of critical approaches that the past half century has brought. Who would now doubt that the behaviour of men in public life was a theme to engage Shakespeare's interest, and to stretch his powers, to the full? Who would assume, as John Palmer did in his *Political Characters of Shakespeare* in 1945, that Shakespeare was 'forced' by the public demand for history plays to 'take the political field' (p. vi)?

On the face of it, the new political awareness ought to add to our understanding of Shakespeare. In the sixteenth and seventeenth centuries the relationship between literature and politics had an intimacy which the modern world has lost. Writers and politicians were so often the same people. The interaction of political and literary aspirations in the career of a Sir Thomas More or a Sir Thomas Wyatt or a Sir Philip Sidney, or of a John Milton or an

Andrew Marvell, is so insistent that we cannot hope to understand the one without the other. Our appreciation of major writings of the sixteenth and seventeenth centuries – of *Utopia*, of *Arcadia*, of *The Faerie Queene*, of *Samson Agonistes* – can be profoundly enhanced by a knowledge of the political circumstances in which they were written. Why, then, is the same not true of Shakespeare's plays? A knowledge of Renaissance politics can, as I hope to intimate, illustrate themes of those plays. But it will not take us to their heart.

Of course, we would not expect to be able to relate Shakespeare's writings, as we can the writings of More or Sidney or Milton, to their author's life, for the obvious reason that so little about Shakespeare's life is known – or, at any rate, so little that illuminates his character. Sometimes evidence of his biography is detected in his writings, a method which can sometimes be fruitfully applied to other writers, but to which Shakespeare's resistance is quickly evident. I have heard it said by eminent scholars that only a man who had fought in a war could have written *Henry V*; that only a huntsman could have written Theseus' description of his hounds; that only someone with personal experience of the court could have composed the precepts delivered by Polonius to Laertes that so resemble the recorded maxims of Lord Burghley. The former cabinet minister Mr Enoch Powell, speaking in a television programme on the authorship of the plays, was certain that they are the creation of a man who, like himself, has been at the centre of power. Even Shakespeare's childhood can be re-created on the same principle. Caroline Spurgeon, in one of a series of such discoveries, assures us that Shakespeare 'was clearly, in boyhood at any rate, a keen and strong swimmer, and had probably, with schoolfellows, often plunged and buffeted in the angry waters of the Avon, as did Cassius once with Caesar in the Tiber'.[1] If we were to credit Shakespeare's life with every experience into which his imagination finds an entry we would soon establish for him a career far too active and varied to have left time for the composition of plays – unless perhaps he wrote them at night, during those protracted periods of insomnia that are doubtless re-created in the nocturnal musings of his troubled kings. The relationship between an artist's biography and his writing is always a difficult subject, but there can be no other important writer since the invention of printing for whom we are unable to demonstrate any relationship at all.

Alone of the major artists of the Renaissance, Shakespeare has no tangible personality outside his art. How striking is the contrast between the vividness and sharpness of his stage characterizations and the pale elusiveness of the author of the Sonnets! None of his contemporaries left behind a strong impression of him. Unable to verify a personality for Shakespeare, we can each envisage our own. Mine is that of an actor, whose infirm identity, at any moment of writing as of performing, merges with that of the character he is creating. His heroes – Antipholus of Syracuse, wandering the world in search of his other half; Prince Hal, ceasing (but does he?) 'to be himself' in the tavern; Hamlet, putting (but does he?) an antic disposition on – can have as much problem with their identities as their creator has with his own. Politics, like all the world, is a stage: the stage on which Richard II and Richard III and Marcus Brutus and Coriolanus test the political possibilities of playacting, and on which they lose or forget their parts. If Shakespeare ever settles upon a view of the world, if he ever achieves the sense of wisdom that his audiences carry away from the plays, it is only within the successive confines of his creations.

Whether or not that speculative characterization of him is correct, our ignorance of the man is one of the many considerations to invite caution in the assessment of the political perspectives of his writing. His beliefs and opinions, no less than his *curriculum vitae*, have been located in the plays. E. M. W. Tillyard tracked down 'Shakespeare's political opinions',[2] and Tillyard's successors – sometimes even his critics – have located Shakespeare's 'political position' or 'views'.[3] Yet all we have on the page are speeches which conform to the characterizations of their speakers. It is hard enough to know how far Ulysses speaking on 'degree', or Henry V's Archbishop of Canterbury on the commonwealth of bees, believes in the vision he articulates, let alone to identify the playright's own 'position'. The essence of drama being conflict, it is not surprising that his characters' opinions often contradict each other. Hamlet, and Kent and Gloucester in *King Lear*, propose that men's destinies are ruled by the heavens: Edmund, Cassius and Helena declare that belief to be self-deceptive.[4] Or what are Shakespeare's 'views' on suicide? Brutus and Cassius kill themselves to defy tyranny, but Macbeth declines 'to play the Roman fool', while Hamlet and Imogen think 'self-slaughter' to be forbidden.[5]

---

[1] *Shakespeare's Imagery* (Cambridge, 1939), p. 99.

[2] *Shakespeare's History Plays* (London, 1944, repr. 1962), p. 227.

[3] John Danby, *Shakespeare's Doctrine of Nature* (London, 1949), pp. 77, 79; Irving Ribner, 'The Political Problem in Shakespeare's Lancastrian Tetralogy', *Studies in Philology*, 49 (1952), 171, 179; David Bevington, *Tudor Drama and Politics* (Cambridge, Mass., 1968), pp. 245, 248; H. A. Kelly, *Divine Providence in the England of Shakespeare's Histories* (Cambridge, Mass., 1970), p. 214; C. C. Huffman, *Coriolanus in Context* (Cranbury, New Jersey, 1971), p. 65; R. H. Wells, *Shakespeare, Politics and the State* (London, 1986), p. 100.

[4] *Hamlet* 5.2.10–11; *Lear* Q 2.113–16, 15.35, 16.34–5; *Caesar* 1.2.141–2; *All's Well* 1.1.212–13.

[5] *Macbeth* 5.10.1–2; *Hamlet* 1.2.132; *Cymbeline* 3.4.76.

Tillyard regarded Shakespeare, sympathetically, as a representative of the political orthodoxy of his age. Although that judgement still occasionally resurfaces, in a form less sympathetic to the orthodoxy and in a less lucid vocabulary, a number of scholars have rejected or refined it. Yet Tillyard's answers have been challenged more often than his questions. There are two principal elements in his thesis and in its legacy. First there is the supposition that Shakespeare wrote against rebellion and in favour of unhesitating obedience to God's anointed rulers. It is true that Shakespeare's kings invoke that principle – the usurpers King John and Richard III among them.[6] But then they would, wouldn't they? The pronouncements of Shakespeare's kings on the subject of rebellion are not to be depended on. Claudius, who has murdered royalty, and Richard II, who knows the sad stories of the death of kings, none the less announce – what may comfort them, and what may be useful for monarchs to have their subjects believe[7] – that kings are untouchable. They learn better – Richard after discovering that kings must do 'what force will have us do', and after dust has been thrown on his 'anointed head'.[8] Like kings, their loyal subjects need not be taken at their word. In *Richard II*, first John of Gaunt and then the Duke of York stand on the principles of submission and resignation and obedience.[9] If their view is sympathetically presented, so is its opposite. What Gaunt calls 'patience' his sister-in-law labels 'cold cowardice'.[10] History brushes Gaunt and York aside.

Tillyard and others have taught us much about what Tudor Englishmen were told to think of rebellion, but we know less about what they did think. In *Richard II* the Earl of Northumberland hints at a public opinion different from the one Tillyard leads us to expect: if Richard will 'confess' his crimes 'the souls of men / May deem that you are worthily deposed' (4.1.216–17). In *Richard III*, at Bosworth, Richmond vindicates his rebellion, with a boldness worthy of a Huguenot resistance theorist, by appealing to the legitimacy of tyrannicide, a daringly unorthodox principle that is given more prominence in Shakespeare's version of the speech than in Hall's, from which he takes it.[11] In the Henry VI plays there is little about the impiety of rebellion, and much more about the validity of the Yorkist claim. A Tudor spokesman would have explained that, although Henry IV had sinned in usurping the crown, Englishmen were obliged to obey him and his successors. Yet Shakespeare's Henry VI concedes that 'my title's weak' (*3 Henry VI* 1.1.135); the Earl of Exeter's 'conscience' prompts him to agree (1.1.151); the lawyers take the same view (*1 Henry VI* 2.4.39–58); and the Lancastrians depend for their support on thugs like the Duke of Suffolk, who regards the 'law' as subordinate to his 'will' (*1 Henry VI* 2.4.7–9), and Lord Clifford, who, as he tells Henry, will back him 'be thy title right or wrong' (*3 Henry VI* 1.1.160–1).

It is true that 'rebellion' is always a pejorative term in Shakespeare, as it was always in Tudor England. By the 1590s, when noblemen and gentlemen had ceased to offer leadership to popular discontent, the word had become associated, as the Earl of Westmoreland in the Forest of Gaultres associates it, with 'base and abject routs' (*2 Henry IV* 4.1.32–3), an argument which Westmoreland prefers, in his reproof of the rebel leaders, to the charge that rebellion is sinful. But who decided who the rebels were? No Tudor rebels thought of themselves as rebels. 'He calls us "rebels"', complains the Earl of Worcester of Henry IV (*1 Henry IV* 5.2.39). At the battle of Shrewsbury, in Morton's account of it, 'the word "rebellion"' 'froze up' the Percies' soldiers 'As fish are in a

---

6 *King John* 3.1.73–4; *Richard III* 4.4.150–1.
7 *The Winter's Tale* 1.2.357–62.
8 *Hamlet* 4.5.122–4; *Richard II* 3.2.53 (but cf. 3.3.78–80), 3.4.205, 5.2.30.
9 2.1.164–71, 2.2.78–9, 2.3.108, 5.2.37–8.
10 1.2.37–8; cf. *2 Henry VI* 2.4.27–69.
11 5.5.193–210. Passages of Hall and Holinshed quoted or cited in this essay can be found in the appendixes to the Arden editions of the plays under discussion.

3

pond.' Yet they gain fresh heart from the Archbishop of York, who 'Turns insurrection to religion' and 'Derives from heaven his quarrel and his cause' (*2 Henry IV* 1.2.197–205). The archbishop's case is unimpressive: his vindication of the uprising uses metaphor not to illustrate an argument but as a substitute for one, and – not alone among Shakespeare's conspirators – he tacks an appeal to the common good on to statements of sectional grievance that seem more keenly felt (4.1.53–94). Yet it would be a confident critic who asserted that Shakespeare's sympathies lie with the archbishop's enemies in Gaultres, the Machiavellian Westmoreland and Prince John – or indeed who claimed to discern any consistent relationship in Shakespeare between the legitimacy or illegitimacy of a cause and the virtues or vices of its champions.

The second principal element in Tillyard's thesis, which has likewise lost authority yet retained influence, is the contention that the English history plays witness a pattern of providential retribution for the usurpation of Bolingbroke. (Perhaps we should rather say, retribution for the murder of Richard that follows and secures it. Bolingbroke expresses no unease about deposing Richard. Like Macbeth and like Claudius he becomes a study in the psychological consequences of committing a murder, not of seizing a throne.) At the conclusion of the histories, the Chorus of *Henry V* proposes no unifying providential theme. Instead, looking back to the Henry VI plays, the Chorus observes that 'so many had the managing' of Henry VI's 'state' that 'they lost France and made his England bleed'. There is nothing in the earlier plays to question the sufficiency of that secular diagnosis (even though critics find a larger element of providentialism in the first tetralogy than in the second). Early in *Henry VI Part 1* the English soldiers in France blame their 'want of men and money' on the English nobles, who 'maintain several factions' (1.1.69–71), the failing which explains the 'negligent and heedless discipline' that fatally prevents relief from reaching Talbot (4.1.187–94, 4.2.44). The other military disasters of the play are attributed by the characters to the cowardice of Falstaff and to the superior cunning of the French.

Sometimes critics invite us to take Joan la Pucelle's estimate of herself in *Henry VI Part 1* as the 'scourge' of England (1.3.108) to be an authoritative allusion to the Christian scheme of retribution; or to see the civil wars of the first tetralogy as divine punishments for the marriages of Henry VI and of Edward IV; or to suppose that the secular causes apparently at work in the Henry VI plays are to be seen, in accordance with the conventional Christian understanding of providence, as secondary to a divine cause. There is no textual foundation for those suggestions. We do not need to invoke providence to understand what happens to England from 1399 to 1485: to see why a usurpation diminishes the awe on which majesty depends, or why the disputed succession which it produces is a recipe for instability. We do not need providence to explain why a monarchy that has been thus undermined should break down under Henry VI, who inherits the throne as a child; who in adulthood abandons the responsibilities of kingship and retreats into his 'ease';[12] who loses foreign conquests in which his rivals have a stake; and who is duped into a politically foolish marriage.

Of course, the Henry VI plays are full of prophecies and auguries and curses. Yet we would be no more entitled to claim that Shakespeare believed in the supernatural apparatus of the early histories than to infer from *Macbeth* that he believed in witchcraft or from *Romeo and Juliet* that he believed the lovers to be star-crossed. Whether or not the history plays are tragedies, they have the elemental dimension of tragedy. First and foremost they are plays, where history is organized, and reorganized, to accommodate the imagination of a writer who reinvents the universe with every

---

[12] *2 Henry VI* 1.3.104–5, 3.1.195–6; *3 Henry VI* 4.7.52.

play, or at least with every sequence of plays, that he begins. Within a play – whether a history or a tragedy – he will build a self-sufficient cosmology that supplies a scale of time and history, or gives dimensions to order and chaos, or indicates the size or frailty of human aspiration, or summons hidden springs of hope and fear. The one history play that lacks a cosmology, *King John*, perhaps proves a rule, for it is also the play where (whether or not by design) the balances of sympathy are confusing: nowhere more so than in the exposure by the Pope's representative Cardinal Pandolf – of all people – of the English people's proneness to superstitious explanation of natural phenomena (3.4.149–52, 4.2.143–6).

If the doctrine of providence held a political sanction in Tudor England it was as a Christian doctrine (even though its exponents could usually accommodate pagan or semi-pagan ideas of fortune within it). Yet the cosmology of the history plays is not predominantly Christian. In the Henry VI trilogy it is predominantly astrological. The 'planets of mishap' govern the 'heavens' (not heaven).[13] Christian doctrine has, too, a smaller place in the trilogy than has classical mythology. It is true that in the two plays that conclude the tetralogies, *Richard III* and *Henry V*, we do find a Christian cosmology. *Richard III* takes us into a late medieval world of beads and rosaries and images and sanctuaries and of oaths sworn over sacraments: a world too where broken men and women lament the judgement of a Christian God upon their land or yearn for 'All-seeing heaven' (2.1.83) to exact retribution upon their enemies. It is a world which Richard expertly manipulates and profanes, clothing 'my naked villainy / With odd old ends, stol'n forth of Holy Writ', seeming 'a saint when most I play the devil' (1.3.344–6), declaring that 'God will revenge' the murder of Clarence (2.1.40), and 'meditating with two deep divines' (3.7.75). The Christian *motifs* summon the play's themes of vulnerability and violation, but need be no closer to any religious convictions Shakespeare

may have had than the astrological framework of the Henry VI plays. Henry V, whose Christianity is unmistakable, and who takes the idea of divine retribution so seriously, fears it not only for 'the fault / My father made in compassing the crown' (4.1.290–1) but for the sinfulness of his troops, and stipulates the death penalty for soldiers who 'take that praise from God / Which is his only' (4.8.106–16). Even Oliver Cromwell, who shared Henry's premises, did not go so far. But nowhere else did Shakespeare go so far either.

II

When Shakespeare's characters contradict each other we notice how rarely or how little the feelings with which we respond to his plays depend upon our taking sides. Yet his characters do not always contradict each other. Some political positions are left unchallenged. They are the conventional positions of Shakespeare's time. Whether they correspond to assumptions consciously or unconsciously held by him, or whether he merely enters into them in order to forge a bond with his audiences, is anyone's guess. Yet it is as well to acknowledge them, for they are the material on which the view of Shakespeare as an expounder of orthodoxy or conservatism must draw. In the history plays, which are written in wartime, love of England and love of victory generally seem desirable. Rich and powerful Catholic churchmen are undesirable or even despicable, Puritans – or characters with Puritan characteristics – no less so: the texts invite not an ounce of sympathy for the beliefs or behaviour of Cardinal Beaufort, or for those of Angelo or Malvolio. There is a horror of demos – of the lynch mob in *Julius Caesar* – and there is a tendency to represent the lower orders as figures of fear or fun or else of unmodulated fidelity. Even in *Coriolanus*, where the citizens are for once given

---

[13] *1 Henry VI* 1.1.1–5, 23, 54; 1.2.1; 1.3.123; 1.6.76; 1.7.9; 2.1.48.

distinctive voices, they are not given names; and after Agincourt, and at the outset of *Much Ado About Nothing*, the good news is brought that none 'of name' are slain.[14]

Some modern critics are indignant to discover that Shakespeare's plays do not seem to be the work of a democrat. Alternatively they uncover democratic aspirations hidden by the allegedly repressive conditions of censorship. It would be as surprising to find a Renaissance playwright hoping for democracy as it would be to find a modern playwright arguing against it. It would be no less surprising to find a Renaissance playwright questioning the institution of monarchy. In Shakespeare's England there was admiration for classical (and aristocratic) republican virtue, but no suggestion that England could or should become a republic. The rebels in Shakespeare's English history plays want not to abolish kingship but either to usurp it or to restore it to the health they believe it to have enjoyed under Edward III or Henry V. While the inconveniences of monarchy that had long been recognized are amply represented in Shakespeare – its tendency to degenerate into tyranny or to break down into the alternative evil of anarchy; the risk of succession disputes and of the rule of minors – its virtues are amply represented too. Kingship has, or should have, a unitive force. When it works well, as in *Henry V*, the nobles are patriotic and unselfish, and the people follow them. When it works badly, as under Henry VI, the nobles are selfish and quarrelsome and infect the commons with their bad example. Folly below corresponds to folly above – as in *Henry VI Part 2*, when the fraud of Saunder Simcox and the fraud of the Duchess of Gloucester are juxtaposed (2.1).

Challenges to the rule of a single person produce selfishness and fragmentation. The rebels in *Henry IV Part 1* squabble, each for 'my' land, as they carve up the map of England (3.1); the conspirators of *Julius Caesar* fall apart; so do the triumvirates that succeed to Caesar's rule. In the representations of Richmond in *Henry VI Part 3* and in *Richard III*, and in the prophecy of Cranmer in *Henry VIII*, Shakespeare solemnizes the Tudor achievement of unity and peace. Is it the distance between the political preconceptions of our time and those of Shakespeare's, or is it some difficulty or embarrassment on Shakespeare's part, that can make those passages seem the sore thumbs of the history plays? Nothing in late Renaissance politics is harder for us to enter – though the theme is widespread in the literature of the period and is the starting-point of the masque – than the idealization of kingship and the longing for a monarch to be a fairy-tale prince. Even in the middle of the seventeenth century, when the collapse of monarchy created the conditions for republicanism, republicans – Milton among them – yearned for an Aristotelian king, who would rule by virtue of divinely appointed merit.[15]

If Shakespeare's age could be kingstruck, it could also, it is true, be more sceptical. He writes when the political realism associated with Tacitus and Machiavelli is making a novel and profound impact on imaginative literature; and the political realism of his plays – whether or not he has read Tacitus or Machiavelli – could surely not have been achieved in an earlier age. Yet his writing shows none of the self-conscious and risky preoccupation with the new politics and the new history to be found in Jonson or Chapman or Daniel. The language of public liberty, so widespread in the plays of his contemporaries, rarely appears in his English history plays and looks like dangerous self-delusion in his Roman ones.[16] He writes *Richard II*, not *Woodstock*. It seems possible that, like his choruses, he wished not to offend.

Yet how little the conventional framework of the plays tells us, and how little it matters! If

---

[14] *Henry V* 4.8.105; *Much Ado* 1.1.7.

[15] B. Worden, 'Milton's Republicanism and the Tyranny of Heaven', in G. Bock, Q. Skinner and M. Viroli, eds., *Machiavelli and Republicanism* (Cambridge, 1991), p. 229.

[16] *Caesar* 3.1.77–80, 110–19; cf. *2 Henry VI* 4.2.182.

Shakespeare can communicate the majesty of power, there is nothing he does not know about the emptiness or the duplicity of 'man, proud man, / Dressed in a little brief authority'. His kings remind us that 'a dog's obeyed in office', that the crown is hollow, that 'ceremony' is an 'idol'.[17] In Shakespeare, as in life, virtue mingles insensibly with *realpolitik*. Henry V is an ideal king, who conquers France with an ideal nobility: he is also the king who has been advised to 'busy giddy minds / With foreign quarrels' (*2 Henry IV* 4.3.342–3); who strikes a murky deal with the Church; and whose triumphs bring plunder and devastation in their wake. Critics wonder which is the true Henry, the hero or the politician. Both are.

Shakespeare's history plays might alternatively be called war plays, for it is in war that man's character is fully extended. He writes no play about the peaceful passages of medieval history. (There is the peacetime play *Henry VIII*, but that, as we shall see, is another exception to prove a rule.) In writing about Rome he would have been cramped by the peaceful tyranny of the period of the emperor Tiberius, to which Jonson, in *Sejanus his Fall*, brought the most *avant-garde* techniques of political analysis. Shakespeare gives little time to the machinery of politics or the workings of constitutions. His interest is in the psychological rather than the institutional basis of politics. Perhaps there is a danger here for modern interpreters, who write in a century which has been preoccupied with psychology and devastated by ideologies. We instinctively think less well of a statement of political principle – as Shakespeare may not have done – when we believe we detect its psychological roots, a habit which may equip us, for example, to comprehend the flaws of Marcus Brutus better than his nobility. Yet whatever our response to Brutus's decision to assassinate Caesar we cannot derive it from a like or dislike of his constitutional programme, for there is no evidence that he has one.

It may be a mistake even to ask whether Brutus is justified in killing Caesar. Shake-speare's instincts are always descriptive, never prescriptive. He provides maps of political conduct, not tests of political theory. The political views – the conflicting political views – of his characters are instructive in a way parallel to that in which their conflicting interpretations of their dreams are instructive. They illustrate the interaction of belief and conduct, and show us how political doctrine is adhered to or abandoned or manipulated, but they do not tell us who is right. When Richard II has lost his power, but not yet his throne, the Earl of Northumberland forgets the reverence owed to a king and omits 'To say "King Richard"' (3.3.7–8). Yet once Bolingbroke is installed, the Earl wishes all happiness to the usurper's 'sacred state' (5.6.6) – a sentiment he subsequently learns to forget, when Henry has banished him from court. Northumberland's record reveals much about his character, and much about the suppleness of political theory before facts of power, but nothing about the legitimacy or illegitimacy of Richard's overthrow.

Shakespeare dwells not on the justice of men's causes but on their perceptions of it. In the opening scene of *Richard II* he shows us two rivals, Mowbray and Hereford, passionately convinced of the truth of the competing versions of past events they give, and offers no indication which version (if either) is correct. The pinning down of political or historical explanation is, in any case, not one of Shakespeare's habits. He prefers the formula, favoured too by his chronicle sources, that gives his audience's imagination the space to roam among differing explanations of events: 'whether 'twas . . . or whether 'twas . . .' (e.g. *3 Henry VI* 2.1.122–8). The plays are full of such openness – and, of course, of historical and biographical imprecision. There is no more beautifully drawn a politician in literature than Polonius. Yet to ask the most elementary question about his political past – whether he had

---

[17] *Measure* 2.2.120–1; *Lear* Q20.152–3; *Henry V* 4.1.237.

served King Hamlet, or has been brought in by Claudius – is to ask in vain.

If Shakespeare's history is imprecise, it is none the less more penetrating than that of his more up-to-date contemporaries: more penetrating for example than that of Ben Jonson, whose historical plays are much more faithful than Shakespeare's to the historical record. The intimate links between the writing of history and the writing of drama in Shakespeare's time, illustrated in the career of Jonson or Daniel or Greville, remind us how far historical insight rested (as perhaps it ought always to do) on a historian's doing what a dramatist does: ask himself how a given character would have thought and acted in a given situation. In that method Shakespeare had no rivals. Has justice ever been done to the power of his historical imagination, or to the interlinear penetration that he brings to his reading of Holinshed and Hall and North?

Consider his Roman plays. Some bold and stimulating claims have been made, it is true, for Shakespeare as a historian of Rome. There is the proposal that the contrast between the austere imagery of *Coriolanus* and the bucolic world of *Antony and Cleopatra* shows Shakespeare to have been alive to the evolution of Rome from a primitive to a sophisticated or corrupted society.[18] There is the thesis that he realized from Livy that Coriolanus' sentiments had outlived their time.[19] Perhaps those arguments are too bold. It is not clear that Shakespeare, or anyone else in his time, had a sharp sense of historical evolution. It is not clear either that he had the interest in the constitutional arrangements of republican Rome with which he has been credited.[20] The scene (3.1) where Coriolanus speaks for his class – for 'we' – against the power of the tribunes draws on a main theme of Shakespeare's sources, but goes against the grain of Shakespeare's characterization, which, by emphasizing the hero's idiosyncrasy and solitariness, reduces the playwright's scope for the sort of political analysis that had engaged Livy, and substitutes psycho-

logical for constitutional perception. Yet if Shakespeare is not a Livian or a Machiavellian commentator on Rome, there is no mistaking his gift for capturing, from the merest hints in his sources, the textures and the sentiments of the societies he re-creates on the stage. What a profundity of insight into the conflict between republican and imperial values is encapsulated, and what a volume of political commentary made redundant, by Julius Caesar's 'Let me have men about me that are fat' (*Caesar* 1.2.193). No doubt, in bringing Rome alive, Shakespeare creates as well as re-creates. Yet his Rome is, at the least, as persuasive a feat of historical recovery as any accomplished by the historians of his time.

The achievement is reflected in the differences between the language of Shakespeare's Romans and that of his Englishmen. His Romans hail 'liberty', which they applaud (as most of Shakespeare's contemporaries did not) as an abstract ideal: his Englishmen instead address questions of resistance and obedience and divine right which exercised Tudor England much more than they had Rome and which are not raised in Shakespeare's Roman plays, even in connection with the assassination of Caesar. There is a more profound perception too. Shakespeare's Romans exclude private from public life: his Englishmen mingle the two. In England, 'love' is both a public and a private word. It belongs both to the masculine loyalties of politics and to private happiness between the sexes. In Rome the word belongs to the public world but is barred from the private one. It has no place in Volumnia's despairing imprecations to Coriolanus at the climax of the play, or in the speech with which he yields to them. In *Julius Caesar* the 'vows of

---

18 P. A. Cantor, *Shakespeare's Rome* (Ithaca and London, 1976); Vivian Thomas, *Shakespeare's Roman Worlds* (London, 1989), pp. 1–2.

19 Anne Barton, 'Livy, Machiavelli and Shakespeare's *Coriolanus*', *Shakespeare Survey 38* (1985).

20 Huffman, *Coriolanus in Context*.

love' which Marcus Brutus once gave to Portia sound to have been formal pledges (2.1.271). At all events a man who is so free with the word 'love' in public life does not use it when protesting his present devotion to her. Instead he calls her, with a word taken from public life, his 'honourable' wife (2.1.287); it is, after all, 'the name of honour' that Brutus 'love[s]' (1.2.90–1). Yet when we turn from Portia's despair at Brutus's broken sleep, and at her own exclusion from her husband's thoughts, to the identical problem troubling Hotspur's wife Kate in *Henry IV Part 1*, we find the English couple able to tease each other about their love (2.4). Or we may compare the tribute of Messala who has brought news of Portia's death to the impassive Brutus – 'Even so great men great losses should endure' (4.2.245) – with the response to the slaughter of his family by Macduff, who agrees to 'Dispute it like a man' but who 'must also feel it as a man' (*Macbeth* 4.3.221–3). Equally we would not find in Shakespeare's Rome a scene comparable to the comical family confrontation in *Richard II* where Bolingbroke overrules his uncle and yields to his aunt in extending leniency to their son Aumerle.[21]

Shakespeare's contemporaries combined their intense interest in England's past with a preoccupation no less intense with the similarities and parallels between past and present. His English history plays subtly delineate a world which is recognizably different from the present, but which also harbours many of the features of that present. If Shakespeare's texts tell us nothing certain about the man by whom they were written, they leave little doubt when they were written. A look at the place of contemporary preoccupations in his plays may help us (provided we do not ask too much of the exercise) to bring some of their themes into focus.

III

The tensions of late Tudor and early Stuart politics are the tensions reported, sometimes more lengthily and loudly, by his fellow dramatists too. They are the tensions between the gains and the losses of the Tudor achievement. On the one side there has been the attainment of order and unity and of the stability that makes the cultural achievement of the late Renaissance possible. On the other there has been the challenge to old values and old ways. The martial concepts of honour and nobility have been undermined. The power of the new monarchy, and the artificiality and effeminacy of its court, have mounted threats to integrity and independence of character and to freedom and frankness of expression. Hotspur confronts the perfumed popinjay. Late Elizabethan England has seen the final taming of the feudal nobility, most dramatically in the north, where the rebellions of 1536 and 1569 have conspicuous resemblances to the Percy uprisings in Shakespeare; the King's charge in *Henry IV Part 1* that the rebels' grievances had been 'proclaimed at market crosses, read in churches' (5.1.73) must have reminded Tudor audiences of those later crises. By the late sixteenth century the medieval nobility had been largely extinguished.[22] It had yielded power to a new service nobility, or carpet nobility, which owed its rise to royal favour and to courtly employment. The manly, warlike, chivalric age was past, or was felt to be. Amidst such gains and losses there was an inevitable ambivalence about the court, the centre of power and of stability and of officeholding. On the one hand it was looked to as a civilizing force and as a model of courtesy and manners. On the other it was reviled, with a persistence and a repetitiveness as striking in literature as in life, as a humiliating arena of flattery and servility. There was a darker side

---

[21] The primacy of public life in the Roman plays is a theme of Robert S. Miola, *Shakespeare's Rome* (Cambridge, 1983).

[22] Frail as its statistical base has been shown to be, Lawrence Stone's *The Crisis of the Aristocracy* (Oxford, 1965) remains essential to an understanding of the changing composition and character of the nobility.

too to the dislike of the court, as a centre of intrigue and suspicion and fear, where the ubiquity of spies and informers made duplicity endemic and frankness politically suicidal.[23]

There are ideal courtiers in Shakespeare. Or rather there once have been, for in *All's Well That Ends Well* the model courtliness of Bertram's father was nurtured in a happier age, before the 'constancies' of courtiers had come to 'Expire before their fashions' (1.2.36–7, 62–3), and in *Cymbeline* too we are taken back to a pristine time, when young Posthumus Leonatus had 'lived in court – / Which rare it is to do – most praised, most loved; / A sample to the youngest' (1.1.46; cf. 3.6.79–84). Yet if courts have been corrupted, they retain an improving function. Henry V, jestingly telling Katherine that princes are 'the makers of manners', touches on a recurrent theme in Shakespeare. In *Twelfth Night* Olivia, who has courtly failings, none the less silences Sir Toby, whose debauchery has so disordered her court: 'Ungracious wretch, / Fit for the mountains and the barbarous caves, / Where manners ne'er were preached'; Lear's knights 'infect' the 'court' of Goneril by their ill 'manners'; Hotspur, excluded from the court, is let down, Worcester tells him, by his 'Defect of manners'; at the exiled court of *As You Like It* Orlando is initially taken for 'a rude despiser of good manners, / That in civility thou seem'st so empty'. If Corin has not been to court, says Touchstone, he 'never sawest good manners'. But of course Corin's riposte – 'Those that are good manners in the court are . . . ridiculous in the country'[24] – is a link in a long chain in Shakespeare of mockery and dislike of the court, of its painted pomp and affected falsity.

In Tudor England the court is the institution which everyone affects to despise, and where everyone wants to be. The Shakespearian character who best expresses that ambivalence is Iden, the slayer of Jack Cade in *Henry VI Part 2*. Perhaps he is a descendant of another inhabitant of Kent, Sir Thomas Wyatt, who when out of favour at the court of Henry VIII had written

poems of Senecan detachment in his native county, but who stayed there no longer than he needed to. Or perhaps Iden is a neighbour of Sir Robert Sidney at Penshurst, Sir Philip Sidney's younger brother, who experienced the same tension between the claims of court and country, a tension caught by Jonson's poem on the house while Sir Robert was its master. When we meet Iden he is asking, with the insistence on the first person singular that had characterized Wyatt's meditations on the theme, 'who would live turmoiled in the court / And may enjoy such quiet walks as these? This small inheritance my father left me / Contenteth me, and worth a monarchy . . .' Yet when the king, knighting Iden for his exploit, commands 'that thou henceforth attend on us', he appears to jump at the chance (4.9.16–23, 80–2).

Of all the sins of the court, none is more pervasive in Shakespeare's plays than flattery. His characters condemn it as the enemy to good counsel,[25] or see in it the necessary route to advancement,[26] but those who fail to practise it become alien figures. The virtuous outcast Kent, and the wicked outsider Richard III, have a common affliction: they 'cannot flatter'.[27] Flattery disarms candour and perverts speech. So does suspicion. The warnings against unguarded speech in commonplace book after commonplace book in Shakespeare's time witness to the pervasiveness of distrust.[28] In *All's*

---

[23] The literary expression of hostility to the court is surveyed in A. H. Tricomi, *Anticourt Drama in England 1603–1642* (Charlottesville, Virginia, 1989). More sympathetic attitudes are traced in Kevin Sharpe, *Criticism and Compliment* (Cambridge, 1987).

[24] *Henry V* 5.2.269–70; *Twelfth Night* 4.1.46–8; *Lear* Q 4.237; *1 Henry IV* 3.1.180; *As You Like It* 2.7.92–3, 3.2.39–40, 44–5.

[25] *Pericles* 2.41–53, 64–7; *Lear* Q 1.140–1; *Timon* 1.2.250–1; *As You Like It* 2.1.9–11.

[26] *King John* 1.1.213–16; *Hamlet* 3.2.54–60.

[27] *Lear* Q 7.94; *Richard III* 1.3.47; cf. *Much Ado* 1.3.28–9.

[28] The phenomenon is amply documented, and the habitual suspicion of the Elizabethan court vividly related, in Lacey Baldwin Smith, *Treason in Tudor England. Politics and Paranoia* (London, 1986).

Well That Ends Well the Countess warns the 'unseasoned courtier' Bertram to 'trust' only 'a few' (1.1.61, 68), while at the court of *The Winter's Tale* Leontes boxes himself into the belief that 'All's true that is mistrusted' (2.1.50). The politician's first lesson is to watch his tongue. In *Henry VI Part 1* Richard Plantagenet speaks wildly against the 'bloody tyranny' of the house of Lancaster, but so far heeds Mortimer's warning to be 'with silence . . . politic', so well learns 'to lock his counsel in my breast' (2.5.100, 117–18), that he becomes the Machiavel of the trilogy.

Alongside the flattery and suspicion and calculation of Renaissance courts there is fear: fear of spies and informers, fear of treason trials. The effect of terror on language is a theme of *Richard III*. In the opening scene Richard shows himself to be in command by standing the rules that restrict free speech at court on their head, and by mocking Brackenbury with the assurance that 'We speak no treason' (1.1.90). Yet when Richard becomes king he does to speech what Macbeth does to sleep: he murders it. A single word – 'if' – occasions the execution of Hastings (3.4.76). The fearful silence of the court, observed by the Scrivener (3.6.12), extends to the desolate capital, whose 'citizens are mum, say not a word' when Buckingham woos those 'tongueless blocks' (3.7.3, 42). The lamentations of the women in Act 4 Scene 4 are made a nightmare by the insistence of the words 'say', 'speak', 'word', 'talk', 'tongue', in a world where words can be uttered only if they lack truth or meaning. Later in the same scene a messenger brings Richard news of Buckingham's army. Messengers know what to expect, but Richard's response – he strikes the messenger for what he takes to be bad news and then, realizing his error, rewards him for good (437–45) – seems an apt expression of the tyranny he has established of power over speech and of speech over truth.

On its retreat from Tudor politics, candour is accompanied by oratory. Here is another late sixteenth-century ambivalence. Oratory, the swaying of free men, is a manly accomplishment. Yet its role has been made doubtful by the decline of the representative institutions of late medieval Europe, which have yielded their power to the courts and cabinets of the Renaissance.[29] The phrase 'play the orator' echoes through Shakespeare's first tetralogy in a way that emphasizes the impotence of rhetoric.[30] In *Richard III* Buckingham tries and fails to 'play the orator' (3.5.93) to help Richard to his throne; Richard turns instead to Tyrrel, to whom 'Gold were as good as twenty orators' (4.2.39); and Edward's Queen Elizabeth is left to lament that words have become mere 'orators of miseries' (4.4.129).

IV

In the respects I have been describing, Shakespeare's middle ages are interchangeable with the England of his time. Yet there are differences too. They stand out when we turn from the tetralogies to the late play *Henry VIII* (of which, scholars now seem generally to agree, Shakespeare was at least the main and perhaps the sole author). Outwardly that play, which may have been written for a royal wedding, is a celebration of the peace and plenty bequeathed by the Tudors. The portrait of Henry is altogether more favourable than that by Shakespeare's contemporary Sir Walter Ralegh, who presented him as an unexampled pattern of a merciless prince. Cardinal Wolsey testified eloquently to the resolution with which, in matters of state, Henry had pursued his 'will and appetite'.[31] Shakespeare's Henry, by contrast, announces his resolve to rule by 'our laws' rather than by 'our will' (1.2.94–5); he rebukes flattery (5.2.157–8); he puts a stop to improper

---

29 B. Worden, 'Constancy', *London Review of Books*, February 1983.
30 *1 Henry VI* 4.1.175; *3 Henry VI* 1.2.2. Cf. *2 Henry VI* 3.2.227; *Richard III* 3.1.37.
31 Peter Gwyn, *The King's Cardinal* (London, 1990), pp. 637–8.

taxation when (rather belatedly, we may think) he becomes aware of it.

Yet Shakespeare's imagination cannot be confined within the play's complimentary purpose. The hushed tones of *Henry VIII* reveal to us something quite different from what we might call – in a phrase we could not properly use of any other play of Shakespeare – its official position. We are taken into a Renaissance court: the court of the monarchy that has broken the medieval nobility and imposed new values and new rules of conduct. The ceremonialism of the play, its account of the competitive pomp of the Field of the Cloth of Gold, its careful re-creation of the pageantry of Anne Boleyn's coronation: those features may take their cue from the aesthetic preferences of the Jacobean rather than of the Henrician court, but the play brings out, once more through Shakespeare's historical intuition, the ways in which the two courts had more in common with each other than either had with the medieval courts before them. In the court of Shakespeare's medieval plays there are occasional Renaissance features, like the anachronistic susceptibility of the youth of *Richard II* to 'Report of fashions in proud Italy' (2.1.21). But there is no ceremonial apparatus to emasculate the prowess and independence of the nobility. There is dread of particular kings but not of the institution of monarchy, and there is no institutional ceremonial procedure to encloud the personalities of monarchs or to insulate them from home truths, as Henry VIII is so long insulated from the truth about Wolsey's taxation.

A detail will highlight the contrast. Shakespeare's contemporaries insisted time and again that the key to power was 'access' to the monarch. Queen Elizabeth, as Bishop Goodman said, was 'ever hard of access',[32] a characteristic exasperating to the courtiers of her later years, to whom 'access' was an obsessive goal.[33] The Renaissance had given a new resonance to the word, as Shakespeare understood. When in the medieval world of *Henry IV Part 2* the rebels complain of being denied 'access' to

the king's person (4.1.78), they merely mean, by access, permission to be present at court. The court from which they are excluded is a frank and manly place, free from flattery. Shakespeare, who takes the word 'access' from Holinshed, omits those with which Holinshed follows it, where the rebels attribute their exclusion to the 'multitude of flatterers' about the king. But when in *Henry VIII* the Lord Chamberlain tells the discontented nobles that their only hope of toppling Wolsey is to cut off the 'access' which the king so readily allows him (3.2.16–19), the word has a new meaning. The problem for the nobles now is not access to the court, the arena which renders them harmless and at which they are welcome: it is access, within the court, to the royal ear. Shakespeare's medieval nobility had been a warlike nobility, its power resting as much on its estates and on its ability to arm its tenantry as on royal favour. By contrast the nobles at the court of Shakespeare's Henry VIII cower in the royal antechambers, dreading the royal anger (2.2.64–74). The institutions and conventions of Henry VIII's court are designed to keep truth at bay: Buckingham must acknowledge the fair conduct of his trial (2.1.63–4); Katherine must be judged not openly, as she wants, but in 'a corner' (3.1.30–1). Wriggle as they occasionally may, the courtiers have swallowed the new rules of the game. We see the transformation in the awed, *sotto voce* pleasantries about the rise and fall of greatness ventured by the 'gentlemen', the choric figures of the play, as the coronation pageant passes before them, dazzling them with the glitter of a court that allows them a peripheral and passive role (4.1.54–7, 96–101).

Shakespeare's medieval plays had occa-

---

[32] Robert Ashton, *King James I by his Contemporaries* (London, 1969), p. 76.
[33] William Camden, *The History of . . . Princess Elizabeth* (London, 1630 edn), p. 182; J. Spedding et al., eds., *The Works of Francis Bacon* 14 vols. (1857–74), vol. 8, pp. 238, 241.

sionally touched upon the emasculation of the nobility, as when Talbot recalls the initial purpose and status of the Order of the Garter (*1 Henry VI* 4.1.33–44). The threat posed to the ancient peers by upstart favourites, a stock theme of the drama of the period (of Marlowe's *Edward II*, for example, or Jonson's *Sejanus*), and a preoccupation of the Earl of Essex,[34] surfaces in *Richard III*, when Richard exploits the argument that the nobility are 'Held in contempt; while great promotions / Are daily given to ennoble those / That scarce some two days since were worth a noble' (1.3.80–2). The Tudor determination to replace feudal loyalties by royal ones is reflected at the beginning of *Richard II*, where Richard resolves to bring to heel the 'time-honoured' noble families who fright 'fair peace' by valuing the resolution of their feuds above obedience to their king.[35] Just so, at the outset of *Romeo and Juliet*, does the prince (perhaps a Renaissance prince, for he succeeds where Richard fails) confront the 'ancient grudge' (Prologue, 3), the bloodfeud, of the rival households, which makes them 'Rebellious subjects, enemies to peace' (1.1.78).

In Henry VIII's England peace has been won – and we are shown the price. The nobles are not sentimentalized: we glimpse their snobbery and selfishness and petulance. Yet we also learn of the shift of power and hence of values that the early Tudors have achieved. The upstart Wolsey, who has 'contemned ... or at least strangely neglected' men of 'ancestry', is turning them 'From princes into pages' (1.1.59, 2.2.48, 3.2.9–13). Their 'slavery' (2.2.44) is breaking their economic power: Lord Abergavenny knows 'Kinsmen of mine – three at the least – that have / By this so sickened their estates that never / They shall abound as formerly' (1.1.80–3).

If the power of the medieval nobility is passing, so too is their concept of honour. 'Honour' can mean many things in Shakespeare, but in politics it is mostly the mark of esteem and independence that (as Falstaff is alarmed to perceive) men value above their lives, or at least above their safety or their comfort.[36] Associated with fighting, honour is denied to those left at home or at court, like Bertram in *All's Well That Ends Well*, who frets at the prospect of 'Creaking my shoes on the plain masonry / Till honour be bought up' (2.1.31–2). Yet in the Renaissance the world is changing.[37] We see the ensuing conflict of values even in the comedy of *Much Ado About Nothing*, in the holiday world which turns brave soldiers into soft wooers, but which is shattered by Beatrice, who declares that 'manhood is melted into courtesies, valour into compliment' and demands of Benedick the fulfilment of 'a man's office', the enactment of an old code of honour (4.1.268, 319–20).

In *Henry VIII* honour has come to mean something quite different. Now it is defined and circumscribed by the court. The term congratulates the court's control of power and of reward and of display. The coronation of Anne is celebrated by 'shows, / Pageants, and sights of honour' (4.1.10–11), and the barons of the cinque ports, now carpet nobles, bring in 'The cloth of honour' (4.1.47–9). Buckingham's threat, from which his colleagues prudently dissuade him, to confront the king, and to tell him the truth about Wolsey from 'a mouth of honour' (1.1.137–8, 158–9), momentarily recalls the strained passion that Hotspur had brought to the theme of honour. But the Percies could raise armies. How many divisions has Buckingham? Henry has become the fount of honour while Wolsey, as the Duke of Norfolk observes, has become its monopolist

---

34 Mervyn James, *Society, Politics and Culture* (Cambridge, 1986), pp. 423.

35 1.1.1, 1.3.131. Cf. York's dilemma at 2.2.111–15.

36 *3 Henry VI* 1.1.247, 4.3.15; *1 Henry IV* 4.3.89; *Caesar* 1.2.90–1; *The Winter's Tale* 3.2.41–4; *Antony* 4.16.49–50; *Troilus* 5.3.226–8.

37 See the invaluable essay on this subject by Mervyn James, 'English Politics and the Concept of Honour, 1485–1642', reproduced in his *Society, Politics and Culture* (ch. 8) from *Past and Present*, Supplement no. 3 (1978).

(2.2.47–9). When in *Henry IV Part 1* Hal calls Hotspur a 'child of honour' (3.2.139) he is commending his manliness and courage: when in *Henry VIII* Katharine of Aragon calls Wolsey 'the great child of honour' (4.2.6) she is alluding to his receipt of royal favour. It was 'my power', Henry VIII reminds the cardinal, that had 'rained honour' on him (3.2.186), and the same power takes it away. Henry's rebuke, later in the play, to the courtiers who have brought charges against Cranmer makes lucid the semantic revolution that Henry has accomplished: 'So I grow stronger, you more honour gain'(5.2.215).

Henry VIII's Whitehall is one of the two carefully drawn Renaissance courts in Shakespeare. The other is Elsinore: the court whose language Hamlet, as we discover when we first meet him, will not speak; the court that houses Polonius, who agrees that a cloud is very like a whale, and the fop Osric, who concedes that hot weather is cold and cold hot. In the way of Renaissance courts (or at least of their contemporary literary representation), that of Claudius is full of spies. Spies indeed lurk everywhere in the courts and in the households (the mini-courts) of Shakespeare's plays. Macbeth, in what Malcolm calls his 'watchful tyranny' (5.112.33), knows the secrets of his nobles, for 'There's not a one of them but in his house / I keep a servant fee'd' (3.4.130–1).[38] The Duchess of Gloucester in *Henry VI Part 2* (1.2.70–107), and Buckingham in *Henry VIII* (1.1.123–4), are undone by servants whom their enemies have hired as informers. In the comedies, of course, there is much spying, or intentional overhearing, which even the present age might hesitate to term 'political', but there are informers even in Leonato's household in *Much Ado About Nothing*, where the conversation in Act 1 Scene 1 in which Claudio tells Don Pedro of his love for Hero is overheard both by 'a good sharp man' who serves Leonato's brother Antonio (1.2.9–16) and by Borachio, who has 'whipped me behind the arras' (1.3.56–7).[39]

Common as spies are in Shakespeare, we can once again observe a subtle difference between his medieval world and his Renaissance one. He omits from his portrayal of Henry VI's court the spy set by Beaufort whom Hall mentions as lurking 'behind the tapet of' the 'chamber', and omits too Hall's information that 'all the king's doings were known to' the Earl of Warwick 'by espials'. Shakespeare's Henry IV is a troubled and dissimulating king, but not quite the prisoner of suspicion that he appears in Holinshed. At Elsinore, by contrast, suspicion and surveillance are a way of life. No sooner has Reynaldo been dispatched to spy on Laertes than Rosencrantz and Guildenstern are summoned to sound out Hamlet. It does not take the prince long to guess that they have been 'sent for' (2.2.276–94) and have agreed to do the crown's dirty work: that is what courts do to people, even to one's boyhood friends, and Hamlet resolves to 'trust' them 'as I do adders fanged' (additional passage H; 3.4.185). His conscience is unmoved by their deaths, for 'they did make love to this employment' (5.2.58), a claim borne out by their fawning language in the royal presence. Rosencrantz, as Hamlet says, is a 'sponge' that 'soaks up the King's countenance, his rewards, his authorities' (4.2.13–15). Guildenstern's promise to keep Hamlet 'safe' (3.3.8–10) reveals a quick mastery of the sinister euphemism characteristic of Claudius's régime, and anticipates the King's decision to send the prince to England 'for thine especial safety' (4.3.39). No sooner are Rosencrantz and Guildenstern set to work than Polonius, that congenital eavesdropper ('What is't, Ophelia, he hath said to you?'), proceeds to 'contrive' with Claudius the 'lawful espials' in which they will overhear Hamlet and Ophelia, 'seeing unseen' (1.3.88; 2.2.165, 214–15; 3.1.32–5). No privacy is safe from their

---

[38] Cf. Jonson, *Sejanus his Fall*, 2.2.444–5.

[39] For other spies in Shakespeare: *1 Henry VI* 3.1.166; *King John* 4.1.128; *Caesar* 1.3.116, 5.1.7; *Henry VIII* 1.1.153–6, 5.2.143–5.

vigilance: 'You need not tell us what Lord Hamlet said; / We heard it all' (3.1.182–3). Small wonder Hamlet is suspicious of Ophelia: 'Are you honest? . . . Where's your father?' (3.1.105, 132–3). Soon Polonius will be behind another arras, in the privacy of the Queen's chamber, for Claudius has 'wisely' resolved 'that some more audience than a mother, / Since nature makes them partial,' should 'o'er-hear' Hamlet and his mother (3.3.30–3).

If *Hamlet* is partly a story about spies, it is also partly a story about poison. When Shakespeare's contemporaries thought about the court, the word poison came readily to their minds. It was a fact of courtly life. Attempts were made to poison both Queen Elizabeth and Essex, and even when poison was not to blame for a royal death it was liable to be suspected, as on the death of Prince Henry or later on that of James I. If poison was a fact, it was also a habitual metaphor for the evils of the age. First, it was associated with suspicion and surveillance. Jonson wrote of the 'black poison of suspect' (*Every Man in his Humour.* 2.3.55–67), while in Donne's fourth satire the courtier, the 'privileged spy', 'by poison hastes to an office's reversion'. Secondly, poison was a metaphor for flattery. In *Woodstock*, which opens with an (unhistorical) attempt to poison a tableful of leading nobles, the 'flattering minions' around Richard II are 'vipers':[40] in Shakespeare's *Richard II* the king succumbs to the 'venom' of the 'flattering sounds' of 'lascivious metres' (2.1.17–20). 'Flatteries,' explains Apemantus in *Timon of Athens*, are of a piece with 'poisonous spite and envy' (1.2.133–5). The Bastard in *King John* intends to rise by flattery, the 'Sweet, sweet, sweet poison for the age's tooth' (1.1.213). 'Sugared words', both in *Henry VI Part 2* (3.2.45) and in *Richard III* (3.1.13–14), conceal the 'poison' of the heart, and in *Henry V* the king asks of the 'idol ceremony' 'What drinkst thou oft, instead of homage sweet, / But poisoned flattery?' (4.1.247–8).

There are a number of poisonings and attempted poisonings in Shakespeare, but rarely, outside Elsinore, does that method of extermination assume a symbolic significance. Once again there is a difference between the medieval and the modern worlds. In the Henry IV plays Shakespeare bypasses Holinshed's observation that the king lived in fear of poison, and in *Richard III* he bypasses Hall's information that it was probably through poison that Richard disposed of Queen Anne. At Elsinore, poison is the standard method of assassination: first in the orchard, an episode twice re-enacted in the player scene while Hamlet underlines the word 'poison' (3.2.223, 249, 277), and then in the clean sweep of poisonings at the end of the play, where Claudius has thoughtfully provided a reserve method – the poisoned chalice – in case the envenomed swords let him down.

It is time to end. Perhaps the boundaries beyond which the politics of Shakespeare's time cease to illuminate his writing make *Hamlet* the appropriate work to have ended with, as the play at once most subject to critical interrogation and most evasive of it, and as the play whose hero sees off the spies who 'would pluck out the heart of my mystery' (3.2.353–4). Shakespeare will preserve his mystery too.

---

[40] Ed. A. P. Rossiter (London, 1946), p. 161: 5.3.28–30.

LANGUAGE, POLITICS, AND POVERTY IN SHAKESPEARIAN DRAMA

WILLIAM C. CARROLL

In an essay published in *Shakespeare Survey 38*, the historian E.W. Ives analysed the ways in which history and literature mutually illuminated (or did not) each other in the study of Shakespeare. After reviewing the distressing conditions of poverty during Shakespeare's lifetime, Ives concluded that 'to the historian, the remarkable thing – and a contrast to Shakespeare's sensitivity to the realities of politics and the Court – is the distance there seems to be between his plays and the socio-economic realities of Elizabeth[an] and Jacobean England'. *Coriolanus*, Ives notes, 'stands alone' as an exception, and in any event 'takes very much an establishment point of view'. Yet it is possible, Ives concedes, 'to show by a study of language and imagery that Shakespeare was aware of much of this, but it gave him few explicit themes'.[1] There is much to agree with in Ives's essay, particularly his argument that 'the reaction against literary evidence in history has gone too far',[2] but there is so much to disagree with in the passages I have quoted that it is difficult to know where to begin. Leaving aside the myriad contradictions and curious theoretical assumptions of Ives's argument, I want to suggest that Shakespeare's language not only reveals his sensitivity to the discourse of poverty in his day, but that his language, in crucial instances, *is* his 'theme'. After some general remarks, I will proceed with three particular examples, two of which Ives does not mention in his essay.[3]

That Shakespeare was aware of, and sensi-

tive to, the beggars and vagabonds in country and city is indisputable, but the many references in his plays also indicate more particularly his awareness of the political realities of their condition: as Calpurnia says in *Julius Caesar*, 'When beggars die there are no comets seen; / The heavens themselves blaze forth the death of princes' (2.2.30–1). The marginalized status of beggars is in Shakespeare *always* their defining characteristic: when a 'holiday-fool' in England 'will not give a doit to relieve a lame beggar, they will lay out ten to see a dead Indian' (*Tempest* 2.2.29–33). Shakespeare's plays are filled with reminders of 'famished beggars, weary of their lives' (*Richard III* 5.6.59), of 'seely beggars, / Who, sitting in the stocks, refuge their shame / That many have, and others must, set there' (*Richard II* 5.5.25–7). He knows their weak and feeble cries, 'puling, / like a beggar at Hallowmas' (*Two Gentlemen* 2.1.24), and he knows that they abandon their children, that one could 'with charitable hand / [Take] up a beggar's issue' at the city gates (*Much Ado* 4.1.133–4). Bolingbroke's sense of outrage over Richard's seizure of his inheritance is shaped in part by his treatment as one of these marginalized outcasts:

---

[1] E. W. Ives, 'Shakespeare and History: Divergencies and Agreements', *Shakespeare Survey 38* (1985), 19–35; p. 28.

[2] Ives, 'Shakespeare and History', p. 35.

[3] The best general works on the problem of poverty in Shakespeare's time are A. L. Beier, *Masterless Men: The Vagrancy Problem in England 1560–1640* (London, Methuen, 1985), and Paul Slack, *Poverty and Policy in Tudor and Stuart England* (London, Longman, 1988).

'Will you permit that I shall stand condemned / A wandering vagabond, my rights and royalties / Plucked from my arms perforce and given away / To upstart unthrifts?' (*Richard II* 2.3.118–21). Later, as Henry IV, he will articulate another, more threatening, political association: 'And never yet did insurrection want / Such water-colours to impaint his cause, / Nor moody beggars starving for a time / Of pell-mell havoc and confusion' (*1 Henry IV* 5.1.79–82); so too the official rhetoric of state authority frequently linked masterless men and the threat of sedition.[4] One way of dealing with the excess population of rogues and vagabonds was through involuntary impressment for war or colonization, a technique Falstaff has mastered as he finds 'food for powder' for the wars; Westmorland says Falstaff's soldiers are 'exceeding poor and bare, too beggarly', but Falstaff blithely dismisses his concern, 'for their poverty, I know not where they had that' (*1 Henry IV* 4.2.65–71). Kate in *The Taming of the Shrew* is confident that 'beggars that come unto my father's door / Upon entreaty have present alms, / If not, elsewhere they meet with charity' (4.3.4–5), but most of the plays offer instead visions of 'begging hermits' (*Titus* 3.2.41), whippings, country beadles on the watch for what Dogberry calls 'all vagrom men' (*Much Ado* 3.3.24), the 'poor beggar [who] raileth on the rich' (*King John* 2.1.593), the 'farmer's dog [which] bark[s] at a beggar' (*Lear* F 4.5.150–1), and the further ironies of economic injustice, as the Fisherman explains to Pericles: 'Here's them in our country of Greece gets more with begging than we can do with working' (*Pericles* Sc.5.104–6). In these and dozens of other allusions and figures of speech, Shakespeare's language reveals a strong and consistent awareness of the political, economic, and spiritual subjection of beggars and vagabonds: they are invariably 'poor and loathsome' (*Shrew* Ind.1.121), 'unfortunate', distressed, crying, suffering, thoroughly marginalized. 'Our basest beggars / Are in the poorest thing superfluous' (*Lear* F 2.2.438–9), Lear knows; there are even those

who would 'show charity to none, / But let the famished flesh slide from the bone / Ere thou relieve the beggar. Give to dogs / What thou deniest to men' (*Timon* 4.3.528–31). The 'disease of all-shunned poverty' (*Timon* 4.2.14) is an epidemic throughout the plays. 'Fortune, that arrant whore', as Lear's Fool says, 'Ne'er turns the key to th'poor' (*Lear* F 2.2.227–8).

But beyond the dense texture of metaphor and allusion, Shakespeare's language and his politics are inextricably linked in more complex and suggestive ways. In three instances which I will discuss, from early, middle, and late in his career, Shakespeare creates a language at once individualized and typical which functions as a counter-discourse to what Ives would term the 'establishment point of view'. In examining these instances, I will however attempt to resist this kind of terminology, in which Shakespeare's own political views are imputed as 'establishment' (bad) or 'subversive' (good) because such binarism seems to me to falsify the complex dialogical events of the plays. My three examples are from *The First Part of the Contention* (*2 Henry VI*), *King Lear*, and *The Winter's Tale*.

I

In the inflammatory rhetoric of the early and mid-1590s, memories of Kett, Jack Cade, and Wat Tyler were frequently evoked; sedition was a genuine concern. Bartholomew Steer, the ringleader of the Oxfordshire Rising of 1596, sounded little different from his cousins on the stage. A group of poor petitioners told the lord lieutenant then 'that yf they Could not have remedie, they would seek remedie themselves, and Cast down hedges and dytches, and knocke

---

[4] For a recent consideration of this connection, see Annabel Patterson, *Shakespeare and the Popular Voice* (Oxford, Basil Blackwell, 1989), pp. 32–51, and Roger B. Manning, *Village Revolts* (Oxford, Oxford University Press, 1988).

down gentlemen'.[5] Steer himself told his interrogators that 'the poore did once Rise in Spaine and Cutt down the gent[lemen], and sithens that tyme they have lyved merily there'. He believed that 'manie would Rise' in the kingdom, and that 'yt was but a monthes work to overrun England'.[6] He also intended to march on London itself, as Jack Cade once did, joining up with the mobs who had recently rioted in the city: 'when the prentices heare that wee bee upp, they will Come and Joine with us'. He was induced to think this, his interrogator reports, 'by reason of the late intended insurrection in London, and that Certain Prentices were then hanged'.[7]

Steer's rising failed spectacularly, but the association between certain forms of sedition and masterless men was quite close here and elsewhere. The rebel Falconbridge in Heywood's *1 King Edward IV* (*c.* 1599), to take another example, is at some pains to distinguish himself from the usual kind of sedition, invoking a social class contempt which demonstrates the allegedly 'natural' association of the poor with rebellion, but distinguishes theirs from his own:

> We do not rise like *Tyler*, *Cade*, and *Straw*,
> *Bluebeard*, and other of that rascal rout,
> Basely like tinkers or such muddy slaves,
> For mending measures or the price of corne,
> Or for some common in the wield of Kent
> Thats by some greedy cormorant enclos'd,
> But in the true and antient lawfull right
> Of the redoubted house of *Lancaster*.[8]

The real economic injustices of the period which did in fact lead to rebellion are not relevant here; rather, like most actual risings in the period, this one is led not by the peasantry but by a discontented nobleman.

In *The First Part of the Contention* (*2 Henry VI*), Shakespeare dramatizes one of the most notorious instances of plebeian revolt in English history, Jack Cade's rising in 1450. Cade's ancestry was notorious. Hall reports that 'divers idle and vacabonde persons, resorted to him from Sussex and Surrey, and from other partes

to a great number. Thus this glorious Capitayn, compassed about, and environed with a multitude of evil rude and rusticall persones, came agayn to the playn of *Blackeheath*.'[9] In one of the rogue pamphlets of the period – *Martin Mark-all* (*c.* 1608) – Cade is in fact said to be the 'originall and beginning' of the Regiment of Rogues of the kingdom – essentially, the Ur-vagabond. Cade's rebellion and march on London are joined, in this version, by the 'Rakehels and Vagabonds . . . [and] masterlesse men' of Kent.[10] So too Shakespeare's Cade is followed by an army of vagabonds, 'a ragged multitude / Of hinds and peasants' (4.4.31–2). Cade himself has all the cultural marks of a vagabond: he was 'born, under a hedge', his father's house was 'but the cage', and he is himself a 'valiant' beggar, who has been 'whipped three market days together', and has been 'burned i'th'hand for stealing of sheep' (4.2.52–65); in elaborating the fantasy that he is the son of Edmund Mortimer, finally, Cade himself offers that he is the older, hitherto unknown child who, 'being put to nurse, / Was by a beggar-woman stol'n away' (4.2.140–1).

Cade's language perfectly embodies the mixture of political and sociological sources which went to create him. His speech is by turns oracular, contradictory, comically inept, full of righteous indignation. At some points he sounds the violent note of class warfare: 'We will not leave one lord, one gentleman – / Spare none but such as go in clouted shoon, / For they

---

5 Quoted in John Walter, 'A "Rising of the People"? The Oxfordshire Rising of 1596', *Past & Present*, 107 (1985), 90–143; p. 98.

6 Walter, 'A "Rising of the People"?', p. 108.

7 Walter, 'A "Rising of the People"?', pp. 107–8.

8 Thomas Heywood, *The Dramatic Works*, vol. 1 (New York, Russell & Russell, 1964; rpt. 1874), p. 9. On enclosure as a continuing cause of disorder and riot, see Roger B. Manning, *Village Revolts*.

9 Geoffrey Bullough, *Narrative and Dramatic Sources of Shakespeare*, vol. 3 (London and New York, 1960), p. 114.

10 Samuel Rowlands, *The Complete Works*, vol. 2 (New York, Johnson Reprint, 1966; rpt. 1880), pp. 44–5.

are thrifty honest men, and such / As would, but that they dare not, take our parts'. Told that they 'are all in order', marching toward them, Cade makes a memorable reply: 'But then are we in order when we are / Most out of order' (4.2.183–9). Above all, Cade's utopianism needs to be recognized as a complex linguistic creation, not simply, as some have argued, a mockery engineered by Shakespeare (himself allegedly on the side of the establishment) to discredit Cade.[11] Part of a long tradition of radical utopian impossibility, echoing the land of cockayne, naïvety and cunning cynicism fused together, Cade's vision is expressed in an idiosyncratic rhetoric which is also part of a long-running political dialogue: 'There shall be in England seven halfpenny loaves sold for a penny, the three-hooped pot shall have ten hoops, and I will make it felony to drink small beer. All the realm shall be in common, and in Cheapside shall my palfrey go to grass' (4.2.67–71). The real suffering and grievances of the poor, the injustices perpetrated by the nobles: these energies lose their force when embodied in Cade's buffoonery, yet the grievances *are* spoken on the stage, and the very sources of his energy and his language derive from such contradictions. He will condemn those who teach reading and writing, or speak Latin, yet he speaks Latin himself (4.7.121). Cade's eloquence against social injustice cannot be separated from, nor is it cancelled by, his grotesqueries. His charge against Lord Say includes the absurd accusation that 'Thou hast most traitorously corrupted the youth of the realm in erecting a grammar school', but that is soon followed by something more compelling: 'Thou hast appointed justices of the peace to call poor men before them about matters they were not able to answer. Moreover, thou hast put them in prison, and, because they could not read, thou hast hanged them when indeed only for that cause they have been most worthy to live' (4.7.30–43). These complaints are real ones, frequently heard outside the theatres; this representation of Cade both subverts their poli-

tical and ideological power *and* enhances it, even explaining, on one level, the rebels' desire to 'burn all the records of the realm' (4.7.13).

Cade's language is part of a political discourse which dates back to More's *Utopia* and earlier. Crowley and other polemicists had accurately represented the voices of protest, and there is little difference to be heard between Thomas More's warning that the displaced poor must either rob or beg, 'and a man of courage is more likely to rob than to beg'[12] and Richard Morison's warning that 'men wylle steale, thoughe they be hanged, excepte they may lyve without stelyng'[13] (in 1516 and 1536, respectively), and Thomas Lodge's personification of Sedition – 'it is a paradox of his, That it is better [to] live a Rebell than die a beggar'[14] – and Edward Hext's reports of desperate countrymen who 'styck not to say boldlye they must not starve, they will not starve'[15] (both

---

11 Among the recent commentaries on the play's ideological position, see especially Robert Weimann, *Shakespeare and the Popular Tradition in the Theatre* (Baltimore, Johns Hopkins University Press, 1978); Michael Bristol, *Carnival and Theatre: Plebeian Culture and the Structure of Authority in Renaissance England* (New York, Methuen, 1985); Richard Wilson, '"A Mingled Yarn": Shakespeare and the Cloth Workers', *Literature and History*, 12 (1986), 164–80; Michael Hattaway, 'Rebellion, Class Consciousness, and Shakespeare's *2 Henry VI*', *Cahiers Élisabéthains*, 33 (1988), 13–22; and Patterson, *Shakespeare and the Popular Voice*. In *Shakespeare's Prose* (Chicago, University of Chicago Press, 1951), Milton Crane described Cade's prose as simply 'scurrilous and incoherent' in comparison with 'the noble and simple verse of Lord Say' (p. 133). In *The Artistry of Shakespeare's Prose* (London, Methuen, 1968), Brian Vickers offers an excellent technical analysis of Cade's prose, acknowledging the rhetorical variations in it, but still concludes that Shakespeare creates a 'totally unsympathetic portrait' (p. 26).

12 Thomas More, *Utopia*, ed. Robert M. Adams (New York, Norton, 1975), p. 15.

13 Richard Morison, *A Remedy for Sedition* (London, 1536), E3ᵛ.

14 Thomas Lodge, *Wits Miserie and the Worlds Madnesse* (London, 1596), p. 67.

15 R. H. Tawney and Eileen Powers, eds., *Tudor Economic Documents*, vol. 2 (London, 1924), p. 341.

Lodge and Hext writing in 1596). Jack Straw's question, 'Who would live like a beggar, and may be in this estate[?]'[16] was asked more than once during the sixteenth century, particularly in the 1590s. Another version of that question occurs in Cade's language, and his desire that 'all the realm shall be in common' (4.2.70), repeated and even more generalized later into 'And henceforward all things shall be in common' (4.7.17), places him clearly in the line of inflammatory utopian rhetoric perhaps most associated with his cousin on the stage, Parson Ball, who in *The Life and Death of Jack Straw* (*c.* 1593) argued for all things in common: 'it were better to have this communitie, / Than to have this difference in degrees'.[17] At the end of *2 Henry VI*, when Jack Cade climbs over the brick wall into Alexander Iden's garden like any poaching vagabond, Cade describes Iden as the 'lord of the soil' who holds his 'fee-simple' as an inheritance (4.9.24–5), and claims to be vanquished by 'famine' alone. To the end, Cade enacts the discourse of property, dispossession, and poverty. His rise and fall reveals no simple ideological position of subverting or subverted. Rather, his voice forms part of a complex socio-political discourse marked most of all by heteroglossia.

II

My second example is Edgar, in *King Lear*. As I have argued elsewhere,[18] Edgar's disguise as Poor Tom, the outcast beggar, is an incarnation of everything antithetical to the order of law represented in his initial identity as 'legitimate' son and heir. A Poor Tom was supposedly a lunatic beggar, an escaped or released inmate of Bedlam Hospital. For most Elizabethans, he seems also to have been understood as a fraud, an ingenious counterfeiter skilled in grotesque makeup, real and pretended self-mutilation, and recurring street scenarios worthy of the *commedia dell'arte*. The Poor Tom is also known in English rogue books as an 'Abraham' or 'Abram' man, but the type is also evident in

Continental literature on the subject, such as the *Liber Vagatorum*. The English rogue pamphlets – Awdeley, Harman, Dekker, and others – elaborate every feature of Poor Tom's rôle, including his self-declaration of name and origin in Bedlam. Poor Tom's language is also specified in some descriptions: he 'nameth him-selfe poore Tom';[19] 'Every one of these *Abrams* hath a severall gesture in playing his part. Some make an horrid noyse, hollowly sounding; some whoope, some hollow, some shewe onely a kind of wild distracted ugly looke';[20] one, it is reported, 'sweares hee hath beene in Bedlam, and will talke frantickly of purpose . . . he calls himselfe by the name of *Poore Tom*, and com-ming neere any body *cries* out *Poore Tom* is a colde'.[21] Jonson describes a '*Bethl'em*-like' speaker as 'a vaine sound of chosen and excellent words, without any subject of *sen-tence*, or *science* mix'd'.[22] The surviving printed sources, if that is where, rather than life, Shake-speare found his information, give little other evidence about the language spoken by Poor Toms: they utter their own names and tell their own histories while begging, they often make 'an horrid noyse, hollowly sounding' and 'talke frantickly of purpose'. When he puts on the disguise of Poor Tom, Edgar understands that the type speaks 'with roaring voices' and 'Sometime with lunatic bans, sometime with prayers / Enforce their charity' (*Lear* F 2.2.177–

---

[16] *The Life and Death of Jack Straw (1594)* (Oxford, Oxford University Press, 1957), line 247.

[17] *The Life and Death of Jack Straw (1594)*, lines 84–5.

[18] William C. Carroll, '"The Base Shall Top Th'Legiti-mate": The Bedlam Beggar and the Role of Edgar in *King Lear*', *Shakespeare Quarterly*, 38 (1987), 426–41.

[19] John Awdeley, *The Fraternitye of Vacabondes* (London, 1561), printed in *The Rogues and Vagabonds of Shak-speare's Youth*, ed. Edward Viles and F. J. Furnivall (London, 1907), p. 3.

[20] Thomas Dekker, *O per se O* (London, 1612), M2ʳ.

[21] Thomas Dekker, *The Belman of London* (London, 1608), D3ʳ.

[22] *Timber, or Discoveries*, in *Jonson*, eds. C. H. Herford and Percy Simpson, vol. 8 (Oxford, Oxford University Press, 1947), p. 574.

83). Beyond the usual beggar's line, some aspects of Edgar's language are also linked, as is well known, to Samuel Harsnett's *A Declaration of Egregious Popishe Impostures*. Yet even Harsnett and the rogue pamphlets cannot entirely account for such phantasmagoric visions as this self-definition by Edgar, who answers Gloucester's question 'What are you there?':

Poor Tom, that eats the swimming frog, the toad, the tadpole, the wall-newt, and the water; that in the fury of his heart, when the foul fiend rages, eats cowdung for salads, swallows the old rat and the ditchdog, drinks the green mantle of the standing pool; who is whipped from tithing to tithing, and stocked, punished, and imprisoned; who hath had three suits to his back, six shirts to his body,

> Horse to ride, and weapon to wear;
> But mice and rats and such small deer
> Have been Tom's food for seven long year.

(*Lear* F 3.4.121–31)

What I would like to stress here is the often explicitly political dimension of Poor Tom's language, an element which seems to have been Shakespeare's own addition to the stereotype in the sources. Certainly the play as a whole undertakes an interrogation of the political,[23] from such signal moments as Lear's prayer for the 'poor naked wretches' of the kingdom, whose 'houseless heads and unfed sides . . . looped and windowed raggedness' (*Lear* F 3.4.28–31) reflect Edgar's disguise and re-inforce his perception that 'the country gives me proof and precedent' of the proliferation of such beggars, and Gloucester's parallel prayer that the 'superfluous and lust-dieted man' should feel the heavens' power, and 'So distribution should undo excess, / And each man have enough' (*Lear* F 4.1.61–4). Beggars never have enough, though 'Our basest beggars / Are in the poorest thing superfluous'. Poor Tom's hallucinatory speeches enact these concerns in another way. He represents among other things the inversion of royal and social power.[24] To the mad king, Tom announces his past as that of 'A servingman, proud in heart and mind . . . False of heart, light of ear, bloody of hand' (*Lear* F 3.4.79–86). This speech not only links

him with the other false servingmen of the play – Edmund and Oswald – but in its fractured shards of the Ten Commandments and the Seven Deadly Sins re-enacts the Fall on a number of levels, including that of the social hierarchy. It is ironically appropriate that Poor Tom should become a 'learned justice' in the mad trial of 3.6 (Sc. 13 in Q); a 'robed man of justice' and 'yokefellow of equity' with the Fool, Tom takes his place as one 'o' th' commission' along with Kent. It is Poor Tom who begins the trial, 'Let us deal justly', but ends it with the vagabond's cry to move on to new targets, 'Come, march to wakes and fairs / And market-towns. Poor Tom, thy horn is dry' (*Lear* Q Sc. 13.17–69). The oppressed conditions of the poor continue as an issue in the play in Lear's language, in the confrontation between Edgar (now speaking as a rustic peasant) and Oswald, and in the general problematic of justice. 'Thou hast seen a farmer's dog bark at a beggar?' Lear asks Gloucester, 'An the creature run from the cur, there thou mightst behold the great image of authority'. 'Change places', the king says, and, 'handy-dandy, which is the justice, which is the thief?' (*Lear* F 4.5.148–55). That is a question to which the play gives various answers, none of them simple or reassuring.

III

My third example is Autolycus, in *The Winter's Tale*, where we will in fact see a beggar-thief change places with a prince in the fourth act. When Simon Forman reported his account of seeing *The Winter's Tale* at the Globe on 15 May 1611, he reported the Leontes–Polixenes plot with some care, with the abandonment and recovery of Perdita explicitly noted; from

---

[23] See elsewhere in this volume Margot Heinemann's fine essay on *King Lear*.

[24] For a stimulating discussion of the dynamics of symbolic inversion, see Peter Stallybrass and Allon White, *The Politics and Poetics of Transgression* (Ithaca, Cornell University Press, 1986).

the second half of the play, however, Forman notoriously did not mention the Chorus of Time (though he did note that Perdita was sixteen years old then), the infamous bear, or the great statue scene (he had not even noted Hermione's apparent death). But one feature of the second half of the play does seem to have struck his attention greatly: 'Remember also the Rog that cam in all tottered like coll pixci. and howe he feyned him sicke & to have bin Robbed of all that he had and howe he cosoned the por man of all his money. and after cam to the shep sher with a pedlers packe & ther cosoned them Again of all their money And howe he changed apparrell w^t the kinge of bomia his sonn. and then howe he turned Courtiar &c'. The message was clear to Forman: 'beware of trusting feined beggars or fawninge fellouss'.[25] Autolycus is an entirely different kind of 'feined beggar' from Poor Tom, of course – not a lunatic but part of the tradition of the merry beggar; he enters singing of the red blood reigning in the winter's pale and the sweet birds, O how they sing. As a matter of economic and political theory, such wandering beggars – Christopher Sly in *The Taming of the Shrew* seems to be another – were subject to all the same harsh laws as any other masterless man, though they were also frequently used as necessary vehicles of distribution in local economies. As one contemporary described the type, 'A Ballad-seller . . . hath a whole Armie of runnagates at his reversion, that swarme everie where in *England*, and with theyr ribauld songs infect the Youth of this flourishing Commonweale.'[26]

Although Autolycus' character seems derived primarily from literary sources – something of the picaresque, and of a tradition which romanticized the freedom and openness of the tramp's life – still the language Shakespeare has created for him receives its life from a number of other wellsprings. The songs link Autolycus with a popular tradition of festive natural celebration; many analogous songs have been reported with the same peddler's cry, 'what do you lack?'[27] On the other hand, the language of Autolycus also reveals a strong indebtedness to the cony-catching pamphlets of Robert Greene, not only in the specific trick which Forman recalled, but in the vocabulary and diction of his language. Autolycus is given many of the specialized terms of the thieves' trade: 'doxy', 'pugging' (or 'prigging'), 'die and drab', 'prig', 'cut-purse', 'I picked and cut most of their festival purses', and so forth. More, his voice is both unique in its colloquial eccentricities and almost Jonsonian in its sharp familiarity with the conventions of thieving:

you might have pinched a placket, it was senseless. 'Twas nothing to geld a codpiece of a purse. I could have filed keys off that hung in chains. No hearing, no feeling but my sir's song, and admiring the nothing of it . . . had not the old man come in with a hubbub against his daughter and the King's son, and scared my choughs from the chaff, I had not left a purse alive in the whole army.   (4.4.610–19)

This language is Shakespeare's closest approximation to what was sometimes known as 'Pedlar's French', or beggar's cant. The origins of the canting language are obscure – the *Liber Vagatorum* (1509), translated by Luther, offers a list of over 200 words; the English rogue pamphlets often featured a vocabulary list and sample dialogues in canting language. Language historians have shown that there were different jargons for various marginalized subgroups, but the vocabulary lists offered for vagabonds in the rogue pamphlets were quite consistent – indeed, often plagiarized from one another.[28] Nor was this language a purely

---

25 Quoted in the Arden *The Winter's Tale*, ed. J. H. P. Pafford (London, Methuen, 1963), p. xxii.

26 E. de Maisonneuve, *Gerileon of England* (1592); quoted in the Arden *The Winter's Tale*, p. 100.

27 See, for example, *The Pedlers Prophecie* (London, 1595): 'What lacke you, what buy you, any good pinnes etc', D3^r.

28 An extensive list of cant terms appears in Thomas Harman's *A Caveat or Warening for Commen Cursetors Vulgarely Called Vagabones* (London, 1568). Harman's *Caveat* went through four editions, followed by more or less open plagiarisms in *The Groundworke of Conny-Catching* (1592) and Dekker's *The Belman of London*

literary construct, for documentary evidence from court transcripts and interrogations demonstrates that Pedlar's French was actually used by peddlers and vagabonds throughout the Tudor–Stuart period; Fleetwood, as one example, recorded in 1585 the use of such terms as 'foyste', 'nyppe', 'lyft' and others at a school of pickpockets in London.[29] One must of course admit that Shakespeare's employment of beggar's cant is in no way as extensive or obsessive as for example Middleton and Dekker's in *The Roaring Girl* or Brome's in *A Jovial Crew*; Shakespeare's interest seems much less journalistic and sociological than theirs.

In considering the general issue of beggar's cant, one important historian of poverty in this period, A. L. Beier, has concluded, 'It is doubtful whether Pedlar's French represented an alternative ideology. It provided a means of communication, but its parameters were quite narrow.'[30] I of course want to argue the opposite point here, that an alternative language does represent an alternative ideology, and that the beggar's language in particular is a counter-discourse within the play. Autolycus is indeed a merry-hearted, jovial vagabond, but he also knows that 'Gallows and knock are too powerful on the highway. Beating and hanging are terrors to me' (4.3.28–9). He can flourish now because 'I see this is the time that the unjust man doth thrive' and he observes that 'The prince himself is about a piece of iniquity, stealing away from his father with his clog at his heels' (4.4.674–80). Autolycus' exchange of clothing with Florizel, the beggar and the prince switching rôles, comically stages the political fear of the lower class replacing a higher one. Autolycus' language does not change, however, as he assumes the trappings of 'great authority' (4.4.800–1): 'Whether it like me or no, I am a courtier. Seest thou not the air of the court in these enfoldings? Hath not my gait in it the measure of the court? Receives not thy nose court-odour from me? Reflect I not on thy baseness court-contempt? Thinkest thou, for that I insinuate to toze from thee thy business, I

am therefore no courtier? I am courtier cap-à-pie' (4.4.730–6).

Autolycus is 'cap-à-pie' a courtier, while Jack Cade, we were told in *The First Part of the Contention* (*2 Henry VI*), expected men to treat him '*in capite*' (4.7.121). Cade's attempted ascent to a kind of peasant kingship, Poor Tom's elevation to the position of 'learned justice', Autolycus' comical reversal in status from vagabond peddler to gentleman and courtier – these reversals suggest that the beggar's status in these plays is therefore not only to speak the voice of the dispossessed, which they do insistently, and not only to represent a socio-political inversion which impersonates the voice and values of those above them, but also to be that force which naturally seeks to *rise*, and therefore constitutes a politicized energy.

Though they are very different characters, Cade, Poor Tom, and Autolycus share many common attributes in their language: it is almost exclusively prose, highly colloquial, filled with puns and dramatic irony, semantically and syntactically unstable, invariably refracting the imagery and thematic concerns of the 'high' language of the plays. But beyond the obvious political themes *in* their language, the most political aspect of it is that it exists at all. As discourse, the voices of Cade, Poor Tom, and Autolycus enact their own ideological positions. Shakespeare may not have quoted his knowledge as frequently as some playwrights, and he certainly seems to have known less about beggars and vagabonds than Dekker did, but that was true of everyone. What he does understand, perhaps better than others, is the profound connection in the underclass between their politics and their language.

(1608); Dekker's plagiarism was pointed out by Samuel Rid, *Martin Mark-all, Beadle of Bridewell* (1608), who nevertheless quoted, and amplified, the list once again.

[29] *Tudor Economic Documents*, vol. 2, p. 339.

[30] Beier, *Masterless Men*, p. 126.

SOME VERSIONS OF COUP D'ETAT, REBELLION AND REVOLUTION

PIERRE SAHEL

This study will be a commentary on some Shakespearian dramatizations of coup d'état, rebellion, and revolution. These three concepts, which imply an obvious gradation within the theme of political violence, can be defined as follows. A coup d'état refers to a rather sudden attempt made by a few men to grasp the power of state at the top level; often, though not always, the attempt is supported by armed forces. A rebellion is a more general armed rising in defiance of the established authority. A revolution is a movement aiming at a lasting change in the social order. These definitions are simple and clear-cut[1] so as to be acceptable by all readers. It may be doubtful whether they would be fully understood by a Renaissance mind, but too minute developments would lead to what Montaigne called 'cette infinie contexture de débats', which, it is felt, should be avoided here.

In Act 2, Scene 7 of *Antony and Cleopatra*[2] a coup d'état does *not* take place, but many of the ingredients contributing to the making of one are gathered. The failure of the coup, *a contrario*, points out the missing constituents. The scene takes place on board Pompey's galley, off Misenum. As host, Pompey is the master of his guests' fates. He is supposed to treat and feast them, but, isolated as they are from the *terra firma*, what cannot Pompey and Menas, his ally, perform upon the unguarded Antony, Lepidus, and Caesar? While the merry feasters speak of crocodiles, pyramids, and quicksands (18–58), Menas unfolds to Pompey

the project that might give him 'all the world':

> These three world-sharers, these competitors,
> Are in thy vessel. Let me cut the cable;
> And when we are put off, fall to their throats.
> All there is thine.   (69–72)

This projected coup, were it actualized, would, at little cost, erect a new single pillar of the Roman world to replace the three old ones. It is conceived in secrecy, amidst the noisy background of feasting and drinking. Menas and Pompey exchange asides and whispers only. Menas' project fails when it is spoken out:

> POMPEY
> Ah, this thou shouldst have done,
> And not have spoke on't . . .
> . . . Repent that e'er thy tongue
> Hath so betray'd thine act. Being done unknown,
> I should have found it afterwards well done.
>   (72–8)

The world of words has invaded the amoral vacuum of political brutality and suddenness. With language, moral consideration creeps into the realm of secrecy: soon, Pompey will evoke his honour and reputation.

At the beginning of *3 Henry VI*, an actual

---

[1] These definitions agree with the explanations and comments of W. F. Wertheim's classical work, *Evolution and Revolution: The Rising Waves of Emancipation* (London, 1974).

[2] References to Shakespeare are from *The Peter Alexander Edition* (London and Glasgow, 1951).

coup d'état is effected in the House of Parliament. In the House of Parliament, a parley might well have been admitted. But the Yorkists (who are going to perform the coup) are determined; language will not conquer them. Force is insisted upon:

RICHARD
Arm'd as we are, let's stay within this house.
WARWICK
The bloody parliament shall this be call'd.
(1.1.38–9)

Henry VI is aware that his enemies' superior might has led them to where they now stand. He confesses that 'they have troops of soldiers at their beck' (68). He may well use language, torrents of words on equity, patience, gentleness, etc. – from his entrance, three lines out of four are his: language, this time, will not subvert action. A stage direction reads:

[Warwick] stamps with his foot and the Soldiers show themselves.

This stamped foot suppresses the whining and pleading. Henry VI quickly capitulates:

I am content. Richard Plantagenet,
Enjoy the kingdom.   (174–5)

And he accepts a political compromise.

Apart from such dramatizations of sheer violence, a coup d'état is liable to be most untheatrical. It may be realized with some surprise that it is likely that Fortinbras, at the end of *Hamlet*, seizes power after a successful coup. Indeed, after carrying out his expedition against Poland, he passes *pat* by Elsinore to receive the unpossessed Danish crown. It is only when Hamlet is about to die that the warlike noises of Fortinbras' approaching army are heard. The path is open for him, and Hamlet does 'prophesy the election lights on [him]' (5.2.347–8). Backed by his soldiers, the conqueror enters the Danish court and orders Hamlet's corpse to be borne away by four of his captains. He pays a compliment to the prince who, to him, is certainly good being gone, and smoothly carries out his coup:

I have some rights of memory in this kingdom,
Which now to claim my vantage doth invite me
(5.2.381–2)

– a most apposite recollection. With these scanty words but amidst the 'soldier's music' and 'the rite of war' speaking loudly, the man of history succeeds the man of tragedy on the stage. Action subverts language. The rest is silence. Fortinbras has Hamlet's dying voice. The living voice of tragedy is not heard any more.

The unobtrusive achievement of Fortinbras conforms with the definition of a coup d'état, which is here effected by a military force and in the absence of any spectacular concourse of people. But theatre will often be more theatrical, and the paradox of hardly noticeable yet effective action on the stage may be superseded by another paradox. In *Richard III*, Shakespeare allows his protagonist to stage the coup that crowns him king by calling upon the clamorous people. But it is noteworthy that, here too, the soldiery is called out. This is suggested by the 'rotten armours' (3.5 stage direction) worn by Richard and Buckingham, and also by the military references in the show-within-the play which the two accomplices give for the Lord Mayor's benefit. These allude to drum (3.5.16), drawbridge (3.5.15), walls (3.5.17), and enemies (3.5.19). They conjure up a background of war which is sham but indispensable to what follows, namely the illegal liquidation of Richard's last foe: Hastings. Against this background, Richard and Buckingham pretend to be engrossed in warlike preoccupations and to have just overcome some military threat. Against this background, Hastings' freshly severed head will seem to be, not the testimony of Richard's ruthless way of dealing with his opponents, but the proof that an attack or rising found rebuke and was deftly handled by Richard and Buckingham – providential victors, *milites ex machina*. It could not be asserted that with Richard the army seizes power, but his soldierly qualities are underlined: being warlike is here a value to be boasted of, more than an actual means to reach the top. More strikingly, the people of London, stimulated by Buckingham's paid applauders, his *claque* (3.7.34–6), and by the Mayor's compliance, become an agent in Richard's enterprise. Richard III is the only Shakespearian sovereign to reach power 'democratically', after an admittedly fake popular election. We certainly feel inclined to smile, or laugh, at the all-but-impossible success of Richard, and Shakespeare's endeavour, presumably, was not the dramatization of high politics but the transformation of coup into farce, of coup d'état into coup de théâtre.[3] He introduces a measure of distancing between the gullible spectators of Richard and Buckingham's show and us, the audience who watch *Richard III*. To us, the final step of Richard's coup, the pseudo-popular offer of the crown, looks like a grand display of theatrical fireworks. But to the gullible spectators-within-the play, it is a political bludgeoning. For they must be convinced that the morally lofty pretender shrinks from seizing the crown and even from showing himself to his supporters. His – deliberately rehearsed – reluctance is proclaimed in various ways. It is first reported by Catesby who describes the still unseen Richard allegedly engrossed in his pious meditations (3.7.61–4). Then this emblematic vignette is commented upon by Buckingham ('when holy and devout religious men / Are at their beads, 'tis much to draw them thence, / So sweet is zealous contemplation', 3.7.92–4). It is afterwards directly dramatized, as a stage direction reads: *Enter Gloucester aloft between two Bishops*. Fourthly, the Mayor describes the scene ('See where his Grace stands 'tween two clergymen', 3.7.95), while (fifthly) Buckingham stresses the moral emblem ('Two props of virtue for a Christian prince, / To stay him from the fall of vanity . . .' 3.7.96–7). This accumulation is an extraordinary technique – the superimposition of dramatized scene and reported scene – resulting in scenic pleonasm when Richard is being watched at the very same time as he is described and commented upon.[4]

When the next concept of violent political means, rebellion, is analysed, it is no surprise to find that a greater number of *personae* are directly and consciously involved than in a coup d'état. Not more than a coup d'état, however, is a Shakespearian rebellion supposed to upset fundamentally the traditional order of things. The old critical dichotomy between order and rebellion is probably regarded by now as an obsolete opposition.[5] The affirmation of a new description is perhaps needed at this time, and it may be formulated as follows: *a rebellion often aims at restoring, not destroying*.

At the beginning of *Richard II*, Bolingbroke's father listens to the protests against the novel Italianate fashions whose adopter is no less than the king (2.1.17–23), before he recalls the chivalric tradition of his sceptred isle, chary of her reputation through the world (40–80). When the first unofficial manifesto of the rebels of the play is issued, it proclaims the regenerative ambition of the enterprise now about to be launched:[6]

---

[3] See Pierre Sahel, 'The Coup d'état of Shakespeare's *Richard III*: Politics and Dramatics', *Aligarh Journal of English Studies*, 10, 1 (1985), 2–8.

[4] The paradox of a political change decided upon by one or few men but involving popular elements reappears in *Henry VIII*, after the palace revolution against Wolsey. See Pierre Sahel, 'The Strangeness of a Dramatic Style: Rumour in *Henry VIII*', *Shakespeare Survey 38* (1985) 145–51, p. 149.

[5] See, for example, R. H. Wells, *Shakespeare, Politics, and the State* (London, 1986), p. 115: 'What we find in Shakespeare is not the didactic assertion of an "orthodox" doctrine of absolute obedience to kingly authority, but a recognition, first of the horrors of civil war, and second, of the fact that in practice a usurper of ability may contribute more to social harmony than an irresponsible king with impeccable hereditary credentials.'

[6] Graham Holderness, *Shakespeare's History* (Dublin and New York, 1985) also finds that Bolingbroke represents feudal reaction rather than political revolution. See also Clayton G. Mackenzie, 'Paradise and Paradise Lost in *Richard II*', *Shakespeare Quarterly*, 37, 3 (1986), in particular p. 324.

> If then we shall shake off our slavish yoke,
> Imp out our drooping country's broken wing,
> Redeem from broking pawn the blemish'd
>   crown,
> Wipe off the dust that hides our sceptre's gilt,
> And make high majesty look like itself,
> Away with me in post to Ravenspurgh.
>
> (291–6)

When Aumerle, in turn, wishes to launch his rising, he hopes to restore Richard (who is still alive) to the throne. He rejects the 'new come spring' of the now established usurper (5.2.46–8). In other words, he would like to go upstream, to call back yesterday, like the earl of Salisbury asking his king to bid time return (3.2.69).

In *1 Henry IV*, Hotspur, while his protest is as yet merely verbal, rejects the world of milliners, pouncet-boxes and fresh bridegrooms of the snobbish civil servant appointed by the new power and who, popinjay-like, is only good to repeat his master's voice (1.3.30–64). As stage managers and directors have sometimes noted, rebellions are launched against the central power by traditional minded Northerners speaking with unaffected regional accents.[7] In the Henry IV plays, Shakespeare dramatizes the rebels' rising as the absurd struggles fought on behalf of a past the death of which they refuse to acknowledge. In particular he shows that the attempt of the rebels of the second Part is nearly as suicidal as the moral combat led by their predecessors in the first Part. They reiterate the doomed resistance made against Henry IV since his accession. Moreover, if the political origin of their attempt is clear, its political aim is blurred into uncertainty. Indeed, if the rebellion against the crowned usurper and supported for a while by Aumerle could, in case of success, restore (as has been seen above) the deposed king, no such possibility exists in the Henry IV plays. None of the rebels of *1 Henry IV* ever mentions the possible coronation of Mortimer. It is, at least, remembered that the same Mortimer was proclaimed 'By Richard that dead is the next of blood' (1.3.146). But the pretender does not even appear in *2 Henry IV*.[8] One of the confederates merely refers to what could hardly be defined as a political platform when he speaks of

> this great work –
> Which is almost to pluck a kingdom down
> And set another up.   (1.3.48–50)

The most significant word in this pronouncement may well be *almost*: it is *almost* to pluck a kingdom down. But what is it *exactly*? What pre-Bolingbrokian state is to be thus set up? The kingdom with a dead king or a resuscitated political saint? The Archbishop of York's rising, indeed, looks more like a resurrectional than an insurrectional movement. He 'doth enlarge his rising with the blood / Of fair King Richard, scrap'd from Pomfret stones' (1.1.204–5). The present régime is thus opposed by means of relics – the symbols of the dead past. The rebels in *2 Henry IV*, not unlike those in *Richard II* and *1 Henry IV*, challenge time. Their enemy's general speaks them true when he warns them:

> it is the time,
> And not the king that doth you injuries.
>
> (4.1.105–6)

Rebels in Shakespeare repeatedly express their awareness that their struggle is a losing fight, for example in *2 Henry IV*:

> We see which way the stream of time doth run
> And are enforc'd from our most quiet there
> By the rough torrent of occasion.   (4.1.70–2)

Elsewhere, they are engaged in a race against time ('O, let the hours be short', *1 Henry IV* 1.3.301; 'Come, let me taste my horse', *1 Henry IV* 4.1.119). But they are fighting against odds. Time is the king their enemy's ally, and they precipitate the armed clash instead of waiting

---

[7] John Dover Wilson and T. C. Worsley, *Shakespeare's Histories at Stratford* (London, 1952), p. 35.

[8] On the question of Mortimer's disappearance, see Kristian Smidt, *Unconformities in Shakespeare's History Plays* (London, 1982), pp. 104–6.

(in *1 Henry IV*) for Northumberland's (possibly problematical) recovery, or for Glendower, who, allegedly, 'cannot draw his power this fourteen days' (4.1.126), or till Worcester's cavalry forces have rested (4.3.21). The flow of time, 'a current roaring loud' (*1 Henry IV* 1.3.192), carries away the rebels in *1* and *2 Henry IV*. Rebellion, passion, family faithfulness, and emotional engagement are done away with at the ambush of Gaultree forest (*2 Henry IV* 4.2). Rebellious risings in Shakespeare may then, through a further paradox, be styled, *stricto sensu*, reactionary.

At first sight, even at second sight, it does not appear that Shakespeare's dramatizations include revolution. There exist in his plays special moments when the advent of a thorough political and social change seems imminent. But these are merely part of a dramaturgical strategy, aspects of an emphasizing rhetoric, suggesting that the whole population is agog. Nature then co-operates with choruses of anonymous voices to foresee a total upheaval and picture some anarchistic *grand soir* – the fatal hour before the big change. On the eve of Richard II's downfall, for example, warning is given:

> The bay trees in our country are all wither'd,
> And meteors fright the fixed stars of heaven;
> The pale-fac'd moon looks bloody on the earth,
> And lean-look'd prophets whisper fearful change;
> Rich men look sad, and ruffians dance and leap.
>
> (*Richard II*, 2.4.8–12)

The vagueness of such terms as 'looks', 'whisper', or 'fearful' only enunciates the unusually negative character of the event to come. Yet it leaves no doubt about the outcome of the unknown event. That rich men look sad while ruffians dance leads one to believe that the 'have-nots' will somehow possess what the 'haves' now possess, and that the established institutions will cease to exist. In *King John*, while the monarch is still in power, a similar warning is voiced:

> . . . as I travell'd hither through the land,
> I find the people strangely fantasied;

> Possess'd with rumours, full of idle dreams,
> Not knowing what they fear, but full of fear.
>
> (4.2.143–6)

A similar vagueness ('through the land', 'strangely', 'the people') seems purposefully maintained here. Something exceptionally frightful is to take place. If the dreams are 'idle', it may mean that the hopes, or the aspirations, or the cravings are not logically channelled in agreement to known patterns; if fantasy prevails, the bourns to some unpathed country may tomorrow be crossed. Yet no sun shall that morrow see, and we soon discover that such words were rhetorical hinges evoking a moral disquiet, or a general mood of uncertainty. As it happens, no revolution ensues. The events so momentously foreseen turn out to be but these: extended palace revolutions, games only, albeit political games, arousing terror in some, expectation in others (in theatrical terms, suspense or excitement), but contemplated by outsiders, as once Cordelia and Lear talking of court news as a kind of gambling – 'Who loses and who wins; who's in, who's out' (*King Lear* 5.3.15). A Henry simply replaces a Richard, or a Richard a Henry. Elsewhere, the evocation of revolution is not an aspect of dramaturgical rhetoric. It is just as negative. Revolution may be conjured up as 'base and bloody insurrection' (*2 Henry IV* 4.1.40), or 'pellmell havoc and confusion' (*1 Henry IV* 5.1.82), or 'hurlyburly innovation' (*1 Henry IV* 5.1.78). Its actors may be viewed as 'fickle changelings and poor discontents' (*1 Henry IV* 5.1.76) or 'moody beggars' (*1 Henry IV* 5.1.81). But these terms are used as so many political tools, propagandistic slanders hurled at the enemies who, in the Henry IV plays, have launched military risings the purpose of which is, as has been seen, rebellious, perhaps reactionary, but certainly not revolutionary.[9]

---

[9] The deprecation of the rebel armies, also described as tattered hosts of beggars, may well be fraught with irony since we know that, among the loyalist forces themselves, stand – witness Falstaff's recruits – 'pitiful rascals', 'exceeding poor and bare' (*1 Henry IV* 4.2.62–6).

It is (of course) in *King Lear* that the most genuinely revolutionary pronouncements are made. The sinning monarch 'takes physic' and wishes to expose himself to 'feel what wretches feel' (3.4.33–4). Knowing, moreover, that the basest beggars 'Are in the poorest thing super-fluous' (2.4.264), he tears off his clothes (3.4.108), debases the great image of authority to the vignette of a dog obey'd in office (4.6.159), and denounces the judge who's obey'd in office too, not because of his virtue and integrity, but because a corrupt and re-pressive society has appointed him. Money, indeed, can 'seal th' accuser's lips' (4.6.170), and the beadle hotly lusts to use the whore he is whipping in that kind for which he whips her (4.6.162–3). But if revolutionary messages are thus voiced in *King Lear*, its hero does not dream of hurling the world into complete reforma-tion: the usurer will continue to hang the cozener (4.6.163). In a fine exemplification of his ambivalent attitude to revolution, Shake-speare allows the villains of the play to sub-stantialize revolutionary programmes. The steps they take can be understood as practical moves towards a general alteration of the social and moral establishments. Edmund the base, refusing 'to stand in the plague of custom', tops 'th' legitimate' (1.2.21). His voice is often that of the leftist, or the radical, or the dissenter, trying to give legitimacy to his cravings. More generally speaking, the torturers of Lear and Gloucester try to superimpose a *new* order of things upon what is established. Regan's ges-ture, as she plucks Gloucester's beard (3.7.34–5), is a symbolic abuse at respectable age and even at man and virility. Goneril's courtship of Edmund (4.2.20–5) is a protest against woman's traditional position as a being to *be* wooed. As she contemplates her husband's assassination, she boldly writes, like a feminist freedom-seeker:

His bed [is] my gaol; from the loathed warmth
    whereof deliver me.   (4.6.266–7)

Her protests agree with Edmund's plea in favour of *union libre* and against the legally sanctioned matrimony, which only offer 'a dull, stale, tired bed' to create 'a whole tribe of fops / Got 'tween asleep and wake' (1.2.13–15). Regan, when she publicly asks Edmund to marry her, wishes to use the habitually mascu-line privilege of 'taking the initiative'. She also expresses her readiness to replace the officiant:

Witness the world that I create thee here
My lord and master.   (5.3.78–9)

Should the aggressive actions of these revo-lutionists be thoroughly successful, the world would be topsy-turvy.

Shakespeare's ambivalent treatment is also discovered in his dramatization of popular revolution. The description as a real revolution of Cade's rising in *2 Henry VI* is not to be taken for granted. It might be called a *jacquerie* – but the listing of revolutionary elements in a *jac-querie* would lead us astray. It might be called an exacerbated protest against the loss of the con-quests in France. It might be called a sinister farce. It might be regarded as the popular parody/imitation of the butchery achieved by the aristocracy of the play. It might be pointed out that Cade is inconsistent in his principles since he insists on presenting himself as the lost son of Edmund Mortimer (4.2.131–41), dubs himself a knight (4.2.115–16), and mentions the restoration on his behalf of *jus primae noctis* (4.7.113–15). Indeed it might. Yet it is, above all, a genuine revolutionary attempt, with its popular legitimacy, ideology, and also mille-nary dreams into which it eventually flounders. The true background of the Cade scenes is neither whatever incident, commotion, or anecdote we might select from Elizabethan history, nor our own knowledge of revolutions past and present, but simply – and logically – *2 Henry VI*. In the first acts and scenes of the play, Humphrey of Gloucester was the protec-tor of the people just as he was the Protector of the kingdom. He 'would not tax the needy commons' (3.1.116). Petitioners would deliver their supplications to him (see 1.3.1–24). His enemies had chosen to murder, not impeach, him because they dreaded a popular rising to save his life (3.1.240). A riot takes place immediately after the news of his death:

> The commons, like an angry hive of bees
> That want their leader, scatter up and down.
>
> (3.2.125–6)

The fundamental injustice of Humphrey's death legitimizes the beginning of Cade's movement. Certainly Cade and his followers do not claim to follow the ways of the justice which Suffolk and Co. have so often twisted to their own advantages. A form of counter-justice appears instead. The brutality and buffoonery of the Cadians reveal a vital and rough desire to have sin 'struck down, like an ox' or 'iniquity's throat cut like a calf' (4.2.25–6). This is assuredly a brutish figurative language, but it is not necessarily unlike the forms of the official justice which was called, in the very words of its titular head, the king, the road 'to the bloody slaughter-house' (3.1.212). The frantic will to destroy law – the Inns of court are to be pulled down (4.7.2–3) – goes together with a desire to abolish knowledge. Is not knowledge a means, for those who possess it, to master those who do not possess it? It increases the gap between the poor and the rich. *Adequation* exists between 'All scholars, lawyers, courtiers, gentlemen' (4.4.36). Evidence is brought against the Lord Say that poor men, if unable to read, were hanged, or, if unable to answer their charges, were sent to prison (4.4.38–40). The Cadians, knowing that the letter has killed, now want to kill the letter. But their violence, because it is revolutionary violence, does not strike at abstract things only. Scapegoats are soon found, and the Clerk of Chatham is sentenced to death by a popular jury: he is hanged 'with his pen and inkhorn about his neck' (4.2.104–5). From a philosophical viewpoint, it is to be added that the purpose of knowledge is to study what is either real or possible. To the Cadians, what is real must disappear. Their wild action is not channelled into what is really possible or poss-

ibly real. Unreality lurks behind their evocations of those moments of plenty, in the time of Henry V, when 'boys went to span-counter for French crowns' (4.2.153). This is no reactionary hankering, or a wish to regain a lost paradise, though it may be remarked, in passing, that the most acknowledged revolutionists, Marx and Engels, did not dispense with an appeal to a more or less imaginary past. For the Cadians, a revolutionary leap is contemplated rather; it is stimulated by the defeat of two royal armies sent against them. This all but impossible success must bring about a marvellous future, a *near* future. The ideology of the rising demands egalitarianism, *hic et nunc*:

> it is said 'Labour in thy vocation'; which is as much to say as 'Let the magistrates be labouring men'; and therefore should we be magistrates. (4.2.15–18)

This is, in a few words, the clearest voicing of a theory of the revolution in Shakespeare. It is also couched in the embryo of a communist programme in four points: collective ownership, one livery for each and all, abolition of money, and a . . . very special economic policy. The essence of Cade's attempted revolution is often akin to a millenary utopia. Were the rioters realistic, they would soon accept the king's mercy offered by Humphrey Stafford. But this would mean their return to social nonentities. Stafford indeed calls them 'the filth and scum of Kent' (4.2.117). Instead of realism, imagination activates the wretches, and penetrates their speeches. Their cataclysmic rising has a touch of magic rendered, for example, by Cade's proclamation when, Moses-like, he strikes his staff on London stone and decrees:

> Now is Mortimer lord of this city. And here, sitting upon London Stone, I charge and command that, of the city's cost, the pissing-conduit run nothing but claret wine this first year of your reign. (4.6.1–4)

When eventually another messenger from the king, Clifford, pacifies the rioters, he will succeed in doing so by appealing to some of the very dreams of the men of Kent:

Is Cade the son of Henry the Fifth,
That thus you do exclaim you'll go with him?
Will he conduct you through the heart of France,
And make the meanest of you earls and dukes?

(4.8.33–6)

The suggestion that, with the king, they will radically transform their lives meets some of the dreams of the Cadians. France, assuredly, will not be reconquered; Henry VI is not Henry V; but Clifford's skilful words speak magic too. Cade's revolution soon collapses.

What is to be made of these excursions into Shakespearian dramatization of some violent political means, coup d'état, rebellion, and revolution? No complete conclusion should be advanced since the treatments of these concepts are more than once ambivalent or contradictory – and probably more so than has been suggested here. Moreover, such politically important plays as *Julius Caesar* or *Coriolanus* have not been dealt with though they too are about coup d'état and revolution; and some of the concepts which have been examined may also be touched on in *Henry V, Troilus and Cressida, Macbeth* or *The Tempest* – whereas only some of the histories and a couple of tragedies have been under consideration. It is doubtful, in any case, that the whole of Shakespeare's work contains any real doctrinal development, even less any ideological unity. Many questions have assuredly remained unanswered here – what distinctions, for example, does Shakespeare make between those who fight for their own ends and those who act selflessly; does he support the *status quo*, etc.? It is enough if these developments somehow tend to increase our knowledge of the playwright's political insight. They reveal or confirm that realism is at the heart of Shakespeare's treatment of the turbulent life of the City: those who can play the fox and the lion do win, without being necessarily right, while those who lose are not necessarily wrong. Shakespeare is also realistic in that he pays the minutest attention to the political moments in his plays even when they have no major impact on the evolving plots. Indeed, Menas' attempted coup does not take us anywhere in particular; nor does the freshly learnt ideology of the reformed Lear; as for Cade's revolutionary moves, they are a parenthesis of utopia and popular frenzy. These developments also reveal or confirm that a civil war of a kind exists between the two pillars of traditional stage: action and speech. They reveal or confirm that rebellion is often restorative or even reactionary, and, perhaps more importantly, that existential questions are raised by the paradoxes of rebellion. Lastly, these developments may reveal the relevance of Shakespeare's dramatizations to these our days, when coup d'état, rebellion, and revolution are frequent means of political action. This is so, probably, because we are (more than ever?) Shakespeare's contemporaries.

WOMAN, LANGUAGE, AND HISTORY IN
THE RAPE OF LUCRECE

PHILIPPA BERRY

Recent feminist criticism of Shakespeare's *The Rape of Lucrece* (or *Lucrece*, as it was titled in its first five quartos) has stressed the extent to which the idea of woman which it represents is one overdetermined by patriarchal ideology, and has typically interpreted Lucrece herself as a sign used to mediate and define men's relationships to men.[1] While I am partially in agreement with such interpretations of the poem, I want here to question the view that at no point in the poem is Lucrece represented as posing any contradiction, any *aporia*, within patriarchal discourse. Nancy Vickers, in her celebrated essay, '"The blazon of sweet beauty's best": Shakespeare's *Lucrece*', argues that:

In *Lucrece* occasion, rhetoric, and result are all informed by, and thus inscribe, a battle between men that is first figuratively and then literally fought on the fields of woman's 'celebrated' body. Here, metaphors commonly read as signs of a battle between the sexes emerge rather from a homosocial struggle, in this case a male rivalry, which positions a third (female) term in a median space from which it is initially used and finally eliminated.[2]

Of course Vickers is right in her assertion that Lucrece, as a third and female term, occupies 'a median space' in the poem. She identifies this inbetween space with Lucrece's body (as Georgianna Ziegler has recently pointed out, this space is also the private domestic space associated with female identity by patriarchal culture).[3] Lucrece's body does indeed begin and end the poem as the object of masculine rhetoric. None the less, it is strange that Vickers, in focusing

her influential feminist analysis upon men's use and abuse of language in Shakespeare's poem, failed to discuss Lucrece's own language – her speech at her death, and her more private but much longer rhetorical performance, in the privacy of her chamber, immediately before and after her rape. For Lucrece's 'inbetweenness' can also be related to the importance which her voice assumes at the dead centre of the poem, in a textually constituted space which corresponds to the very depths of night according to Shakespeare's narrative. It is in this median and very dark space, under the threat of rape and death, that Lucrece utters her first words in the poem, thereby beginning a long rhetorical performance (albeit one that is occasionally interrupted) which runs from line 575 until her death at line 1722, and in which the number of lines actually spoken by Lucrece is 645 – in other words, just over a third of the total number of lines in the entire poem.

The greater part of this long speech is an extended lament or complaint by Lucrece for her lost virtue, and here Shakespeare departs

---

[1] See in particular Coppélia Kahn, 'The Rape in Shakespeare's *Lucrece*', *Shakespeare Studies*, 9 (1976), 45–72; and Nancy Vickers, '"The Blazon of Sweet Beauty's Best": Shakespeare's *Lucrece*', in *Shakespeare and the Question of Theory*, ed. P. Parker and G. Hartman (London, 1985), pp. 95–115.

[2] Vickers, 'The Blazon of Sweet Beauty's Best', p. 96.

[3] Georgianna Ziegler, 'My Lady's Chamber: Female Space, Female Chastity in Shakespeare', *Textual Practice*, 4, 1 (Spring 1990), 73–90.

most strikingly from his sources in that throughout most of this lament Lucrece is alone. In the classical sources of the poem, notably Ovid's *Fasti* and Livy's *History*, Lucrece's lament is much shorter, and always addressed to an audience – her husband Collatine, her father, and their two friends, Junius Brutus and Publius Valerius. The same masculine audience for this utterance is posited in the rather longer speech found in the extremely popular *Declamatio Lucretiae*, written by the Florentine humanist Coluccio Salutati in the fourteenth century. Not only does Shakespeare's Lucrece speak most of her lament while she is alone; Shakespeare also added a number of details to the quite simple form of the lament found in his sources: in particular, Lucrece's three impassioned apostrophes to Night, Time, and Opportunity, and her meditation upon a painting of the fall of Troy. Yet while these changes have been noted by critics, they do not appear to have provoked much interest. Even a fairly extensive consideration of this part of the poem, by Don Cameron Allen, concentrates only upon the second stage·of the lament, in which Lucrece meditates upon a painting of violated Troy.[4]

In this essay, therefore, I will consider the complex implications of the often forgotten centrepiece of the poem, which is one of the most extended tragic utterances attributed to a woman in English Renaissance literature, and will assess its possible importance for a feminist – and a political – reading of this poem. My contention is that Lucrece is represented in the poem as an important but unorthodox example of Renaissance *virtù*, for this quality is given most powerful expression in the poem, not through her actions, but through her private use of language – a use which implicitly stresses its performative, even magical powers. It is in fact in this secret and powerful feminine eloquence that we can find the clearest indication of republican political ideals in the poem. The Earl of Southampton, to whom the poem is dedicated, is known to have been interested in

republican thought, and Shakespeare's choice of subject matter for his poem naturally suggests such an interest, since it was of course Lucrece's death which caused the end of Roman kingship with the downfall of the Tarquins, and the establishment of the Roman republic by Junius Brutus.[5] Significantly, the connection of Shakespeare's narrative with republican politics is never directly stated in the poem (presumably for reasons of political expediency). It is in Lucrece's lament, however, that the question of political justice is raised most directly.

Of course Lucrece's utterances in Shakespeare's poem are always to some extent implicated within a masculine poetic discourse: a discourse which is framed by the two male poetic exemplars of Orpheus and Virgil, as well as by the voice of the implicitly male narrator. Yet in contrast to the poem's emphasis upon the vulnerability of the female body, the female voice is here represented, not only as much less susceptible to manipulation by men, but even as the catalyst of an extraordinary political force: Lucrece's complaint enables her to replace Tarquin as the controlling figure in the narrative until the moment of her death. She only speaks, of course, when she is forced into the position of social outcast and scapegoat through the loss of her chastity – as in many other examples of English Renaissance literature, it is not until a female figure assumes a position of obvious marginality to conventional society (as opposed to the unacknowledged marginality to which all women are condemned in a patriarchal society) that she finds a voice. But through her discovery of a voice at the moment of personal disaster, Lucrece also develops a plan of action.

---

[4] Don Cameron Allen, *Image and Meaning*, 2nd edn (Baltimore, 1968), ch. 4.

[5] See Margot Heinemann, 'Rebel Lords, Popular Playwrights, and Political Culture: Notes on the Jacobean Patronage of the Earl of Southampton', *Yearbook of English Studies: Politics, Patronage and Literature in England 1558–1658*, 21 (1991), 63–86.

Without disputing the oft-stated feminist view that Lucrece's suicide is closely related to her acceptance of a patriarchal ideology of female chastity, I would suggest that this central section of Shakespeare's narrative challenges any interpretation of his Lucrece as being simply history's victim. Instead, it positions her as a partially independent, if somewhat un-orthodox (and confused) historical agent, who uses an Orphic private utterance to initiate historical change. Close analysis of her lament reveals Lucrece as the deliberate rather than accidental cause of that historical change which follows her death, and which leads to the expulsion and death of the Tarquins and the establishment of the Roman republic (although as I shall show later on, Lucrece never fully grasps the implications of the historical change which she initiates). It also shows her to be a figure who is learning, along with vocal self-expression, a political art of dissembling or concealment – a skill which will be most apparent in her planning of her suicide. Seemingly, Lucrece acquires and exercises a certain degree of political skill specifically through her use of language; in the first instance, she does this by appealing to a series of ideas which figured prominently in Renaissance mythographies: Night, Time and Opportunity (Opportunity being usually referred to as Occasio or Fortuna).[6] In this part of her lament, she expresses a powerful desire to reshape history and, specifically, to make it just. This struggle with history is seen primarily as a struggle with supernatural forces.

The effort of the man of *virtù* to shape fortune to his will was of course an important theme of Renaissance humanism, a theme especially prominent in the political thought of Machiavelli.[7] In his *Discourses*, which extolled the virtues of republican government, Machia-velli praised Junius Brutus as the Roman whose exemplary *virtù* led to the establishment of the Roman republic. But he also referred to the frequently important rôle played by women in the downfall of tyrannical rulers:

we see how women have been the cause of many troubles, have done great harm to those who govern cities, and have caused in them many divisions. In like manner we read in Livy's history that the outrage done to Lucretia deprived the Tarquins of their rule ... Among the primary causes of the downfall of tyrants, Aristotle puts the injuries they do on account of women, whether by rape, violation or the breaking up of marriages.[8]

Shakespeare's Lucrece is represented through her lament as a woman attempting to replace a loss of a specifically feminine 'virtue' with a *virtù* which can enable her to take control of her tragic fate. Yet her feminine discovery of this quality is importantly different from the typically public manifestation of *virtù* usually associated with men. Her attempt to master the forces which have led to her tragedy – Night, Time and Opportunity (or Fortune) – is con-ducted privately, and through a highly poetic use of language which simultaneously stresses language's magical, incantatory properties. This lament begins with Lucrece according supernatural priority to a primordial female divinity, Night. Only as a result of this private struggle to assert her *virtù* is Lucrece able to express it in more public terms at the end of the poem, with her speech and suicide before the four men whom she has summoned.

---

[6] For the frequent identification of Fortune with Oppor-tunity or Occasio, see Howard R. Patch, *The Goddess Fortuna in Medieval Literature* (London, 1927), pp. 115–16.

[7] The view of several Florentine humanists was that *virtù vince fortuna*: fortune need not overwhelm a man who does not fear to swim with her fierce current. Niccolò Machiavelli explored the problematic relationship between man and fortune (a personification whose feminine gender he stressed) in chapter 25 of *The Prince*. This book, together with Machiavelli's *Discourses*, was printed in England (in Italian) in 1584, under a false Italian imprint.

[8] Machiavelli, *The Discourses*, ed. Bernard Crick, trans. Leslie J. Walker SJ (London, 1983), 3, p. 26. I am indebted to Patricia Klindienst Joplin for the discovery of this quotation, which she cites in '"Ritual Work on Human Flesh": Livy's Lucretia and the Rape of the Body Politic', *Helios* 17, 1 (Spring 1990), 51–70.

In its appeal to Night, Lucrece's speech seems on one level to represent an early attempt by Shakespeare to use a figurative association of woman with darkness or blackness to challenge Petrarchan emphasis upon appearances in the poetic representation of women – it is her red and white perfection whose praise by Collatine at the beginning of the poem has contributed to Lucrece's tragedy. As in his use of images of darkness in connection with women in works which include the *Sonnets*, *Love's Labour's Lost*, and *Romeo and Juliet*, Shakespeare seems in *The Rape of Lucrece* to be trying to define an unorthodox, dynamic version of female identity in terms of hiddenness or concealment. Lucrece appeals to Night to protect her reputation by concealing her under shadow of darkness:

O night, thou furnace of foul reeking smoke,
Let not the jealous day behold that face
Which underneath thy black all-hiding cloak
Immodestly lies martyred with disgrace!
Keep still possession of thy gloomy place,
  That all the faults which in thy reign are made
  May likewise be sepulchred in thy shade.

Make me not object to the tell-tale day:
The light will show charactered in my brow
The story of sweet chastity's decay,   (799–808)

Yet at the same time, Lucrece's speech makes clear the moral ambiguity of Night: an ambiguity which is also suggested in its invocation by two such different tragic heroines as Juliet and Lady Macbeth.[9] Indeed, when considered in relation to the political themes of this poem, the associations of Night with concealment also imply a connection with the sixteenth-century humanist motif of politic dissembling, set out most explicitly in Machiavelli's *The Prince*. Breaking with earlier humanist emphasis upon the morality of *virtù*, Machiavelli had stressed that its practitioner must often dissimulate, and certainly a concealment and dissimulation associated with Night is central to Lucrece's practice of *virtù*. Not only does she conceal the fact of the rape until her husband and father are in her presence; the

theme of hiddenness also characterizes Lucrece's lament or complaint, most of which is uttered secretly, under cover of darkness.

But the aesthetic and political implications of Lucrece's emphasis upon Night become clearer when these are related to the metaphysical significance of this concept. Night figured prominently in Orphic theology, a web of ideas which was granted considerable importance in the syncretic Christian Platonism of the Renaissance. For Renaissance Platonists, because Orpheus was described in myth as imposing order upon chaos through his extraordinary eloquence, he was seen not only as the inspired poet par excellence, but also as a magician, one of the *prisci theologi* – the ancient theologians whose thought was held to have prefigured Platonism as well as Christianity.[10] Pico della Mirandola asserted that: 'In natural magic nothing is more efficacious than the Hymns of Orpheus', and identified the Orphic principle of Night with the supreme deity of the Jewish Kabbalists, the En Soph.[11] Within the Orphic cosmogony, Night was represented as a force which could overturn the authority even of the king of the gods.

The Orphic hymns, first published in the Renaissance at Florence in 1500, were an important literary influence upon the French Pléiade poets in the mid sixteenth century, but in England interest in this material is not apparent until 1594, when, in the same year as *The Rape of Lucrece*, George Chapman's *The Shadow of Night* was published.[12] This poem was explicitly indebted to the Orphic hymns. The first of its two parts was a long hymn or incantation to Night as a primordial goddess.

---

9 *Romeo and Juliet* 2.2.10–16; *Macbeth* 1.5.50–4.
10 See D. P. Walker, *The Ancient Theology: Studies in Christian Platonism from the Fifteenth to the Eighteenth Century* (London, 1972).
11 Pico della Mirandola, 'Conclusiones secundam propriam opinionem . . . hymnos Orphei', II and XV, in *Conclusiones* (Rome, 1486).
12 See Françoise Joukovsky, *Orphée et ses disciples dans la poésie française et néo-latine du XVIe siècle* (Geneva, 1970).

Night is represented by Chapman as inspiring her poet with a *virtù* which is expressed through eloquence rather than strength, but which is none the less capable of ending human injustice and vice. For Chapman, Orpheus' attempt to rescue Eurydice from hell is an allegory of his fervent desire to restore justice on earth.[13] As the new Orphic poet, he appeals to Night to stage an apocalyptic overthrow of all present 'tyrannies':

> O then most tender fortress of our woes,
> That bleeding lye in vertues overthroes,
> Hating the whoredome of this painted light:
> Raise thy chaste daughters, ministers of right,
> The dreadful and the just Eumenides,
> And let them wreake the wrongs of our disease,
> Drowning the world in bloud, and staine the
>   skies
> With their spilt soules, made drunke with
>   tyrannies.[14]

The relationship between the works of Shakespeare and Chapman has of course been a subject of controversy since Arthur Acheson, Frances Yates and Muriel Bradbrook asserted that a reference to the 'school of night' in *Love's Labour's Lost* represented a satiric attack on the intellectual views of Chapman's circle (whose members included Raleigh and the Earl of Northumberland).[15] In my view, however, the rhetorical importance accorded to Night in *The Rape of Lucrece* (together with the use of similar imagery in several other works by Shakespeare) should prompt a reconsideration of this question; especially since the poem's date of composition seems likely to have been quite close to that of *Love's Labour's Lost*.

That Shakespeare's version of Night is indebted to the Orphic tradition is further suggested when Lucrece is herself directly compared to Orpheus, just before the first time that her words to Tarquin are reported by the narrator:

> Here with a cockatrice' dead-killing eye
> He rouseth up himself, and makes a pause,
> While she, the picture of pure piety,
> Like a white hind under the gripe's sharp claws,

> Pleads in a wilderness where are no laws
>   To the rough beast that knows no gentle
>   right,
>   Nor aught obeys but his foul appetite.

> But when a black-faced cloud the world doth
>   threat,
> In his dim mist th'aspiring mountains hiding,
> From earth's dark womb some gentle gust doth
>   get
> Which blows these pitchy vapours from their
>   biding,
> Hind'ring their present fall by this dividing;
>   So his unhallowed haste her words delays,
>   And moody Pluto winks while Orpheus
>   plays.   (540–53)

The reference suggests that while Lucrece's powers of language are comparable to those of Orpheus, at this stage they are unable to help her. It is not until after the rape, when Tarquin has fled, that her eloquence finds unconstricted expression. It is now that she appeals to 'comfort-killing' Night – a force which, as the poem emphasizes, has indirectly served as Tarquin's accomplice – to desert to her side, and stage a reordering of time:

> O hateful, vaporous, and foggy night,
> Since thou art guilty of my cureless crime,
> Muster thy mists to meet the eastern light,
> Make war against proportioned course of time.
>   (771–4)

She appeals to Night:

> Let my good name, that senseless reputation,
> For Collatine's dear love be kept unspotted;
> If that be made a theme for disputation,
> The branches of another root are rotted. (820–3)

---

[13] *The Poems of George Chapman*, ed. Phyllis Brooks Bartlett (New York, 1941), 'The Shadow of Night: Hymnus in Noctem', lines 151–2.

[14] Ibid., lines 247–54.

[15] See Arthur Acheson, *Shakespeare and the Rival Poet* (London, 1903); M. C. Bradbrook, *The School of Night: A Study in the Literary Relationships of Sir Walter Ralegh* (Cambridge, 1936); F. A. Yates, *A Study of 'Love's Labour's Lost'* (Cambridge, 1936).

A few lines later, Lucrece makes explicit this metaphoric connection between natural mutability and the sphere of politics, in what seems a restatement of the Machiavellian theme that all states are subject to decay, because of the natural depravity of man. Her words hint at a covert criticism of all models of kingship:

> Why should the worm intrude the maiden bud,
> Or hateful cuckoos hatch in sparrows' nests,
> Or toads infect fair founts with venom mud,
> Or tyrant folly lurk in gentle breasts,
> Or kings be breakers of their own behests?
>   But no perfection is so absolute
>   That some impurity doth not pollute.
>
> (848–54)

Lucrece follows her invocation of Night with an attack on Time and 'thy servant opportunity' (or Fortune) for behaving unjustly in betraying her to this misfortune. She demands of Opportunity:

> When wilt thou be the humble suppliant's friend,
> And bring him where his suit may be obtained?
> When wilt thou sort an hour great strifes to end,
> Or free that soul which wretchedness hath chained,
> Give physic to the sick, ease to the pained?
>   The poor, lame, blind, halt, creep, cry out for thee,
>   But they ne'er meet with opportunity.
>
> (897–903)

Finally, she asks Time:

> Why work'st thou mischief in thy pilgrimage,
> Unless thou couldst return to make amends?
>
> (960–1)

And she urges Time to punish Tarquin:

> Thou ceaseless lackey to eternity,
> With some mischance cross Tarquin in his light.
> Devise extremes beyond extremity
> To make him curse this cursèd crimeful night.
>
> (967–70)

Lucrece's lament is therefore also both invocation and imprecation. Through its language, she figuratively seizes control of history, rather than remaining its passive victim. Thereby, from the magical perspective of Orphic poetics, she actually begins to change it. Thus the poem seems to be associating a new, feminine model of *virtù*, expressed through the language of grief and mourning, with the capacity to disorder time and its processes.

But it would be a mistake to overestimate Lucrece's understanding of her own relationship to language or to history. Her desire for a universal justice is confusedly interwoven in this part of her lament with concern for Collatine's honour; moreover, she seems to underestimate the power of her own language, seeing her apostrophes to Night, Time, and Opportunity as having been made in vain. This lack of self-knowledge is even more apparent in the second phase of her solitary lament, which reveals her as extraordinarily anxious about the association of certain kinds of language with historical change, and as unable to face the implications of her desire to be revenged. While it was a Greek poet, Orpheus, who had influenced her invocations of Night, Time, and Opportunity, Lucrece's contemplation here of a painting of the fall of Troy is indebted to the writings of a Roman poet: to Books I and II of Virgil's *Aeneid*. And in this episode, the Greeks are identified with the treacherous power of language for deceit and destruction, through references to the 'golden words' of Nestor and the 'enchanting story' of Sinon. This emphasis upon the Greeks' powers of language suggests that the narrator may regard them with some sympathy and admiration; but Lucrece certainly views them with loathing, and grieves for ruined Troy. The episode indicates that at the same time as desiring justice, she is extremely fearful concerning the possible outcome of such a demand. Lucrece asks of Paris' cause of the fall of Troy through his abduction of Helen:

> Why should the private pleasure of someone
> Become the public plague of many moe?
> Let sin alone committed light alone
> Upon his head that hath transgressèd so;
> Let guiltless souls be freed from guilty woe.

THE RAPE OF LUCRECE

For one's offence why should so many fall,
To plague a private sin in general? (1478–84)

As her identification with Troy shows, Lucrece is profoundly implicated in the hierarchical system of values and government which her appeal for revenge will eradicate. We are told of the fall of Troy:

the skies were sorry,
And the little stars shot from their fixèd places
When their glass fell wherein they viewed their
faces. (1524–6)

Thus in spite of her concern about Collatine's honour, Lucrece does not grasp the extent to which she is now a traitor to that system. Shakespeare would have known from his sources that the expulsion of the Tarquins would ultimately mean a loss of political power for the family of her husband Collatine, who was cousin to Tarquin. It is striking that in her meditation upon the Troy painting, Lucrece directs especial hostility, firstly, towards Helen, a woman whose rape, like her own, causes the fall of a dynasty of kings; and secondly, towards 'perjured Sinon':

whose enchanting story
The credulous old Priam after slew;
Whose words like wildfire burnt the shining
glory
Of rich-built Ilion, (1521–4)

We are told, moreover, that Sinon had:

Cheeks neither red nor pale, but mingled so
That blushing red no guilty instance gave,
Nor ashy pale the fear that false hearts have.
(1510–12)

and that 'For every tear he falls a Trojan bleeds' (1551).

In other words, although Lucrece compares this traitor to the Trojans to Tarquin, he seems more closely to resemble herself. While her face is first described in the poem as a picture of red and white beauty, when she appears before the four men at the end of the poem the misfortune she has experienced is 'carved in it with tears' (1713), and this clearly adds to her rhetorical impact. Hence in her intense hostility to Helen and Sinon, Lucrece may imply a buried anxiety about her own ambiguous status as both member of and traitor to her society. At the same time, her criticism of Sinon also articulates a profound uncertainty about the ethics of a use of language to produce political change. Yet in spite of such reservations, Lucrece never fully acknowledges either her own contradictory historical position, or her personal recourse to the manipulative and performative resources of language. She goes on to stage the last act of her own tragedy, unaware of the full political and historical implications of the private as well as the public phases in this compelling performance.

LOVE IN VENICE

CATHERINE BELSEY

I

Love in Venice generally has a poor record. For Othello and Desdemona, as three centuries later for Merton Densher and Kate Croy, things work out badly. Love in Venice withholds happiness from Henri and Villanelle, the protagonists of Jeanette Winterson's novel, *The Passion*. It is fatal, of course, to Thomas Mann's Gustav Aschenbach. And Jessica, the twentieth-century heroine of Erica Jong's *Serenissima*, goes to Venice to play her namesake, and has the misfortune to fall in love with Shakespeare.[1] Though the nature of their tragedies changes with cultural history, Venice is generally no place for lovers.

In the circumstances, this essay, which is about *The Merchant of Venice*, should perhaps have been called 'Love in Belmont'. Belmont, after all, is so evidently the location in the play of happy love. Belmont is a fairytale castle, where three suitors come for the hand of the princess, and undergo a test arranged by her father in order to distinguish between true love on the one hand and self-love and greed on the other. It is a refuge for eloping lovers, who flee the precarious world of capital and interest and trade, to find a haven of hospitality, music, poetry, old love stories retold in the night – and the infinite wealth (without origins) which makes all this possible. Belmont is the conventional critical *other* of Venice, its defining romantic opposite. Belmont, it is widely agreed, is feminine, lyrical, aristocratic – and

vanishing – while Venice represents the new world of men, market forces and racial tensions.

And yet it is the relationship between Venice and Belmont which generates the romantic plot of the play. Portia's princely suitors are in the event an irrelevance: true love turns out to rely on credit. And when Portia takes an active hand in the affairs of capital, true love undergoes, I want to argue, a radical transformation which has continuing repercussions for us now.

It is surely perverse in a volume on Politics and Shakespeare to talk about *The Merchant of Venice* without discussing Shylock, who has quite properly come for twentieth-century criticism, particularly since the Second World War, to represent the crucial issue of this puzzling and in many ways disturbing play. The history of anti-semitism in our own epoch demands that this question be accorded full attention. If I say nothing about it, that is not because I regard it as less than central, but only because I have nothing of value to add to the existing debate.[2] And meanwhile, the play also

---

[1] I owe this reference to Kristina Engler.

[2] For an account of the debate (and selective bibliography) see Walter Cohen, *Drama of a Nation: Public Theater in Renaissance England and Spain* (Ithaca, 1985), pp. 196–7. See also Cohen's own analysis, pp. 195–211; Thomas Moisan, '"Which is the Merchant here? and Which the Jew": Subversion and Recuperation in *The Merchant of Venice*', in *Shakespeare Reproduced: The Text in History and Ideology*, ed. Jean E. Howard and Marion F. O'Connor (New York, 1987), pp. 188–206; Kiernan Ryan, *Shake-*

presents a sexual politics which is beginning to be the focus of feminist criticism and the cultural history of gender.[3] This essay is offered as a contribution to that discussion.

A reading of the sexual politics of the play might begin where interest in Shylock ends, in Act 5. The action of the play seems to have been completed already: the conflict, for better or worse, is over. Act 5 constitutes a coda to the main plot, a festival, set in Belmont, of love and concord and sexuality, combining elements of poetry and comedy, just as weddings do. Although it has no part in the main events of the play, Act 5 is conventionally held to complete its 'harmonies', to dissipate tension and reconcile differences.[4] The classic analysis is surely C.L. Barber's:

No other comedy, until the late romances, ends with so full an expression of harmony as that which we get in the opening of the final scene of The Merchant of Venice. And no other final scene is so completely without irony about the joys it celebrates.[5]

It is true that Act 5 *alludes to* harmony in Lorenzo's account of the music of the spheres. But it also reminds us that we cannot hear the celestial concord 'whilst this muddy vesture of decay / Doth grossly close it in' (5.1.64–5), and this way of talking about the body might seem, if not ironic, at least incongruous in an unqualified celebration of the joy of love. So too, perhaps, is the choice of love stories the newly married Lorenzo and Jessica invoke so lyrically: Troilus and Cressida, Pyramus and Thisbe, Dido, Medea (5.1.1–14). Nor does the text select from their tragic narratives moments of reciprocal happiness. On the contrary, Troilus is represented on the walls of Troy, sighing his soul towards the Greek camp and the absent Cressida. Thisbe is fearful and dismayed, Dido already deserted. Medea, gathering enchanted herbs, has not yet murdered her children in revenge for Jason's infidelity, but the text hints at her demonic powers and begins her characterization as a witch.[6]

The stories of Troilus and Cressida, Dido and Aeneas, and Pyramus and Thisbe are also represented on the walls of the temple of Venus in Chaucer's *Parliament of Fowls* (lines 289–91).[7] The temple, with its near-naked goddess lying on a bed of gold in the scented half-light, is surely a perfect allegory of desire. But desire is predicated on deprivation: love's acolytes in the temple include pale-faced Patience and bitter Jealousy; two young people kneel to the goddess crying for help; the altar-candles flicker, fanned by lovers' sighs. The stories painted on the walls tell more of sorrow than of joy. Happy love, as Denis de Rougemont repeatedly reminds us, so that the phrase becomes a kind of refrain running through *Love in*

speare (London, 1989, pp. 14–24; and John Drakakis, 'The Merchant of Venice, or Christian Patriarchy and its Discontents', In Mortal Shakespeare: Radical Readings, ed. Manuel Barbeito (Santiago de Compostela, 1989), pp. 69–93.

[3] See for example Linda Bamber, Comic Women, Tragic Men: A Study of Gender and Genre in Shakespeare (Stanford, 1982), pp. 109–33; Keith Geary, 'The Nature of Portia's Victory: Turning to Men in The Merchant of Venice', Shakespeare Survey 37 (1984), 55–68; Lars Engle, '"Thrift is Blessing": Exchange and Explanation in The Merchant of Venice', Shakespeare Quarterly, 37 (1986), 20–37; Karen Newman, 'Portia's Ring: Unruly Women and Structures of Exchange in The Merchant of Venice', Shakespeare Quarterly, 38 (1987), 19–33; Jean Howard, 'Crossdressing, the Theatre, and Gender Struggle in Early Modern England', Shakespeare Quarterly, 39 (1988), 418–40.

[4] See for example Lawrence Danson, The Harmonies of 'The Merchant of Venice' (New Haven, 1978), pp. 170–95.

[5] C. L. Barber, Shakespeare's Festive Comedy: A Study of Dramatic Form and its Relation to Social Custom (Princeton, NJ, 1959), p. 187.

[6] The specific reference is to Ovid, Metamorphoses vii, 162 ff. Medea treats Aeson with rejuvenating herbs. When the daughters of Pelias subsequently ask for her help, she deliberately offers them inefficacious herbs and thus causes them to bring about his death. I owe this point to Michael Comber. See also Jonathan Bate, 'Ovid and the Mature Tragedies: Metamorphosis in Othello and King Lear', Shakespeare Survey 41 (1989), 133–44, pp. 134–5.

[7] Geoffrey Chaucer, Works, ed. F. N. Robinson (London, 1957).

the Western World, happy love has no history.[8] In Chaucer's poem the parliament of the birds, to which the account of the temple of Venus is no more than a prelude, would have no story at all if Nature simply prevailed, and the fowls unproblematically chose their mates and flew away. But the narrative is sustained by the courtly eagles, all three in love with the same mistress, so that two at least are doomed to despair, and all three compelled to wait in hope and fear and longing.

'The moon shines bright. In such a night as this . . .' The rhythms and the internal rhymes, in conjunction with the climatic conditions, 'When the sweet wind did gently kiss the trees' (*The Merchant of Venice* 5.1.1–2), all serve to contain and dissipate what is most distressing in Shakespeare's classical and Italian narratives transmuted into medieval romance. The effect is thrilling to the degree that pleasure is infused with danger. It is also profoundly nostalgic in that it looks back to a world, fast disappearing in the late sixteenth century, where love was seen as anarchic, destructive, and dangerous. In the play this world is no longer dominant. Love in *The Merchant of Venice* means marriage, concord, consent, and partnership. It means mutual compatibility and sympathy and support. But the older understanding of love leaves traces in the text, with the effect that desire is only imperfectly domesticated, and in consequence the extent to which Venice is superimposed on Belmont becomes visible to the audience.

II

Desire, as characterized in Western culture, is dangerous. It depends on lack: you desire what you don't have; desire fulfilled is desire suspended. Psychoanalytically, desire can be satisfied only at the level of the imaginary, in that it insists upon absolute recognition from the other.[9] Lacan distinguishes desire from demand, the appeal for love which can be formulated – and met. Desire is the residue of demand, the unutterable within or beyond it. Lacan calls it the 'want-to-be' ('manque-à-être') that demand 'hollows within itself'. Because love cannot be fully present in the signifier, desire is brought to light precisely by the signifying chain itself, the otherness of language, in which it can never be met, since language too lacks being.[10]

Western literature presents desire as immoderate, disproportionate, unstable, thrilling precisely because it is hazardous. Villanelle, Jeanette Winterson's web-footed, cross-dressed Venetian croupier heroine, consistently associates desire with gambling, gambling with passion. Both are compulsive and urgent; both risk the possibility of loss. 'Somewhere between fear and sex passion is.'[11] Gustav Aschenbach is paradoxically elated by the discovery of disease in Venice because he senses a correspondence between the concealed, physical threat to the population and the dangerous secret of his own emotional condition.

Desire is perilous because it annihilates the speaking, knowing, mastering subject, the choosing, commanding self so precious to the Free West. Lovers are conventionally speechless (what can they say that would do justice to desire?). They are uncertain, irrational, out of control; transformed, transported, other than they are. Gustav Aschenbach, the rational, disciplined writer, knows that he ought to warn the Polish family about the pestilence and then leave Venice, but he also knows that passion will prevent him from doing either. 'It would restore him, would give him back himself once

---

8 Denis de Rougemont, *Love in the Western World*, trans. Montgomery Belgion (Princeton, NJ, 1983), p. 15 and *passim*.

9 Jean Laplanche and J.-B. Pontalis, 'Wish (Desire)', *The Language of Psychoanalysis*, trans. Donald Nicholson-Smith (London, 1973), pp. 481–3. Cf. Jacques Lacan, *Écrits: A Selection*, trans. Alan Sheridan (London, 1977), p. 58.

10 Lacan, *Écrits*, pp. 263, 265.

11 Jeanette Winterson, *The Passion* (London, 1988), p. 62. Cf. pp. 55, 66.

more; but he who is beside himself revolts at the idea of self-possession.'[12] For these reasons, desire also undermines the *idea* of the self, calling in question the dualism on which it is founded, deconstructing the opposition between mind and body, as each manifests itself in the province of the other.

We know from endless accounts of burning, freezing Petrarchan lovers, still pursuing, still disdained, wrecked and racked by love neglected, that the Renaissance took full account of the element of danger in desire.[13] And we know it too from the efforts of Astrophil to resist his own destruction, from the ambivalence of Antony towards his strong Egyptian fetters, and from countless tragedies of love in the period, most particularly, perhaps, the work of Middleton. Passion turns women to whores; it renders men effeminate, incapable of manly pursuits; it threatens identity, arousing fears that subjectivity itself is unstable.[14]

Bassanio is able to solve the riddle of the caskets not only because he sees through outward show, but also because he alone among the suitors recognizes the appropriate emblem of desire: 'thou meagre lead / Which rather threaten'st than dost promise aught, / Thy paleness moves me more than eloquence . . .' (3.2.104–6).[15] The Prince of Aragon thinks of his own desert, and the silver casket acts as a mirror for his narcissism, revealing the portrait of a blinking idiot (2.9.30–2, 50, 53). Morocco resolves to take his own desert for granted (2.7.31–4) and thinks of Portia's value: 'never so rich a gem / Was set in worse than gold' (2.7.54–5). The golden casket contains death, the destiny of those who serve mammon. Only Bassanio is motivated by desire and knows that lovers give and hazard all they have. His choice vindicates Portia's conviction: 'If you do love me, you will find me out' (3.2.41).

Even in his triumph Bassanio displays all the symptoms of passion: he is bereft of words; only his blood speaks in his veins, reducing subjectivity to sensation. Turmoil within the subject confounds the familiar system of differences: 'Where every something being blent together / Turns to a wild of nothing save of joy / Expressed and not expressed'. And in case it should all be too easy from now on, he willingly accepts the new hazard that Portia has set him: 'when this ring / Parts from this finger, then parts life from hence' (3.2.175–84). Even Portia's picture, which is no more than her 'shadow', is full of metaphorical dangers. Her parted lips are sweet friends *sundered*; her hair is a spider's web, 'A golden mesh t'untrap the hearts of men / Faster than gnats in cobwebs'. And in a strange, baroque conceit, Bassanio argues that the rendering of her eyes should surely have blinded the painter: 'having made one, / Methinks it should have power to steal both his / And leave itself unfurnished' (3.2.118–29).

III

Riddles too are traditionally dangerous because they exploit the duplicity of the signifier, the

---

[12] Thomas Mann, *Death in Venice, Tristan, Tonio Kröger* (London, 1955), p. 74.

[13] See Scott Wilson, 'Racked on the Tyrant's Bed: The Politics of Pleasure and Pain and the Elizabethan Sonnet Sequences', *Textual Practice*, 3 (1989), 234–49.

[14] Laura Levine, 'Men in Women's Clothing: Antitheatricality and Effeminization from 1579–1642', *Criticism*, 28 (1986), 121–43; Stephen Orgel, 'Nobody's Perfect: Or Why Did the English Stage Take Boys for Women?', *South Atlantic Quarterly*, 88 (1989), 7–29.

[15] Freud argues that Bassanio's choice (which is really a choice between three women) betrays an acknowledgement of ineluctable death, masked as the choice of a desirable woman (Sigmund Freud, 'The Theme of the Three Caskets', *Complete Psychological Works*, SE 12, ed. James Strachey (London, 1958), pp. 291–301). Sarah Kofman, developing Freud's argument, sees the episode as a representation of the 'ambivalence' (or duplicity) of love: the wish for love is superimposed on the awareness of death, but the imagery prevents the complete success of the process, so that the audience is satisfied at the level of fantasy but also at the level of the intellect (Sarah Kofman, 'Conversions: *The Merchant of Venice* Under the Sign of Saturn', in *Literary Theory Today*, eds. Peter Collier and Helga Geyer-Ryan (Cambridge, 1990), pp. 142–66).

secret alterity that subsists in meaning. They prevaricate, explicitly deferring and obscuring the truth. Riddles demonstrate that meaning is neither single nor transparent, that words can be used to conceal it. They show that language itself seduces and betrays those who believe themselves to be in command of it, who imagine it to be an instrument for their use, at their disposal. Riddles equivocate: Portia is what many men desire; but so is death. His own portrait is what Aragon deserves precisely because he supposes that he deserves Portia.

'What has one voice, and goes on four legs in the morning, two legs in the afternoon, and three legs in the evening?' The sphinx posed her riddle to the Thebans, and each time they got it wrong, she devoured one of them. In the play suitors who fail to solve the riddle of the caskets undertake never to marry. Penalties of this kind are common. Riddles are posed by the wise to isolate the foolish. Solomon delighted in them. They feature prominently in the book of Proverbs. The riddle for Portia's hand has the sacred character of a trial by ordeal. As Nerissa explains:

Your father was ever virtuous, and holy men at their death have good inspirations; therefore the lottery that he hath devised in these three chests of gold, silver, and lead, whereof who chooses his meaning chooses you, will no doubt never be chosen by any rightly but one who you shall rightly love.

(1.2.27–32)

Traditionally riddles are no joke. It is only the Enlightenment regulation of language, with its insistence on the plain style, affirming the transparency of the signifier, that relegates riddles to the nursery,[16] along with ogres and fairies and all the remaining apparatus of the uncanny.

In folk-tales riddles are a common way of exalting the humble and meek. The youngest of three brothers or the poorest of three candidates has only ingenuity or virtue to draw on. Success depends on quick wits or the help of a grateful friend. One of the commonest situations in folk-tales is a contest for the hand of the princess, and the motif of winning a bride

by solving a riddle goes back to the Greek romances, and reappears in the middle ages.[17] Bruno Bettelheim proposes a broadly Freudian interpretation of this recurrent phenomenon:

Solving the riddle posed by a particular woman stands for the riddle of woman in general, and since marriage usually follows the right solution, it does not seem farfetched that the riddle to be solved is a sexual one: whoever understands the secret which the other sex presents has gained his maturity.[18]

In a broadly Lacanian reformulation of this proposition it could be argued that the riddle for the hand of the princess is a riddle about the nature of desire, and that the text of The Merchant of Venice comes close to making this explicit. In the presumed source in the Gesta Romanorum, where the protagonist, interestingly, is a woman, the inscription on the lead vessel is providential: 'Who so chooseth mee, shall finde that God hath disposed for him.'[19] Shakespeare's change locates the meaning of the lead casket firmly in the realm of the secular and the sexual.

Moreover, riddles could be said to enact at the level of the signifier something of the character of desire. Both entail uncertainty, enigma. Both are dangerous. Riddles tease, torment, elude, challenge, and frustrate. Once the answer is known the riddle ceases to fascinate, just as desire evaporates once the *otherness* of the other is mastered. Both riddles and desire depend on a sense of the unpresentable within the process of representation, though desire imagines a metaphysical presence, a real existence elsewhere, while riddles refer to the unpresented, the meaning which is not there but which can be found, and found nowhere else

---

[16] Mark Bryant, *Dictionary of Riddles* (London, 1990), p. 51.

[17] Stith Thompson, *The Folktale* (Berkeley, 1977), pp. 153–8.

[18] Bruno Bettelheim, *The Uses of Enchantment: The Meaning and Importance of Fairy Tales* (London, 1978), p. 128.

[19] John Russell Brown, ed., *The Merchant of Venice* (London, 1959), p. 173.

but there.[20] In this sense the wooing of Portia displays a perfect appropriateness, a ceremonial decorum which endows it with all the traditional impersonality of the Anglican marriage service itself (this man . . . this woman, making a formal undertaking).[21]

IV

The riddle for Portia's hand is posed, appropriately enough, by a dead father, and solved by the romantic hero. Portia, who also has immoderate desires, cannot act on them but waits, a sacrificial virgin, for the happy outcome of the ordeal (3.2.111–14, 57). The news from Venice, however, changes everything. Antonio's predicament also poses a riddle: how can he fulfil his contract without losing his life? This time, Bassanio stands helplessly by while Portia and Nerissa turn to men, and Portia-as-Balthasar finds the equivocation which releases her husband's friend: flesh is not blood. An apparently archetypal and yet vanishing order is radically challenged by cross-dressed women who travel from Belmont to Venice and, uniquely in Shakespearian comedy, intervene not only in the public world of history, but specifically in the supremely masculine and political world of law, with the effect of challenging the economic arrangements of the commercial capital of the world.

And then in the final episode of the play it is the women who produce a series of equivocations which constitute yet another riddle, this time concerning the meaning of gender difference within a new kind of marriage, where a wife is a partner and a companion. The exchanges in Act 5 between Lorenzo and Jessica about old tales of love and death and the unheard music of the spheres are interrupted by the voice of Portia (5.1.110, 113), and her first words to them constitute a riddle to which, of course, the audience knows the answer: 'We have been praying for our husbands' welfare, / Which speed (we hope) the better for our words' (5.1.114–15). The remainder of the play

(almost 180 lines of it) consists largely of a series of increasingly bawdy puns and doubles entendres about rings, and this festival of plurality at the level of the signifier poses a riddle about sexual identity which presumably pleases the audience, but entirely baffles Bassanio.

George Puttenham discusses riddles in his handbook for vernacular writers, *The Arte of English Poesie*, printed in 1589. For Puttenham, with his clear humanist and Renaissance commitments, riddles are already becoming childish, though it is possible to see more in them than children might.

My mother had an old woman in her nurserie, who in the winter nights would put us forth many pretty riddles, whereof this is one:

> I have a thing and rough it is
> And in the midst a hole Iwis:
> There came a yong man with his ginne,
> And he put it a handfull in.

The good old Gentlewoman would tell us that were children how it was meant by a furd glooue. Some other naughtie body would peradventure have construed it not half so mannerly.[22]

Evidently for Puttenham riddles are engaging, harmless equivocations or ambiguities (unless they're unduly lewd), and the answer can be deduced from the terms of the puzzle itself, though it is not necessarily the first solution a grown-up might think of.[23]

---

[20] Wyatt exploits the parallel in his riddles of forbidden desire. See for example 'A ladye gave ne a gyfte she had not' . . . and 'What wourde is that that chaungeth not?', *The Collected Poems of Sir Thomas Wyatt*, ed. Kenneth Muir and Patricia Thomson (Liverpool, 1969), pp. 238, 36.

[21] The view that Bassanio is no more than a fortune-hunter who desires Portia only, or primarily, for her money seems to me anachronistic, probably filtered by Victorian fiction, where love and money are commonly opposed.

[22] George Puttenham, *The Arte of English Poesie*, ed. G. D. Willcock and A. Walker (Cambridge, 1936), p. 188.

[23] William Dodd identifies a structural analogy between riddle and comedy, which also sets a puzzle and finally solves it, though not in the most obvious way. See

But Puttenham also identifies another category of equivocation, this time profoundly disturbing, to which Steven Mullaney has drawn attention. This is the kind that seduces and betrays Macbeth, because it lies like truth, making it impossible to tell where truth resides. Puttenham calls this figure *amphibology*, and he condemns it roundly as a threat to order. Amphibologies are frequently without evident human or social origin: they emanate from oracles, pagan prophets – or witches, of course. And they particularly constitute the figure of insurrection, misleading the people in times of rebellion,

as that of Iacke Straw, & Iacke Cade in Richard the seconds time, and in our time by a seditious fellow in Norffolke calling himself Captaine Ket and others in other places of the Realme lead altogether by certaine propheticall rymes, which might be constred two or three wayes as well as that one whereunto the rebelles applied it.[24]

Amphibologies depend on an indeterminacy of meaning which only events can resolve. Puttenham has no patience with them because they have unexpected consequences, and because he associates them with challenges 'to' the social order.

It is difficult to identify with any confidence a clear formal distinction between Puttenham's amphibologies and his riddles. Both depend on ambiguity; both prevaricate and equivocate. Both use words to conceal what is meant, paradoxically bringing out into the open the hidden alterity of meaning. The difference seems to lie in the question of mastery. Riddles promise closure: the old woman in the nursery has the answer, and the children can expect to be told if they have guessed correctly. Like Macbeth, however, Captain Ket has to wait until experience reveals the truth. The proof of the pudding is deferred until it is too late to be any use. Amphibologies mislead. Riddles instal the knowing subject: amphibologies undermine the subject's power to know and consequently to control events.

The riddles posed by Portia and Nerissa in the rings episode of *The Merchant of Venice* mostly concern the sex of the lawyer. 'In faith, I gave it to the judge's clerk. / Would he were gelt that had it for my part', Graziano stoutly affirms (5.1.143–4). The clerk *is* 'gelt', of course, to the extent that in the Renaissance, as in a different way for Freud, women are incomplete men,[25] and the pleasure for the audience lies in identifying a meaning which is not available to the speaker.

NERISSA   The clerk will ne'er wear hair on's face
    that had it.
GRAZIANO   He will an if he live to be a man.
NERISSA   Ay, if a woman live to be a man.
GRAZIANO   Now by this hand, I gave it to a youth
    . . .   (5.1.158–61)

All these utterances are true. By a radical transgression of the differences that hold meaning in place, the youth and the woman are the same person, though Nerissa and the woman she speaks of are not the same. The speed of the exchanges requires some agility on the part of the audience, though not, perhaps, the degree of mobility needed to follow the dizzying series of shifts in the meanings Portia attributes to the 'doctor':

Since he hath got the jewel that I loved,
And that which you did swear to keep for me,
I will become as liberal as you.
I'll not deny him anything I have,
No, not my body nor my husband's bed:
Know him I shall, I am well sure of it.
Lie not a night from home. Watch me like Argus.
If you do not, if I be left alone,
Now by mine honour, which is yet mine own,
I'll have that doctor for my bedfellow.

                                        (5.1.224–33)

Misura per misura: la transparenza della commedia (Milano, 1979), pp. 203 ff.

24 Puttenham, *Arte*, pp. 260–1. Steven Mullaney, 'Lying Like Truth: Riddle, Representation and Treason in Renaissance England', *ELH*, 47 (1980), 32–47.

25 Stephen Greenblatt, 'Fiction and Friction', *Shakespearean Negotiations: The Circulation of Social Energy in Renaissance England* (Oxford, 1988), pp. 66–93.

Here Bassanio once again confronts three apparently exclusive options. First, the doctor is a woman (but not Portia, whose honour is still her own), and the woman has taken the 'jewel' that Bassanio promised, by marrying her, to keep for Portia herself. Second, the doctor is a man, and Portia is willing to share her bed with him. And finally the doctor is Portia, her bedfellow when she is alone. Each of the options contains part of the answer. No wonder Bassanio is baffled, and Portia has to spell out the truth for him (5.1.269–70).

The full answer to the riddle of the rings is that Portia has more than one identity. There is a sense in which the multiple meanings here recapitulate the action of the play. Portia has always been other than she is. The fairytale princess, a sacrificial virgin, as she characterized herself, was not only 'an unlessoned girl' but also (and in the same speech) 'the lord / Of this fair mansion, master of my servants, / Queen o'er myself' (3.2.159, 167–9). Evidently to be an heiress is already to disrupt the rules of gender. But her marriage in conjunction with her Venetian journey (and the deferred consummation confirms them as inextricable) invests her with a new kind of polysemy. The equivocations and doubles entendres of Act 5 celebrate a sexual indeterminacy, which is not in-difference but multiplicity.

In this sense the episode of the rings surely resembles Puttenham's category of amphibology rather than his concept of the riddle. The answer cannot be deduced from the terms of the puzzle itself. At one level, of course, the solution to the ambiguities and equivocations of the scene is readily available: the doctor and his clerk are also women. That knowledge sustains all the puns and resolves all the contradictions, and thus ensures for the audience the pleasure of mastering a succession of rapidly shifting meanings. This pleasure may help to account for the feeling of harmony which so many critics derive from Act 5. But there is another sense in which the implications of the episode are more elusive. The double act be-

tween Portia and Nerissa takes their performance beyond the realm of the individual, endowing it with a representative quality, and the reference back through the text which the episode invites, suggests a more metaphysical question: what, in a world where Belmont encounters the values of Venice, does it mean to be a wife?

Portia claims the ring in return for rescuing Bassanio's friend and thus, indirectly, Bassanio himself. Like Britomart, the lady becomes a warrior, and the equal of her man. 'If you had known,' she says to Bassanio, 'half her worthiness that gave the ring . . .' (5.1.199–200). The role of desire is fully acknowledged in the casket scene, and the importance of sexual difference is repeatedly affirmed in the bawdy double meanings of Act 5. This is evident in the final pun, delivered, appropriately, by Graziano: 'Well, while I live I'll fear no other thing / So sore, as keeping safe Nerissa's ring' (5.1.306–7), though Stephen Orgel points out that an element of indeterminacy remains even here. Anatomical rings may be masculine as well as feminine, and the preceding lines are: 'But were the day come, I should wish it dark / Till I were couching with the doctor's clerk.' But the other non-sexual, non-differential 'half' of Portia's worthiness as a wife is made apparent in her performance as Bassanio's fellow-warrior, partner and friend. The solution to the riddle of the rings is thus a utopian vision of the new possibilities of marriage. The riddle does not originate with Portia and Nerissa, nor even entirely with their author, for all his familiar human wisdom. On the contrary, it is the effect of a specific cultural moment when the meaning of marriage is unstable, contested, and open to radical reconstruction.[26] The riddle is also deeply socially

---

[26] See Catherine Belsey, 'Disrupting Sexual Difference: Meaning and Gender in the Comedies', in *Alternative Shakespeares*, ed. John Drakakis (London, 1985), pp. 166–90; *The Subject of Tragedy: Identity and Difference in Renaissance Drama* (London, 1985), pp. 129–221.

disruptive in its fundamental challenge to the patriarchal order.

In the episode of the rings happy love acquires a history by superimposing a similitude on the existing difference. The otherness which is the condition of desire is brought into conjunction with a comradeship which assumes a parallel, a likeness of values and dispositions. The gap that lies between these two 'halves' of what constitutes conjugal worth is dramatized both in the disjunction between the two parts of Act 5 and in the multiple identity that is required of Portia.

v

If the term 'wife' absorbs the meaning of 'friend', what place in the signifying chain, what specific difference is left for the meaning of friendship? We can, of course, reduce the metaphysical burden of Antonio's apparently unmotivated melancholy to disappointed homoerotic desire. This is a possible reading and not one that I wish to discredit.[27] Certainly the play constructs a symmetry between Antonio and Portia. It is Antonio who assures Bassanio, 'My purse, my person, my extremest means / Lie all unlocked to your occasions' (1.1.138–9), but it might equally have been Portia who said it (see 3.2.304–5). And certainly in Acts 4 and 5 this symmetry turns into the contest between two kinds of obligation which is evident in the episode of the rings. But my view is that the play here presents to the audience the implications of a contest for meaning, including the meaning of sexuality, which throws into relief something of the distance between the culture of Renaissance England and our own.

In court in Act 4 Bassanio declares:

Antonio, I am married to a wife
Which is as dear to me as life itself,
But life itself, my wife, and all the world
Are not with me esteemed above thy life.
I would lose all, ay, sacrifice them all
Here to this devil, to deliver you. (4.1.279–84)

Bassanio's priorities are surely shocking to a modern audience. Men are not supposed to prefer their friends to their wives. On the contrary, in our normative society, while adolescent sexuality is allowed to include homosocial or even homoerotic desire, this phase is supposed to be left behind by adults, who 'naturally' privilege heterosexual marriage. (At least one recent reading of *The Merchant of Venice* takes this pattern of 'normal' development for granted.[28])

But Bassanio's position is not without a Renaissance pedigree. In Sir Thomas Elyot's *The Governour* (1531) Titus and Gysippus grow up together and are inseparable until Gysippus falls in love and decides to marry. But when Titus meets his friend's proposed bride, to his own horror, he instantly falls in love with her too. Overcome by the double anguish of desire and disloyalty, Titus takes to his bed. At last Gysippus prises the secret out of him, and once he knows the truth he is easily able to resolve the problem. The friends agree to substitute Titus for Gysippus on the wedding day. Thus friendship is preserved. Gysippus is publicly embarrassed, and has to leave town for a time, but otherwise all is well, and Elyot triumphantly cites the story as an 'example in the affectes of frendshippe'.[29] The values here resemble those of Chaucer's *Knight's Tale*, where love tragically destroys chivalric friendship. The relationship between Palamon and Arcite is

---

Eighty years later it would be possible for a good woman to propose that it would be 'nobler' to be her husband's friend than his wife (John Dryden, *Troilus and Cressida* 2.1.143–5, *Works*, vol. 13, ed. Maximillian E. Novak (Berkeley, 1984). I owe this point to M. C. Bradbrook.

27 This has been a recurrent interpretation of the play at least since Tillyard toyed with the idea in 1966. See Danson, *Harmonies*, pp. 34–40.

28 W. Thomas MacCary, *Friends and Lovers: The Phenomenology of Desire in Shakespearean Comedy* (New York, 1985), especially pp. 167–8.

29 Sir Thomas Elyot, *The Governour* (London, 1907), p. 183.

heroic; love, on the other hand, is high folly, according to Theseus, and the text does nothing to counteract this view (lines 1798–9). According to Geron's aphoristic assessment of the priorities in Lyly's *Endimion*,

Love is but an eye-worme, which onely tickleth the heade with hopes, and wishes: friendshippe the image of eternitie, in which there is nothing moveable, nothing mischeevous ... Time draweth wrinckles in a fayre face, but addeth fresh colours to a faste friende, which neither heate, nor cold, nor miserie, nor place, nor destiny, can alter or diminish.

(3.4.123–36)[30]

Eumenides accepts this evaluation, chooses friendship, and is rewarded with love too.

When Damon is falsely accused of spying in the play by Richard Edwards, his friend Pithias volunteers to take his place in prison and to be executed if Damon fails to return in time. The hangman finds this remarkable:

> Here is a mad man I tell thee, I have a wyfe
>   whom I love well,
> And if iche would die for her, chould iche
>   weare in Hell:
> Wylt thou doo more for a man, then I woulde
>   for a woman(?)

And Pithias replies firmly, 'Yea, that I wyll' (lines 1076–80).[31] It is not clear how seriously we are invited to take the values of the hangman, but it is evident that Pithias is right about the supreme obligations of friendship in this most pedagogic of plays, written in the 1560s by the Master of the Chapel Royal for the Children to perform. Even as late as *The Two Noble Kinsmen* in 1613 the conflicting claims of marriage and friendship are matter for debate – this time between women. Hippolyta reflects without rancour on the affections of Theseus, divided between herself and his friend Pirithous:

>   Their knot of love,
> Tied, weaved, entangled, with so true, so long,
> And with a finger of so deep a cunning,
> May be outworn, never undone. I think
> Theseus cannot be umpire to himself,

Cleaving his conscience into twain and doing
Each side like justice, which he loves best.

(1.3.41–7)

Hippolyta finally concludes that Theseus prefers her (1.3.95–7), but not before Emilia has put the case for friendship between members of the same sex as the stronger force: 'the true love 'tween maid and maid may be / More than in sex dividual' (1.3.81–2). In the end Hippolyta and Emilia agree to differ.

Both *The Governour* and *Endimion* are cited by Bullough as possible sources of *The Two Gentlemen of Verona*, where Valentine offers his beloved Silvia to his friend Proteus.[32] Bullough finds Valentine's gesture 'Quixotic', as presumably most twentieth-century commentators would.[33] And indeed the play has so enlisted our sympathy for Julia that we cannot want Proteus to accept his friend's generosity. Elsewhere too Shakespeare's texts tend to opt, however uneasily, for the nuclear couple. Othello, who should prefer his wife, tragically listens to his friend. More specifically, in *Much Ado About Nothing*, which is chronologically closer to *The Merchant of Venice*, Beatrice's imperative to Benedick on behalf of her cousin also foregrounds the conflicting obligations of lovers and friends. The loyalty of Beatrice to Hero is absolute, and at the moment when Benedick declares his love for Beatrice, her immediate concern is Hero's honour. Beatrice's challenge necessarily threatens the loyalty of Benedick to Claudio.

BENEDICK Come, bid me do anything for thee.
BEATRICE Kill Claudio.
BENEDICK Ha! Not for the wide world.

(4.1.289–91)

---

[30] John Lyly, *Endimion*, *The Complete Works*, ed. R. Warwick Bond (Oxford, 1902), 3 vols., vol. 3. Cf. Elyot, *The Governour*, II.xi, and Montaigne, 'Of Friendship', cited in Eugene Waith, ed., *The Two Noble Kinsmen* (Oxford, 1989), p. 50.

[31] Richard Edwards, *Damon and Pythias* (Oxford, 1957).

[32] Geoffrey Bullough, *Narrative and Dramatic Sources of Shakespeare*, vol. 1 (London, 1957), pp. 203–17.

[33] Bullough, *Sources*, vol. 1, p. 203.

Whether or not Benedick's moment of recoil is played as comedy, the play goes on in the event to realign him explicitly as Beatrice's 'friend' (4.1.319) and thus as Claudio's enemy. Later the text reverts to this issue when, in the course of a series of teasing exchanges, an instance of the verbal friction characteristic of desire,[34] Beatrice sets up an opposition between Benedick's friendship and his 'heart'. But this time she opts for friendship with Benedick even at the price of love:

BENEDICK   . . . I love thee against my will.
BEATRICE   In spite of your heart, I think. Alas, poor heart. If you spite it for my sake I will spite it for yours, for I will never love that which my friend hates.   (5.2.61–4)[35]

This *is* comedy. The play's treatment of the issue is more complex: Beatrice's challenge to Benedick to fight for her evokes classical myth and medieval romance, rather than the new model of marriage. At the same time, we are invited to understand that Benedick qualifies as a husband to the degree that he is prepared to sacrifice his friend. It is no surprise, therefore, that in *The Merchant of Venice* Bassanio's declaration that his friend comes first does not go unchallenged. At once Balthasar, uniquely in the court scene, draws the attention of the audience to his/her other identity: 'Your wife would give you little thanks for that / If she were by to hear you make the offer' (4.1.285–6). When Bassanio surrenders the ring to Balthasar it is in response to Antonio's persuasion, and the conflict of obligations is made explicit:

My Lord Bassanio, let him have the ring.
Let his deservings and my love withal
Be valued 'gainst your wife's commandëment.
                                   (4.1.446–8)

Bassanio subsequently excuses himself to Portia in the vocabulary of chivalry:

Even he that had held up the very life
Of my dear friend. What should I say, sweet lady?

I was enforced to send it after him.
I was beset with shame and courtesy.
My honour would not let ingratitude
So much besmear it.   (5.1.214–19)

And here, perhaps, is a pointer to the residual meaning of friendship in the period. Georges Duby gives a graphic account of the life of chivalry among the 'youth' of twelfth-century France. These men constituted a substantial proportion of the audience, and therefore, no doubt, much of the motive, for the new romantic love stories and troubadour poems of the period. A version of their image survives in ideal form in the nostalgic culture of late sixteenth-century England, most obviously in texts like *The Faerie Queene*, in response to the Queen's enthusiastic cultivation of the heroic and courtly ideal.

Duby's 'youths' were fully grown knights who were not yet fathers. This stage of life might last, it appears, for upwards of twenty years. During this period the 'youth', often accompanied by a slightly more experienced 'youth', or as one of a group of fast friends who loved each other like brothers, roamed in pursuit of adventure and, more specifically, in quest of a wife. The eldest son could expect in due course to inherit his father's property. But in a world where the patrimony was expected to provide a living for the couple as well as a marriage settlement for the wife, younger sons had usually little to hope for outside a career in the church, unless they could locate an heiress, secure her father's approval and marry her.

Since the life of the 'youth' was violent and dangerous, whole male lineages were in practice eliminated, and rich women were not as rare as might be expected, though only a tiny minority of the 'youth' could hope to secure one. In the mean time, groups of men, officially celibate, lived and fought together. We may assume that in such circumstances the virtue of loyalty was paramount: at least in their ideal-

---

[34] Greenblatt, 'Fiction and Friction', pp. 88–91.
[35] I owe this point to A. D. Nuttall.

ized, literary form, the knights were conventionally bosom friends and inseparable companions. Once married, and a father, the knight gave priority to his own establishment, though he might well retain some of his former comrades in his household, and indeed help them to find suitable brides.[36]

Duby's account gives no indication of a conflict between love and friendship. In a chivalric culture love endangers friendship when it becomes rivalry, as *The Knight's Tale* shows, but wives do not supplant friends: their rôle is quite different. The new model of marriage in the sixteenth century, however, identified wives precisely as friends, and the texts of the period bring to light some of the uncertainties and anxieties which attend the process of redefinition. Antonio is sad because he is in mourning for friendship. Of course, Portia does it nicely. She gives the ring to Antonio to give back to Bassanio, so that Antonio feels included. But he knows from the beginning of the play that things will never be the same again.

And what about the place of homoerotic desire? Perhaps we shall never know. Eve Kosofsky Sedgwick is surely right to urge that 'the sexual context of that period is too far irrecoverable for us to be able to disentangle boasts, confessions, undertones, overtones, jokes, the unthinkable, the taken-for-granted, the unmentionable-but-often-done-anyway, etc.'[37] It seems unlikely that medieval knights were as chaste as the chivalric code required. On the other hand, while sodomy was consistently identified as an abominable crime, homosexual acts were very rarely prosecuted in England in the middle ages or the Renaissance.[38] In practice the whole issue seems to have generated relatively little anxiety. Stephen Orgel in a brilliant contribution to the cultural history of the sixteenth century argues that homosexual acts were perceived as less dangerous to men than heterosexual love, because it was association with women which was effeminating.[39]

A single example may indicate the difficulty we have in construing the meanings of a vanished culture. In *The Two Noble Kinsmen* the relationship between Palamon and Arcite is treated in remarkable detail. They love each other; they lighten each other's imprisonment. Arcite declares, apparently without embarrassment, that since imprisonment will prevent them from marrying, 'We are one another's wife, ever begetting / New births of love' (2.2.80–1). At the same time, it is clear that their explicit sexual preferences are heterosexual. The whole plot depends on this. And besides, the text makes clear that they admire each other greatly for their former heterosexual conquests (3.3.30–42).

Possibly our difficulty resides in the plurality of the word 'love'? Palamon loves Arcite; Arcite loves Palamon; but both Palamon and Arcite love Emilia. Perhaps it is not only our difficulty: Palamon explicitly distinguishes between love and desire, in order to be sure that his cousin is really his rival. 'You love her then?' 'Who would not?' 'And desire her?' (2.2.159–61). It could be argued, then, that the play sets up its own system of differences: that while love might or might not be sexual, desire is erotic in this text. It could be argued, were it not for Palamon's final words to the dying Arcite, which surely deconstruct any such opposition:

> O cousin,
> That we should things desire which do cost us

---

[36] Georges Duby, 'Youth in Aristocratic Society', *The Chivalrous Society*, trans. Cynthia Postan (London, 1977), pp. 112–22. I owe this connection to Mary Beth Rose, *The Expense of Spirit: Love and Sexuality in English Renaissance Drama* (Ithaca, 1988), pp. 178–235, though she reads the texts with a rather different emphasis.

[37] Eve Kosofsky Sedgwick, *Between Men: English Literature and Male Homosocial Desire* (New York, 1985), p. 35.

[38] For a discussion of the available evidence see David F. Greenberg, *The Construction of Homosexuality* (Chicago, 1988).

[39] Orgel, 'Nobody's Perfect'.

The loss of our desire! That nought could buy
Dear love, but loss of dear love.

(5.6.109–12)

Here heterosexual passion and homosocial friendship are defined in exactly the same terms: both are dear love; both are desire. It remains for the audience to determine whether Palamon's words are best understood as conflating difference (one love, one desire, at the price of its similitude) or as turning to account the difference within the signifier (one love, one desire, at the cost of its distinguishing, differentiating other).

VI

A tentative history of our own cultural moment emerges from all this. Our more carefully regulated meanings impose narrow limits on the range of possibilities available to us. Since Freud we have learned that all intense emotion is 'really' sexual; since the Enlightenment we have known how to classify and evaluate deviance; and since *The Merchant of Venice* we have known that marriage, which includes every imaginable adult relationship, ought to be enough for anyone.

I wonder . . .

TWO KINGDOMS FOR HALF-A-CROWN

DOMINIQUE GOY-BLANQUET

I thought of calling this chapter 'A Tale of Two Bishops', in homage to the two figures who appear at regular intervals in the history plays framing the person of the king, but on second thoughts, that had too medieval a ring for such an innovative experiment as the dual monarchy, or the union of the two crowns as it was called at the time. It is ideally defined at the end of *Henry V*:

> God, the best maker of all marriages,
> Combine your hearts in one, your realms in one.
> As man and wife, being two, are one in love,
> So be there 'twixt your kingdoms such a spousal
> [...]
> That English may as French, French Englishmen,
> Receive each other, God speak this 'Amen'
>
> (5.2.344–53)[1]

words probably well designed to make any true-blooded French or Englishman shudder, but which faithfully echo the hopes expressed by the treaty of Troyes in Hall's report,

> that [...] bothe the crounes [...] of Fraunce and England perpetually be together in one and in thesame persone [...] that there shalbe fro hence forwarde for euermore peace and tranquillitee and good accord and common affeccion and stable frendship betwene thesame realmes and their sub-iectes.[2]

Such were the terms of the union designed by Henry V and so fatally mishandled by his successors.

My hesitations over the title were the sum of doubts about Henry's double dealings in the concluding tale of the histories. The success story in five acts and as many prologues is defeated at the end by the flat statement that it was of no avail, leaving us to wonder what exactly we have been watching. Policy or politics? Bishops or crowns? Duck or rabbit? We know how much depends on the way we look at the design.[3] And we know how English cats may look at kings' crowns, where French dogs dare only look at bishops, which is but the beginning of our differences.

Perhaps the most irritating point about the histories is the fact that Shakespeare wrote them the wrong way round. Or did he? One might argue that starting with the loss of France and England, then going back to the original cause is the proper way of research. Yet Henry V carries a sense of the pastness of the past which makes him look like the great-grandson of Henry VI, who does belong to a former age in more ways than one.

It must have required much wisdom and research from Shakespeare the scholar to reach the heart of matters made hopelessly unclear by the chronicles. The abortive attempt to unite the two crowns of England and France was the conclusion of a long feud, much older than the

---

[1] *Henry V*, The Oxford Shakespeare, ed. Gary Taylor (Oxford, 1984).

[2] *Hall's Chronicle*, ed. Sir Henry Ellis (London, 1809), p. 99.

[3] Norman Rabkin, *Shakespeare and the Problem of Meaning* (Chicago, 1981).

Hundred Years War over lands held in France as vassals by English kings who found their dependence on French monarchs irksome. They had been fighting for centuries to gain complete sovereignty over their possessions, when Henry V offered this unprecedented solution to the conflict. In spite of its original character, the experiment itself has not attracted much interest, and twentieth-century reactions do little more than reprove or reflect contemporary feelings. Most French historians express their relief at the terrible fate which was then averted – to think that we might have become English! The British ones share this relief, which they find only natural, and in their view, the failure was finally turned to advantage, since the loss of its continental foothold released England for greater adventures. Was Henry too late with the remnants of a medieval dream of Godly union, or was he too early, since we are not ready yet for what he then attempted, still trying to solve what needed another four, perhaps five and a half centuries to mature. Critics remain violently divided on issues which suggests that Shakespeare's point must be hard to take.

But back to our tale. The one unfolded by the two bishops is in no way a fair statement of the matter, as the audience soon understands. For one thing, it very properly ignores the fact that whatever rights Henry might have in France, the French king's title to his throne as fourth of his line must be stronger than Henry's to the crown of England, a fact which was repeatedly, sometimes rudely underlined by the French ambassadors at the time. Nor does it give a fair idea of what is at stake. The feudal conflict had gradually developed into a more serious quarrel over a long list of material benefits then vital to Britain. The claim to the French crown used to come up regularly in the arguments without being seriously pressed. Edward III had even agreed to give it up in the treaty of Bretigny, in 1360, but since his other conditions had not been met, the matter was still open when Henry V took it up. At first, his claim was taken on both sides for what it was, no more than the usual opening to further negotiations. Britain's commercial interests were certainly a powerful motive, but the real point of his war appears to have been the one made by Shakespeare, that this campaign was necessary to establish his position at home and abroad. By all accounts, he was quite as pious and orthodox as he is advertised to be by our two bishops. It seems, besides, that he had a strong belief in his rights and saw the claim in the light of a duty, as the descendant of Edward III, repeatedly insisting on the borderlines defined at Bretigny, and using his ancestor's Great Seal at the signature of the peace treaty. We hear in the play that

> Your highness [. . .]
> Did claim some certain dukedoms, in the right
> Of your great predecessor, King Edward the
> Third   (1.2.246–8)

when he has already made up his mind to the war, just as the original Henry was declaring his peaceful intentions to the world while actually arming at great speed for an invasion.[4]

It was years later that the state of affairs opened greater possibilities. The division of the French nobility, culminating in the murder of the Duke of Burgundy at Montereau in 1419, had brought the kingdom to such confusion that both Armagnacs and Bourguignons began to think an appeal to a third party was the only remedy left. As King Francis I was told a century later, when shown the murdered Duke's skull, 'It is through this hole that the English entered France': Henry saw his opportunity and rode straight in.[5] What his motives may have been for actually investing the French throne remains unclear. It is thought that by joining the two most powerful monarchies of the time, he had hoped to reunite Christendom

---

[4] J. H. Wylie, *The Reign of Henry V* (Cambridge, 1914–29), vol. 1 pp. 159–490, vol. 3, p. 170.
[5] Paul Bonenfant, *Du meurtre de Montereau au traité de Troyes* (Bruxelles, 1958).

under his leadership and defeat the ambitions of the Turks. Henry V has been defined as the typical medieval hero.[6] Apart from his victorious deeds, this quality appeared in his attempt to bind domestic policy, religious reform and European diplomacy in one great design, and the fact that all his achievements depended so heavily on his personality. Once released from his strong hold, they all went to pieces. 'Hence kingdoms which depend on the virtue of one man do not last long, because they lose their virtue when his life is spent,' Machiavelli reminds us.[7]

The treaty of Troyes instituting the dual monarchy is generally considered 'infamous' by modern French historians,[8] though in fact it was welcome to many at the time, for a variety of reasons, most of them far removed from politics. It seems to have answered many needs on both sides of the Channel. In England, the war brought material advantages to a large section of the middle class, merchants and traders, who were Henry's staunch supporters. In France, the state of anarchy created by King Charles's madness and the civil strife was such that it was often felt 'que de deux maulx le moins pire est a eslire',[9] and Henry V was to a comfortable majority the lesser of two evils. The population at large who were exhausted by war, famine, violence and disorder wanted peace at any cost. The University, Parlement, and citizens of Paris called Henry in, banking on his reputation for justice and efficiency, in the hopes that he would restore the realm to its former health. They made sure that he would guarantee the maintenance of their liberties and privileges, which are carefully listed in the treaty. Patriotism and national spirit had not been quite invented yet. The two countries were close to each other, the Plantagenets were more than half French anyway, and French spoken with an English accent was still the language of administration, justice, and aristocracy. There was no apparent reason why the two partners could not successfully be matched.

But it was not to be. The terms of the agreement were ambiguous, and certain articles were liable to create new difficulties. The treaty makes no mention of Henry's lineal rights, a point which caused much displeasure then in his own country, 'as by the makyng of this peace it shuld appeare that England had no right to Fraunce' and made the whole war appear unjust. It inspires Hall with angry comments on the king's detractors, but he wastes little interest on the arrangement itself, which provides that the two crowns will be joined perpetually together

kepyng neuerthelesse in all maner of other thynges to ether of ye same realmes their rightes, liberties, customes, vsages and lawes, not makyng subiecte in any maner of wise one of thesame realmes to the rightes, lawes or vsages of that other. (p. 99)

Henry V becomes adopted heir to the French king by his marriage to Princess Katherine, while the Dauphin is attainted for his complicity in the murder of Burgundy, and declared unfit to succeed, 'indigne de succession'. King Charles keeps his title as long as he lives, and Henry is to rule France in his name, but

---

[6] C. L. Kingsford, *Henry V, the Typical Medieval Hero* (London, 1901).

[7] Niccolò Machiavelli, *The Discourses*, trans. Leslie J. Walker, ed. Bernard Crick (Harmondsworth, 1970), I.II, p. 141.

[8] Françoise Autrand, *Charles VI* (Paris, 1986), p. 577, gives a fair idea of the general tone: 'Comment des hommes avisés, lucides et, parfois, honnêtes ont-ils pu croire à l'avenir de la double monarchie?' The feelings of Régine Pernoud, *Christine de Pisan* (Paris, 1982), *Jeanne devant les Cauchons* (Paris, 1970) are quite as passionate as her heroines', and François Neveux, *L'Évêque Pierre Cauchon* (Paris, 1987), has made himself most unpopular by defending the man who condemned our national saint, which drew a prompt reindictment from Emmanuel Bourassin, *L'Évêque Cauchon* (Paris, 1988).

[9] Originally the words of Burgundy's advisers (Bonenfant, 216), echoed by various writers of the time like Le Religieux de Saint Denys, *Chronique de Charles VI*, ed. L. F. Bellaguet (Paris, 1839–52), vol. 6, p. 376. See also C. A. J. Armstrong, 'La Double Monarchie France-Angleterre et la maison de Bourgogne (1420–1435): le déclin d'une alliance', *England, France and Burgundy in the Fifteenth Century* (London, 1983), pp. 343–74.

whether it is as Regent or conqueror of the said realm is left unclear, and the frontiers of his conquests remain equally vague. The treaty also stipulates that he will endeavour to conquer the rest of his kingdom from the revolted Dauphin, and that at his father-in-law's death, all the conquered lands will revert to the French Crown. All these articles will be submitted for approval to the three Estates of both realms.[10]

In France, the treaty was welcomed with great rejoicing, which cooled quickly when the war was resumed, the food shortages continued, and the attempted reordering met with indifferent success.[11] In fact, Henry continued fighting till the end and had little leisure to reform the French system of government, though he tried to reduce the waste of public revenues and took measures to reform the currency. In spite of his efforts, the prices kept going up, and none of the former evils occasioned by war – banditry and famine – could be eradicated. The effort took the necessary but unpopular form of taxation, and a general levy of silver was ordered to produce better coinage, for its successive debasements were commonly felt to be the source of all economic troubles.

Meanwhile the Dauphin's allies were advertising the 'royauté des lys' and enlisting such passionate support as that of Joan of Arc, developing powerful hatred against all invaders, English wolves and French renegades, 'Français reniés'. If national feelings were shapeless or still in the making, it is generally accepted that a sense of national identity was forged at that time in both countries by repulsion and rejection of each other's national traits, embodied in the rival claims of rival kings and defeating all attempts at fusion.[12] The budding States built their identity around the persons of their monarchs, the living embodiments of national sovereignty, and the dual monarchy found itself with one king too many. The dilemma is far from being solved: Mrs Thatcher recently asked what would be the fate of her 'poor Queen' once the States of Europe were united. The Nouvel Observateur took up the question

three months later, what are we to do with this surplus of kings who stand in the way of supranationality?[13]

In 1415, the English Parliament had greeted Henry's victories with obvious pleasure and generous grants of money, but the terms of the peace treaty in 1420 seemed to have caused some anxiety. The Commons begged for reassurance that the realm of England should never be placed in subjection to the Crown of France, that the two realms would be kept wholly separate and independent. One explanation for this was that they were afraid they might be made French overnight. Another, more convincing, is that having rashly awarded grants of subsidies to Henry for his lifetime, they were anxious about his own promise to bring his other kingdom to obedience and did not want to be accountable for the expense. Now that the two countries were at peace, they were under no obligation to finance a war he had engaged to fight as regent and heir of France, not as king of England. The advantages of conquering Normandy and Gascony for commerce, shipping and defence were obvious to all, the conquest of the whole of France was not, especially as the treaty specified that the conquered lands would never belong to the English Crown. And indeed, for nearly seven years after Henry's death, the Parliament offered no subsidy for the wars in France. It was

[10] E. Cosneau, Les Grands Traités de la Guerre de Cent Ans (Paris, 1889), gives the full text of the articles, with their corresponding references in Rymer's Foedera and the other contemporary accounts.

[11] The anonymous Journal d'un Bourgeois de Paris 1405–1449, ed. Colette Beaune (Paris, 1990), faithfully reflects those variations and is very detailed on food prices, especially for the years 1418–22, pp. 135–84.

[12] P. S. Lewis, 'War Propaganda and Historiography in Fifteenth Century France and England', Essays in Later Medieval French History (London, 1985), pp. 192–213. A. Gransden, Historical Writing in England (London, 1982), vol. 2. Colette Beaune, Naissance de la Nation France (Paris, 1985).

[13] The Independent on Sunday, 29 April 1990. Le Nouvel Observateur, 16–22 August 1990.

only under threat of losing all that they agreed to provide their troops overseas with adequate support, too late, which oft our stage hath shown.[14]

Where Hall loses himself in a verbose catalogue of reasons, the first scene of *1 Henry VI* deftly seizes on the main cause of disaster, 'No treachery, but want of men and money', and pictures an army of starved Englishmen abandoned by a convocation of politic worms who are safe at home, while their enemies rally around the Dauphin. The links between the loss of France and the civil wars are equally well observed, for the king's government had been seriously discredited by the mismanagement of French affairs, and public opinion would not be reconciled to a loss which had cost such enormous waste of blood and treasure.

Shakespeare's interpretation of history underlines a number of facts which modern research has established as particularly significant. Yet he leaves out an equally significant number of important features, like the death of the first Dauphin, the murder of Montereau, and the five eventful years which ran between Agincourt and the treaty of Troyes. In those years, the foreign policy of Henry V underwent a complete change, from a war fought on traditional grounds of feudal rights, an attempted settlement in Normandy, to a bid for a whole kingdom culminating in the union of the two crowns, with a possible hope of leading Christendom to its last crusade. Ironically, France and Constantinople were lost within two years of each other, putting an end to all dreams of medieval Europe.

The history plays offer flashes of insight on the main causes of this ultimate failure, which is the ambiguous sum of triumphant war, as well as its relevance to Shakespeare's own time. The dual monarchy never came to life for the ostensible reason which defeated all the attempts of his own age at colonization: the inability to maintain a steady stream of supplies overseas. His dramatic treatment shows in one clear stroke how ineffective the union of the two crowns actually was, and what unavowed form of expansionism hid behind peaceful terms of amity. It also reminds us that for years after, England's foreign policy was bent on gaining ground in France, that even the first decades of Elizabeth's reign were spent in a vain attempt to recover Calais.

The Tudors still had to solve some of the difficulties met by Henry V, though in different circumstances,[15] which are suggested obliquely on stage by historical perspective. The glorious termination of the medieval dream screens the design of Renaissance European politics. By way of the Prologue and other metadramatic devices, Shakespeare brilliantly demonstrates what the theatre is able to do, contract several layers of time in one telling scene, just as Hamlet's *Mousetrap* will show in the same movement past murder and vengeance to come. *Henry V* achieves the same chiasmus on a larger scale: leitmotivs from the past, disturbing intimations of what is brewing in a near and distant future which reaches up to the present.

Shakespeare's reading of history is perfectly sound. Whatever the degree of union vouched for in the articles of the treaty, there is little doubt that Henry's aims were expansionist, and his first designs on Normandy an attempted colonization. When Harfleur surrendered, a proclamation was issued at Westminster to merchants, victuallers and craftsmen, offering houses and special privileges to all who would come to settle there. Meanwhile the French burghers were ransomed or shipped to England, and the poorer residents sent away to find new homes in other towns. The same policy was carried out on a lesser scale in all the main towns of Normandy.[16] Henry is reputed to have refrained from wholly anglicizing his

---

[14] Maurice H. Keen, *England in the Later Middle Ages, A Political History* (London, 1973), pp. 359–75. Wylie, vol. 2, pp. 237–40.

[15] Kingsford, pp. 395–8, for a parallel between Henry and the later Tudors.

[16] Wylie, vol. 2, pp. 61–5. Kingsford, pp. 133–232.

conquered territories, but this was probably due to lack of time more than consideration for local feelings. The ambiguities of amiable conquest find their dramatic reflection in the discrepancies between the staged picture of a merciful hero and his terrifying images of war.

The division of the languages is pleasantly treated in the play where Katherine anticipates the victory of the conqueror, but one should pay heed to her warning 'dat de tongues of de mans is be full of deceits', for it had been in fact a standing argument in the negotiations between the two countries. The dispute was finally won by the English side, with long-term effects. Henry had strongly opposed the use of French as the universal diplomatic language, on the grounds that neither he, his council nor his envoys could properly write, understand or speak French, and it was finally agreed that all documents would be translated in Latin and English, while Henry himself promoted the use of the English tongue 'by example and precept' in diplomacy, business, and language composition.[17] Then did our ways begin to part.

These various points are evidence of Shakespeare's excellent understanding of his subject, as was Prince Hal's early preoccupation with the 'crack'd crowns' and general debasement of values in his father's realm. But a number of clues point to later political concerns. Though it really is the sequel of the first cycle of histories, the second set of plays goes back to an earlier time as to the only way left open by Richmond's entrance. The victory of Bosworth provides a happy ending to the first series, but does not tell us how the new Godsent hero will succeed in keeping due order where pious Henry VI and wise Humphrey of Gloucester so signally failed. Thanks to Richard III it must be obvious to all by then that the traditional virtues are ineffective and more apt to produce their extreme opposites. The accession of Richard is the crowning evil of the civil wars. His appearance between two bishops, parodying the saintly figure of Henry VI, has shown the traditional image to be still emotionally

powerful, and probably required by public sentiment. How pious Richmond would reconcile it with the controlled cruelty of *real politik* could hardly be investigated on stage. Having drawn so close to the heels of truth, the author retraced his footsteps to an earlier dynastic change rather than pry any further into those 'mysteries of State' which Queen Elizabeth and her forefathers kept so jealously to themselves. It must be left to Henry V to draw the line between private virtues and State violence before he hides the breach under a cloak of ceremony. Such knowledge acquired from dramatic experience does make him the heir of Henry VI.[18]

Shakespeare's Harry has none of the self-righteousness of his model, but all the well-known traits of the original are turned to political advantage in the dramatic creation. Sharing the Tudors' care for genealogy and founding myths, Henry is concerned with the story of origins. The yarn spun by the two bishops, going back to Pharamond, establishes the legitimacy of his claim and grounds the national union in a common epic. Thus Henry takes his place in a line of heroes, Edward III, the Black Prince, which conveniently by-passes the usurpation and establishes his own legitimacy. Bolingbroke is hardly ever mentioned in the play. Indeed Henry finds he is the best author of himself, better even than Chorus or learned bishops:

Either our history shall with full mouth
Speak freely of our acts, or else our grave,
Like Turkish mute, shall have a tongueless mouth,
Not worshipped with a waxen epitaph. (1.2.230–3)

To make sure this is done properly, he goes on to tell the story himself – tales of his wild youth and reformation to the French ambassadors,

17 François L. Ganshof, *Histoire des Relations Internationales*, ed. Gaston Zeller (Paris, 1953), vol. 2, pp. 250–3. Wylie, vol. 3, p. 425.
18 Dominique Goy-Blanquet, 'Des Histoires Tristes', *Mythe et Histoire*, ed. M-T. Jones-Davies (Paris, 1984), pp. 31–48.

tales of victory and eternal fame to his army before the battle is even fought:

> This story shall the good man teach his son,
> And Crispin Crispian shall ne'er go by
> From this day to the ending of the world
> But we in it shall be rememberèd,
> We few, we happy few, we band of brothers.
>
> (4.3.56–60)

Borrowing freely from the historical character, Shakespeare's Henry conquers France, 'best garden of the world', to atone for his father's ruined Eden. His virtues are confirmed by his sycophants, he 'whipped th'offending Adam out of him', yet it is plain that 'miracles are ceased', old beliefs answer Machiavellian or Baconian views of religion as the natural cement of society. If Henry finds old customs 'a little out of fashion', he is too wise to break openly with approved traditions. He is 'no tyrant, but a Christian king', still he proves to be a very modern one by divorcing his more tender self from the merciless machinery of State.

If Henry's triumphant 'discourse of war' has a truly medieval ring, his and his soldiers' qualms about the justice of this particular war do not appear much in the chronicles of his time, when writers plainly thought that 'regular blood-letting reduced the excessive humours in the body politic'.[19] It certainly kept the nobility pleasantly occupied. But Renaissance men appear to have been more self-conscious on this score. Erasmus' resounding plea for peace may have had little actual effect, but it gave contemporary rulers a few uneasy moments. And though conclusive evidence is hard to come by, Erasmus had undoubtedly read *Henry VI* when he advised monarchs to think twice before conquering another kingdom:

Thus neither of the two countries will have a ruler for, while he abandons the first of his realms, the other will not accept him on the grounds that he is alien, and born in a different world. And while he is attempting to establish his regal right through conquest and bargaining in his second realm, he wears and wastes the former one. Sometimes he loses both by trying to rule the two States when he is hardly able to govern even one.[20]

Erasmus quotes Seneca in a letter of advice to King Francis I: there are many princes who have erased the borders of other kingdoms, none who have set limits to their own [. . .] Alexander the Great wished for another world when he reached the Ocean, for this one was too small for his ambition.[21] Which shows Erasmus had also read *Henry V*. And there were other considerations. As Machiavelli recalls from Juvenal,

the acquiring of foreign lands familiarized the minds of the Romans with foreign customs, so that, in place of frugality and its other high virtues, 'gluttony and self-indulgence took possession of it and avenged the world it had conquered'.[22]

Shakespeare who had been brought up on Plutarch knew the risks of absorbing barbarian realms: the extension of dominion had made the Empire ungovernable, and fatally diluted pure Roman virtue. Even his Trojan Henry is exposed to contamination:

> forgive me, God,
> That I do brag thus. This your air of France
> Hath blown that vice in me. I must repent.
>
> (3.6.149–51)

Despite such classical wisdom, Renaissance monarchs went on fighting happily as ever. Still, the wording of their treaties shows an acute need for virtuous justifications: they are generally full of concern for public morality or zeal for religion. In a speech to her troops, Queen Elizabeth, like Henry himself, claimed that she had no other wish but to be a brother to them all:

---

[19] Garrett Mattingly, *Renaissance Diplomacy* (London, 1955), p. 134.

[20] 'The Complaint of Peace' (1517), *The Essential Erasmus*, ed. John P. Dolan (New York and Ontario, 1983), p. 194.

[21] *Opus Epistolarium Desiderii Erasmi*, ed. P. S. Allen (Oxford, 1906–28), vol. 2, p. 207.

[22] *The Discourses*, II.19, p. 138.

I am come amongst you [. . .] not for my recreation and disport; but being resolved in the midst of the heat of the battle to live or die amongst you all; to lay down for my God and for my Kingdom and for my people my honor and my blood even in the dust

and repeatedly vowed that, unlike some others, she desired nothing but peace:

I think foul scorn that Parma or Spain or any prince of Europe should dare to invade the borders of my realm [. . .] All this time of my reign I have not sought to advance my territories and enlarge my dominions [. . .] My mind was never to invade my neighbors or to usurp over any. I am contented to reign over mine own and to rule as a just prince.[23]

This edifying picture is slightly marred by comments like Camden's who welcomed the Peace of Vervins in 1598 with the thought that now England would no longer be branded a disturber of the whole world.[24] Which sounds closer to the facts of European political life at the end of the sixteenth century. The dilemma of all Renaissance Europe, overpopulation, shortage of food and employment, makes the question of expansionism central, while European princes are increasingly aware there is no real future in conquering each other's lands, no possibility of lasting peace. The community uneasily maintained by Empire and theocracy throughout the Middle Ages has been exploded by religious divisions, leaving no arbiter to come in between the combatants.[25] The only alternative to endless strife is to find new outlets for those 'natural and instinctive impulses of any healthy society'. Queen Elizabeth delivers Letters Patent to discover and occupy 'lands not possessed by any Christian prince', virgin lands as it were, her apt choice of a name for her first settlement. A group of West Country men sail out to conquer those portions of the world reserved for the English 'by God's providence', for 'England has many inhabitants and little land'.[26]

The literature of voyagers and projectors is full of the marvellous benefits for shipping, marketing, God's Word and gold digging to be drawn from their ventures. In contrast, most sixteenth-century political thinkers have strangely little to offer on this vital issue. With his unique talent for saying aloud what everybody else thinks but dares not mention, Machiavelli states flatly that 'it is impossible for a state to remain for ever in the peaceful enjoyment of its liberties and its narrow confines' and he considers as a natural phenomenon 'the colonies sent out either by a republic or a prince to relieve their towns of some of the population'.[27] On the continent, isolated French and Spanish theorists apply their efforts to matters of international law and the status of new territories.[28] In England, at both ends of the century, Thomas More recommends colonization of the whole world by Utopians as the remedy to all evil, while Spenser's *View of the Present State of Ireland* finds room for improvement there and also advises colonization. Apart from these few originals, the main stream of essayists are too involved in domestic broils, religious struggles and questions of national sovereignty to waste much thought on distant savages or lonely pioneers. One must wait for Bacon's complaint that 'it is a shameful and unblessed thing to take the scum of people and wicked condemned men, to be the people with whom you plant', just as 'it is the sinfullest thing in the world to forsake or destitute a

---

[23] 'To the Troops at Tilbury, 1588', 'Dissolving Parliament, 1593', *The Public Speaking of Queen Elizabeth*, ed. G. P. Rice (London, 1951), pp. 96, 101.

[24] *Annals*, pp. 545–50, in Edward P. Cheyney, *A History of England from the Defeat of the Armada to the Death of Elizabeth* (London, 1914–26), vol. 1, p. 448.

[25] J. H. Elliott, *Europe Divided 1559–1598* (Glasgow, 1968).

[26] A. L. Rowse, *The Expansion of Elizabethan England* (London, 1955), pp. 2–3, 180, 211.

[27] *The Discourses*, II.19, p. 335, I.1, p. 101.

[28] In the survey of Pierre Mesnard, *L'Essor de la Philosophie Politique au XVIe Siècle* (Paris, 1936), Guillaume Postel (*La République des Turcs*), Francisco de Vitoria (*De Indis*), Jean Bodin (*La République*), Suarez (*Defensio Fidei*), are the only forerunners of Grotius' *De Jure Belli ac Pacis*, the first comprehensive theory of international public law.

plantation once in forwardness'[29] to consider their plight. Although, as modern history has it, England is 'stretching fingers of Empire to East and West', and 'more blood is to be spilt over the clove than all the past dynastic wars',[30] the political implications of this conquering mood are hardly ever broached. Unless we discover in Shakespeare some early intuition that the country's soul needs 'elbow-room'.

The intrusion of Ireland and its gracious Empress in the midst of Henry's French wars seems to point that way – Westward Ho! England is to be released from its traditional anchorage in 'the narrow seas', the shift of scene from the Channel to the Atlantic reflects the major political change of the era. In the 1590s, the public is informed that continental wars are obsolete. It hardly matters then if French poodles are less barbarous than Irish curs, the current enemy is the rival Armada, the dream of Empire for the next centuries must be a fleeting one. Now that England's hopes lie to the West, wars are no longer fought by landed gentry for territorial gains but by seamen, merchant adventurers, for freedom of the seas and access to the wealth of the New World, trading kingdoms for liquidities, for such liberty of space and movement as the Prologue enjoys.

---

29 'Of Plantations', *The Essays*, ed. John Pitcher (Harmondsworth, 1985), pp. 162–4. In 'Of Empire', pp. 115–19, Bacon treats of just and unjust wars.

30 Thorold Rogers, in André Maurois, *Histoire d'Angleterre*, (Paris, 1963, rev. 1978), p. 263.

'FASHION IT THUS': *JULIUS CAESAR* AND THE POLITICS OF THEATRICAL REPRESENTATION

JOHN DRAKAKIS

In David Zucker's 1988 film of *The Naked Gun*, a hapless Los Angeles Chief of Police, Lieutenant Frank Drebin, is warned by his relatively pacifist Mayoress employer to curb his propensity for violence. Drebin, himself an exaggerated post-modernist collocation of easily recognizable film texts, counters with a policy statement of his own sufficient to rival any pronouncement of Clint Eastwood's Dirty Harry:

Yes, well when I see five weirdos dressed in togas stabbing a guy in the middle of the park in full view of a hundred people, I shoot the bastards. That's my policy.

The response of his outraged employer is the embarrassed revelation that: 'That was a Shakespeare in the park production of *Julius Caesar* you moron. You killed five actors: good ones.' The choice of the assassination scene from *Julius Caesar* to illustrate the violence necessary to redress an alleged crime echoes parodically one of two familiar critical readings of this Shakespearian text. In Zucker's film the comic extolling of Caesarism through the wholly inept efficiency of a law enforcement officer unaware of his own representational status and also, at the same time, unable to distinguish other forms of representation, is reinforced by the reactionary nature of his task: the protection of a visiting English queen against the threat of assassination. The latter, ironically republican critical perspective is exemplified in Alex Cox's film *Walker* (1988) which utilizes a scene from *Julius Caesar* to explore, in the thinly veiled allegorical setting of nineteenth-century Nicaragua, the ironies and contradictions inherent in an imperialist project.[1]

The case of Lieutenant Drebin is not unlike that of Julius Caesar himself, who, according to Thomas Heywood, was so accomplished an 'actor' that on at least one occasion he was involuntarily taken in by the veracity of representation itself. In *An Apology for Actors* (1612), in an argument designed, astonishingly, to advance the cause of acting, Heywood relates the following incident:

Julius Caesar himselfe for his pleasure became an Actor, being in shape, state, voyce, judgement, and all other occurrents, exterior and interior excellent. Amongst many other parts acted by him in person, it is recorded of him, that with generall applause in his owne Theater he played *Hercules Furens*, and amongst many other arguments of his compleatenesse, excellence, and extraordinary care in his action, it is thus reported of him: Being in the depth of a passion, one of his seruants (as his part then fell out) presenting *Lychas*, who before had from *Deianeira* brought him the poysoned shirt, dipt in the bloud of the Centaure, *Nessus*: he in the middest of his torture and fury, finding this *Lychas* hid in a remote corner (appoynted him to creep into of purpose), although he was, as our Tragedians vse, but seemingly to kill him by some false imagined wound, yet was *Caesar* so extremely carried away

---

[1] See Geoffrey Bullough, *Narrative and Dramatic Sources of Shakespeare*, 8 vols. (London and New York, 1977), vol. 5, pp. 58–211, for the full range of source material for *Julius Caesar*.

with the violence of his practised fury, and by the perfect shape of the madnesse of *Hercules*, to which he fashioned all his actiue spirits, that he slew him dead at his foot, & after swoong him *terq; quaterqu;* (as the Poet sayes) about his head.[2]

This incident is not recorded, unfortunately, in North's translation of *Plutarch's Lives*, and it has all the hallmarks of an apocryphal story. Indeed, apart from Caesar's allegedly acting in a Senecan play, at least some forty years before the birth of Seneca, it is likely that Heywood confused two stories from Philemon Holland's translation of Suetonius' *The Historie of Twelve Caesars* (1606), conflating episodes from the lives of Julius Caesar and Nero.[3] For Heywood Julius Caesar forsakes his status as an historical personage and becomes an actor himself, a focus for a range of narratives invested with sufficient authority to underwrite the activities of other 'actors'. In short, Caesar is adapted for a particular purpose, endowed with what Roland Barthes might call 'a type of social *usage*',[4] accorded the status of a 'myth' which is then used to legitimize an institution whose preoccupation is the business of representation itself. As a mythical entity, the figure of Caesar consisted of material that, as Barthes would say, had *already* been worked on so as to make it suitable for communication.[5]

Some twelve years before the appearance of Heywood's *An Apology for Actors*, and in the newly built Globe Theatre, on 21 September 1599, the Lord Chamberlain's Men mounted a production of *The Tragedie of Julius Caesar*. A Swiss visitor, Dr Thomas Platter, saw the performance, and recorded that 'at the end of the play they danced together admirably and exceedingly gracefully, according to their custom, two in each group dressed in men's and two in women's apparel.'[6] *Julius Caesar* is hardly a play to set the feet tapping, and if, indeed, this was the play that was written, as Dover Wilson conjectured, 'expressly for the opening' of the Globe[7] then the dance about which Dr Platter enthused may have had more to recommend it than mere 'custom'. Indeed, in the light of a

persistent outpouring of anti-theatrical sentiments throughout this period, combined with what Jonas Barish identified as 'a deep suspicion toward theatricality as a form of behaviour in the world',[8] such a gesture, in a newly opened theatre, may be interpreted as an act of flagrant political defiance.[9] This view receives some general reinforcement from Steven Mullaney's persuasive argument that the suburbs where the public theatres were situated constituted 'a geo-political domain that was crucial to the symbolic and material economy of the city . . . traditionally reserved for cultural phenomena that could not be contained within the strict or proper bounds of the community'.[10] Moreover, the potential for resistance derived from this contextualization of the theatre is reinforced by his suggestion that dramatic performance may be defined as 'a performance *of* the threshold, by which the horizon of community was made visible, the limits of definition, containment and control made mani-

---

[2] Thomas Heywood, *An Apology For Actors*, I. G., *A Refutation of The Apology For Actors, The English Stage: Attack and Defense 1577–1730* (New York and London, 1973), sig. E3v.

[3] C. Suetonius Tranquillius, *The Historie of Twelve Caesars, Emperors of Rome*, trans. Philemon Holland (London, 1606), sigs. c2v–3, and sigs. R4–4v. See also Suetonius, *The Twelve Caesars*, trans. Robert Graves (Harmondsworth, 1957), pp. 26ff. and pp. 219ff.

[4] Roland Barthes, *Mythologies*, trans. Annette Lavers (St Albans, Herts., 1973), p. 109.

[5] Ibid., p. 110.

[6] William Shakespeare, *Julius Caesar*, ed. A. R. Humphreys (Oxford and New York, 1984), p. 1.

[7] William Shakespeare, *Julius Caesar*, ed. J. Dover Wilson (Cambridge, 1941), p. ix.

[8] Jonas A. Barish, *The Antitheatrical Prejudice* (Berkeley, Los Angeles, and London, 1981), p. 133.

[9] See John Drakakis, *The Plays of Shackerley Marmion (1603–39): A Critical Old-spelling Edition*, 2 vols. unpublished PhD thesis, University of Leeds (1988), vol. 1, pp. 494ff. for a full account of the controversial position of dancing during the late sixteenth and early seventeenth centuries.

[10] Steven Mullaney, *The Place of The Stage: License, Play and Power in Renaissance England* (Chicago and London, 1988), p. 9.

fest'.[11] In other words, the liminal position of the theatre, which it shared with other forms of festivity, far from simply ventriloquizing the discourses of political domination, engaged in forms of representation through which other, potentially subversive voices could be heard.

A useful model for this complex process might be Volosinov's reformulation of the Freudian opposition between the 'conscious' and the 'unconscious', as a conflict between 'behavioural ideology', which, he argues, is, in certain respects, 'more sensitive, more responsive, more excitable and livelier' and 'an ideology that has undergone formulation and become "official"'.[12] In an attempt to recuperate the Freudian unconscious for a political account of the relationship between the individual and society, Volosinov insists that what is repressed or censored represents a *conscious* expression of 'behavioural ideology' in so far as it expresses 'the most steadfast and the governing factors of class consciousness'.[13] More recently, Antony Easthope has challenged the notion of a 'political unconscious' as it emerges in the work of Pierre Macherey and Fredric Jameson, on the grounds that while the notion of 'class' as a means of positioning the individual 'is involuntary and acts against the individual's will ... it is not *unconscious* or *repressed* in the psychoanalytic sense of these terms'.[14] For Volosinov, where forms of human behaviour which are not divorced from what he calls 'verbal ideological formulation', but which remain 'in contradiction with the official ideology', it is manifestly not the case that they 'must degenerate into indistinct inner speech and then die out', but rather that they 'might well engage in a struggle with the official ideology'.[15] It is the resultant maintenance of contact both with society and with communication that gives to certain forms of behavioural ideology their revolutionary potential. Volosinov grounds the motive for such a struggle on '*the economic being of the whole group*', but he goes on to suggest that such motives develop within 'a small social milieu'

before being driven into 'the underground – not the psychological underground of repressed complexes, but the salutary political underground'.[16] This is not to suggest that the Elizabethan public theatre was a fully conscious proponent of 'revolutionary ideology', but it does go some way to ascribing intention of a sort within a very complex social formation, while at the same time designating this emergent institution as responsive, excitable, and lively. Indeed, when we consider the timing of performances, the constraints of official censorship, the social heterogeneity and consequent volatility of public theatre audiences,[17] along with the desire for respectability amongst practitioners, and the attempts to secure influential patronage, it becomes clear that the liminal status of a theatre such as the Globe effectively guaranteed its relative 'openness' to the production of contradictory cultural meanings. In addition, Volosinov goes on to suggest that where there is discontinuity between behavioural and official ideologies, then the result is a radical decentring of the individual human subject; he argues:

Motives under these conditions begin to fail, to lose their verbal countenance, and little by little really do turn into a 'foreign body' in the psyche. Whole sets of organic manifestations come, in this way, to be excluded from the zone of verbalized behaviour and

---

[11] Ibid., p. 31.
[12] V. N. Volosinov, *Freudianism: A Marxist Critique*, trans. I. R. Titunik (New York, San Francisco and London, 1976), p. 88.
[13] Ibid., p. 88.
[14] Antony Easthope, *Poetry and Phantasy* (Cambridge and New York, 1989), pp. 36–7. For a fuller articulation of the debate to which Easthope responds, see Pierre Macherey, *A Theory of Literary Production*, trans. Geoffrey Wall (London, 1978), pp. 85ff., and Fredric Jameson, *The Political Unconscious: Narrative as a Socially Symbolic Act* (London, 1981), pp. 17–103.
[15] Volosinov, *Freudianism*, pp. 89–90.
[16] Ibid., p. 90.
[17] Cf. Andrew Gurr, *Playgoing in Shakespeare's London* (Cambridge, 1987), pp. 51–7.

may become *asocial*. Thereby the sphere of the 'animalian' in man enlarges.[18]

We see some evidence of this decentring, and of the crisis of representation which results from it, in Shakespeare's second tetralogy, and especially in *Henry V*, a play very close temporally and thematically to *Julius Caesar*, where theatrical production itself is something for which a choric apology is required as the precondition of a larger revisionary justification for authority.[19] For Henry V, like his father before him, authority resides primarily in those ritual representations through which class interests and force are articulated: the 'idol ceremony' which is defined, somewhat defensively, in terms of a rhetorical question which discloses the operations of ideology: 'Art thou aught else but place, degree, and form, / Creating awe and fear in other men?' (*Henry V*, 4.1.243–4). As Jonathan Dollimore and Alan Sinfield have cogently argued, at this point the king 'claims to be an effect of the structure which he seemed to guarantee',[20] but he also manipulates those symbols from which he seeks some temporary disengagement in order to elicit sympathy for what we might call, with the benefit of hindsight, 'the management interest'. Of course, the figure of the king is what Derrida, in another context, identifies as a 'central presence',[21] responsible for the ordering, extending, and multiplying of a range of signifiers. And it is precisely this presence, 'which has never been itself, has always already been exiled from itself into its own substitute',[22] which the decline and death of Richard II reinforces as what we might call an '*imaginary* signification'.[23] The difficulty for *Henry V* arises directly from the confrontation which takes place in the play between a central organizing signification charged with the task of reconstituting its authority, and the behavioural ideology which challenges, on the terrain of history itself, its efficacy as an instrument for restricting meaning. The relocation – which is also to some extent a dislocation – of this process in the setting of the beginnings of Imperial Rome, and the invocation of a narrative *differentially* constructed along the axis of an opposition between 'popular' and 'humanist' readings of the Caesarian myth, makes *The Tragedie of Julius Caesar* an exemplary text whose own 'ambivalence' is brought into constitutive alignment with the openness and instability of the theatre itself. Indeed, as I shall try to show, the play's concern is not with the *subject* of representation: that is, of rendering a hitherto inaccessible reality present whose ontological status is not in question; but rather with what Robert Weimann has identified as the 'difference within the act of representation' through which a struggle for 'material interests' is articulated.[24] Indeed, if the theatre deals in representations and metaphors it also has the capability to disclose the power that authority *invests* in them, sometimes in the very act of denying their efficacy.

As a number of commentators have shrewdly observed, *Julius Caesar* contains no king; that is, absent from the play is what Derrida calls 'a re-assuring certitude which is itself beyond the reach of play'.[25] Caesar's appropriation of the feast of Lupercal, historically and mythically a festival of origins, clearly has the effect of suppressing *difference*, although this ceremonial affirmation of presence is

18 Volosinov, p. 89.
19 See John Drakakis, 'The Representations of Power in Shakespeare's Second Tetralogy', *Cosmos: The Yearbook of the Traditional Cosmology Society*, vol. 2 (1986), ed. Emily Lyle, pp. 111–35.
20 Jonathan Dollimore and Alan Sinfield, 'History and Ideology: the instance of *Henry V*', in John Drakakis, ed., *Alternative Shakespeares* (London, 1985), pp. 222–3.
21 Jacques Derrida, *Writing and Difference*, trans. Alan Bass (London, 1978), p. 280.
22 Ibid.
23 See Cornelius Castoriadis, *The Imaginary Institution of Society*, trans. Kathleen Blamey (Cambridge, 1987), pp. 146–56.
24 Robert Weimann, 'Towards a Literary Theory of Ideology: Mimesis, Representation, Authority', Jean E. Howard and Marion O'Connor, eds., *Shakespeare Reproduced: The Text in History and Ideology* (New York and London, 1987), p. 271.
25 Derrida, p. 279.

rendered ambivalent by the anti-theatrical puritanism of Flavius and Marullus who challenge this specific *use* of 'holiday'.[26] In his instruction to Marullus to 'Disrobe the images / If you do find them decked with ceremonies' (1.1.64–5), Flavius initiates a deconstruction of the very representations which are a constitutive element of Caesar's success. They are the signifying practices which position Caesar 'above the view of men' at the same time as they reinforce the social hierarchy by keeping 'us all in servile fearfulness' (1.1.74–5). The following scene firmly inscribes Caesar in the process of 'ceremony' both as a producer and an actor, of whom Antony can say: 'When Caesar says "Do this", it is perform'd' (1.2.12), and who insists upon a complete performance: 'Set on, and leave no ceremony out.' (1.2.13) By contrast, Brutus admits, 'I am not gamesom'; (1.2.30), although this anti-festive expression is quickly belied by a tacit admission of consummate acting: 'If I have veiled my look, / I turn the trouble of my countenance / Merely upon myself' (1.2.39–41); and similarly, the Cassius who eschews ritual but articulates his political desires through its language is later affirmed by Caesar as an enemy of theatrical performance: 'He loves no plays' (1.2.204). But it is ironical that while one performance is taking place elsewhere, to which the audience is denied full access, Cassius proposes to Brutus a performance of another kind, deeply dependent upon the mechanics of representation. In an attempt to disclose his 'hidden worthiness' (1.2.59), Cassius constructs a 'self' for Brutus which the latter identifies as both dangerous and alien, and it is one which involves the exposure of the means through which the allegedly tyrannical image of Caesar is sustained. Ironically, the demythologizing of Caesar, which involves divesting his name of political resonance, is itself dependent upon a representation: 'I, your glass, / Will modestly discover to yourself / That of yourself which you yet know not of' (1.2.70–2). Here the 'self' is not that ontologically stable '*Center* of my circling thought' of

Sir John Davies's *Nosce Teipsum*,[27] but a fabrication that can be persuaded that it is fully the subject of its own actions:

> Men at some time were masters of their fates.
> The fault, dear Brutus, is not in our stars,
> But in ourselves, that we are underlings.
>
> (1.2.140–2)[28]

Indeed, it is characteristic of all the conspirators that they oppose 'truth' to a distinctly theatrical falsity, as evidenced in the opposition Casca sets up between Caesar the theatrical performer and himself as a 'true man': 'If the tag-rag people did not clap him and hiss him, according as he pleased and displeased them, as they use to do the players in the theatre, I am no true man.' (1.2.258–61). Also, it is not entirely inappropriate that Messala's eulogy over the body of Cassius at the end of the play should focus upon the ambivalence of representation itself: 'Why dost thou show to the apt thoughts of men / The things that are not?' (5.3.67–8). Indeed, in the play as a whole, one man's truth is another man's theatre. If, as Ernest Schanzer speculated, 'perhaps there is no real Caesar, that he merely exists as a set of images in other men's minds

---

26 Cf. Richard Wilson, '"Is this a Holiday?": Shakespeare's Roman Carnival', *English Literary History*, 54, no. 1 (Spring, 1987), 31–44. See also Mark Rose, 'Conjuring Caesar: Ceremony, History, and Authority in 1599', *English Literary Renaissance*, 19, no. 3 (Autumn, 1989), 291–304. For a more general discussion of the anti-authoritarian notion of festivity, see also Mikhail Bakhtin, *Rabelais and His World*, trans. Helene Iswolsky (Cambridge, Massachussetts, and London, 1968), pp. 21ff., and Peter Burke, *Popular Culture in Early Modern Europe* (London, 1979), pp. 182ff.

27 Sir John Davies, *The Poems of Sir John Davies*, ed. Robert Kreuger (Oxford, 1975), pp. 182ff.

28 I have followed the reading of 1.140 in *William Shakespeare: The Complete Works*, ed. Stanley Wells, Gary Taylor, John Jowett, and William Montgomery (Oxford, 1986). However, the Folio reading of the line is: 'Men at sometime, are Masters of their Fates', and this is followed in A. R. Humphreys, ed., *Julius Caesar* (Oxford and New York, 1984), and T. S. Dorsch, ed., *Julius Caesar* (London, 1965). The use of the present tense of the verb lends greater immediacy to Cassius's machiavellian proposition to Brutus.

and his own.',[29] then the same is doubly true of Brutus, a self fashioned in accordance with the demands of an ambivalent narrative which elicits, to use Schanzer's phrase, 'divided responses'.[30]

Cassius, the stage machiavel, whose metaphorical location in the play, despite protestations in principle to the contrary, is 'Pompey's Theatre' (1.3.152) – significantly, also, the place where Caesar's own death will be staged in accordance with the generic demands of *de casibus* tragedy – initiates here a theatrical process which resonates through the remainder of the play. Casca, plucked by the sleeve, will, like a metropolitan drama critic, 'after his sour fashion, tell you / What hath proceeded worthy note today' (1.2.181–2). Cassius himself will script the representations of an alternative theatre where language itself is an irreducibly material phenomenon, and where signifiers such as 'offence', 'virtue' and 'worthiness' will depend for their meanings upon the alchemical process produced by an appearance: 'that which would appear offence in us / His countenance, like richest alchemy, / Will change to virtue and to worthiness' (1.3.158–60). As a subject of this discourse, where the stakes are political supremacy, Brutus, to use Althusser's phrase, works by himself. Indeed, in a speech which, in part, echoes Marlowe's Machevil,[31] he fabricates a narrative which radically opposes personal obligation – the friendship and 'love' through which imperial politics articulate their hierarchical interests – against a republican view which justifies human intervention in the social order:

> But 'tis a common proof
> That lowliness is young ambition's ladder,
> Whereto the climber-upward turns his face;
> But when he once attains the upmost round,
> He then unto the ladder turns his back,
> Looks in the clouds, scorning the base degrees
> By which he did ascend. So Caesar may.
> Then lest he may, prevent. And since the quarrel
> Will bear no colour for the thing he is,
> Fashion it thus: (2.1.21–30)

Brutus, like Cassius before him, conjures here a representation of a Caesar that the play never allows us to observe as anything other than a wholly fabricated identity, and as a consequence the action is pushed further into that liminal realm already occupied by the theatre itself.

Cassius and Casca's 'fashioning' of Brutus is an indispensable precondition for the success of the conspiracy, and Brutus's soliloquy at the beginning of Act 2 moves the action deeper into that liminal area where ideology and subjectivity intertwine. It is also the area where strategies for the controlling and contesting of meaning are formulated. There is very little in the play as a whole that does not generate alternative readings, whether it be public display, ritual sacrifice, or psychic phenomenon, and it is this hermeneutic instability, the consequence of the existence of two radically opposed forms of authority in Rome, that returns the analysis of motive and action to the space occupied by the theatre which can now claim both to produce *and* to interrogate ideologies. The theatre itself achieves this complex objective, to use Michael Holquist's formulation, through bending language 'to represent by representing languages';[32] and we can see precisely what is involved here in Brutus's response to Cassius's suggestion that Antony and Caesar should 'fall together' (2.1.161). In this debate, as elsewhere in the play, critics of the most liberal

---

[29] Ernest Schanzer, *The Problem Plays of Shakespeare* (London, 1963), p. 32.

[30] Ibid., p. 6.

[31] Cf. Christopher Marlowe, *The Jew of Malta*, ed. N. W. Bawcutt (Manchester, 1978), p. 63:

> Though some speak openly against my books,
> Yet will they read me, and thereby attain
> To Peter's chair; and when they cast me off
> Are poisoned by my climbing followers.
> (Prologue: lines 10–13)

[32] Michael Holquist, 'The Politics of Representation', in *Allegory and Representation*, ed. Stephen Greenblatt (Baltimore and London, 1981), p. 169.

of persuasions have sided with Cassius,[33] but it is Brutus more than Cassius who grasps the importance of mediating the conspiracy through existing rituals and institutions.[34] Here representation accumulates a level of irony which discloses it as misrepresentation:

> Let's be sacrificers, but not butchers, Caius.
> We all stand up against the spirit of Caesar,
> And in the spirit of men there is no blood.
> O, that we then could come by Caesar's spirit,
> And not dismember Caesar! But, alas,
> Caesar must bleed for it.   (2.1.166–71)

Clearly, liberation from alleged tyranny cannot be permitted to result in absolute freedom for all. If so, authority and power are not worth having. Resistant though the conspirators are to the Caesarian control of institutions and meanings, they formulate a strategy of temporary release and restraint which parallels the *ideological* usage of festivity, extending the potential for containment to the affective power of tragic form itself. These concerns are concentrated with remarkable economy in Brutus's appeal to his fellow conspirators: 'And let our hearts, as subtle masters do, / Stir up their servants to an act of rage, / And after seem to chide 'em' (2.1.175–7). From this point on the talk is of 'fashioning', of manufacturing, and hence of historicizing, truth, and, inevitably, of theatrical representation. The fully fashioned Brutus will now undertake to 'fashion' Caius Ligarius (2.1.219), an assertion that may well have received an added irony in the original performance where it is thought that the parts of Cassius and Caius Ligarius may have been doubled.[35] Such a suggestion would give added ironical point to Cassius's own speculation in his soliloquy at 1.2.314–15: 'If I were Brutus now, and he were Cassius, / He should not humour me.' Also Cassius's bid to revive Roman self-presence with his exhortation to the conspirators to 'Show yourselves true Romans' (2.1.222) is expanded by the one character whose 'countenance' is endowed with transformative power: 'Let not our looks put

on our purposes; / But bear it as our Roman actors do, / With untired spirits and formal constancy' (2.1.224–6). Here theatrical representation is neither illusion nor self-delusion, rather it is the ground upon which the symbols of authority are contested. It is no accident that Thomas Beard could refer to the conspirators as those who 'were actors in this tragedy',[36] or that William Fulbecke could refer to Brutus as 'chiefe actor in Caesars tragedie'.[37]

If the conspirators are exhorted to sustain a 'formal constancy', then the Caesar which the first two acts of the play reveals is as consummate a Roman actor as his adversaries. To recuperate the assassination as the *origin* of a theatrical tradition in which the tragic protagonist is the unwitting participant, as Cassius later does, is simultaneously to expose the discursive mechanisms, at the moment that it seeks to reinforce, the historical and material determinants, of political power: 'How many ages hence / Shall this our lofty scene be acted over / In states unborn and accents yet unknown!' (3.1.112–14). In an augmentation of the practice of scripting, Brutus urges his accomplices to:

---

[33] Cf. Irving Ribner, *Patterns in Shakespearian Tragedy* (London, 1969), p. 60. See also Ernst Honigmann, *Shakespeare: Seven Tragedies: The Dramatist's Manipulation of Response* (London, 1976), p. 50; Alexander Leggatt, *Shakespeare's Political Drama: The History Plays and The Roman Plays* (London, 1988), p. 144; and Vivian Thomas, *Shakespeare's Roman Worlds* (London, 1989), p. 76.

[34] For a more negative view, see Robert S. Miola, *Shakespeare's Rome* (Cambridge, 1983), p. 93, where it is suggested that 'Brutus's words reveal the savagery of the impending Roman ritual; in addition they expose the self-delusion of the conspirators.'

[35] A. R. Humphreys, ed., *Julius Caesar*, pp. 80–1. I am also grateful to Professor Gunther Walch for having drawn this possibility to my attention in his unpublished paper '"Caesar did never wrong, but with just cause": Interrogative Dramatic Structure in *Julius Caesar*'.

[36] Thomas Beard, *The Theatre of God's Iudgements* (London 1597), p. 249, *STC* 1659.

[37] William Fulbecke, *An Historicall Collection of the Continuall Factions, Tumults, and Massacres of the Romans and Italians* (London, 1601), p. 170, *STC* 11412.

'Let's all cry "Peace, freedom, and liberty"!' (3.1.111), but this is followed almost immediately by the entry of a 'servant' who produces, not the voice of a free subject, but that of his 'master' Antony which he proceeds to ventriloquize. In the following scene it is the plebeian voice, emanating from an onstage audience credited with a dutiful quiescence which the actual Globe audience was unlikely to have reflected, which, ironically, through a replication of conspiratorial locutions, confirms the continuity of the rhetoric and symbols of political power: 'Let him be Caesar', 'Caesar's better parts / Shall be crowned in Brutus.' (3.2.51–3). As in the later play *Coriolanus* the 'audience' is simultaneously empowered and disempowered, allotted a rôle from which it cannot escape. In the later play, where the Roman populace is given a more substantial critical voice, the *irony* of this position is laid open to question as the Citizens are obligated to support a patrician in whom they have little confidence:

We have power in ourselves to do it, but it is a power that we have no power to do. For if he show us his wounds and tell us his deeds, we are to put our tongues into those wounds and speak for them; so if he tell us his noble deeds we must also tell him our noble acceptance of them. Ingratitude is monstrous, and for the multitude to be ingrateful were to make a monster of the multitude, of the which we, being members, should bring ourselves to be monstrous members. (*Coriolanus* 2.3.4–13)[38]

If this is so, then it is extremely doubtful whether such self-consciously theatrical allusions serve, as Anne Righter has argued, 'pre-eminently to glorify the stage'.[39] This representation of the workings of political power, irrespective of intention, discloses an unstable institution proceeding gingerly into a terrain fraught with considerable political danger. Cast in a subversive role, confronted with the demands of official censorship, but nevertheless seeking legitimation, the actual choice of dramatic material would have been crucial. In *Julius Caesar* the Chamberlain's Men could

displace their own professional anxieties onto a narrative which, by virtue of its very ambivalence, offered a space for the exploration of the ideology which governs the exchange of representations which take place between society and theatre, centre and margins.

In a culture in which those who would oppose theatrical representation continued to insist upon the power that inheres in the theatrical image itself, *Julius Caesar* is not so much a celebration of theatre as an unmasking of the politics of representation per se. The play does not *express* meaning; rather, in its readings of Roman history it *produces* meanings. Moreover, in its shuttling between the generic requirements of *de casibus* tragedy, and the Senecan tragedy of revenge, historical possibilities are simultaneously disclosed and withdrawn, in such a way as to propose an alignment of enjoyment with danger and with resistance. In its vacillation between 'fate' and human agency as the origins of action, and hence of history itself, *Julius Caesar* enacts the precarious position of the Globe itself. This is not the Shakespeare that we have been encouraged to regard as 'profoundly moving, or spiritually restoring, or simply strangely enjoyable', as recently proposed by Professor Boris Ford;[40] this carefully tailored brand of anti-intellectual prophylactic consumerism demands a kind of passivity that refuses to contemplate, among other things, the popular significance of that unsettling carnivalesque dance that closed the Globe performance of *Julius Caesar*. It subscribes tacitly to a teleological conception of Art not too far removed from the advice proffered by the Arts Minister, Richard Luce, as part of an argument in support of the

---

[38] See John Drakakis, 'Writing The Body Politic: Subject, Discourse, and History in Shakespeare's *Coriolanus*', *Shakespeare Jahrbuch*, ed. Gunther Klotz (forthcoming, 1992).

[39] Anne Righter, *Shakespeare and The Idea of The Play*, (Harmondsworth, 1967), p. 141.

[40] Boris Ford, 'Bardbiz', *Letters: The London Review of Books*, vol. 12, no. 14 (2 August 1990).

suppression of modern 'popular' theatre: 'You should accept the political and economic climate in which we now live and make the most of it. Such an attitude could bring surprisingly good results.'[41] Of course, as we know from our own media representations of a crisis

which is much nearer to us than Renaissance readings of the origins of Imperial Rome, no gun is ever naked.

---

[41]John McGrath, *The Bone Won't Break: On Theatre and Hope in Hard Times* (London, 1990), p. 161.

'DEMYSTIFYING THE MYSTERY OF STATE': *KING LEAR* AND THE WORLD UPSIDE DOWN

MARGOT HEINEMANN

King Lear is very much a political play – that is a play concerned with power and government in the state, with public and civil life, and not solely with private relationships and passions. Of course it is not *only* political; but it seems necessary to restate the point because recent productions so often try to make it a *purely* personal, familial, and psychological drama (much in the manner of A.C. Bradley, though a Bradley who has read Freud, Laing, and Foucault). However, even if this is intended to render the play acceptable to modern audiences (who are assumed to be very simple-minded), it is still a distortion, and makes much of the action unintelligible. As Peter Brook put it, the fact that the play is called *King Lear* does not mean that it is primarily the story of one individual[1] – or, one may add, of one family. Shakespeare himself, by introducing the Gloucester parallel plot from quite another source, seems concerned to generalize the issues, to show that Lear's personal psychology or 'character' is not the only force at work.

There was a period, of course, when an exclusively timeless, ahistorical way of reading was more or less taken for granted. It was a great illumination for me, then, to read studies like John Danby's *Shakespeare's Doctrine of Nature* (1949), and the chapters by Kenneth Muir and Arnold Kettle in *Shakespeare in a Changing World* (1964), which attempted to read the play in the light of its contemporary historical and political significance, whatever reservations one may now have about some of

their particular interpretations. Many years later, when my own highly intelligent and dominating mother reached the age of eighty-six, my sister and I discovered in ourselves marked Goneril and Regan tendencies. In one sense, as Goethe has it, 'an old man is always a King Lear'. The frustrations of old age ('I will do such things / What they are yet I know not, but they shall be / The terrors of the earth!'); the pain of confusion and weakness, are superbly given. The play needs inescapably to be seen *both* as an individual's loss of power and control *and* as the breakdown of a social and political system: that is indeed its point.

Why, for instance, some critics ask, does not Cordelia humour her old father, in the opening scene, by telling him what he wants and expects to hear – that she loves him above everything? If he were *only* her father, that could perhaps be a reputable argument. But he is also the King, he wields absolute power in the state, and for Cordelia to join in the public competition of flattery and cadging would be to collude with the corruption of absolute power – a matter which preoccupied many of James I's most politically thoughtful subjects in 1604–7. This she cannot do, as Kent cannot do it, and we admire their courage, come what will. If we take it only as a personal story (which the legendary history of course does not), it becomes plausible to imagine Cordelia as culpably

---

[1] Peter Brook, *The Empty Space* (London, 1968), p. 91.

stubborn, opinionated, self-righteous and self-ish, the inherited mirror-image of Lear's personal failings. But one cannot play it like this without destroying the force of the legendary narrative and the interaction in the theatre.

DEMYSTIFYING THE MYSTERY OF STATE

The main political thrust is not, of course, to propound an ideal, simplified, harmonious solution for conflicts and contradictions that were genuinely insoluble in the society of the time. Shakespeare is not writing Agitprop. School pupils and students who ask: 'What is Shakespeare putting over?' can be given only a negative answer – some things he is clearly not putting over.

The political effect is, rather, sharply to represent the complex conflicts of interest and ideology in his own world; to dramatize them as human conflicts and actions, not ordained by fate; to present images of kings and queens, statesmen and counsellors as simultaneously holders of sacred office and fallible human beings who may be weak, stupid, greedy or cruel (in itself a central contradiction). Hence the drama empowers ordinary people in the audience to think and judge for themselves of matters usually considered 'mysteries of state' in which no one but the 'natural rulers' – the nobility and gentry and professional élites – should be allowed to meddle. Sir Henry Wotton commented after seeing *Henry VIII* at the Globe that it was 'sufficient in truth within a while to make greatness very familiar, if not ridiculous'. If this was what he thought about *Henry VIII*, the most spectacular and ceremonious of Shakespeare's history plays, what would he have said of *King Lear*, which produces this effect in its extremest form?

REINFORCING DOMINANT IDEOLOGY?

It has been argued that the dramatists necessarily reinforce the dominant ideology which holds the society together, within which insti-

tutions such as the theatre function and provide them with a living, so that on balance criticism is safely 'contained'. In the early seventeenth century, however, it becomes increasingly evident that no single dominant ideology or consensus is capable of holding the society together. The existence of different ideologies and of deep ideological and political conflicts over the nature and limits of monarchic power and prerogative, and the rights and liberties of subjects (however masked by the pervasive censorship), has been clearly demonstrated and documented for the years 1603–40 by younger historians, notably J.P. Sommerville, Richard Cust, and Peter Lake.[2] The Essex circle, where so many contesting ideological viewpoints were articulated and discussed in the 1590s, was a marvellous seedbed for Shakespeare's multi-vocal historical and political drama. But that complex clash of ideologies – bastard-feudal, politique, scientific-Machiavellian, republican, radical-Puritan crusading and anti-clerical – ended in the disaster of the Essex revolt. In the drama, optimistic confidence in political and military action to fulfil national destiny gave place to a sense of history as tragedy, and modern English history became for the time being a banned subject.

WHAT THE POLITICS OF *KING LEAR* CANNOT BE

The politics of the play cannot then be the assertion of absolute monarchal power, prerogative, and magnificence against mean-spirited Parliamentary attacks on royal expenditure and pleasures, symbolized allegorically in Goneril and Regan, though this has been seriously argued. The Parliament of 1604 was certainly no flatterer of the monarch. Neither does the play show that any interference with or dimin-

---

[2] See in particular the chapters by these authors in *Conflict in Early Stuart England*, ed. R. Cust and A. Hughes (London, 1989); and J. P. Sommerville, *Politics and Ideology in England, 1603–1640* (London, 1989).

ution of the King's absolute power is unnatural and must lead to chaos: for it is Lear's refusal to listen to wise counsel, his insistence on his own will as paramount and absolute, that opens the way to chaos and disintegration. The patriarchalist view of monarchy, that equates kingly power with the power of the father within the family, is strongly present in the play, above all in the mind of Lear himself. Patriarchalism does not, however, necessarily entail an absolutist view of kingly power; the importance of paternal power was supported by many anti-absolutist and even some revolutionary and Leveller political thinkers.[3] Yet Cordelia, who challenges her father's use of absolute power, retains the audience's sympathy in so doing. To read the play as unequivocally patriarchalist is to read against the grain.

The assertion of the traditional and necessary rights and privileges of Parliament against government by royal prerogative was not something invented in the 1620s and 1630s, just in time for the Civil War, but goes back to the moment of *King Lear* and beyond it. James I was confused and annoyed by the institution of Parliament as he found it in his new kingdom, and the loyal Commons tried to explain to him that their right to be consulted and to criticize Crown policies did not imply disloyalty. The 'Apology of the Commons' in 1604 expressed their fears, based on what was happening to elected assemblies elsewhere in Europe:

What cause your poor Commons have to watch over our privileges is manifest in itself to all men. The prerogatives of princes may easily and do daily grow: the privileges of subjects are for the most part at an everlasting stand. They may be by providence and good care preserved, but being once lost are not recovered but with much disquiet.[4]

The Apology itself (never finally passed through parliament or officially presented) was drafted by Sir Edwin Sandys, MP, thereafter a close associate of Shakespeare's former patron the Earl of Southampton, with other surviving Essexians (such as Sir Thomas Ridgway) taking an important part. Sandys himself, one of the foremost exponents of anti-absolutist thinking in Jacobean times, claimed that the King's power had originally been introduced by popular consent; he declared in Parliament that now 'it is come to be almost a tyrannical government in England'.[5] The tension between King and Parliament was indeed to continue throughout James's reign.

We do not know very much about Shakespeare's later connections with Southampton and his circle, but there is no evidence that they were broken off. Shakespeare apparently celebrated his former patron's release from the Tower with a congratulatory sonnet (No. 107), and continuing links with his circle are demonstrated by G.P. Akrigg.[6] *The Tempest*, begun around the time when Southampton (with Sandys) helped to found the Virginia Company, shows continuing cross-fertilization, and revolves (though sceptically) the colonialists' dream of creating a juster empire in the New World.[7]

In the context, it seems that Goneril, Regan, and Edmund were likely to be identified by the audience not with the Parliamentary oppositionists, but with what they saw as con-

---

[3] Sommerville, *Politics and Ideology*, pp. 28–32.

[4] From 'A Form of Apology and Satisfaction', drawn up at the end of the 1604 session by a Committee of the House. Cited Conrad Russell, *The Crisis of Parliaments* (London, 1971), p. 270.

[5] Cited Derek Hirst, *Authority and Conflict in England 1603–1648* (London, 1986), p. 117.

[6] G. P. Akrigg, *Shakespeare and the Earl of Southampton* (London, 1968), pp. 264ff.

[7] Other links with Parliamentarian circles can be traced through the Digges brothers, who are connected in various ways with Shakespeare and later with anti-absolutist opposition trends. Their stepfather, Thomas Russell, was overseer of Shakespeare's will. Leonard Digges published eulogies of Shakespeare in 1623 and 1640. (*Shakespeare, Complete Works* (Oxford, 1986), pp. xlvi and xlviii). Dudley Digges, who is believed to have shown Strachey's confidential report on the state of Virginia to Shakespeare (see *The Tempest*, ed. Frank Kermode (London, 1964), pp. xxvii–xxviii) was a prominent anti-absolutist MP, and in 1629 drafted the Petition of Right.

temporary flatterers, cadgers, and upstarts at the Jacobean court, who were being rewarded for their obsequiousness with land, monopolies, offices and gifts – people like James's unpopular Scottish favourites. The land and the peasants who live on it are given away by Lear as if they were his private property. The decay of the old social order, with an alternative not yet ready to be born, gives rise to such morbid growths – as Gramsci expresses it.

NATURE OF THE POLITICAL INTEREST

The heart of the political interest is not in the division of the kingdom or the issue of unification with Scotland, though there may well be allusions to this. The *division* as such does not in fact cause the war and barbarity that we see. The sole rule of Goneril, the eldest, would scarcely make for peace and harmony, and the single rule of Cordelia could only be secured if primogeniture were ignored. The causes of disaster lie deeper than that. The central focus is on the horror of a society divided between extremes of rich and poor, greed and starvation, the powerful and the powerless, robes and rags, and the impossibility of real justice and security in such a world. Lear himself, like the faithful Gloucester, discovers this only when his own world is turned upside down, when he himself is destitute and mad, and at last sees authority with the eyes of the dispossessed. Central to the language as well as the stage images is the opposition between 'looped and window'd raggedness', utter poverty, and the 'robes and furred gowns' that hide nakedness and crimes. All the difference lies in clothes and ceremony: 'a dog's obeyed in office'.

This crazy world is directly the responsibility of the King and of the rich and powerful in general, and the verse continually underlines this: 'You houseless poverty', cries Lear on the heath,

> O, I have ta'en
> Too little care of this. Take physic, pomp,
> Expose thyself to feel what wretches feel,

> That thou mayst shake the superflux to them
> And show the heavens more just. (3.4.32–6)

And Gloucester, blind and helpless, echoes this conclusion:

> Heavens deal so still!
> Let the superfluous and lust-dieted man
> That slaves your ordinance, that will not see
> Because he does not feel, feel your power quickly.
> So distribution should undo excess,
> And each man have enough. (4.1.60–5)

This is a note not struck in the earlier Histories, and certainly not in the other 'deposition play', *Richard II*.

The indictment is still, for us, very direct and near the bone. Audiences going to the South Bank to see in 1990 *King Lear* at the National Theatre passed by Cardboard City, the modern equivalent of Edgar's hovel, where the homeless shelter in cardboard boxes on the pavement. Mother Teresa of Calcutta, visiting London, said on television that she had seen such sights in the Third World, but in a rich country like Britain she could not understand it. Many of those sleeping rough are the mentally disturbed and the old, made homeless by the closing of mental hospitals and old people's homes, the cuts in home helps, the lack of funds for care in the community. Lear bitterly tells Goneril, 'Age is unnecessary'. It still is.[8]

---

[8] During the year to October 1990 London local authorities had to place over 31,000 families in temporary accommodation (a new high), and 8,000 in bed and breakfast accommodation. (Chairman of Association of Local Authorities Housing Committee, the *Guardian*, 12 October 1990). Even in prosperous Cambridge, 307 homeless families had to be rehoused in the year 1990–1, an increase of 44 on the previous year and the highest number on record. For England as a whole official statistics show homeless households have increased by 131 per cent in 1979–89 to a total of 122,680: recent research (by Professor John Greve) shows that in 1990 some 170,000 households were accepted as homeless by Local Authorities, amounting to about half a million people. Estimates of single homeless (who are not entitled to be rehoused) in London vary between 65,000 and 125,000: according to the housing charity *Shelter*, about 3,000 are currently sleeping rough in London.

This interest, and the rôle-reversal of riches and poverty, power and powerlessness, is stressed in Quarto and Folio alike, despite the many alterations. Nor is it just our modern prejudice that leads us to focus on this as a central concern. It is surely significant that so many of what are now widely believed to be Shakespeare's own revisions relate to this aspect of the play – the inverted world, the counterposing of king and clown, wisdom and madness, insight and fooling. Clearly he was particularly anxious to get this right. He has two goes at presenting the 'upside-down' view of monarchy and absolute power. Once this appears as a powerful stage image, the 'mock-trial' of the Quarto text, in which the very possibility of securing justice in such an unjust and unequal society is parodied and mocked. This scene can be much more effective on the stage than it looks on the page (*pace* Roger Warren),[9] since the parallel with Lear dispensing 'justice' from his throne in the opening scene can be made visually much sharper and more shocking.

In the Folio text the upside-down view of justice is presented purely in language, in the extended speech of Lear to Gloucester, which, after the brilliant images (already in Quarto) of the dog obeyed in office and the beadle lashing the whore he lusts for, adds the explicit general moral:

> Plate sin with gold,
> And the strong lance of justice hurtless breaks;
> Arm it in rags, a pygmy's straw does pierce it.
> None does offend, none, I say none. I'll able 'em.
> Take that of me, my friend, who have the power
> To seal th'accuser's lips.   (4.5.161–6)

The 'upside-downness' is emphasized and made more explicit verbally in Folio – *extended* from Quarto but not *amended*. 'None does offend' suggests that no one has the right to accuse or judge since all are sinners, or that no one will dare to accuse if the king opposes it and has the power to silence the accusers and pardon the offenders. But there may also be an echo of antinomian discourse, implying that our categories of right and wrong, sin and righteousness, are meaningless and evil. The dreams

of persecuted underground Familist groups at the time when *King Lear* was written surface again in the revolutionary years in the antinomian vision of Abiezer Coppe:

> Sin and transgression is finished and ended . . . Be no longer so horribly, hellishly, impudently, arrogantly wicked, as to judge what is sin, what not.[10]

Although I understand Roger Warren's point about the difficulty of staging the 'mock-trial', which *may* have prompted the revision, it has (as he concedes) been successfully done, for example in our time by Peter Brook, and it is difficult to accept that by cutting it Shakespeare made a better play. For the 'mock-trial' vividly makes the case not against a particular legal injustice or the corruption of individual judges (as Middleton does in, say, *The Phoenix*), but against the whole intrinsically ridiculous pretence of justice in an unjust society.

Warren criticizes the scene as ineffective on the grounds that the Fool and Edgar as Poor Tom, seated on the farmhouse bench alongside Lear, fail to keep to the legal-satirical point, though Lear himself does so.[11] But this is surely the essence. The entire set up is absurd – the rich and respectable are no more qualified to dispense justice than the whores and thieves, or the fools and madmen. To make this strike home and shake our complacency, the speech of madness and folly at this moment needs to sound truly mad, wild and disorganized, not the coherently composed discourse of a satirist in disguise. The image flashes on us as a moment of dreadful insight – enough, one might say, to drive the beholder mad.

Christopher Hill perceptively notes that many prophets of the upside-down world in

---

[9] Roger Warren, 'The Folio Omission of the Mock Trial: Motives and Consequences', in Gary Taylor and Michael Warren, eds., *The Division of the Kingdoms* (Oxford, 1983), pp. 45ff.

[10] Abiezer Coppe, *A Fiery Flying Roll*, pt 1, ch. 8 (London, 1649).

[11] R. Warren, p. 46.

the seventeenth century were thought by contemporaries to be mad, and some probably were – the vision was too much for their sanity.[12] But in some cases madness was a useful protection for the expression of opinions dangerous to the social order. There can be no doubt that the Ranter Thomas Webbe was being prudent when he called himself Mad Tom in a pamphlet foretelling the downfall of Charles II in 1660.[13]

This reversal of degree finds no easy resolution in the play. Edgar's final speech provides no strongly felt reassurance that the world is now once more firmly the right way up. It is deliberately quiet and bleak.

RESISTANCE UPSIDE DOWN

The resistance to evil too has an 'upside-down' dimension, coming first from the weak, the oppressed lower orders, the peasants and servants. This is highlighted in the first violent check to tyranny, when the Nazi-type brute Cornwall, about to put out the other eye of Gloucester, is defied and wounded by his own servant. In the few lines he speaks this unnamed man declares himself a lifelong servant of the Duke, not a casual hireling; but the bonds of feudal loyalty and rank cannot hold in face of such dishonourable cruelty:

> I have served you ever since I was a child,
> But better service have I never done you
> Than now to bid you hold.   (3.7.71–3)

This echoes Kent's justification of his insubordination to Lear. A 'villein' of Cornwall's draws on his lord as an equal, and Regan screams out the indignation of the 'natural rulers':

> A *peasant* stand up thus!   (3.7.77)

She kills him, running at him from behind. But the resistance has started, and Cornwall will not be there to help crush it.

For the audience, this action – quite unprepared – by one of the stage 'extras' is startling, and evidently meant to be so. It is followed, in Quarto, by the sympathy and indignation of the horrified servants, who despite their terror do their best to help Gloucester and bandage his wounds. This first tentative rallying of humane forces against the tyrants was cut in the Folio text, and also in a famous production by Peter Brook, who said he wished to prevent reassurance being given to the audience. One wonders why. The reassurance provided in these depths of agony hardly seems excessive. Was the suggestion of a justified *popular* rising against despotic power perhaps felt to be going too far? However that may be, Edgar when he kills Oswald is disguised as a peasant, wearing the 'best 'parel' provided by the honest old man, Gloucester's tenant, and talking stage country dialect. His peasant cudgel beats down the gentleman's sword and his fancy fencing:

> I's' try whether your costard or my baton be the harder ... 'Chill pick your teeth, sir. Come, no matter vor your foins.   (4.5.240–4)

Ordinary countrymen were of course forbidden to wear a sword, which was the exclusive privilege of gentlemen.[14] Hence this victory must register in the theatre as symbolic of the common people defeating the hangers-on of court and wealth, though since Edgar is really a nobleman in disguise, and the audience knows this, the effect is less subversive than it might be. However, if we compare this fight with the concluding duels between Hamlet and Laertes, Prince Hal and Hotspur, or Coriolanus and Aufidius, this image is strikingly a contest of social unequals, in which the plain but righteous man wins against the odds. It may also have suggested a further symbolic meaning for some in the audience. The Surrey group of

---

[12] Christopher Hill, *The World Turned Upside Down* (London, 1972), p. 224. The whole chapter 'The Island of Great Bedlam' is illuminating on the relation between lower-class prophecy and accusations of madness.

[13] Hill, p. 227.

[14] Oswald, as Kent points out earlier, while technically allowed to wear a sword, is too dishonourable to have a right to it.

Familists, whose pacifist principles forbade them to bear arms, found that this made them too conspicuous, and therefore compromised by carrying staves (cudgels).[15]

Lear's Fool is of course the most obvious source of upside-downness in both texts, speaking wisdom in the proverbial idiom of the people, often coarsely, in contrast to the hypocrisy and folly of formal and ceremonial utterance by the great. (The distinction that has been suggested between a 'natural' Fool in Quarto and an 'artificial', skilful courtier-Fool in Folio has to my mind been greatly overstated.) The Fool's jokes and aphorisms are consistently in the irreverent upside-down style, often literally so, and some as old as Aesop:

e'er since thou madest thy daughters thy mothers . . . and puttest down thine own breeches . . .
(1.4.153–4)

May not an ass know when the cart draws the horse?
(1.4.206)

When thou clovest thy crown i'th' middle and gavest away both parts, thou borest thine ass o'th' back o'er the dirt.   1.4.142–4)

This echoes the images of the topsy-turvy world in scores of songs and broadsides,[16] such as the popular ballad, 'Who's the fool now', favoured by James's own provocative Fool Archy Armstrong (and still in use at folksong festivals to this day). Textual revision has not substantially changed this effect. The King himself reduced to a fool is a key image in both texts. The main difference may be in the greater emphasis given to it in the Quarto:

LEAR   Dost thou call me fool, boy?

FOOL   All thy other titles thou hast given away.
That thou wast born with.   (Q.4.143–5)

And one may note also the obviousness of the topical application in Quarto, which it is suggested the censor may have jibbed at.[17] Among the lines excised is the Fool's jingle:

That lord that counselled thee
To give away thy land,
Come, place him here by me;
Do thou for him stand.
The sweet and bitter fool

Will presently appear,
The one in motley here,
The other found out there.   (Q.4.135–142)

So too is the Fool's complaint that he has failed to secure a monopoly of folly, because:

lords and great men will not let me. If I had a monopoly out, they would have part on't, and ladies too, they will not let me have all the fool to myself – they'll be snatching.   (Q.4.147–50)

There is indeed a double topical reference here (1) to the land given away by the King to his favourites, and (2) to anti-monopoly pressure by the Commons, culminating in the Apology of 1604.

The Fool stands in a direct theatrical tradition from Tarlton, appearing as Simplicity in the 'medley' plays of the 1580s. Even his jokes are traditional.[18] The clown as prophet appears in *The Cobbler's Prophecy* (printed 1594) where the poor cobbler, endowed with prophetic gifts by the gods, denounces the rich and foresees the world turned upside down at the Day of Judgement, when widows and starving children will be avenged. The most direct analogy, however, is with Rowley's comic-historical presentation in 1605 of Henry VIII and his famous jester Will Summers, who in this rendering is an iconoclastic, egalitarian, anti-Popish clown and a champion of the poor. It would be better, he

---

[15] See Janet E. Halley, 'The Case of the English Family of Love', in *Representing the English Renaissance*, ed. Stephen Greenblatt (London, 1988), pp. 319–20. See also John Rogers, *The displaying of an horrible sect of gross and wicked heretics* (London, 1578).

[16] See Peter Burke, *Popular Culture in Early Modern Europe* (London, 1978), especially the illustrated broadsides of the mice burning the cat; the woman with the gun and the man with the distaff; and the peasant riding on the nobleman's back (between pp. 98 and 99).

[17] See Gary Taylor in *The Division of the Kingdoms*, pp. 104–9.

[18] The Fool's joke about the cockney's brother who, 'in pure kindness to his horse, buttered his hay' (*Lear* 2.4) is anticipated by Tarlton's story about the inn where they greased the horses' teeth to prevent them eating, and so saved the cost of the fodder (*Three Ladies of London*, Dodsley's *Old Plays* (London, 1874), vol. 6, p. 255).

says, if Henry had their prayers rather than the Pope's, for the Pope is at best St Peter's deputy, 'but the poor present Christ, and so should be something better regarded' – an old anti-clerical aphovism traceable back to the Lollards.[19]

NOT ONLY 'CARNIVALESQUE'

The upside-down discourse here is not simply 'carnivalesque', if by that we mean providing a recognized safety-valve for the release of tensions in a repressive society – a temporary holiday from hierarchy which enables it to be reimposed more effectively afterwards, as we see in the Feast of Fools, the Lords of Misrule, or the iconoclastic Christmas entertainments customary to this day in the London teaching hospitals.

The deriding of accepted categories of sin, adultery, property and officially enforced law echoes Utopian ideas which survived in a serious and organized form, more or less underground, in late-Elizabethan and Jacobean times, among radical religious sects such as the Family of Love, and were to surface again forty to fifty years later in the revolutionary years, first with the Levellers, and after their defeat with Ranters and Seekers. A Presbyterian divine, denouncing the sect under Elizabeth, had emphasized the 'topsy-turvy' aspect of Henry Niclaes' teaching as especially subversive of order:

To be brief in this matter of doctrine, H.N. turneth religion upside down, and buildeth heaven here upon earth: maketh God, man; and man, God; heaven, hell; and hell, heaven.[20]

The existence of such ideas was topical knowledge about the time when *King Lear* was first produced. In *Basilikon Doron* King James had particularly attacked Familists as an example of *dangerous* Puritanism:

their humours . . . agreeing with the general rule of all Anabaptists, in the contempt of the civil magistrate, and in leaning to their own dreams and revelations.[21]

The Familists, replying to this, petitioned King James for toleration, disavowing any intent to overthrow the magistrate and place themselves in his seat: an appeal almost certainly drafted by Robert Seale, one of a group of Familists in the royal Guard.[22] They did not obtain the toleration they sought. In 1606 a confutation of their *Supplication* was printed (together with the text) and thereafter little is known about the sect as such. The ideas, however, were in the air, and theatre people could have picked up their acquaintance with them around the court as well as in artisan circles (often no doubt in distorted form).

NOT MAD FROM THE BEGINNING

The 'world upside down' effect in the play is easily destroyed, though, if the King is played (as has happened in some recent productions) as deranged, undignified and in senile dementia from his first entrance. Dramatically, no fall or reversal is then possible, and 'Let me not be mad, not mad, sweet heaven!' loses all its agonizing force. No moral or political point can then be made, except perhaps that kings ought

[19] Samuel Rowley, *When You See Me You Know Me* (London, 1605) (Malone Society Reprint, 1952, line 1568).

[20] John Knewstub, *A Confutation of Monstrous and Horrible Heresies* (London, 1579). Preface.

[21] Cited by Halley.

[22] Seale was briefly imprisoned on suspicion of Familism in 1580, but was still in a position of trust at court as clerk of the Cheque of the Guard in 1599, a position which he continued to hold in 1606. In the reply confuting the Familists' Supplication (which includes their text) the editor refers (p. 18) to leading Familists 'receiving yearly both countenance and maintenance from her princely coffers, being her household servants': and on p. 28 states that the Elizabethan Familists are 'yet living and in Court', with 'their children in right ancient place about his majesty'. The Familists included both an educated élite and an organized popular following, mainly of artisans, in such areas as Wisbech, Surrey, Suffolk, and Cambridge. See Alastair Hamilton, *The Family of Love* (1981), especially Chapter 6 on the Family in England.

to be retired early, so that they can be replaced by sane people like Goneril and Regan.

It is not a question of the sacred untouchability of the text. As Brecht once said, 'I think we can alter Shakespeare if we can alter him'; but wrong alterations will 'mobilise all Shakespeare's excellences against us'. This particular one seems to me the kind of alteration that distorts the original to the point where the chemistry of the play no longer works. A successful production has to convince us that a King, however grand and mighty he has been, is a fool anyway, and mortal anyway. Lear's fearful experience makes him and the audience aware of this. Hence the need of any king for wise and courageous advisers prepared to tell him the truth and set limits to his power – the role played by Kent here, and in the contemporary political context, unevenly but increasingly, in their own mind at least, by some opposition elements in Parliament.

CENSORSHIP AND THE RECEPTION OF THE PLAY

Direct censorship (as distinct from cautious self-censorship) has been argued as possibly accounting for some of the differences between the two texts – notably the omission of several of the Fool's speeches in Scene 4. It was a tricky moment to write in this tone about a *British* Court and Crown, even if legendary ones. But it may just have been that the bitter jokes against royalty did not please, and some were therefore cut by the dramatist and the players in a revised acting version. That, however, may not have been enough. No London revival of *Lear* after 1606, which might have used a revised text, is actually known, though there were many repeats, at court and elsewhere, of

Othello, Hamlet, Richard II, and the late romances. The chances are that this play, directly representing a King as foolish, the rich as culpable, and the poor as victims, may have been felt as altogether too disturbing and subversive.

There is indeed evidence that the company was in political trouble with the Court around this time. The King's Men had, it seems, displeased James by a play performed 'in their theatre' reported to him as containing many 'galls', 'dark sentences / Pleasing to factious brains,' with 'every otherwhere a jest / Whose high abuse shall more torment than blows'. The company made their peace with a Court performance of the old romantic–heroic popular favourite *Mucedorus*, including a specially rewritten Epilogue, in which the characters appealed on their knees to the 'glorious and wise Arch-Caesar on this earth' to pardon 'our unwitting error'.[23] The references to the offending play in this Epilogue (attributed by several scholars to Shakespeare) sound more appropriate to *King Lear* than to anything else recently performed by the King's Men. However that may be, the company had certainly been warned; and the marked change of tone in Shakespeare's later plays – *Pericles* and *Winter's Tale*, *Cymbeline* and *Tempest* – may in part reflect this.

---

[23] I am grateful to Richard Proudfoot for drawing my attention to the *Mucedorus* Epilogue and its significance. The revised Epilogue, first printed in the 1610 edition, is included in *The Shakespeare Apocrypha*, ed. C. Tucker Brooke (1908), from which all the above phrases are quoted. The matter is discussed in *The Comedy of Mucedorus*, ed. K. Warnke and Ludwig Proeschold (1878); and by R. Simpson in *Academy*, (29 April 1876). The play is described in the Epilogue as a 'comedy' but this does not rule out a reference to *Lear*: Hamlet, after all, referred to *The Murder of Gonzago* as a 'comedy'.

TRAGEDY, *KING LEAR*, AND THE POLITICS OF THE HEART

TOM McALINDON

I should like to begin by expressing two reservations about political criticism of Shakespeare as it is practised today. First, it seems at times to participate in the prevalent blurring of all generic distinctions to the extent of dissolving immensely complex artistic structures and consigning them to an amorphous continuum of ideology and discourse. Thus it is apt to evade a question of perennially absorbing interest: what constitutes the unique quality or singular greatness of this particular play? Why is it that four hundred years of cultural change have not diminished its appeal to audiences and readers alike? Second (and this point is connected with the first), political criticism is largely if not wholly indifferent to the affective dimension of the plays,[1] an indifference which seems least defensible in relation to the tragedies.

In seeking to counteract these tendencies without relapsing into mere formalism, one might mark out an appropriate theoretical position with the combined assistance of Philip Sidney and Mikhail Bakhtin. Bakhtinian poetics postulate that every literary genre is embedded in contemporary history and subject to extra-literary institutions. At the same time each genre has its own past, its own dynamic development, and a set of norms and conventions which help to shape and control the author's representation of reality. The Bakhtinian concept of genre is central to a poetics which fully acknowledges the intrinsic properties as well as the socio-historical determinations of literature.[2] Sidney's relevance to the

question lies in his claim that tragedy serves a political function, that is, works against tyranny, by virtue of its capacity to excite 'admiration and commiseration', to 'draw ... an abundance of tears', and to 'move' and 'mollify' the 'hardened heart'.[3] This perspective on tragedy was widespread in the Renaissance and ultimately goes back to the Greeks, for whom emotional intensity was the form's chief characteristic.[4] It is wholly bound up, moreover, with classical and Renaissance rhetorical tradition, which taught that cognitive and behavioural change should be brought about through an appeal to the affections.

One could cite many tragedies both by Shakespeare and his contemporaries which fully accord with Sidney's generic paradigm. None does so more impressively or more self-

---

1 A point made by Edward Pechter in 'The New Historicism and Its Discontents: Politicizing Renaissance Drama', *PMLA*, 102 (1987), 292–303; p. 299.

2 P. N. Medvedev/M. M. Bakhtin, *The Formal Method in Literary Scholarship: A Critical Introduction to Sociological Poetics*, trans. Albert J. Wehrle (Baltimore and London, 1978), pp. 130–1.

3 *An Apology for Poetry*, ed. Geoffrey Shepherd (London, 1965), p. 118.

4 On the synthesis of *admiratio* (wonder), pity, and fear in the Renaissance theory of tragedy, see J. V. Cunningham, *Woe or Wonder: The Emotional Effect of Shakespearean Tragedy* (Denver, Col., 1951), ch. 2; and for the Greeks, see William Bedell Stanford, *Greek Tragedy and the Emotions: An Introductory Study* (London, 1983).

consciously than *King Lear*;[5] it is the supreme exemplar. Confronting that fundamental question, 'In what consists the peculiar greatness of this play?', one would rightly point to its enormous scope as an enquiry into the nature of humankind and the whole structure of reality within which it operates.[6] Such an answer, however, leaves out of account the extraordinary power with which this play fixes all our attention on its vision of suffering, cruelty, and injustice. Exposing myself to the charge of simple-mindedness, I shall offer as my own answer the fact that it appeals more profoundly both to the heart and the mind than any other play of Shakespeare's. Of course it will be noted that every work of literary art appeals to the understanding through the sensibilities; but *King Lear* is a tragedy of feeling, of the heart, in a unique sense. Its searing effect on the whole self is an extension of its self-conscious engagement at every point with the human heart as the beginning and the end, the source and the explanation, of almost all our concerns. Referred to about sixty times, the heart is arguably the play's major image. To follow only a selection of the passages in which it occurs is to perceive more clearly what the play is about, and why it moves us so deeply.

The tragedy is set in motion by Cordelia's inability to heave her heart into her mouth, and by her claim that she loves her father contractually, according to her bond, no more and no less (1.1.91–3). 'But goes thy heart with this?', asks Lear incredulously (line 104); and when she says that it does, his love turns by way of humiliation and rage to hatred.

When she has gone, Lear begins to wonder how so small a fault could have drawn from his heart all love and added to the gall (1.4.248–9). To intensify his regret, there is the discovery that Goneril and Regan are not only 'empty-hearted' (1.1.153) but also 'marble-hearted' (1.4.237). Complaining to Regan about Goneril's cruelty, he presents himself as another Prometheus; but whereas Prometheus' torment was to have his liver continuously torn by a vulture, with Lear the lacerated organ is the heart: 'O, Regan, she hath tied / Sharp-toothed unkindness like a vulture, here . . . struck me with her tongue / Most serpent-like upon the very heart' (2.2.306–7, 333–4). But Regan joins forces with Goneril, and together they proceed to strip him of all his dignity as a king, as a father, and even as a man, reducing him from 'noble anger' to tears. It is at this point that the first signs of a mental crack-up appear; but it should be noted that the cracking of the mind is figured in terms of the heart, and that the pun on 'flaw' (meaning both 'fragment' and 'sudden burst or squall of wind') intimates that the universe itself reverberates to the cracking of Lear's heart:

> You think I'll weep.
> No, I'll not weep. I have full cause of weeping,
> *Storm and tempest*
> But this heart shall break into a hundred
> thousand flaws
> Or ere I'll weep – O Fool, I shall go mad!
> (2.2.456–9)

At which point he rushes out into the night.[7]

Lear now begins to enquire, for the first time it would seem, into the fundamentals of life. And where should the enquiry lead him? – 'Then let them anatomize Regan; see what breeds about her heart. Is there any cause in nature that makes these hard hearts?' (3.6.34–6). The progress of this enquiry is inseparable from, indeed dependent on, the intensity of his own feelings. He is possessed in turn by a boundless sense of ingratitude; by self-pity;

---

[5] The intense emotionalism and generic self-consciousness of *Lear* has already been emphasized by Cunningham, *Woe or Wonder*, p. 99, and by Nancy R. Lindheim, '*King Lear* as Pastoral Tragedy', in *Some Facets of 'King Lear': Essays in Prismatic Criticism*, ed. Rosalie L. Colie and F. T. Flahiff (Toronto, 1974), pp. 175–8.

[6] R. B. Heilman, *This Great Stage: Image and Structure in 'King Lear'* (Baton Rouge, La., 1948), p. 133. Cf. G. Wilson Knight, *The Wheel of Fire* (1930; London; 1960), pp. 177–8.

[7] I am indebted to my colleague Gilian West for drawing my attention to the pun on 'flaw'.

by the old vindictive rage; by shame; by compassion for the Fool ('I have one part in my heart / That's sorry yet for thee' (3.2.72–3) and for the world's poor naked wretches. The compassionate Gloucester refers to him simply at this point as a 'poor old heart' (3.7.60). The phrase is doubly apt, being paradoxical. Lear's heart is great, and it is coming to full life in old age; and in the life of the heart lies the discovery of true riches.

Lear's Shakespearian prototype, Titus Andronicus, refers to his daughter as 'the cordial of mine age to glad my heart' (1.1.166). There is an etymological pun here on the word 'cordial', since it derives from the Latin *cor* (declined *cordis*, *cordem*), which means both 'heart' and 'feeling'. There is nothing so overt as this in *King Lear*, but clearly Cordelia's name is meant to be descriptive of her nature and her dramatic rôle; it functions as a silent pun from the moment she protests her inability to heave her heart into her mouth.

When she returns from France in Act 4, scenic juxtaposition is used to effect a powerful contrast between Cordelia's tender nature and the hardness of the 'dog-hearted daughters' (Q.17.46) – Goneril, with her contempt for her humane ('milk-livered') husband; Regan, with her tardy acquisition of political acumen: 'It was great ignorance, Gloucester's eyes being out, / To let him live. / Where he arrives he moves all hearts / Against us' (4.2.32, 4.4.9–11). Cordelia's nature is captured in the quarto description of her almost speechless reaction to Kent's letters about her father:

KENT
Made she no verbal question?
[FIRST] GENTLEMAN
   Faith, once or twice she heaved the name of
    'father'
   Pantingly forth as if it pressed her heart,
   Cried 'Sisters, sisters, shame of ladies, sisters,
   Kent, father, sisters, what, i' th' storm, i' th'
    night,
   Let piety not be believed!' There she shook
   The holy water from her heavenly eyes

   And clamour mastered, then away she started
   To deal with grief alone.   (17.25–33)

Proceeding from and summoning the restorative powers of nature ('All you unpublished virtues of the earth, / Spring with my tears'), these same tears restore Lear to his sanity (4.3.16–17). When he awakes from his long sleep, she is unable once more to heave her heart into her mouth, but her tears tell him everything he needs to know ('Be your tears wet? Yes, faith'); and they give an astonishing emotional power to her two famous monosyllables: 'No cause, no cause' (4.6.64, 68).

But just as Cordelia's tears cure Lear's 'heart-struck injuries' (3.1.8), so too her violent death cracks his sanity and ends his life. He dies quite simply of a broken heart; in fact that last terrible scene is all about the piercing and the cracking of the heart. Kent, we learn, broke down and suffered a minor stroke in telling Edgar his 'most piteous tale' of Lear's miseries. 'His grief grew puissant and the strings of life / Began to crack . . . I left him tranced' (Q24.211–15). The strings of life, or the heart-strings, had a literal existence in the old anatomy. So when Kent later sees Lear die, says to himself, 'Break, heart, I prithee break' (5.3.288), and indicates immediately afterwards that he has not long to live, we must assume that he dies literally of a broken heart. Edgar too is distraught in telling *his* tale ('O that my heart would burst!'); but that detail merely points to the climax of his story, the death of his father. Gloucester's 'flawed heart – / Alack, too weak the conflict to support – / 'Twixt two extremes of passion, joy and grief, / Burst smilingly' (lines 174, 188–91). This in turn anticipates explicitly and narratorially what is implicitly dramatized in the death of Lear. Because of his sudden conviction that Cordelia lives, Lear's old heart is struck in swift succession by an ecstasy of grief and an ecstasy of joy, and so breaks at last into a hundred thousand flaws.

Labels are reductive, yet it is surely right to claim that *King Lear* is, in a special sense, a tragedy of the heart. For not only does it exhibit a range and intensity of feeling unique in the canon, it is also deeply preoccupied with the rôle of feeling, both good and bad, in the lives of men and women. We may believe that ideas, discourse, socio-economic forces, or power are the primary determinants of what people say and do; but this text intimates that the clue to thought and action, and ultimately to social change and human history, lies in the heart. A sentimental notion, it might seem, but consider the text: 'I know his heart' (1.4.309), says Goneril contemptuously of her father, meaning: 'I know exactly how he will behave; how he thinks and acts is how he feels.' So too Edgar tears open Goneril's murderous love-letter to Edmund saying, 'To know our enemies' minds we rip their hearts' (4.5.259).

Jonathan Dollimore interprets this play from a Brechtian perspective, a perspective which is strenuously anti-empathetic and possibly even anti-tragic. So he claims that *King Lear* shows us 'the woeful inadequacy of what passes for kindness' in the context of a society where injustice flourishes; justice, he adds, is shown to be 'too important to be trusted' to 'empathy' and 'pity'.[8] I would not be the first, however, to insist that feeling as unselfish, compassionate love emerges as the supreme value in this play. And by no means, I would add, does it signify a socio-political dead-end. It is shown to be the first prerequisite for socio-political understanding: those who are responsible for injustice will not see because they do not feel (4.1.62–3); and when they begin to see the truth they 'see it feelingly' (4.5.145). Pity also leads to remedial action, both interpersonal and social, medical and political. The partnership between Cordelia with her tears and the gentle Doctor with his simples reminds us that medicine originates in human compassion. The political value of pity is shown in the revolt of Cornwall's servant who, 'thrilled with remorse' – pierced with pity – by the blinding of Gloucester, turns against Cornwall and thus seriously weakens the evil alliance – at the cost of his own life

(4.2.41). The report of this act of compassionate heroism has a powerful effect on Albany, whose horror at the ruthless treatment of Lear is already preparing the ground for his stand against Goneril and Edmund. No doubt too it was the behaviour of this servant which alerted Regan to the political implications of pity ('where he arrives he moves all hearts against us'). But it is in Edgar that the socio-political potential of pity is fully realized. Not only does he nurse his father through his miseries, saving him both from the demon of despair and the sword of Oswald; he also saves Britain from the nightmare future in which it was to be ruled by Queen Goneril and King Edmund. The meaning of his character is to be inferred from Edmund's claim that 'to be tender-minded / Does not become a sword' (5.3.31–2). Edgar disproves this triumphantly. Beginning as an amiable dupe, he emerges in the end as the complete man: mightier than Edmund with the sword, yet 'pregnant to good pity' and enriched with 'the art of known and feeling sorrows' (4.5.221–2). As a ruler, he will not disjoin remorse from power (*Julius Caesar*, 1.3.18–19).

The assault on the heart and the value of pity have an obvious bearing on the rôle of the audience and the status of the play itself as a political intervention. When Edgar is recounting his piteous tale to Albany and Kent, he hesitates to complete it because he senses that to do so would be to 'amplify, too much', and 'top extremity' (Q 24.203–4); and indeed his audience is 'almost ready to dissolve' (24.200; F 5.3.195). At this point in the action, Shakespeare still has the hanging of Cordelia to spring on *his* audience, and he is obviously thinking about what it will do to our feelings. Throughout the play he has been asking how much misery life can inflict on human beings

---

[8] *Radical Tragedy: Religion, Ideology and Power in Shakespeare and his Contemporaries* (Brighton, 1984), pp. 191–3.

and how much they can endure. Now he is wondering how far a tragedy can go, how much an audience will take. And of course he was right to wonder. But having made his oblique apology through Edgar, Shakespeare resolutely brings us to the edge of the abyss. Implicitly, he declares that tragic art has a moral and political function to fulfil through emotional shock and pity. 'Expose thyself to feel' – if only by imagination – 'what wretches feel' (3.4.34), and perhaps the armour of detachment and indifference will crack. We must reply with Edmond: 'This speech of yours hath moved me, / And shall perchance do good' (5.3.191–2).

Our leading exponents of political criticism seem determined not to be moved, however: mindful no doubt of Brecht's insistence that empathy with the sufferings of characters in a play is a form of self-indulgence which inhibits political action. Thus one might wonder if tragedy is not losing its identity in the current critical climate and the word itself becoming meaningless. Leonard Tennenhouse, for example, informs us that generic classification of Shakespeare's plays is a liberal humanist conspiracy – beginning with the First Folio editors and culminating in Northrop Frye – to suppress the political operations of writing. He argues that what really 'determines the differences by which we distinguish literary genres' are 'variations in the behavior of power'. And so Shakespeare's tragedies are dropped into the great melting pot: 'I regard the plays as a series of semiotic events, the staging of cultural materials, the mobilization of political representations.'[9] In *The Subject of Tragedy: Identity and Difference in Renaissance Drama* (London and New York, 1985), Catherine Belsey – unlike Tennenhouse – addresses herself specifically to tragedy rather than to all the dramatic genres; her real concern, however, is not tragedy as such but rather the history of the human subject or self. Tragedies have been chosen for examination because (a) 'the history of the self has to start *somewhere*', and (b) 'Fiction ... tends to

throw into relief the problems and contradictions which are often only implicit in other modes of writing' (p. 9) (emphasis added). In Belsey's methodology, moreover, qualitative as well as generic distinctions are suppressed. Although the tragedies of Shakespeare and his major contemporaries are her main texts, she assures us sternly at the outset that she will not 'privilege these plays but [will] put them to work' – alongside thoroughly minor plays and non-fictional works – 'for substantial political purposes which replace the mysterious aesthetic and moral pleasures of nineteenth-century criticism' (p. 10).

Which seems an ironically appropriate point at which to return to Soviet Russia's most agile critical theorist (Sidney, with his stress on mollifying the hardened heart, has been with us throughout). In the late 1920s, Bakhtin warned prophetically against the 'ideological squeezing' of literary texts and against 'losing touch with the work of art in its artistic specificity' for 'the sake of another reality',[10] no less than he warned against the study of literary works in dissociation from their informing historical contexts. On genre as context, Bakhtin declared that the great mistake made by the formalists was to arrive at the problem of genre last. 'Poetics', he added, 'should really begin with genre.'[11]

From the beginning of his career, Shakespeare thought deeply about genre. He was acutely conscious of the intimate relations and the often uncertain borderline between the different kinds, and especially (as we can see in *A Midsummer Night's Dream* and *Romeo and Juliet*) between the two antithetical kinds. But he had no doubt that tragedy at its best is a highly distinct genre. It is distinguished above all by its capacity to fill the audience with a

---

[9] *Power on Display: The Politics of Shakespeare's Genres* (New York and London, 1986), pp. 5, 12, 13, 16.
[10] *The Formal Method in Literary Scholarship*, pp. 19, 26.
[11] Ibid., p. 129.

sense of woe and wonder, and to leave them at the last mute, and pale, and very thoughtful. As it does, supremely, in *King Lear*. If this is Shakespeare's greatest tragedy, it is so not least because here his consciousness of the nature of the genre is such that tragedy's proper dynamics and effects are even integrated to the play's action and theme.[12]

[12] Shortly before this volume went to press, I received a review copy of Arthur Kirsch's *The Passions of Shakespeare's Tragic Heroes* (Charlottesville and London, 1990), which independently emphasizes the importance of the heart-imagery in *King Lear* (pp. 8–9, 104–6). Although he does not touch on the question of generic expectations, Professor Kirsch contends that the enduring value of Shakespeare's tragedies derives mainly from their dramatization of human passion; and like myself, he takes the New Historicist and Cultural Materialist critics to task for ignoring or neglecting this aspect of the plays. Professor Kirsch finds a likely source for the heart imagery of *Lear* in Ecclesiastes. The undoubted source, however, was *King Leir*: see my forthcoming *Shakespeare's Tragic Cosmos* (Cambridge, 1991), p. 177.

THE POLITICS OF SHAKESPEARE
PRODUCTION

JOHN RUSSELL BROWN

The ways in which plays – including Shakespeare's – are produced today are affected by political forces and structures both within theatres and outside them. Everyone who works in theatre is aware of this. A leading American dramatist has calculated that if the Manhattan Theatre Club produced nothing for one whole year except plays that he had written, and if – somehow – he had managed to direct all of them himself, he would then have earned less that year than the theatre's Artistic Director. And this impossible work-load would also have brought him less money than the theatre's Administrator, and less than its Development Officer. The message he received was that in this organization which is devoted to staging plays by living dramatists (who, unlike Shakespeare, are there to stand up for themselves), the writer has less clout than any of the people responsible for keeping the production machine rolling. It is also evidence that a theatre's main problem today is to stay in business, to be able to produce, to have the funds and the people; and so, when a play is being produced, the task of serving its author is likely to be much less important than that of serving the institution and its administrators.

In Britain, theatres are kept in business by various state subsidies as well as by ticket sales to the public, and so the political forces at work are more evident. If in 1989 a director wished to produce Shakespeare at the Riverside Studios in London, he or she would apply to the local Hammersmith and Fulham Council for a grant,

and would receive a fifteen-page questionnaire. Two pages are for a 'full account of your project' in which you must show 'the need for such a project and its relation to other similar services in the locality/borough'; and you must pay 'particular regard to the implementation of equal opportunities practices'. You must also 'describe how your project proposes to monitor and evaluate its effectiveness'. Three further pages are devoted to financial details, and one to a description of company organization. Three pages provide the necessary instructions for filling out the application, one of these being a list of telephone numbers for contacting council officials.

Being open to all kinds of investigation has become a major task in the theatre during the last few decades. Speaking as Director of the Edinburgh Festival, Frank Dunlop has said that 'the Arts Council is too interested in the details of what you're doing to allow you to take risks; it's like a permanent Gestapo, wanting to know if it is making a good investment' (*The Times*, 7 August 1989).

Considering only English-speaking and European theatres, and not including film or television, an attempt to show the significance of political forces on Shakespeare production should encompass all aspects of theatre; it will be a tour around a vast mansion, stopping only to open the doors of various apartments, each strangely crowded with people, papers, or computers, and then passing on. It may seem that the tour is around an international encampment, where many people are engaged in some kind of conflict, using a strange assortment of weaponry, but not altogether sure of whom they are fighting; what most of them do know, however, is that they fight for their very existence.

It can never be easy for a theatre company to produce Shakespeare's plays. These texts are unlike any written today; they are set in ancient times and fantastic places, they use unusual language and require casts of fifteen to twenty-five actors, with numerous changes of costume. A dozen of the actors should have vivid imaginations, uncommon skills, and some previous experience of acting in these plays; and of course, confidence and availability.

The task is done most spectacularly by the Public Theatre in New York City, a theatre supported by profits from the world's longest-running musical, by grants and endowments, and recently by public subscription to a marathon of all Shakespeare's plays. This theatre can afford full-page advertisements in expensive newspapers. It attracts actors from film and television, and directors from almost anywhere. It has a choice of performance spaces in a large building, and it can move productions to regular commercial theatres. It also performs in Central Park, to an audience of thousands who pay nothing to see a production, but hear its words through loudspeakers, mixed with sounds of the metropolis. All this busy business is uneven in quality, but seemingly unstoppable; it's there, and its audiences are there too.

In Britain, the Royal Shakespeare Theatre and the Royal National Theatre are, as their names imply, 'flagship companies', both staging Shakespeare. Both have been provided with brand new theatres and are supported annually by millions of pounds from public funds. In 1988–9, the RSC received a basic £5.3 million from the Arts Council of Great Britain, more than five times the subsidy of the next largest theatre. The National (whose responsibility is to a 'world repertoire') received £7.9 million,

about eight times the same base-line.[1] But despite these subsidies, both theatres are governed by commercial pressures: to balance their books, they must play to an average of eighty per cent capacity, on all their shows, all the time; and they do not find this easy. Neither company thinks it has enough money to do the job properly, and both have run up large overdrafts. By 1989–90, the RSC's was to have been £2.9 million (see The Times, 10 February 1990); and the company had decided to close its two London theatres for five months, cancelling numerous shows and creating problems for all its support-staff. These theatres keep going only by cutting costs, cutting productions, raising prices, and hoping for more subsidy next year. The outlook can seem desperate, because they dare not fail. The Insolvency Act of 1986, with its concept of 'wrongful trading', has added new urgency to discussion with their Boards of Trustees who are responsible for approving financial policy. Survival is the serious game which both national companies are now playing: innovation, development, research, actor-training, variety of input, sustained touring, assistance to other theatres, star-casting, rapid response to new opportunities – all these must take second place to the task of keeping solvent.

There are, of course, many alternative ways of producing Shakespeare. In North America, Shakespeare Festivals are almost everywhere. Inspiration came originally from the summer performances that had preceded the RSC's year-round programmes at Stratford-upon-Avon; and several of the second-generation festivals in America have also developed in the same way, to become major operations. The Old Globe at San Diego, California, is now equipped with three auditoria and a programme of thirteen productions a year, mixing classics with new plays. Most performances are sold out, and this theatre has little trouble in sustaining a ninety-five per cent capacity; if

---

[1] See Arts Council, 44th Annual Report and Accounts (London, 1989), p. 65.

there were more seats to sell, the company could add to its surplus and spend more on development. As it is, the Old Globe has its Training Programme, in association with the local university, and its Education Programme, called Face to Face, with classes in the theatre and in local schools, and with play-visits, tours, and a summer theatre-camp. A Play Discovery Project provides public readings of new scripts, and studio productions of the best of them. A bicultural Teatro Meta explores the Hispanic heritage and integrates Hispanic artists into all aspects of the Globe's work. Assessment and endorsement come not from officials, but from the audience: the Old Globe has the largest subscription list of all nonprofit theatres in the United States, and earns over sixty-five per cent of its $7.4 million budget from ticket sales. It also has income from individual and corporate sponsors. An extra $10 million is being raised currently, to pay for another rehearsal hall, improved catering facilities, more offices and a bigger endowment – the last, as the appeal literature puts it, to 'further stabilize the Globe against economic changes'. So here, in California, Shakespeare production is at the heart of boom-time theatre.

Other festivals have their own stories. The most famous is at Stratford, Ontario, which still operates on a seasonal basis, but now in three very different auditoria and with a mixed repertoire. Its fortunes have varied over the years, but since the beginnings in a large tent in 1953, the Festival has drawn holiday crowds, playgoers, students, and a host of supporting businesses. In 1990, $14,900,000, or seventy-three per cent of its budget, came from ticket sales. Shakespeare has lifted a small market town into such prosperity that it is now a site for corporate headquarters and a thriving tourist centre. Politically the Canadian Stratford has always been highly visible, a model of enterprise and publicity, and a means of exporting culture around the world.

At first, Stratford drew directors, actors and technicians away from Britain, but later imi-

tations have not started with imported talent. The Alabama Shakespeare Festival was initiated in 1971, soon after Martin L. Platt arrived in 'Annie's Town', Alabama, as a director for its amateur community theatre. He was twenty-two years old and fresh from Carnegie Tech. The following May, Platt borrowed $500 from his mother and went to New York City to audition actors and set about the first festival season of four plays: *The Two Gentlemen of Verona*, *The Comedy of Errors*, *Hamlet* and *Hedda Gabler*. He directed all of them – 'no one else would hire me to direct these plays so I decided to do them myself' – and, as there were no union rules, they all rehearsed for twelve or more hours every day. These were 'small shows with a scruffy company', as Martin Platt will confess today, but from that unlikely beginning the Festival was able to develop, and in 1985 it took possession of a new theatre at Montgomery, Alabama, equipped with two auditoria, two rehearsal halls, workshops, gift-shop, café and offices. As a board member remarked, 'Culture was gaining on agriculture for the first time in Alabama.'[2] The Festival is now a multi-million dollar operation, with Shakespeare at the centre of a diversified programme. It has the physical and financial means to vie with the very best in the world.

Other festivals, in North America and elsewhere, have not expanded so grandly, but remained faithful to the needs and thinking of the university or college which gave them birth: such are Colorado, Utah, Santa Cruz, Indiana, New Jersey. Many are open-air, summer occasions, and their support-staff are students and amateurs. Standards vary widely: productions may be under-rehearsed and under-cast; equipment may be primitive and finance uncertain; but almost all have retained a holiday spirit and pioneering ambitions. Audiences can pronounce their positive assessment

---

2 Jim Volt, *Shakespeare Never Slept Here* (Atlanta, 1986), pp. 3–6, 115–25.

by purchasing season subscriptions and making tax-free donations.

Shakespeare also claims an occasional place in the programmes of many of the richer non-profit theatres throughout the world, productions fitting into established routines as well as circumstances allow. Those theatres which are funded generously by state or municipality and able to employ a permanent company, will develop a production of Shakespeare over many rehearsals, and keep the play in repertoire for as long as it holds public attention. So Lyubimov's *Hamlet* at the Taganka Theatre in Moscow, which opened in November 1971, rehearsed for some two years and then played for nine and a half, until the death of its star actor. Hamlet, standing alone and at odds with his world, lived on that stage and drew strength from the whole company and from its loyal audience. In Poland, Czechoslovakia, Hungary, Berlin, and elsewhere in the East, generously funded state theatres have used their privileges to stage Shakespeare: he is a 'classic' and therefore comparatively safe from censorship, even when a production has raised icons of hope and posed issues of dissent. With care and wit, by means of visual signs, allusions to current politics, coded messages, satirical edge, broad clowning, emphatically used supernumeraries, radical re-interpretations, Shakespeare became part of that amazing theatrical counter-culture which spoke for freedom when little else was able to do so.

Elsewhere in Western Europe – but not in Britain – lavish subsidies and official support have enabled some star theatre directors to create arresting productions of Shakespeare in which their political, philosophical, or aesthetic views have been blazingly and sometimes arbitrarily apparent. Strehler, Zadek, Stein, Bergman, Brook have taken such opportunities indefatigably, and so their names and their messages have resounded around the world. Other Shakespeare productions have taken a more modest place in well-funded programmes, using as well as possible those members of a permanent company who have been in post for many years and must therefore be cast in leading rôles. Such security has disadvantages: Ophelia may be played by an actress far too old, Claudius by an actor too settled in his profession to bring a sense of danger to the stage, and Polonius by the most senior resident comedian for whom no other work can be found. Shakespeare is often a substantial and settled part of a publicly funded repertoire.

Until comparatively recently, regional theatres in Britain also provided regular productions of Shakespeare, some developing distinct traditions and affording a training ground for the national companies. But at Bristol, Birmingham, Liverpool, Nottingham, Sheffield and many other towns, home-produced Shakespeare is increasingly a financial impossibility; besides, their acting companies are seldom held together, even for a single season. So the British regions are deprived of what used to be a staple fare, and recruits to Stratford are less well prepared than previously; a leading member of that company reported that 'some younger actors, perhaps playing important rôles, may arrive unsure of exactly what an iambic pentameter is'.[3]

Shakespeare survives rather better in the regions of North America. Supported by long lists of patrons and subscribers, the more established theatres can readily afford a cast of twenty-five, and are prepared to audition outside the company for crucial rôles; such theatres include Arena Stage (Washington), Hartford Stage and Seattle Repertory. But Shakespeare has to fit into the timetables of a season dominated by very different fare, so that there is little opportunity for basic preparations with the cast. Too often a director's or a designer's 'concept' must be given greatest prominence, because in the time available the actors cannot

---

[3] Edward Petherbridge, in *Players of Shakespeare 2*, ed. Russell Jackson and Robert Smallwood (Cambridge, 1988), p. 40.

know the text and each other well enough to reach full pitch of performance. Some people say that the best American actors will not perform in these conditions; others that even the richest regional theatres cannot compete financially with the calls of television and film.

Occasionally television and film will pay dues to Shakespeare in another way. When schedules and tax regulations permit, one-off productions bring screen stars to Shakespeare productions in commercial theatres. Usually this is at the insistence of the actor who needs the stimulus of working on these texts; but it is a risky business for producers, who will be pleased to cover costs. Al Pacino, Glenda Jackson, Christopher Plummer, Dustin Hoffman, Vanessa Redgrave are among those who have had productions built around them. Just occasionally a theatre director has sufficient public acclaim to float his own company too: Jonathan Miller, Peter Hall, Trevor Nunn. But the auguries are not good, and we cannot rely on film reputations or individual directors to bail Shakespeare production out of its difficulties. There is no beaten path for producers from subsidized theatre, or from cinema or television, to presentations of Shakespeare in theatres which are out to make money for everyone.

Films based on Shakespeare's plays and some that record theatre productions have reached large audiences; they have become one of the commonest ways in which Shakespeare is first encountered in performance. But they spring from a different administrative base from theatre productions, and have little direct reference to the problem of staging live performances, the medium for which the plays were written.

Touring is yet another way to produce Shakespeare in the theatre. Some young companies have had spectacular successes: the Acting Company, in the USA, the Renaissance Theatre Company, the English Shakespeare Company, Odyssey, and Compass, in Britain. Other operations of still smaller scale, some of them offshoots of major theatres, tour around a circuit of small venues, especially those in an educational setting. Mobile, spare, adventurous, hard-working, these are 'growth-points' in the present scene.

But there are problems. They draw on the personnel of the larger companies and on actors straight from school; and they seldom have time to develop a style of their own during rehearsals. Financially, the productions make heavy demands on company members, who are paid close to the permissible minimums and must devote themselves to a tour, away from home and professional contacts for months at a time – that is the only way to recover initial costs. The actors also pay by sustaining long leading rôles eight times a week in varied venues, or for several short stands within a single week. Necessarily these companies are young in spirit and in average age. The pace is hard, so they travel light and deal with one season at a time. Their administrators struggle to seek multiple funding for consecutive engagements, and to drum up audiences unfamiliar with what they have to offer. The companies cannot develop deep roots or reach out far in forward planning. Not surprisingly, their work can show signs of haste, insufficient experience and talent, and false economies. Nevertheless, the small touring companies have made important advances: no one can now doubt that they thrive on their own terms by producing Shakespeare; and that they can make his plays more widely accessible. Despite the large-scale demands of the texts and despite all the opportunities they offer to the most excellent of actors, and to the most careful, subtle and ambitious of directors, Shakespeare's plays are also highly suitable for economic touring and simplified staging.

A glance at the Edinburgh Festival shows how much is afoot. In 1990, the Renaissance Company came to a very temporary rest with *King Lear* and *A Midsummer Night's Dream*. A total of seven touring productions of *Macbeth* was offered to the official programme, and two were accepted by Frank Dunlop.[4] Twenty productions of Shakespeare, in various forms, were among the year's Fringe offerings.

Many small experimental companies, which came into being with no thought of staging Shakespeare, are also drawn to his plays. While Shakespeare productions are frequently expensive to stage, technically advanced, traditional, splendid, or elegant, and employ large, specialist casts, some companies cannot afford, and do not wish, to follow these examples. 'Little pots are soon hot', as the ill-used Grumio would say; and some economically produced and poorly paid performances are alive with new ideas, as inventive and accessible as anything theatre can offer. So *King Lear* has been performed in the tiny Orange Tree theatre at Richmond, London, a bicultural *Romeo and Juliet* in Haifa, a *Richard II* in a bingo hall in Eastbourne, a *Tempest* in a pocket theatre in Prague and another in the Donmar Warehouse in London – all using a small cast, small stage, and the minimum of expense. Even theatre on the bread-line can find ways of staging Shakespeare that are attractive, rewarding and, in some sense, successful.

Shakespeare lives in almost every kind of theatre, not least quantitatively in student, community, and amateur companies. His plays are an endless challenge and a stimulus at almost every pitch of engagement. But they do call for persistence, vigilance, imagination, skill, spirit and cunning, and this survey of the means of production would be incomplete without a recognition that these qualities are often missing. Productions can be negligent, muddled, makeshift, complacent; audiences can be frustrated, bored. Often there has not been time enough, or money enough, for a theatre to do as well as it would and could, or as well as its audience will accept. And producing companies are often short on talent and imagination, as well as time and money.

Some theatres producing Shakespeare are riding high, while others face bankruptcy or are calling out for help – more money, different theatre buildings, better audiences. Why should this be? Cannot those who thrive teach those who struggle? Cannot re-organization, refinancing, new management, and new ideas bring success within the reach of all? And where regeneration proves impossible, should not someone create new theatre companies on successful models? Cannot the pleasures of a good Shakespeare production be part of the public wealth for every citizen to enjoy? These are some of the inter-related political issues involved in Shakespeare production.

To people working in beleaguered theatres, the problem is simple and stark. The Young Vic Theatre in London announced in August 1990 that it would have to close if it could not raise £100,000 by the end of September; and all the company was issued with redundancy notices. Founded twenty years ago as a theatre for young audiences, the Young Vic has an open stage with surrounding auditorium which is well suited for staging Shakespeare. The company has produced numerous of his plays, and has run workshops and classes for students, often to packed houses. It has also been host to visiting productions, notably the RSC's small-scale, star-cast *Macbeth* and *Othello*. But, as David Thacker put it, all this had to stop unless something was done:

There are theatres all over the country that are in danger of closing because of government policies towards the arts. We are in greater danger than most. There is a choice. Either you change the Government's attitude to arts funding or change the Government. (*The Independent*, 7 August 1990)

The Young Vic receives £250,000 a year from the Arts Council and £49,000 from its local council; but these sums are not enough. Even when the theatre raised the £100,000, it could do no more work for children during the financial year, no more educational work, and no more Shakespeare plays.

---

[4] See Interview in *The Times*, 7 August 1989.

The belief that government should find more money for theatres which cannot manage on what they have been given stems from the fact that going to a theatre is a public event, like walking in a park, or using a library or a swimming bath: the individual citizen cannot provide such amenities for him or herself, and so the state has to do so. Moreover, theatre fosters the public good – or the 'quality of life', to use a current phrase which suppresses the political issues involved – and any caring government would *want* to pay for that. This argument is particularly strong with regard to productions of Shakespeare which keep alive a notable part of our cultural inheritance: an object for study; the English language used by one of its greatest masters; and images of life, love and death experienced to the uttermost and considered with infinite care and perception.

The Universal Declaration of Human Rights, endorsed in 1948 by all the victorious powers after World War II, spelled out the importance of the arts in society. The signatories agreed that:

Everyone has the right freely to participate in the cultural life of the community and to enjoy the arts.[5]

The Charter of the Arts Council of Great Britain, in its revised form of 1967, accepts responsibility for ensuring that this basic human right is maintained. The Council's objectives are:

a to develop and improve the knowledge, understanding and practice of the arts;

b to increase the accessibility of the arts to the public throughout Great Britain;

c to advise and co-operate with departments of government, local authorities and other bodies.

How can 'accessibility' be increased if theatres are allowed to close?

Of course, another reason why theatres believe that government should fund them adequately is that government has more money at its disposal than anyone else. But even mega-funds have their limits and we are frequently told that any additional money given to theatres will have to come from budgets for parks, libraries and swimming baths; or from education, hospitals, roads, pensions, the police, the unemployed, the disadvantaged, the armed forces, parliament, and so on. 'Is a Shakespeare production more important than saving a life in a hospital?' – so the issue is presented. But to this there is one very persuasive answer. All the money given to an active theatre is an investment which makes *more* money. It can be shown that the government gets back far more than it ever gives, in savings on unemployment benefits and in positive increments from taxation – not least, in Britain, from the punishing Value-Added, or Sales, Tax. There are also revenues for government, less easily calculated, from the stimulation of tourism, export, and general social vitality.

So why don't all governments support all theatres generously? For some, the reason may be an unspoken fear – fear of artists who speak their own minds freely, and are able to touch the conscience of their audiences. Politicians of all parties and all countries hate adverse criticism (whatever they may say to the contrary), especially when criticism is effective. And then politicians are worried by the fact that no one can know what an artist will do next – that is almost a definition of art. With more justification, they are also suspicious; for how are they to believe that all who proclaim themselves to be artists have even begun to earn that name? May not those who clamour for subsidy be charlatans, self-deluded fantasts, con-artists, or more ordinary people who think, mistakenly, that art is easy and their own work beyond reproach?

But all these reasons are not often disclosed. It is far simpler for politicians to point out that large state subsidies do not necessarily ensure that a production of Shakespeare will do much

---

[5] Quoted by Roy Shaw, *The Arts and the Public* (1987), p. 119.

to 'develop and improve the knowledge, understanding and practice of the arts'. So governments are chary, and they keep their money for safer markets. Besides they know that some theatres manage without asking for subsidy, and so they wonder why all cannot be like that. (They forget that no production is wholly unsubsidized; that those which do make money for impresarios depend on artists and technicians who have developed their skills in subsidized institutions and theatres.)

There are politicians – and a few journalists and well-established artists – who argue against any form of public funding. For them, the Shakespeare Festivals and the regional theatres of North America provide splendid examples of private enterprise. The National Endowment for the Arts does disburse public funds in the United States, but much less per head than is customary in Europe; and it restricts itself to grants for special projects and capital funding, or to support for local Arts Associations. In the United States, not a single theatre is kept in business by the state. However, almost all of them would close without a subsidy given in the form of tax concessions to corporate and wealthy private patrons; this hidden public funding is crucial and very significantly larger than grants from the NEA. The Old Globe in San Diego will, in effect, have two-and-a-half million dollars added to its latest fund-raising initiatives, because a few hundred people will get into ballgowns and bow ties to eat a gala buffet-supper. Public and private support together keep the festivals and larger regional theatres in comparatively easy circumstances; but the arrangement has drawbacks. By respecting the likes and dislikes of their wealthiest supporters, some atrocious productions are supported generously by the state, with no questions asked. And, more seriously, the government does not fulfil its duty to 'everyone', as agreed in the Declaration of Human Rights: not all sections of the public are provided with access to the arts. Many Shakespeare productions in the United States play almost exclusively to people who can pay about $100 per head once or twice a year for a season ticket, who lead such settled lives that they want to invest in their entertainment on a pre-paid and regular basis. This well-established, comfortable audience may be supplemented by purchasers of the few tickets that are not pre-sold, and by young persons in parties from school or college. (But educational visitors are often hived off into special matinées at ten o'clock in the morning, so that most audiences remain highly predictable.)

Shakespeare Festivals may have a more mixed attendance: they take place in school holidays, a time which is free from usual routines and predictabilities; so audiences can take a chance, and bardolators travel long distances to see the plays. But the liveliest audiences for Shakespeare in the States tend to be in small, stubbornly independent theatres, in university theatres, or at the Public Theatre in New York – all places where productions are not part of an extensive, pre-sold subscription season for a limited section of society.

In Britain, an alternative to government subsidy is business sponsorship, widespread in the States and spreading slowly elsewhere. Advocates often explain that this is an extension of princely patronage during the Renaissance (as if this were the best of recommendations). But the analogy is not convincing: because those princes paid for what gave pleasure to themselves, even as they ensured a public demonstration of individual wealth and power. Modern corporate barons spend not to enjoy themselves, but to buy the use of a company or a production as a vehicle for advertising their own goods or services: they spend to sell, and to grow in the public's estimation; they pay to increase their own financial gain, otherwise the money cannot be set against corporation tax-liability. This means that business sponsors in Britain must always be associated with theatres which are already successful and conspicuous, whose achievements are sure to improve their own trading-image and involve no risk of being caught up in failure or controversy. They will support a new venture only if it has good credentials and good relationships with the press; in this way they will benefit from the initial flush of publicity, and they can drop the sponsorship soon after the launch. No theatre company can go to a business sponsor and say that it is having difficulty in balancing its books or is about to take an untried initiative.

The proper purposes of an Arts Council or Endowment for the Arts – the provision of an agreed human right throughout a state, and the development of the arts – will not be served by commercial patronage or by hidden subsidies that promote the pleasures of only one section of society. And yet in no country today is a healthy repertoire of theatre sustainable without some form of subsidy – it never has been, without lavish expenditure by some public body or by some persons. So in a world where government dominates financial affairs and is responsible for the public good, it is to government we must look if Shakespeare productions are to be made available to every kind of audience, and if the plays are to be kept fully alive in the new world in which we live. How much money is provided is a political issue which must be debated in parliament or congress; and it should be a part of every politician's appeal to the electorate. It follows that everyone interested in Shakespeare production should bring their special knowledge and advocacy to that political and public debate.

The difficult questions are how subsidy should be dispensed, and which are the most deserving theatres, the most promising, or the most indispensable.

Different countries have different ways of administering grants to theatre and to the arts generally.[6] In France, for example, a government department does the job, and when questions are debated the Arts Minister can call on the President for support against the Finance Minister; and the Arts Minister must listen to the President when he wants a brand new

opera house or a museum extension. In West Germany, likewise, the state is clearly in charge, but with a stronger devolvement to regional decision-making, each of eleven states having its own Minister of Education and Culture. Municipalities also provide subsidies directly. In the United States, political appointees head a government civil-service organization, which works with panels of professional advisers for each artistic category.

Britain has developed an extraordinary compromise. The Arts Council is charged with the charter objectives already quoted here. This committee is a QUANGO – a Quasi-Autonomous-Non-Governmental Organization – and it is funded by the government. Council members are not representatives (and many of them are not artists); rather they are nominees of the government, who serve for a fixed term of years. They are guided by a Chairman, who is also a government appointee. Everyone is unpaid, which means that Council members cannot fulfil their responsibilities in what is merely their spare time; and so executive and budgetary back-up is provided by salaried officers who are often career bureaucrats. Nor can the Council itself have detailed knowledge of all the arts in all their manifestations, and so there are unpaid committees or 'panels' – at the last count, forty-one of them – to advise on the separate arts and on separate aspects of those arts. This famously complicated system is intended to show that government does not interfere with what the artists do; in its early years it was copied, with variations, in Australia, Canada, New Zealand, and elsewhere. But in practice, that promise has not been fulfilled. Council members have found that they were 'impotent' or 'just a rubber stamp' (to quote two particularly interested in theatre); according to another, they were required to do little more than listen to the government-appointed Chairman, and then

---

[6] John Allen gives an account of these administrative arrangements in *Theatre in Europe* (1981), pp. 67–98.

'nod approval'.[7] A recent Secretary-General, having previously held a post in Business Sponsorship, has described the task of the Arts Council as that of treading a difficult path between 'maintaining the confidence of the arts world on the one hand, and of the Government of the day on the other'.[8]

Time has exposed the pretensions of the Arts Council. How are the endeavours of independently minded theatres to be defended against the more vocal interests of what the Secretary-General has called the 'arts world'? How can the rights of the public at large be maintained against the avowed intentions of government to save money wherever possible? How do council and panel members remain 'unpaid' when they are recompensed with esteem – self-esteem, at any rate – and, more generously, in the very slippery coin of inside-knowledge and influence? Why should a few people who have the luxury of a great deal of spare time be those whose consent has to be gained for any major policy change? Now the processes of subsidy in Britain are being complicated still further by devolution of many tasks to Regional Arts Associations, all modelled to some extent on the Arts Council, but with additional input by local government. The result is a slow-moving mixture of political, professional, socially advantaged and bureaucratic forces, which seems, very often, to be covert in operation.

It is not easy to know who should administer government funds to the theatre. A minister of a democratically elected government might seem the fittest person, but not all politicians will know what is involved, nor will the bureaucrats who work under them. In 1990, the new government in Poland found that there was very much less money for everything, including the arts; and so it was decreed that in future only one in every four theatres would be subsidized.[9] The continuation of the best theatres – or the most famous – with the subsidy to which they had grown accustomed, was preferred to poverty and consequent ineffi-

ciency for them all. Such a decision would save a lot of trouble for administrators, but was it the best decision? Was some restructuring not possible, some economies, or collaborations? The theatre is among the most complicated problems for any government department to deal with – even with a theatre-person in charge, as in Poland.

In December 1988, a special conference was held in the University of London on *Theatre in Crisis*. Here artists, administrators, and academics agreed on a Declaration, which concluded:

that the management and distribution of [public] funding should be democratically organized and devolved.

But this solution would not be easy to put into practice. For how would democratic representatives be elected, and what constituents would they represent? If each theatre union and professional association had its own statutory voice, discussion about subsidy could become a fight between vested interests. And how would theatre audiences be represented in these councils? How would votes be counted, and on what issues? In 1977, in the interests of democratization, a debate took place between representatives of the French theatrical unions and their conclusions were these: that workers in every sector of cultural activity should have a voice in the framing of policy and greater control of their conditions of work; that contracts should be for five and not three years; that subsidy should be related to the cost-of-living index. Moreover, subsidy should be removed from about 100 theatre companies and redistributed to six new Drama Centres for Young People, and to ten new permanent companies – a wholesale realignment which would offer much better conditions of work

---

[7] Roy Shaw, *The Arts and the Public*, pp. 48–50.
[8] Arts Council, *42nd Annual Report* (London, 1987), p. 7.
[9] See Mavor Moore, 'When theatre is buffeted', *The Globe and Mail* (Toronto), 10 April 1990.

and greater stability.[10] Concern for professional safeguards may be the inevitable and sole result of 'democratization'.

If the management of subsidy is difficult to arrange, the grounds for deciding how to distribute it are still more of a problem. Sometimes it is said that money should be the reward for high standards and for 'excellence', but what then about encouraging new and adventurous work? Some people argue that the theatres most suitable for receiving subsidy are those large enough to run smoothly and attract many donations; they won't waste money, and are in a position to improve their programmes and take risks. But others believe that theatres which serve their authors well, or serve their actors or directors well, are putting first things first, and most deserve help. Perhaps a theatre should be supported if minorities are involved in every aspect of its operation, or if it has ambitious plans to extend its audience. Perhaps successful staging of new works should be rewarded: but then who decides what is successful? Confidential assessment by professional advisers may help, but the result of this can prove puzzling and sometimes outrageous. The surest judgement comes only with time, when it can be seen what fruit the old tree or the young sapling has borne – how many new plays have been created, how many new writers or directors have been developed, how many original and powerful actors, how extensive is a theatre's influence on others. But delayed critiques are not very helpful; nothing can then be done to protect and support new initiatives.

Most bureaucratic assessments of theatres use bureaucratic standards, asking if budgets balance and organizations function properly, and insisting that predictions about future finance are realistic and businesslike. When the Arts Council arranged for a 'Scrutiny' of the RSC in 1984, it was undertaken by a management consultant, Clive Priestley. When in 1985 the Board of the National Theatre commissioned its own report on its operations, this was undertaken by the chairman of Marks and Spencer,

Lord Rayner, who had earlier been Adviser to the Prime Minister on improving efficiency and eliminating waste in government. In 1986, the Arts Council set up a more elaborate 'Enquiry into Professional Theatre in England', chaired by Sir Kenneth Cork, an accountant who specializes in bankruptcies. This Enquiry did include a theatre critic, an actress and a theatre director among its members, and it was asked to consider creative as well as financial and practical issues. Yet its main conclusions were still very business-like: either the government must inject an extra 13.4 million pounds a year into its funding for theatre, or one of the two national companies must be closed. In the event neither alternative was followed: Sir Kenneth resigned from the Arts Council of which he had been a member, and theatre in Britain was left to muddle on, trying to survive with inadequate finance, as it did before.

Events have shown that bureaucratic subsidizing bodies cannot deal with artistic questions, which are seldom simple matters of either/or, or of efficient management. They can ensure that theatres are business-like, and they can give more money when they have some to give. They can also close theatres, or take away money. They may issue orders about repertoire or touring, or educational ventures or social engineering. But, at their best, all that politicians and bureaucrats can do is to assess efficiency and respond to demands from the theatres. Only theatre companies and their audiences can protect and increase the true wealth of a nation's theatre, by responding freely and imaginatively to life around them and to writers, actors and other artists, and by developing new policies and conditions of work.

If political forces outside theatre can do little but respond more or less generously, allowing more or less freedom, and insisting on business-like procedures, does that mean that whatever

---

[10] See John Allen, *Theatre in Europe*, p. 96.

programme is offered by theatres should be funded, in whatever way they want to work?

David Thacker, speaking of the crisis at the Young Vic, emphasized the need for more money and fewer productions, but he did not propose a change in the theatre's organization or artistic purpose. Could the Young Vic's resources be used in a different way? Might that Shakespearian stage become the home-base for a company like the Renaissance or English Shakespeare companies? Could the Young Vic collaborate or merge with one of these touring companies, helping them by providing continuity, and helping its own programme by providing more productions? Or could the Young Vic start a London Shakespeare Festival, in something like the North American fashion, with smaller, quicker and more numerous productions than the RSC offers, and for a shorter season? Could the theatre be given over to a director to work with young writers, using mostly student actors and the simplest production-values? Or could that director build up an ensemble from a group of young actors? Some of these policies might cost more money at first; but might they not use that money more effectively than continuing with a programme which is bound to be crippled by under-funding? The Young Vic has served its first purpose well, but have both needs and opportunities altered in twenty years?

Internal politics will nearly always favour established ways of running theatres – just as in railways, hospitals and education. Those in power hang on to power; and they are goaded by lack of funds to cling to their original plans, believing that their job is to survive at any cost. In that small embattled world, it is easy to forget that we are moving into a new social and cultural situation, and gaining the benefits of an astonishing new technology. But as in railways and universities, as in governments and homes, in theatres these new conditions require radical changes. Politicians and bureaucrats have shown that they cannot undertake this on behalf of the arts; and those in charge of theatres

do not seem ready or able to do so – they are too busy trying to survive. That suggests a need for some independent initiative, at least an independent and understanding voice in the present debate. Scholars and critics will never understand from the outside how a theatre is run from day to day, nor can they provide any extra funding; but they could work carefully and tactfully to investigate a crisis, and make sure that their conclusions are publicized.

Theatre history won't provide solutions to current problems, but it is fertile ground in which to discover a whole spectrum of possible stratagems for political change within theatre organizations. Once upon a time, a group of actors ran two theatres and thrived on Shakespeare's plays; they also adapted their work for small-scale touring, taking plays the length and breadth of the country. Does this Elizabethan and Jacobean theatre hold lessons for today, suggestions about a change in the power structure or in the programming of theatres staging Shakespeare? More recently, a popular Member of Parliament, Richard Brinsley Sheridan, served his party and constituency with notable success, but was also one of three men who ran a theatre famous for its Shakespeare productions: how close to active political life can our theatres become? On several occasions an actor has owned and managed a theatre, developed it, and extended its audience, and toured with Shakespeare prominent in his repertoire. Only a few decades ago, three recently graduated students, Terry Hands, Peter James and Martin Jenkins, started the Everyman Theatre in a Temperance Hall in Liverpool, and in their earliest days staged Shakespeare boldly. A few decades earlier, a singer, Lilian Baylis, together with her aunt who happened to run another Temperance Hall, started the Old Vic Theatre Company in London: among other achievements, they explored how cheaply Shakespeare could be produced and sold, and on the way developed the most gifted Shakespearian actors of a generation. Gordon Craig, a brilliant designer and actor, staged a production of *Much Ado about Nothing*, with his mother, Ellen Terry, as Beatrice; and he set the play in action as no one else had done before. Behind these special stories are very special people, and circumstances which will never be repeated, but by considering how they extended the powers and accessibility of theatre in the past, we can extend our views of what might be possible in the present. We should study theatre history conscious of that opportunity, and we should make our discoveries known.

Of course, no old solution can be applied unchanged to the very different theatres and audiences of today, but Shakespeare's texts do remain in use and the scholar's and critic's specialist understanding of them can have direct and timely relevance. From a study of the plays we should be able to suggest answers to such contemporary questions as what kind of acting company can best respond to their challenge. For example, how necessary are star actors, and should they be in charge of repertoire and expenditure? Or are the texts best served by an ensemble, used to playing together? Or should actors in a Shakespeare company be as varied as possible in training and experience, in order to respond to the variety of style in the texts and to represent dramatic contrasts strongly? How important is a large number of supernumeraries and how drilled should they be? Is individual casting necessary for all of Shakespeare's smallest roles, or can they be doubled to advantage? Or could anyone, even someone unskilled, play these parts and do something like justice to them? What plays can best be staged by a very small company, and what are the most helpful simplifications that can be introduced?

Many subjects are awaiting research which would be of great interest to theatres staging Shakespeare in the political conditions of today. Since the theatres have neither the time nor expertise to undertake these enquiries for themselves, universities should become the research branch of Shakespeare production. For example, the *Records of Early English Drama* will document the wide and busy network of tour-ing throughout England in Shakespeare's day; the nine volumes published already have provided a mass of new evidence and have changed very significantly our view of the theatrical profession of the time. These books should be studied carefully for what can be deduced about how plays were staged, how tours arranged, how texts chosen and adapted. The scholars who do this should also study modern touring to help them read the documents and to present their findings in practical terms.

In recent years a change has begun in the way theatres are directed. So demanding are the subsidizing bodies for statistical material and business expertise, and so complicated the technical and public-relations aspects of theatre, that some of the larger companies are now run by two persons, a director and an administrator, in almost equal harness; smaller ones choose a single person to combine both rôles. In most cases the executive head of the organization seems to be moving further apart from the rehearsal and staging processes, and the concerns of that person are becoming less and less those of actors or writers. If this is in fact so, the consequences for the production of Shakespeare could be great. Play directors would have to take orders – such as there must be no modern dress productions, because they would bring a drop of twenty per cent (or whatever) in ticket sales; or there can be no live music, no special casting. Administrative or financial pressures might be allowed to force a change in casting just before rehearsals begin, when the production can no longer adjust to such external directives. Of course, such restrictions and confusions are not in themselves remarkable, but the way in which they come into force affects everyone within a theatre and the very spirit of all its work. Comparative studies of several companies, over some twenty recent years, could show who makes the crucial decisions and why, and their effect on rehearsal methods, repertoire and production.

The Festival Theatre at Alabama has the makings of a major producer of Shakespeare; it has the plant, the funds, and apparently, the audience. Its progress, or otherwise, should be carefully studied, not only to see how much money is made or how much is needed, but to observe how the theatre functions so that others can learn from whatever happens. The same is true of the Old Globe at San Diego. Few theatres are so happily placed as these, and both call for more than journalistic reviews of individual productions.

The large political problems involved in producing Shakespeare's plays should be studied independently and with unhurried care.

The concern of criticism and scholarship is not only with how good or bad this production may be, or this actor or this designer, or whether a particular interpretation has proved to be revealing and exciting. At a time when theatres 'are in danger of closing', it would be good to know which are the theatre organizations, the kinds of subsidy, the artistic policies that will encourage productions which respond imaginatively and skilfully to Shakespeare's texts. How can the public best be served, and how can theatres thrive?

SHAKESPEARE IN THE TRENCHES

BALZ ENGLER

In April 1916 the tercentenary of Shakespeare's death was celebrated both in England and Germany, although the two countries had been at war for almost two years. This may just sound like an intriguing story, but it is also of considerable critical interest, because it illustrates how Shakespeare's international reputation survived under pressure, how conflicting views of him were defined by the political situation, and how these views, in turn, shaped the meaning of Shakespeare's texts, and affected the history of literary studies after the war.

In other words, in tracing these developments here Shakespeare will be considered as a public symbol, as myth.[1] But this will be done in a comparative perspective, which may help to remove the national limitations characteristic of most studies in this area.[2]

I

In England a committee, with the Prime Minister as its honorary president, had prepared elaborate ceremonies.[3] They could not really include 23 April, the day of Shakespeare's birth and death (and, significantly for many, St George's Day), because, in 1916, it coincided with Easter Sunday. Officially suggesting a parallel between Christ and Shakespeare would have meant taking things too far. Therefore the celebrations concentrated on the first week of May. On four days great institutions did homage to Shakespeare, on Sunday the Church, on Monday politics, on Tuesday the arts, on Wednesday education.

Sunday, 30 April, was declared Shakespeare Sunday. In many churches Shakespeare sermons were preached.[4] Shakespeare and patriotism was the most frequent subject. At Holy Trinity Church in Stratford, for example, it was about the strength that Shakespeare must have gained from his early experience of the Warwickshire countryside – strength 'which heartens our England to strive and endure'.[5] One sermon noted how the wave of patriotism that had recently passed over the land had made

---

[1] Cp. Balz Engler, 'The Classic as a Public Symbol', *REAL: Yearbook of Research in English and American Literature*, 6 (1988/9), 217–36, and *Poetry and Community* (Tübingen, 1990); Graham Holderness, ed., *The Shakespeare Myth* (Manchester, 1988); Marion F. O'Connor, 'Theatre of the Empire: "Shakespeare's England" at Earl's Court, 1912', in Jean E. Howard and Marion F. O'Connor, eds., *Shakespeare Reproduced: The Text in History and Ideology* (New York and London, 1987), pp. 68–98.

[2] This seems to be a problem with many books on Englishness. Cp. Brian Doyle, *English and Englishness* (London, 1989); Raphael Samuel, ed., *Patriotism: The Making and Unmaking of British National Identity*, 3 vols. (London, 1989), and its review in *TLS*, 22–8 December 1989, pp. 1407–8.

[3] *The Times*, 29 January 1916, p. 5.

[4] A. J. Carlyle, *The Shakespeare Tercentenary. A Sermon Preached in the City Church of Oxford, April 30th 1916* (Oxford, 1916).

[5] Anthony C., Deane, *His own Place. The Tercentenary 'Shakespeare Sermon' preached in the Church of the Holy Trinity, Stratford-on-Avon, April 30th, 1916* (London, 1916), p. 4.

people understand Shakespeare better again, after shameful neglect, due to gross materialism; 'we who think of him, who after three hundred years risen from the dead still lives and moves and speaks to us in his marvellous creations, must needs thank Him Who is the bringer of all that is good and gracious . . .'[6]

On Monday a public meeting was held at Mansion House, with the participation of the Government, the Archbishop of Canterbury, and the diplomatic representatives of the Empire and the allied and neutral, but not the axis, countries. Lord Crewe (standing in for the Prime Minister), the American ambassador, the representatives of the South African Union and of Sweden, among others, addressed the meeting.

On Tuesday afternoon a special performance took place at Drury Lane, in the words of the organizing committee 'a tribute to the genius of William Shakespeare, humbly offered by the players and their fellow-workers in the kindred arts of music and painting'. It was to be done 'in the spirit of the Bayreuth festivals; and there can be little question but that the audience will find that, as the occasion is worthier, so is the execution finer'.[7] The King and Queen were present; the proceeds went to joint funds of the British Red Cross Society and the Order of St John. A programme of Shakespeare music by living composers was followed by a performance of *Julius Caesar* with Frank Benson as Caesar, and a pageant of Shakespeare figures impersonated by well-known actors and actresses (in the tradition of earlier Shakespeare centenaries).[8] It was after this performance that Frank Benson was knighted – the King borrowed a sword from the property-room.

On this occasion a memorial volume was presented to the public, *A Book of Homage to Shakespeare*, edited again by Israel Gollancz, the indefatigable secretary of the tercentenary. It contained lavish illustrations, the homage of the painters, as well as 166 addresses, poems and critical essays in many languages, from most, but not the axis, countries.[9]

Wednesday, 3 May, was declared Shakespeare Day for the schools and training colleges. In the spirit of Empire Day it was to create 'a bond between the English-speaking children in the United Kingdom, the Dominions and the United States of America'.[10] London schoolchildren were given badges with the Droeshout portrait, offered by the British Empire Shakespeare Society.[11]

The celebrations were to begin with a reading from Ecclesiasticus 44 ('Let us now praise famous men'), followed by the singing of Shakespeare songs, a discourse on the poet, the reading of scenes from his plays, and closing with 'God save the King'. The London County Council had also set up a committee to devise a 'Shakespeare prayer', which was said in all London schools.[12] The beautiful mem-

---

[6] H. D. Rawnsley, *Shakespeare. A Tercentenary Sermon* (London, 1916), p.11. Note also the speech by the Bishop of Birmingham at the Repertory Theatre on 25 April, in which he stated: 'To Shakespeare patriotism and religion were inseparable. Anything less like the real Shakespeare than the one made in Germany had never been seen or dreamed of', *The Times*, 26 April 1916, p. 9.

[7] *The Times*, 21 April 1916, p. 7.

[8] The plays represented were *Romeo, Merchant, Merry Wives, Much Ado, As You Like It, Twelfth Night, Coriolanus, The Winter's Tale*. A cast list is to be found in J. P. Wearing, *The London Stage 1910–1919*, vol. 1 (Metuchen, 1982), pp. 632.5.

[9] Among the essays there is a remarkably generous, but untypical one by C. H. Herford on 'The German Contribution to Shakespeare Criticism', pp. 231–5. Herford, Professor of English at Manchester, had studied in Berlin.

[10] Sir Israel Gollancz in his evidence to the Newbolt Committee. His proposal was taken up favourably by the committee. See *The Teaching of English in England. Report of the Departmental Committee* (London, 1921), p. 319.

[11] The British Empire Shakespeare Society was founded in 1901, with Henry Irving as its first president (Ivor Brown and George Fearon, *Amazing Monument: A History of the Shakespeare Industry* (New York and London, 1939), p. 317).

[12] Unfortunately I have not been able to locate its text. A report in *The Times* on 3 May 1916, p. 7, confirms that such 'a special form of prayer' was indeed used.

orial programme[13] printed for the occasion contains 'Notes on Shakespeare the Patriot', concerning his views on language, patriotism, the fleet, etc., and illustrating them with passages mainly from *Henry V*.

Theatrical activities were few; in London just one Shakespeare season, at His Majesty's, was announced.[14] In particular, one dream once again did not come true in 1916: the foundation of a National Theatre.[15] This had been discussed in the House of Commons in 1913, appropriately on St George's Day.[16] Among the arguments then used for the establishment of such a theatre, two are of particular interest to us: the need for a place where those plays could be adequately performed whose language constituted a bond among the English-speaking people; and, quite explicitly, the model of rival Germany, where much more was being done for Shakespeare on the stage. H. J. McKinder, who moved the resolution, quoted from advance sheets of the *Shakespeare-Jahrbuch*, indicating the number of Shakespeare performances by professionals in Germany, 1,156 in 1912; and he ventured to think 'that we have nothing in this land of Shakespeare to show which is comparable in the least degree to the facts indicated by these figures'.[17]

By comparison with the official English celebrations in 1916 activities in Germany were modest. Max Reinhardt revived a cycle of Shakespeare plays that he had first put on in 1914. There was nothing like the Shakespeare Week in London. At the meeting of the *Deutsche Shakespeare-Gesellschaft* in Weimar, which was afterwards criticized as dull and uninspiring, Rudolf Brotanek, in his 'Festvortrag', found that Shakespeare's opinions, as expressed in his plays, were in accordance with the German position in the war. He closed by saying:

We are satisfied that we still adhere to notions of duty which Shakespeare laid down three hundred years ago in his works, those statutes of free and noble humanity. We are pleased that in our statesmen the feeling of fellowship with the people and of

responsibility towards God is still so strong as in the soul of Henry V, as studied by Shakespeare, that all our leaders may raise their hands and hearts towards the God of battles and may pray, with the victor at Bosworth:

> O thou, whose captain I account myself,
> Look on my forces with a gracious eye. [. . .]
> Make us thy ministers of chastisement,
> That we may praise thee in the victory.
> (*Richard III*, 5.5.61–7)[18]

There were reasons for this relative neglect in 1916 – and we have to move back two years in history to understand them: in 1914 Shakespeare's 350th birthday had been celebrated extensively.[19] This year had been chosen, because the *Deutsche Shakespeare-Gesellschaft* was then also marking its fiftieth anniversary. The festivities, as always, took place at Weimar, the city of Goethe and Schiller, three months before the beginning of the war. They were internationally oriented, in particular reflecting the anglophile attitude of German Shakespearians: Franz Josef I of Austria and Hungary

---

[13] *Shakespeare Day 1916* (London, 1916).

[14] *The Times*, 3 May 1916, p. 7.

[15] Such plans were old, of course. Cf. Geoffrey Whitworth, *The Making of a National Theatre* (London, 1951).

[16] The debate is well documented in Whitworth, *National Theatre*, pp. 100–13.

[17] Whitworth, *National Theatre*, p. 101.

[18] 'Wir sind es zufrieden, noch immer zu Pflichtbegriffen uns zu bekennen, welche Shakespeare vor dreihundert Jahren in seinen Werken, jenem Gesetzbuch freier und hochgemuter Menschlichkeit niederlegte. Wohl uns, dass in unseren Staatsmänneren das Gefühl der Zusammengehörigkeit mit dem Volke und der Verantwortung vor Gott noch so klar ist wie in der von Shakespeare durchleuchteten Seele Heinrichs V., dass ein jeder unserer Führer Hände und Herz zum Gott der Schlachten erheben und mit dem Sieger von Bosworth flehen darf:' etc. (Rudolf Brotanek, 'Shakespeare über den Krieg', *Shakespeare-Jahrbuch*, 52 (1916), xvii–xlviii, p. xlviii). Brotanek quoted of Shakespeare in German, of course.

[19] Shakespeare had the misfortune to die at fifty-two; for the benefit of future admirers poets should ideally die at twenty-five or at seventy-five.

joined the Gesellschaft, but also King George V (the Kaiser had been a member for a long time); Viscount Haldane, the British Lord Chancellor, was made an honorary member.

In England the mood had been similar in 1914. There were few events to mark Shakespeare's birthday in April. But in June a Shakespeare Association was founded, with the purpose of organizing the 1916 centenary. Its thirteen vice-presidents were to include luminaries in English studies from all over the world, among them three representatives from Germany.[20] Beerbohm Tree proposed that, in 1916, an international production of all the history plays should be put on in London, with a cast including Americans, Frenchmen, Germans and Italians.[21] Shakespeare could still be shared with the world.

The outbreak of the war in August almost immediately called in question the high principles extolled on both sides only a few months earlier. In September Max Reinhardt's Deutsches Theater in Berlin, which had been preparing a grand cycle of Shakespeare plays to mark the anniversary, polled important personalities on whether, under the new circumstances, it was appropriate to perform the works of Shakespeare, a British author. The answers were unanimous: there was no reason to stop performing him: 'Shakespeare gehört der ganzen Welt' (Shakespeare belongs to the whole world), as the chancellor, Bethmann-Hollweg, put it; moreover, Germany was at war not with the people of Shakespeare's England, but with their mean and degenerated descendants; and finally, in the words of Fürst von Bülow, Bethmann-Hollweg's predecessor, Shakespeare 'is among the oldest and most beautiful conquests of the German mind, which we shall defend against all the world, like our other spiritual and material possessions'.[22]

War imagery became common on both sides in the following years, the imagery of territorial possession and conquest, of asylum and internment. In a prologue to a Shakespeare performance delivered at Leipzig, in the autumn of 1914, Feste was given a provocative message from Shakespeare to the audience. A translation of it was soon printed in *The Times*:

Ye unto him have been until today
His second home; his first and native home
Was England; but this England of the present
Is so contrarious in her acts and feelings,
Yea, so abhorr'd of his pure majesty
And the proud spirit of his free-born being,
That he doth find himself quite homeless there.
A fugitive he seeks his second home,
This Germany, that loves him most of all,
To whom before all others he gives thanks,
And says: Thou wonderful and noble land,
Remain thou Shakespeare's one and only home.[23]

---

[20] They were Alois Brandl (Berlin), Max Förster (Leipzig), and Josef Schick (Munich), *The Times*, 19 June 1914, p. 13.

[21] *The Times*, 19 June 1914, quoted by Carl Grabau, 'Zeitschriftenschau 1914', *Shakespeare-Jahrbuch*, 51 (1915), p. 240. Grabau does not always indicate his sources. I have checked these wherever possible, which showed that his reports can be relied on.

[22] Grabau, 'Zeitschriftenschau 1914', 242–3. Shakespeare 'gehört zu den ältesten und schönsten Eroberungen des deutschen Geistes, die wir wie unseren sonstigen geistigen und materiellen Besitz gegen alle Welt behaupten wollen. Wir haben Shakespeare längst annektiert und geben ihn nicht wieder her' (243).

[23] Arthur Quiller-Couch, 'Patriotism in English Literature', in his *Studies in Literature* (Cambridge, 1918), 290–322, p. 316. The original runs as follows:

Ihr wäret ihm bisher die zweite Heimat
Gewesen, seine erste, angeborne: England!
Doch dieses England, wie es heute sei,
Sein Handeln und sein Fühlen, sei ihm so zuwider,
Ja, so verhasst dem redlichen und reinen,
Dem Königsgeiste seines freien Wesens,
Dass er sich dort als heimatlos empfände!
Als solch ein stolz aus eigner Wahl Verbannter,
Als Flüchtling käm er heut in seine zweite Heimat,
Ins deutsche Land, das stets vor allen ihn geliebt,
Dem dankbar er vor allen andern sei,
Käm hin und spräche: Treues, tiefes, edles Land,
Was Du mir warst, das sei mir fürder zwiefach:
Des Shakespeare einzige und wahre Heimat [.]

(Ernst Hardt, 'Prolog zu einer Shakespeare-Aufführung im Herbste des Jahres 1914', *Shakespeare-Jahrbuch*, 52 (1916), p. 2.) The tone of this prologue is typical. Cp. also Gerhart Hauptmann's speech at the

Ernest de Sélincourt commented: 'Poor Shakespeare! If you want to crystallize the pathetic situation in a phrase you might call it "Shakespeare interned" or "Germany the snapper-up of unconsidered trifles"';[24] and Arthur Quiller-Couch's commentary summarizes many of the prejudices on the English side:

These men do honestly believe our Shakespeare . . ., whose language they cannot speak, cannot write, can but imperfectly understand . . . our Shakespeare's spirit – has migrated to a nation whose exploits it benevolently watches in the sack of Louvain, the bestialities of Aerschot, the shelling of Rheims cathedral.[25]

II

So far I have been anecdotal, and I should now like to bring some order into what I have reported: how does Shakespeare appear in these events on both sides?

In Germany the claim that Shakespeare was *unser*, ours, presented a problem, of course: nobody could seriously deny that Shakespeare was an Englishman. But there were essentially three strategies to deal with this. One could argue that it was mere coincidence that Shakespeare, the poet of all humankind, was born and lived in England.[26] Then there were the climatic and racial theories, which saw Shakespeare as one of the geniuses of the Germanic North, as against those of the Romance South.[27] This opposition goes back to Herder's attempt in the eighteenth century to free German literature from the grip of French classicism, and to create a sense of German nationhood with the help of literature.[28] In this Shakespeare played a crucial rôle as a genius who, unobstructed by any moral or aesthetic rules, offered direct access to Nature.

Finally, one could claim, as Brotanek and many others did, that Shakespeare had been an English patriot, even an exemplary one. However, his values were no longer upheld by his countrymen, but by the Germans, who had naturalized Shakespeare in a long effort of

appropriation. This rhetoric reached its apotheosis with the publication of Friedrich Gundolf's *Shakespeare und der deutsche Geist* in 1911, one of the most influential books of literary criticism in German.[29]

As such Shakespeare could come to be considered one of the three greatest German authors, along with Goethe and Schiller; and it was no coincidence that the Shakespeare-Gesellschaft established its seat at Weimar. Hamlet, along with Faust, became one of the great myths of German culture;[30] and phrases from Shakespeare's plays permeate the German lan-

---

meeting of the *Deutsche Shakespeare-Gesellschaft* in 1916: Shakespeare belongs to the whole world, but there is no people in the world, 'auch das englische nicht, das sich ein Anrecht wie das deutsche auf Shakespeare erworben hätte. Shakespeare Gestalten sind ein Teil unserer Welt, seine Seele ist eins mit unserer geworden: und wenn er in England geboren und begraben ist, so ist Deutschland das Land, wo er wahrhaft lebt.' [not even the English, who have earned a right to Shakespeare in the way the Germans have. Shakespeare's figures are part of our world, his soul has merged with ours: and if he was born and buried in England, it is in Germany where he truly lives.] (Gerhart Hauptmann, 'Deutschland und Shakespeare', *Shakespeare-Jahrbuch*, 51 (1916), vii–xii, p. xii.)

[24] Ernest de Sélincourt, *English Poets and the National Ideal* (London, 1915), p. 13.

[25] Quiller-Couch, 'Patriotism', p. 317.

[26] E.g., Franz Kaibel, 'Dichter und Patriotismus: Die Betrachtung eines Deutschen zum dreihundertsten Todestag eines Engländers', *Shakespeare-Jahrbuch*, 52 (1916), 36–63.

[27] Climatic theories of this kind became accepted also in England, partly under German influence, cf. Carlyle's writings or Hyppolite Taine, *History of English Literature*, trans. H. van Laun, second edn (Edinburgh, 1872).

[28] The hidden presence of France also in the early twentieth-century debate is made explicit by Josef Kohler, 'Die Staatsidee Shakespeares in *Richard II*', *Shakespeare-Jahrbuch*, 53 (1917), 1–12. Cp. also Jonathan Bate, 'The Politics of Romantic Shakespeare Criticism: Germany, England, France', *European Romantic Review* 1 (1990), 1–26.

[29] Eckhard Heftrich, 'Friedrich Gundolfs Shakespeare-Apotheose', *Jahrbuch der Deutschen Shakespeare-Gesellschaft West*, 1988, 85–102, p. 86–7.

[30] In the German Hamlet myth, Hamlet, the Northern prince, stands for Germany, brooding and unable to act.

guage as much as those from Goethe and Schiller.

In England, as the tercentenary celebrations indicate, Shakespeare was closely associated both with the idea of England and that of the Empire, according to which English and the English way of life had spread their beneficial influence all over the world.[31] In fact, the two ideas are difficult to disentangle: the values that constitute Englishness and those of a world-wide Empire are fused in a complex and ambiguous manner, perhaps best summed up by Rupert Brooke's sonnet 'The Soldier';[32] and we know from more recent European history how national consciousness among the English, under the influence of imperialism, has been only imperfectly developed, unlike that of other nations on British soil. Shakespeare then was both universal, and as such representative of what placed England *above* nationalism, and of what made his own country different from others and placed it *beside* them.

There was nothing as formidable as Gundolf's Shakespeare that could be set against what looked like systematic German attempts to requisition Shakespeare. In this situation, the German challenge to the ownership of Shakespeare was met, at first insecurely, with a more narrowly defined nationalist position, emphasizing borders, denying access to Shakespeare, insisting on what made England and her poet different and difficult to master for other nations.

III

The struggle for Shakespeare during the First World War was to leave deep traces in the history of Shakespeare studies for decades to come; of these I should only like to mention the reception of German Shakespeare criticism and the development of English as a discipline in England. Before the First World War German Shakespeare criticism, within certain limits set by the image of the philologist as pedant, had been taken seriously, especially in

the areas of textual, aesthetic and biographical studies.[33] But now the English began to neglect, even to reject German criticism, an attitude that has persisted in many places. I remember an eminent English Shakespeare scholar advising me not to use Alexander Schmidt's *Shakespeare Lexicon*: 'Schmidt was German and therefore could not understand Shakespeare properly' – clearly an echo of Quiller-Couch's position. He had failed to notice that the *OED* routinely uses Schmidt's definitions where single occurrences of words in Shakespeare are recorded.[34]

In the context of the First World War there were attempts to re-interpret this myth, to turn Hamlet into a warlike hero. See Bernhard Fehr, 'Unser Shakespeare', *Westermanns Monatshefte*, 120, 1 (May 1916), 348–52, one of the most revealing contributions to the Shakespeare tercentenary.

[31] Cp. the Earl's Court exhibition of 1911, as described by O'Connor, 'Theatre of Empire'.

[32] Similar ideas were expressed by F. R. Benson at Stratford ('At Shakespeare's Shrine', *The Times*, 20 April 1915, p. 12. 'At the shrine on this day comes knowledge, clear and unmistakable, that there is no proper shrine to the Shakespeare memory save the hearts of Englishmen. The altar at Stratford is kindled, and again it grows cold; but on Europe's battlefields ten thousand nobler altars enlighten the world with flames which shall not be extinguished. These are Shakespeare's men, though some of them may scarcely be familiar with the name of Shakespeare.' Cp. also the letter from C.L.D., *TLS*, 4 May 1916, quoting J. R. Seeley's essay on 'Milton's Poetry' in his *Lectures and Essays* (London, 1870), pp. 152–3.

[33] The account offered by Sidney Lee, *Shakespeare's Life and Work* (London, (1900) 1907), pp. 193–6, may be typical: 'During the last half-century textual, aesthetic, and biographical criticism has been pursued in Germany with unflagging industry and energy; and although laboured and supersubtle theorising characterises much German aesthetic criticism, its mass and variety testify to the impressiveness of the appeal that Shakespeare's work has made to the German intellect.' Lee specifically mentions Nicolaus Delius (textual criticism); Karl Elze (biography and stage history); F. A. T. Kreyssig, *Vorlesungen über Shakespeare* (1858 and 1874), *Shakespeare-Fragen* (1871), Otto Ludwig, *Shakespeare-Studien*, E. W. Sievers, Ulrici, *Shakespeare's Dramatic Art* (1839) and Gervinus's commentaries (1848–9).

[34] Wolfgang Keller thinks that neglect set in at the time of the Boer war (when the two countries for the first time

In more general terms, one can also see the effects of this struggle for the possession of Shakespeare as a factor in the establishment of English as an academic discipline after the war.[35] Quiller-Couch, in the essay I have already quoted, went as far as blaming the Germans for the neglect of English literature in English schools.

I do not say, nor do I believe for a moment, in spite of a long malignity now unmasked, the Germans have *of set purpose* treated English literature as a thing of the past or imposed that illusion upon our schools, with design to prove that this particular glory of our birth and state is a dead possession of a decadent race. My whole argument is rather that they have set up this illusion, and industriously, because they could not help it; because the illusion is in them: because this lovely and living art which they can never practise nor even see as an art, to them is, has been, must be for ever, a dead science – a *hortus siccus*; to be tabulated, not to be planted or watered.   (p. 314)

Such a view, which acknowledges German influence at an unlikely moment, helped to shape the insistence on literature as a vital force, which we associate with the Cambridge tradition of literary studies, as something that may 'once more bring sanctification and joy into the sphere of common life', as the Newbolt Report put it.[36]

IV

What can we learn for Shakespeare criticism from all this? I should like briefly to mention three points that concern related areas of debate. In 1989 there was a controversy in the *TLS* on whether there were any limits to the interpretation of Shakespeare's plays.[37] The evidence of the First World War supports the view that this is not the case. On both sides, soldiers were sent into battle with the same slogans from Shakespeare;[38] the German Chancellor quoted *Henry V* when German troops stood before Calais;[39] the play was performed in Germany in 1917, and criticism concerned the question why it was not part of a cycle of histories,[40] rather than why it should have been done at all.

This leads me to my second point: What I have said makes it clear that it is the context in which we perceive Shakespeare and his works, *how we use them*, that determines their meaning. In other words, we have to acknowledge the primacy of pragmatics in the study of Shakespeare. And finally: A comparative perspective may be helpful in the study of this – and in giving up entrenched positions.

---

were on opposite sides), but that it really became serious after the First World War (Wolfgang Keller, 'Shakespeare als Dichter der Deutschen', in Paul Meissner, ed., *Shakespeare in Europa* (Stuttgart, 1944), pp. 1–116.

[35] Chris Baldick, *The Social Mission of English Criticism, 1848–1932* (Oxford, 1983), pp. 86–108, 'Literary-Critical Consequences of the War' deals with this topic.

[36] *The Teaching of English in England. Report of the Departmental Committee* (London, 1921), p. 258.

[37] Cf. Terence Hawkes, 'Wittgenstein's Shakespeare', in Maurice Charney, ed., *'Bad' Shakespeare* (Cranbury, NJ, 1988), reviewed by Robert Hapgood, *TLS*, 25–31 August, p. 927, and Terence Hawkes's letter to the editor (*TLS*, 8–14 September 1989).

[38] Cf. Paul Fussell, *The Great War and Modern Memory* (London, 1975, 1977), pp. 198–9; and, for example, Alois Brandl, 'Jahresbericht für 1914/15', *Shakespeare-Jahrbuch*, 51 (1915), v, quoting *Henry V*.

[39] *The Times*, 24 April 1915, p. 9.

[40] Rudolf Raab, '*Heinrich V.* in neuer Bearbeitung am Karlsruher Hoftheater', *Shakespeare-Jahrbuch*, 55 (1919), 223–5.

SHAKESPEARE'S EARLIEST EDITOR, RALPH CRANE

T. H. HOWARD-HILL

Nicholas Rowe is usually taken to be Shakespeare's first editor, 'perhaps', Gary Taylor suggests, 'because he is the first we can confidently name'.[1] The reservation rests on his contention that the editing of Shakespeare's works 'began with the publication of the first editions of his works in the 1590s'. No doubt this is correct in that the translation of a play from study to print is inevitably accompanied by the alteration of textual details and the addition of such accoutrements as title-pages, dedications, commendatory epistles or poems intended to facilitate purchase and reading. Indeed, we may extend this implicit definition of editing further, to apply it to the kinds of adjustments that are made to a playwright's text in order to fit it to the stage and the performance which first publishes it abroad. From the moment a playwright stabilizes his conception in a text that embodies his intention for the work in any satisfactory manner, a series of successive destabilizing processes are set in motion. The function if not the purpose of the stage is to appropriate the playwright's work, willingly relinquished, to represent it in forms that do not respond to the originary moment of creation. On the other hand, publication in print involves a procrustean translation of the work from one arena of performance to another: the attempt to stabilize a final reading text destabilizes the playwright's original text.

Modern editors are properly aware of these processes for the stabilization of textual variation lies at the heart of their mystery. But in modern times it is not useful to extend the noble title of 'editor' undiscriminatingly to the myriad scribes, book-keepers, compositors, friends of the author or of the press, and printers or publishers who have busied themselves with the text of any of Shakespeare's works.[2] Rowe and his successors from Pope (through to Taylor himself no doubt) conceived that they operated with significantly different methods and objects from those of, for instance, the humble scribe or compositor, and observation that their functions are similar in one or another respect should not obscure recognition of the areas of editorial concern which were not usually shared by early scribes, compositors or, even, publishers of individual works. Nevertheless, *Mr William Shakespeares Comedies, Histories, & Tragedies* issued by the Jaggards and Blount in 1623 was just the kind of compilation that involved activities that we can properly characterize now as 'editorial'. It follows, therefore, that there must have been an editor. His identity is naturally a matter of great interest for anyone concerned with the First Folio and the transmission of Shakespeare's text in general.

Various names have been suggested: Hem-

---

[1] Stanley Wells and Gary Taylor, *William Shakespeare: A Textual Companion* (Oxford, 1986), p. 53.

[2] The fact that Taylor's usage gives fresh currency to obsolete senses of 'editor' (cf. *OED*, e.g. *éditeur*) and 'edition' is not helpful in contexts where we need to make distinctions.

inges and Condell, of course, Ben Jonson, the printer Isaac Jaggard or the publisher Edward Blount. Nevertheless, Taylor cannot locate the central authority. In any event, following Greg, he concludes, 'In so far as the King's Men did oversee the volume, the detailed work was probably delegated to their book-keeper (Knight?) and any other scribes who (like Crane) regularly worked for the company.'[3] The production of the First Folio as a collaborative enterprise that involved the co-ordination of several functions and responsibilities can be understood readily by anyone who has 'edited' a play in a modern series as I have recently done. Nominally *the* editor, I nevertheless have a series editor who will doubtless share responsibility for any errors or solecisms he allows to persist in the edition. He himself has an editor, a functionary in the publishing house charged to urge the edition onwards to completion and publication: the Revels Plays *A Game at Chess* has therefore three editors, with different but interlocking responsibilities. The organization of the First Folio does not fit this division exactly but the analogy is close enough to be useful. The first responsibility for the selection of the works and their arrangement in the Folio must have belonged to Shakespeare's old friends and colleagues, Heminges and Condell: they knew what he wrote and how to get access to copies of his plays. The printer virtually selected himself. William Jaggard, besides being Printer to the City of London since 17 December 1610, also enjoyed from 1615 onwards a monopoly of the printing of playbills that had given him constant contact with the London theatre companies. The Jaggards had quite recently been involved in Thomas Pavier's abortive attempt to publish a collection of Shakespearian works and, William being blind, his son Isaac had developed some expertise in the display of dramatic texts. As both printer and co-publisher Isaac Jaggard occupied a crucial position in the execution of the great design.

Despite the prominence of Heminges and Condell as the signatories of the 'Epistle Dedi-

catorie', and the address 'To the great Variety of Readers', it is hardly credible, as Greg points out, that they 'personally performed the arduous duty of detailed supervision; and it is hardly likely that two busy actors, with the management of a large company and two theatres on their hands, would have found leisure for the task'.[4] The same objections may be made to the book-keeper's close involvement with the project.[5] On the other hand, there does exist indisputable evidence of an editorial presence in the Folio over some stretch of time, exerted by one who had a documented close connection with the King's Men about the time copy for the Folio was being gathered together. I refer of course to Ralph Crane whose unexampled notoriety in Shakespearian circles has not furthered a true assessment of his relationship with the editing of the Folio. Nevertheless, there is no need to recapitulate the well-known details of his life and scribal characteristics. Instead, I intend to draw on fresh evidence garnered from close examination of his involvement in the proliferation of texts of Middleton's *A Game at Chess* in 1624 in order to demonstrate his claim to consideration as Shakespeare's earliest editor.

CRANE AS EDITOR OF MIDDLETON'S *A GAME*

Some use has been made of variations amongst Crane's transcripts of *A Game* to illustrate his

---

[3] *Textual Companion*, p. 36. T. W. Baldwin, *On Act and Scene Division in the Shakspere First Folio* (Carbondale, Ill. 1965) attributed the editing of copy for the Folio to 'Knight's predecessor as book-keeper in the company 1621–24, or someone who assisted him . . . they were quite likely the chief, if not the only actual editors, for the First Folio' (p. 54). However, he maintained that Crane was not the 'classical editor' responsible for the scene headings of *TGV*, *Wiv.* and *WT* (p. 59).

[4] W. W. Greg, *The Shakespeare First Folio: Its Bibliographical and Textual History* (Oxford, 1955), p. 77.

[5] That Edward Knight was the King's Company book-keeper in 1620–3 has not been established. No indications of his scribal characteristics in the Folio have been detected.

operations or to show that indifferent authorial readings may exist in manuscripts apparently some distance from their origin.[6] However, because little was known of the transmission of Middleton's work in the six manuscripts and two substantive editions of it that survive, conclusions that could be drawn from comparison of Crane's transcripts are tentative at best and sometimes incorrect. Middleton's play supplies a unique and striking instance in the seventeenth century of a broadly based effort to capitalize on the extraordinary success of a 'nine days' wonder', a play designed to skirt the limits of official tolerance. Crane had worked for Middleton previously – he had made a copy of the 'Invention' performed at the mayoral dinner of Sir Edward Barkham in 1622 – and Middleton seems to have trusted Crane to work without close supervision. Only the earliest of Crane's transcripts bears any sign of the playwright's solicitude for his text, the insertion of a short line omitted from 2.1. Crane's transcripts in 1624, from one of which Q3 was eventually printed, proliferated from a non-extant manuscript (also probably in his hand) copied from Middleton's foul papers, during the performances of the play through the end of the year: his Malone transcript was a new year's gift to Middleton's dedicatee. In the early stage of the transcription process there was necessary commerce between the scribe and the playwright for, as is well known, Crane's Archdall manuscript, apparently completed on 13 August, gives (uniquely) the text of Middleton's early, shorter version of the play. The enhancements of the fuller version, notably the passages incorporating the Fat Bishop, had to be added to the copy Crane used in order to transcribe the manuscript from which Q3 was later printed and also his calligraphic Lansdowne and Malone manuscripts. Moreover, partly because Q3, Lansdowne and Malone are terminal witnesses, Crane must have made other transcripts of the play which have not survived. This must be recalled when his operations on Archdall, Q3, Lansdowne and Malone are described in the

order in which he made them. The complexity is such that each of these witnesses conveys a text of *A Game* significantly different from the others and from the other four witnesses of the play, including of course the two manuscripts (Trinity and Bridgewater–Huntington) in which Middleton himself participated.[7] Consequently, detailed assessment of Crane's function in the multiplication of *Game* witnesses involves not only recognition of the complex inter-relationships amongst the witnesses to which he contributed but also understanding of the influence of other scribes and manuscripts upon his work. Sometimes hitherto, Crane has been credited with innovations which in fact he faithfully transmitted from his sources.

Such textual relationships are not the issue here, however, and there is no need to describe them more precisely than I have done above. The value of textual analysis in this context is that now we can be fairly certain of the provenance of the details which attract interest and, with the aid of Middleton's holographic Trinity manuscript, we can interpret the sequence of Crane transcripts from Archdall to Malone to reveal the evolution of texts progressively liberated from the constraints of original authority and increasingly edited for readers. In this respect, as Crane successively transcribed from

---

[6] Jeanne A. Roberts, 'Ralph Crane and the Text of *The Tempest*', *Shakespeare Studies*, 13 (1980), 213–33; John Jowett, 'New Created Creatures: Ralph Crane and the Stage Directions in *The Tempest*', *Shakespeare Survey 36* (1983), 107–20; E. A. J. Honigmann, *The Stability of Shakespeare's Text* (London, 1965).

[7] Susan Z. Nascimento (*Thomas Middleton's 'A Game at Chess': A Textual Study*. PhD diss., University of Maryland, 1975) examines the textual inter-relationships of the *Game* witnesses statistically and gives extensive collations. I have reconstructed the history of the text's evolution and suggested a stemma in a volume of studies on the play to be published shortly. Quotations from Middleton's Trinity manuscript or his share of B–H use the line numbers of the Malone Society Reprints edition, 1990. The play itself is quoted in modern spelling from my Revels Plays edition (Manchester University Press, forthcoming) with its act, scene and line numbering.

his own copies, his practice is analogous to that of a modern editor who uses an already edited modern text as the basis of his own. It is this lineal succession of sophisticated texts that allows us to detect Crane's editorial function and, as I think, purpose. However, anyone who has read my *Ralph Crane and Some Shakespeare First Folio Comedies* (1972), where Crane's activities as a professional preparer of literary texts for presentation are described, may well be reluctant to give much significance to a new conclusion that Crane 'edited' Middleton's texts. We need to notice, then, that Crane's *Game* transcripts mark a transition between those surviving transcripts which represent him in a predominantly functional role, fulfilling authorial commissions (Jonson's *Pleasure Reconciled to Virtue*, 1618; Middleton's *A Song in Several Parts*, 1622) and the later transcripts ostentatiously written for presentation to patrons on the author's or the scribe's own behalf (Middleton's *The Witch*, 1624/5; Fletcher's *Demetrius and Enanthe*, 1625, and his poetical transcripts from 1626).[8]

The Archdall transcript, the copy for Q3 which does not seem to have been originally intended for publication, and the Lansdowne manuscript all lack dedications. It is commonly assumed that they were made for sale but the only evidence is Middleton's statement in his dedication to the Malone manuscript that no 'Stationers Stall' could display a copy of his work. It is by no means self-evident that the scribe would have entered upon his task as his early professional experience instructed, content to reproduce the substance of a text without elaboration or decoration.[9] In distinction, the Malone transcript itself, as will be seen, is the product of the most constrictive kind of literary editing. The special significance of the Crane *Game* transcripts, I may repeat, is that they follow Crane's involvement with the Folio project and on that account afford instructive indications of his rôle there.

We must recognize that the style of Middleton's manuscripts allowed Crane plenty of

scope to improve the presentation of his text. Both the title-pages of the Trinity and Bridgewater manuscripts in Middleton's hand are unadorned. The pages of the manuscripts are ruled but lack running-titles and pagination; catchwords occur intermittently, without function.[10] With a couple of exceptions Middleton does not vary his mixed hand with italian script, even in the act headings (scenes other than the first are not indicated), and there is no ornamentation other than intermittent broken lines and the occasional periodus (∵) that may identify Middleton's influence in scribal transcripts. Verses often extend the full width of the ruled text area, sometimes cross the right-hand ruling, sometimes are turned up at the right margin but more often are continued into the following line of text. Whole openings are not readily distinguishable as verse: see, for instance, Trinity fols. 22–3. All in all, Middleton's Trinity manuscript is workmanlike but bland, the different parts of the text (e.g. headings, stage-directions, speech-prefixes, dialogue) barely distinguished by handwriting, position or subordination. It is understandable that a scribe like Crane, himself then a published author, might look upon a Middleton manuscript as simply the occasion for preparation of a readable text rather than the thing itself.

Turning now to the Crane witnesses individually, it is interesting to observe that the title-page of the early Archdall manuscript is distinguished from Crane's title-pages for Lansdowne and Malone by its lack of calligraphic ornamentation, and it also fails to identify Middleton as the playwright. This suggests a more modest intention for this transcript than for its successors, obviously prepared for public

---

8 *Sir John van Olden Barnavelt* (1619) is exceptional; it is discussed on pp. 125–6.

9 If literally true, the claim implies that the other previous transcripts were also made for presentation.

10 These observations are fuller in the Malone Society edition.

purposes. Nevertheless, Crane wrote the manuscript as a book: it is paginated, has a running-title above the page rulings, and has catchwords uniformly. (The Lansdowne and Malone manuscripts are similarly arranged except that the running-titles, present also in *The Witch*, are replaced as in *Demetrius and Enanthe* by central pagination.) What most immediately distinguishes Crane's transcripts from Middleton's is the lavish use of ornamental scrolls and rulings to set off parts of the text and the variation of hands for display (in headings and stage-directions) and to emphasize words in the text. Crane used his fine italian hand in Archdall deliberately to distinguish the speech-prefixes and important parts of stage-directions, and for significant nouns (often proper nouns) in the text. It was also employed for the Black King's letter in 2.1 and for passages read from books (in 2.1 by the White Queen's Pawn, Black Bishop's Pawn and Black Knight severally, in 3.1 by the Black Bishop, and the Black Knight reading from the Book of General Pardons in 4.2), for the invocations in 3.3, the Latin oration in 5.1, the song in 5.1, occasional phrases in Latin, and for passages marked as sentences (e.g. '. . . *the Eare of State is quick and iealious*', 1.1.323). The first words of the Induction and each act are written prominently in a display hand. The omission of this feature from the beginning of scenes – which are marked only in the Crane witnesses of *A Game* – gives good evidence of his deliberate attention to his task.

Instructive for consideration of the Folio texts printed from Crane copy is the treatment of these features of the Crane copy for Q3 of *A Game*.[11] The beginnings of acts are displayed distinctively only in the Induction 1.1 and 4.1. Italic type is used for the same passages that were written in italian hand in Archdall but in Q3 there is a general and sporadic diminution of the number of proper nouns and other words distinguished by italic type, probably because the printer's type supply could not cope with Crane's lavish use of the italian hand. A few instances of dashes in Q3 appear to be composi-

torial in origin but others have precedent in Archdall.[12] The quarto witnesses an interesting development in Crane's editorial treatment of a feature which is ambiguous in Middleton's manuscripts. In his Trinity manuscript Middleton has a speech-prefix at 2140 (5.2.77) for the Black Queen's Pawn who apparently had not entered the stage. In fact, as his subsequent 'Intus' directions at lines 2145, 2151 and 2155 show, the Black Queen's Pawn spoke 'within'. In Archdall Crane supplied the speech-prefix in place of 'Intus' but gave no indication that the Pawn's speeches were spoken offstage. Q3 adds a clarifying stage-direction ('*Black | Queens Pawn with- | in*'.) in the right margin at line 2140, and '*within*' directions also in the margin opposite the speech-prefixes at lines 2145, 2151, 2155. Crane's Lansdowne manuscript illustrates the synthesis of the speech-prefixes and stage-directions at the left of the page with '*Bl.Q.P. within*' and a neat curly bracket for all four speeches. (However, he did not give an entrance for the Pawn.) When he came to prepare the Malone transcript Crane progressed further towards economy by omitting the speech-prefix after the first instance of the combined instruction. Such careful attention to textual presentation is characteristic of Crane's active involvement with texts he had for transcription, exemplified most strikingly by his Lansdowne manuscript.[13]

---

[11] Crane prepared the transcript that eventually provided the printer's copy for Q3 from an earlier transcript which had been transcribed from the source of Ar. (Archdall) after that transcript had received the additions and textual adjustments comprising the main revision of the text between Ar. and Tr. (Trinity).

[12] Dashes at the start of verses occur on pp. 32 (Tr. 1126), 35 (1254), 36 (1272) and 37 (1322), possibly relics of casting-off: they serve no textual function. Other dashes with marginal stage-directions on pp. 2 (Tr. 70), 6 (180), and 44 (1572) correspond to Crane's practice in, say, Ln. (Lansdowne) where most of them may be seen, and the dash after 'If he deflowre thee not' (p. 55, Tr. 2000 + 23) could well be, by comparison with Ln., the compositor's misreading of Crane's extended crossbar of the 't'.

[13] Q3 shows seven right-hand multiline marginal stage-directions with curly brackets, on pp. 45, 57, 58, 61 and

Crane manifests his intention to produce a manuscript book attractive to readers in his Lansdowne manuscript. The dated title-page proclaiming Middleton's authorship is ornamented with scrolls and heavy rulings; the pages are ruled and numbered at the head of each page. Catchwords are given regularly. The section and act headings in prominent italian script, and the initial entrances, are further distinguished by thick rulings, as are the ends of scenes. The speeches are indented on the speech-prefixes at the left-hand side of the page and later entrances and other stage-directions are written in prominent italian script after an introductory dash to the right of the main text. The handwriting is deliberately florid and both majuscules and the italian hand are employed lavishly. Besides the portions of the text already mentioned, Crane uses italian script for passages which the White Queen's Pawn reads from the Book of Obedience in 2.1 and the Black Knight's quotations from the Black Bishop's Pawn's notes of intelligence in the same scene. These, like the italicization of the Prologue and Epilogue, are innovations in Lansdowne, all the more significant because they were not indicated in Crane's original copy, in so far as that can be judged from the Trinity manuscript. Because Crane's ministrations are intensive or incremental, most of the features mentioned may be seen again in the Malone manuscript, but before we look at that unique manuscript where Crane functions as an early Maxwell Perkins, it is instructive to examine a couple of well-known Crane features more generally.

Italicization: Middleton used his italian script quite infrequently in his share of the Trinity and Bridgewater manuscripts, reserving it for his title-pages, act headings and endings, and a single Latin phrase ('*Curanda pecunia*', Trinity 446). Consequently, the italicization of words in the texts of Archdall, Lansdowne and Malone was predominantly scribal. The possible influence of this feature on Folio texts printed from Crane manuscripts can be illustrated from Q3. The quarto contains 224

italicized words (excluding headings, speech-prefixes, stage-directions, and passages like the Latin oration), most of which are proper nouns. It would be easy to assume that the quarto compositor/s provided the italics. However, only sixteen of these are not italicized in Archdall and only another eight fail to be italicized in Lansdowne or Malone. Consequently, although many pages of Q3 lack italics, probably because of shortage of type, the italicized terms there are originally scribal rather than compositorial.[14] More interesting is Crane's use of italian script to mark off 'sentences' or sententious verses like his '(Experience is a doctrine medinall [i.e. medicinal]', *The Pilgrim's New Year's Gift* [1625], A2v). The only phrase to persist in italics throughout the Crane witnesses is '*Qui cauté, casté*' which the Black Knight identified as his 'motto' (Trinity 670; 2.1.171), but 'the Eare of state is quick and Iealous' (Trinity 461; 2.1.323) is indicated as a sentence by initial double quotation marks and italian script in Archdall and by the handwriting alone in Lansdowne and Malone. Also in italian in Lansdowne and Malone is Trinity's 'Fond men command, and wantons best obaye' (544; 2.1.64); and the second verse of the couplet that completes 1.1, 'wch path so ere thou takst thour't a lost Pawne' (Trinity 466; 1.1.328) is also written in italian in Lansdowne and Malone even though its sententious significance is not as strong as other verses not particularized in this manner.[15] The second verses of two other couplets are also written in italian script in Malone: 'Palme-oyle will make a Purseuant

---

67. Crane did not use such brackets in Ar. but there are five in Ln., four of which occur also in Q3.

[14] Q3 twice italicizes Crane's 'of' (A4v, G4v), an easy error; two other italicized Q3 words not italicized in Ar., Ln., or Ma. (Malone) are 'all' (G4v) and 'Epicidean' for 'Epicurean' (I2r).

[15] Crane seemed disposed to use italicization to mark the end of an act: the last verse of Act I in Ln. and Ma., the last verse of 2.2 in Ma., and the concluding couplet on 5.3 in Ln. (the last verse only in Ma.) are completely in italian script.

relent' (Trinity 1166; 3.1.98–9) and 'pawnes that are lost, are euer out of playe' (Trinity 1424; 3.1.308). These instances confirm G. K. Hunter's observation that 'gnomic pointing is not normally a part of the working text' but is added to presentation copies as to 'definitive editions to give an impression of scholarship and moral weight'.[16] In short, it is the product of editorial care and intention.

Couplet: Outside the Prologue, Epilogue, invocations and song, Middleton has thirty-five couplets in *A Game*, setting aside those which may occur unintentionally in any stretch of blank verse. For all but six couplets he used eye-rhymes,[17] adjusting the spelling of the rhymes so the unity of the couplet was readily perceptible.[18] The compositor/s of the quarto obscured the rhymes by varying the spelling in four cases but all but one of these are 'correct' in the Crane transcripts: the exception is Middleton's 'suffize/rize' (Trinity 2309–10; 5.3.98–9) which Crane rendered as 'suffise/rise' in Ar., but 'suffice' thereafter. In no other instance does Crane injure the eye-rhyme.[19] Even when he varies the spellings (e.g. Trinity 'confest/ unblest', Archdall 'confessed/vn-bless'd', 219–20, 1.1.106–7; Trinity 'Lawe-tost/crost', Lansdowne 'tosd/Crosd', 1588–9, 3.3.59–60), Crane is attentive to the desirability of preserving the rhyme.[20]

Parentheses: Crane's meticulous attention to the text is tellingly illustrated by his famous parentheses, banished from the recent Oxford *Complete Works* of Shakespeare (1986) as 'inappropriate to a dramatic text'.[21] Yet it has not hitherto been appreciated how deftly Crane used parentheses – at least in *A Game* – to indicate asides and changes of address from one character to another, supplying by parentheses editorial directions to readers for which no other means were available to him at the time. Some examples are instructive, the first where Crane preserves Middleton's intentions. In 1.1 the Black Knight's Pawn enters and in an aside comments on the Black Bishop's Pawn's likely corruption of the White Queen's Pawn

(1.1.208–19); he resolves to address her. Middleton's Trinity manuscript has parentheses around 'most noble Virgin' (Trinity 344), the start of a speech which is abruptly interrupted by the indignant female Pawn. Crane's later Lansdowne and Malone transcripts retain Middleton's parentheses, but in Archdall Crane instead left the speech open, without terminal punctuation.[22] In other instances, Crane substituted his parentheses for the dashes of the

16 'The Marking of Sententiae in Elizabethan Printed Plays, Poems, and Romances', *The Library*, 5, 6 (1951), 171–88; p. 179.

17 E.g. 'bee/Integritie' (Tr. 1250–1; 3.1.171–2), 'Sun/ Donne' (Tr. 1327–8; 3.1.233–4).

18 Crane 'improved' the spelling of three of the couplets: Middleton's 'drawen/Pawne'(Tr. 465–6; 1.1.327–8) becomes 'drawne' from Ar. onwards, in 'Feate/great' (Tr. 1989–90; 4.4.40–1) 'great' becomes 'greate' in Ln. and Ma., and in 'destroy/Ioye' (Tr. 2433–4; 5.3.218–19), 'Ioye' loses the terminal '-e' from Q3 onwards. Crane could do nothing with 'mee/companie' (Tr. 1425–6; 3.1.309–10) and 'see/dignitie' (Tr. 1995–6; 4.4.45–6) and did not avail himself of 'delite' in 'delight/White' (Tr. 1997–8; 4.4.47–8).

19 Middleton's 'waye/obaye' (Tr. 543–4; 2.1.63–4), 'obey' in Q3; 'men/agen' (Tr. 2000 + 71–2; 4.4.59–60), 'againe' in Q3; 'her/stir' (Tr. 2426–7; 5.3.202–3), 'stirre' in Q3.

20 In Tr. Middleton consistently used the spellings 'blessed/blest' for metrical purposes (Tr. 120, 319, 1304, 1772, 2000 + 40; 270, 1247, 1537, 1692, 1724; 220); his intentions are preserved in all Crane witnesses.

21 From Stanley Wells's editorial guidelines for the edition, quoted in Ann Thompson's 'Casting Sense between the Speech: Parentheses in the Oxford Shakespeare', paper circulated to the Seminar on the Oxford Shakespeares, Shakespeare Association of America, April 1990, p. 1.

22 This may not be significant because both Crane and Middleton not infrequently failed to terminate speeches. The Q3 compositor supplied a period. However, Crane would normally reproduce parentheses: 49 of Middleton's 52 parentheses in Tr. appear in the Crane witnesses. B–H preserves Middleton's parens, the Rosenbach manuscript and Q1 do not. At 1.1.287–9 the Black Knight has an aside unnoticed by modern editors; Middleton indicated his change of address to the Black Bishop's Pawn with an open paren before 'now Sir weere in private' (Tr. 418). Crane closed the parenthesis in his witnesses.

Trinity manuscript.[23] Of far greater editorial significance are eight asides which Crane identified by the insertion of parentheses where the Trinity manuscript had no distinguishing signs at all. Four are not marked in Q3 on which the early editors (Dyce and Bullen) based their text' but all modern editors mark 'Aside's at 3.1.177, 3.1.206, and 4.1.147–8, and elsewhere where Q3 and Crane transcripts agree in the use of parentheses: 2.1.156, 3.1.181–2 and 184–8. An aside at 4.1.130 marked first by a single paren in Malone was not picked up until the Brooke and Paradise edition of 1933 where a change of address is indicated somewhat ambiguously by an initial dash; Harper (New Mermaids, 1966) is the first editor to note the 'Aside'. An aside at 2.1.222–3 marked in Q3, Lansdowne and Malone was not adopted by modern editors: they apparently believed that the Black Knight would address the White King's Pawn, to whom he was promising rewards, directly with the comment 'And such a one had your corruption need of; | There's a state fig for you now.' Here, notably, whether or not he appreciated it, Crane marked an aside within an aside. Furthermore, Crane supplied parens in two other editorial situations. In Malone in the Epilogue spoken by the White Queen's Pawn the first couplet reads:

My Mistris (the White-Queene) hath sent me forth,
and bad me bowe (thus Lowe) to all of worth.

Here the parens seem designed to mark off a direction for action in the text. No editor has taken Crane's hint and provided a marginal stage-direction, and perhaps one is not strictly necessary or desirable. It will be interesting to learn whether the editor of the forthcoming Oxford *Middleton* will elect to use dashes for Crane's parentheses, following the general practice of the Oxford *Shakespeare*: 'and bad me bow – thus low –'to all of worth'. Finally, Middleton's gnomic interjection at Trinity 1660 – 'Knowledge is a Mastrie' – is furnished with parens in Archdall, followed by Q3. The phrase is intruded into the structure of the

speech and affords a characteristic example of George Puttenham's 'unnecessary parcel of speach'.[24] Nevertheless, one can wonder whether Crane intended by this means also to identify it as a sentence. In any event, the whole verse does not occur in Crane's Lansdowne or in Malone. A textual variation required to make the speech coherent after the omission strongly suggests that the omission was deliberate.[25]

Crane's use of elisions in order to regularize the metre of the texts he transcribed has been discussed in adequate detail already in *Ralph Crane* (pp. 43–54). Amplification here is unnecessary in order to show that in performing such operations, Crane consciously undertook editorial responsibilities. Nevertheless, his decision in Malone to indicate the omission of the verb from the second clause of 'This is the room he did appear to me in; | And look you, this the magical glass that showed him' (3.2.1–2) by the insertion of an apostrophe after 'this' may be mistaken, but it does illustrate his scrupulous attention to textual details in the service of comprehensibility. Crane's attention to metrical regularity and the methods he adopted to achieve it are not essentially different from those of most modern editors and they too, as a glance at the collations of modern editions of early plays confirms, are just as disposed to impose other kinds of consistency on texts. For instance, even though Middleton only occasionally used 'mine' or 'thine' for euphony when the following word began with a vowel

---

23 At 1.5.89 (1879), 93 (1884), 96–7, 98 (1888) where the Black Knight interjects his comments as he reads from the *Taxa Poenitentiaria*. Middleton did not employ dashes consistently here and some editing was necessary.

24 *The Art of English Poesy* (Menston, Scolar Press, 1968), p. 141.

25 Tr. reads: Bl.Qs.p.

> but tis in our power now
> to bring time neerer, Knowledge is a Mastrie, 1660
> and make it obserue vs, and not wee it:

Ln. and Ma. omit 1660 and have 'to' for 'and' at line 1661.

(e.g. Trinity 108, 547, 612, 652, 2181, 2386), Crane accepted all of Middleton's '-ine' spellings and, almost without exception, added to their number appropriately in his transcripts. His use of the morphological variants as hiatus breakers is seen advantageously in this line quoted from his Archdall transcript: 'with thine owne venom: thy prophaine lifes vomit' (Trinity 2175) where 'thine' – occurring only in Crane's Archdall, Q3 and Lansdowne – also reinforces Middleton's telling concentration of nasal sounds. But such regularizations are not so important for an editor of a text printed from a Crane transcript as other more far-reaching editorial activities Crane undertook.

For instance, the introduction and variation of elisions like 'I'm' or 'they're' was not the only means by which Crane sought to fit Middleton's often wayward verses to the Procrustean bed of metrical regularity. Collation of the *Game* witnesses reveals other instances in which Crane inserted and added words or phrases for the sake of the metre.[26] Of course, an indeterminable number of these may result from unconscious processes common in textual transmission, but other more complex variations suggest the range of Crane's influence on the verse of any work he transcribed. At 2.1.135 where Middleton wrote 'take heede I take not both, wch Iue | vowde since' (Trinity 626–7), Crane dropped 'since' and expanded the elision to 'I haue' so that the verse is a tidy iambic pentameter in Q3, Lansdowne and Malone. Again, at 3.1.229 Middleton's 'that startled his Attempt, and gave her libertie' (Trinity 1323) was a licentious hexameter that cried out for reformation. Crane simply altered 'his Attempt' to 'him' (Lansdowne, Malone) and all was well. A final instance is more informative about Crane's editorial mind-set because Middleton's 'I feele no tempest not a Leafe winde stirring' (4.2.38; Trinity 1823) could have been regularized simply by omitting the final extrametrical syllable. However, Crane revised the verse in Lansdowne to read 'I never feele a Tempest a Leaffe-wind'. It

has ten syllables but Middleton's verse is better.

Crane was disposed to get things right. A number of other variations in his witnesses are less readily classified but reveal his persistent reformist tendency. For instance, although on occasions he marked ellipsis with an apostrophe (as in 3.2.2 discussed on p. 120), sometimes he went so far as to supply the deleted item, even, in one instance, at the expense of metrical regularity.[27] Other 'improvements' have larger scope and significance even though it is not always possible to understand fully what benefits Crane sought in the particular event. At 1.1.321 Crane appears to have been troubled by Middleton's use of the active rather than the passive mood in his second pentameter (or the fact that it was a syllable short) in 'keepe all Supplies back both in meanes and men | that maye rayse agaynst you, wee must part' (Trinity 458–9) and inserted 'Strength' after 'rayse' in Q3, Lansdowne, Malone, and Rosenbach. Both sense and metre were improved without implicating the playwright.[28] At 2.1.163–4 the Black Bishop boasts 'this Act will fill the Aduersaries mouth | and blowe the Lutherans cheeke, tillt crack agen' (Trinity 661–2). The

---

[26] Insertions are 1.1.248 (Tr. 376) *Incendiarie? one*] ~ and ~ Ar., Q3, Ln., Ma., Rs.; 254 (Tr. 381) *haue*] I'haue Ar., Q3, Ln., Ma., Rs.; 303 (Tr. 437) *they*] they'ue, they'have Ar., Q3, Ln., Ma., Rs. Omissions occur at 1.1.97 (Tr. 208) *that*] om. Ln., Ma.; 240 (Tr. 366) *a*] om. Ln., Ma.; 2.2.45 (Tr. 807) *that*] om. Ln., (Ma.); 92–3 (Tr. 861) *I must confesse*] om. Q3; 263 (Tr. 1055) *why*] om. Ln., Ma.; 4.2.100 (Tr. 1890) *too*] om. Ar., Ln., Ma.; 4.4.17 (Tr. 1963) *a*] om. Ln., Ma.; 5.2.83 (Tr. 2149) *a*] om. Ar., Q3, Ln., Ma., Q1, Rs. (The occurrence of these features outside the Crane witnesses is explained by the stemma mentioned earlier.)

[27] 1.1.302 (Tr. 432 *think*] I ~ Q3, Ln., Ma.; 5.2.48 (Tr. 2107) *hope*] I ~ Q3, Ln., Ma., Q1.

[28] One might take the insertion of 'Strength' as an authorial revision entered in the early manuscript from which Rs. was made but the variant's absence from the other early witnesses besides its concentration in Crane witnesses (the verse does not occur in Ar.) tells against that. Also, there is some evidence that the source of Rs. was also in Crane's hand.

thought of just one of the Lutheran's cheeks being blown troubled Crane: Q3, Lansdowne and Malone read 'blow the Lutheran's cheek*s*, till *they* crack again'. There was another apparent difficulty at 2.2.64–5 where the Black Knight vows revenge against the Fat Bishop 'for the phisick hee provided | and the base Surgeon hee inuented for mee' (Trinity 830–1), perhaps in the current sense of 'invent' as 'to find'. For whatever reason, Crane revised the verbs so that in Lansdowne and Malone the physic is 'prescribed' and the surgeon 'provided'. However, at 4.1.147 there is a clearer basis for Crane's variation. At the end of the scene the Black Queen's Pawn announces her intention to deceive both the White Queen's Pawn and the Black Bishop's. Whereas Trinity has an exeunt for the three to go off immediately afterwards, the Black Queen's Pawn's final two verses presumably being spoken aside, modern editors provide the other two with an exeunt that allows the Black piece to linger on stage alone to proclaim her secret intention to the audience. Crane appears to have agreed with this staging. He noticed that when she announces 'Ile enioye the Sport and coozen you both' (Trinity 1781) the Black Queen's Pawn refers to characters whom she is not addressing and who are not on stage. Consequently, Lansdowne and Malone have 'cozen 'em' for 'coozen you'.[29]

It is often forgotten nowadays that the obligation to censor a text was taken – often tacitly – to be an important editorial responsibility. Editors of all periods willingly undertake to shield their tender readers from words and concepts from which they – hardened by long exposure to the very worst textual variations – escape unblemished. Crane was no exception. Middleton's text compelled him to pen repeatedly expressions which he found offensive but must leave intact. What he could alter he did, but not consistently and not in every witness. It is unnecessary to discuss the eleven instances of variations of oaths I have noticed in Crane witnesses but it is worth mentioning that

their distribution does not suggest that Crane was influenced by the 1606 Act to Restrain Abuses of Players against actors who 'jestingly or prophanely speake or use the holy Name of God or of Christ Jesus, or of the Holy Ghoste or of the Trinitie'.[30] Crane apparently did not approve of swearing of any kind.[31] He also shows a certain sensitivity to sexual and scatological references. The Jesting Pawn's scene (3.2.1–39; Trinity 1471–520) might have been omitted deliberately from Lansdowne and Malone, as I mentioned earlier, because Crane considered the scene unnecessary and to omit it would shorten his task, but to a modern eye at least the scene is full of sexual innuendo not likely to find approval from a pious Calvinistic scribe. He had in any event blunted Middleton's bawdy reference to 'penis' in 'they put theire pens the Hebrewe waye mee thinkes' (1.1.303; Trinity 437) by writing 'P'ees' in Archdall[32] and his Lansdowne transcript alone omits 'Priapus, Guardian of the Cherrie Gardens' (1.1.269; Trinity 396); this was a liberty that the syntax of the speech allowed him to take. A somewhat different sensibility is revealed by Crane's treatment of the Fat Bishop's penultimate speech at the end of the play. After the Black Knight is bagged, the Fat Bishop expostulates

---

[29] Similar variations are 2.2.12 (Tr. 483) *hah? a Seald Note, whence this?*] hah? what haue we here? a seald Note Q3; 4.1.35 (Tr. 1648) *oh my heart!*] 'tis he Ln., Ma.; and the omission of line 1660 discussed in note 25.

[30] E. K. Chambers, *The Elizabethan Stage*, 4 vols. (Oxford, 1923), vol. 4, p. 339.

[31] These expressions were omitted from the Crane witnesses: 1.1.208 (Tr. 333) *by this hand*] Ln., Ma.; 2.1.103 (Tr. 590) *blesse mee*] Ma.; 3.2.8 (Tr. 1482) *a pox on you*] Q3; 30 (Tr. 1508) *by this hand*] Q3, Q1; 36 (Tr. 1516) *masse*] Q3; 4.2.96 (Tr. 1886) *masse*] Q3, Ln., Ma.; 5.2.87 (Tr. 2156) *light*] Ar., Q3, Ln., Ma., Q1; 5.3.188 (Tr. 2408) *sfoote*] Q3, Ln. Three substitutions are: 2.1.198 (Tr. 706) *by this hand*] ~ ~ light Ar., Q3, Rs.; 5.2.84 (Tr. 2152) *a pox*] mischief Ar., Q3, Ln., Q1, Rs.; 5.2.116 (Tr. 2194) *Death*] how Q3, Ln., Ma.

[32] Richard Levin ('Dekker's Back-door'd Italian and Middleton's Hebrew Pen', *Notes and Queries*, 208 (1963), 338–40) provides the context of this line.

with the play's bluntest reference to Gondo-mar's renowned fistula:

foh, youre polititian is not sound ith Vent,
I smell him hether   (5.3.209–10; Trinity 2434–5)

The lines do not occur in Crane's Q3, Lans-downe, Malone, or in Q1 which depends on a Crane transcript hereabouts.[33]

Precedents for these kinds of alterations occur in Crane's transcript of *Sir John van Olden Barnavelt* (1619) and his more far-reaching re-formations may be studied in the variations between his *Demetrius and Enanthe* transcript (1625) and the printed text, *The Humorous Lieutenant* (1679). In *Barnavelt* Crane substituted 'a kind wench' for 'a fresh whore' (206) and deleted 'upon my soule' (2425), apparently un-prompted by the censor.[34] In the Fletcher play the situation is somewhat complicated in that the manuscript and the Folio text show differ-ent patterns of suppression of oaths. Crane avoided using 'pox', 'death', 'God', and 'plague' where Folio prints the expressions, but the Folio was less tolerant of 'heaven' than the scribe.[35] Nevertheless, *Demetrius and Enanthe* omits five of the oaths that the Folio prints[36] and substitutes weaker expressions for ten others.[37] As example, where the Folio reads 'O God, my head', Crane's manuscript has 'oh, my head: my head': (3.2.69) and for the Folio's repetition of 'God a mercy' at 3.3.81–2 Crane substitutes repeated 'I thanck thee's as he would do later at 5.2.22, 30. On the other hand, there are another twenty-nine oaths or similar expressions that the manuscript and printed texts share: Crane was never quite so consistent as we sometimes might wish him to have been.[38]

But all this is small beer compared to the scope of Crane's activities in his Malone manu-script. Here Crane skilfully reduced the text of *A Game* in Trinity by about 787 lines, thus producing a unique version of the play to which the nearest analogue is the Dering ver-sion of *Henry IV*.[39] There is no more substantial evidence that Middleton had anything to do

with the condensation of the play than the bald fact that later Middleton inserted his holograph dedication to his friend William Hammond into the completed transcript. This is ambi-valent for Middleton's involvement with the

33 The failure of 'Venerie!' (5.3.125; Tr. 2340) to appear in Ar. probably identifies it as a late revision that was not entered in Crane's copy. The phrase 'the gelder & the gelded' (1.1.206; Tr. 330) was added to Ar. by another hand, and a related revision, 'but none for Gelding' (4.2.128; Tr. 1923), was not incorporated. – The varia-tion 1.1.219 (Tr. 344) *Virgin*] Lady Ma. may not be significant in this context.

34 The line references are to the Malone Society edition (1980); see also T. H. Howard-Hill, 'Buc and the Cen-sorship of *Sir John Van Olden Barnavelt* in 1619', *Review of English Studies*, 39 (1988), 39–63, pp. 51, 62.

35 Philip Oxley (ed., *A Critical-Edition of John Fletcher's 'The Humorous Lieutenant'* (New York, 1987)) suggests that as 1625 was a plague year, Fletcher himself dying of it, 'Crane or someone with access to his copy evidently saw fit to expunge the terrible word' (p. 14). References to plague occur in the Folio but not the manuscript at 2.2.91, 2.3.8, 2.4.172, 3.3.69, 4.4.88, 128 (Hoy's line-ation). Crane himself composed the dedication to Sir Kenelm Digby in which he hopes that it 'will not be much in oportune, after a season so sad, to present you with a Matter *Recreatiue*'. Fletcher was dead and Crane wrote on his own behalf. He therefore was the most likely to have altered the text to avoid remembrance of the past sad season.

36 1.1.51 'Death, 53 [what] a devill, 2.2.85 Pox upon it, 3.3.86 Pox take thee, and 3.5.23 'Life.

37 1.2.65 F *Pox*] fye; 2.2.23 F *'Death*] sure; 2.4.13 F *by this hand*] by heaven; 111 F *'death*] 'pray; 3.2.21 F *a Pox*] out; 4.4.17 *By—he's*] beware he's; 4.4.8 F *By this hand*] by thy leave; 5.1.24 *Od's precious*] 's' pretious; 5.2.22, 30 F *God a mercy*] I thank thee.

38 At 1.1.36, 230, 359; 2.2.19, 69, 84, 2.5.96, 110; 3.2.3, 33, 51, 63; 3.3.10; 3.5.34; 4.1.57; 4.2.36, 50, 123; 4.4.13, 69, 90; 4.5.24; 4.8.2, 31, 84; 5.1.3; 5.3.34, 67, 79. It should be clear that my earlier view that there was no evidence that Crane would have reformed offensive language 'on his own initiative' (*Ralph Crane*, p. 135) was wrong. Nevertheless, his attention was intermittent rather than consistent. The distribution of his 'reformations' in his witnesses demonstrates clearly that he did not purge his copy (the source of Ar., particularly) before transcribing it.

39 '*The History of King Henry the Fourth*' *as Revised by Sir Edward Dering, Bart*, ed. G. W. Williams and G. B. Evans, 1973.

textual process which produced the Malone manuscript. He may indeed have marked up the manuscript from which Crane copied Malone but there is no indication that he did, and the quality of the omitted material suggests Crane's sensibility rather than Middleton's. Besides the reduction of the offensive material previously mentioned, the Malone version deals quite summarily with the gelding of the White Bishop's Pawn: Crane seems to have seized this opportunity to purge the play of material he had found offensive but essential in earlier transcripts.[40] However, the single editorial virtue Crane lacked was consistency and, as with the oaths of *Demetrius* so with similar items in Malone: some instances are purged, others are not. Besides deletions and the skilful splicing together of half-verses, Malone shows Crane in a more inventive capacity, writing transitional textual adjustments and occasional phrases to compensate for deletions.[41] Clearly in preparing the contracted version of the play Crane went far beyond the usual scope of editorial activity and it simply isn't possible any longer to regard him merely as a scrivener who copied texts mechanically for a fee. However, the authority he exerted over Middleton's play in the Malone manuscript was not that of a rebellious hireling; rather, Crane appropriated the play to edit in accordance with his own principles but with considerable attention to the *gestalt* of the work. We cannot doubt that Crane would have thought that his version was superior to Middleton's: shorter, less trivial, less bawdy, in fact, a play rendered more powerful by condensation. In short, the Malone version shows the application of a literary intelligence to familiar material. While it demonstrates the scope of Crane's interaction with texts in 1624, it also points the way to his historically attested development as a literary scribe.

For a few months in 1624 Crane was engaged in editing the raw material of Middleton's dramatic manuscripts into finished literary texts designed to allow readers to create freshly a performance of the play in the theatre of their imagination.[42] Crane imposed a decorum on his copy that was physical in details of display, arrangement and ornamentation, textual in its marking of emphasis and subordination by the use of italics and parentheses, and persistently reformative by means of the indication of metrical values and their adjustment, emendation of the text, and attention to matters which might be distressing to readers. If not consistent, Crane was attentive to the meaning of the texts he transcribed and exercised a responsibility to transmit a meaningful text. In brief, when working on Middleton's *A Game* he functioned as an editor.

CRANE AND THE KING'S MEN

But all this happened in 1624 while the First Folio was already on the bookstalls, and besides, Crane wrote his copies of *A Game* for the playwright, not the company which had performed the play in August. In all the *Game* witnesses and documents nothing proves or even strongly suggests that Crane prepared or saw a theatrical document or ever saw the play performed. It would be surprising if he hadn't, indeed, but no feature of his transcripts indicates the intrusion of experience of performance into his literary transcripts.[43] Nevertheless,

---

40 Nascimento (pp. 47–9) gives a concise description of the abbreviated text. A notable exclusion is the speech of the White King condemning his traitorous Pawn (3.1.263–76; Tr. 1369–82) which contained a crucial passage of the 'Middlesex' revision. The playwright is unlikely to have deleted such topical material himself but Crane, like most later readers, could well have failed to recognize its significance.

41 When Tr. 786–94 of the Fat Bishop's soliloquy in 2.2. were cut, Crane inserted 'But' before Tr. 795 (2.2.33) for a smooth transition. Note also 2.1.179 (Tr. 681) *I haue don't then]* Be it thus then Ma.; 2.2.17 (Tr. 778) *Distribute 'mongst the white house]* Goe, be gon Ma.; 4.5.15 (Tr. 2000 + 19)] there is no remedie Ma.

42 In this respect Crane was more enlightened than succeeding editors: he never attempted to supply additional indications of scene locations.

43 The discovery of the Black House at 5.3.160–1 (Tr. 2379–80) is marked uniquely by 'A great shout and

we can ask what was his relationship with the King's Men through the period in which he transcribed *Barnavelt* and the copies for the First Folio plays associated with him. In particular, we seek information that would put him with the company during the compilation of the Folio, eligible for the editorial function I suggest was his.

Crane's first dramatic transcript, a copy of Jonson's *Pleasure Reconciled to Virtue* (1618), seems to have been privately commissioned by the playwright; there is no connection between the masque and the King's Men. Nevertheless, his next literary work shows him working closely with the company. Crane's transcript of the King's Men's play *Sir John van Olden Barnavelt* was written between 17 May 1619, when the first account of Oldenbarnevelt's execution was licensed for publication, and around 14 August when the Bishop of London was reported to have stayed the first performance.[44] The interesting characteristics of this manuscript having been described in some detail elsewhere, we need make only two broad observations here. First, Crane was obviously not the company's book-keeper, stage-keeper or prompter; that is, he was not a functionary of the theatre charged to bring an authorial text to performance on the stage. Crane's manuscript is quite copiously annotated with directions for production in another hand but even though Crane wrote some similar directions, the playhouse annotations and therefore the responsibility of preparation for performance were not his. Second, on the other hand, neither of the two collaborators, Fletcher and Massinger, left a trace of his presence in the manuscript. *Barnavelt* is one of the most heavily censored extant dramatic manuscripts of the age and it was substantially revised and then passages of the text rewritten by the scribe. Nevertheless, none of the consequential textual adjustments whether more or less extensive is in the hand of either of the playwrights. It is as if they had abandoned their composition to the playhouse scribe. Indeed, Crane's rôle is doubly

anomalous. It is usually assumed that after playwrights had submitted their plays to the players it was the company that sought the Master of the Revels' licence for performance. Yet analysis of the book-keeper's markings in the manuscript shows absolutely clearly that – in this instance at least – he was not at all involved in fitting the text to the censor's demands: his concerns were exclusively theatrical. Crane then appears to have represented both the authors and the company in dealing with the Master of the Revels. Such a rôle indicates the confidence they had in him and testifies to his competence.

We need also to recall that by 1619 Crane had lived a long full life. His biography is versified in the preface to his *The Works of Mercy* (1621)[45] and amplified in the induction to the revised edition, *The Pilgrim's New Year's Gift* (1625?) where he mentions his 'almost seventie yeares' (p. 1). This would make him about sixty-three years old when he worked on *Barnavelt*, two or three years short of seventy when the First Folio was published. When we review Crane's activities during the crucial 1619–23 period we need to remember both that he was a mature, widely experienced scribe and too, that – as he documents repeatedly in his own writings – his powers were failing; he was falling into the unhappy condition of anyone who survives too long in a society that does not provide for the aged.

The amount and extent of the work Crane did for the King's Men is obscure. Many plays

---

flourish' in Q1, a direction likely to reflect performance, but that seems to have occurred after Crane's influence (through the copy of Q3) was exerted on the last part of Q1.

44 T. H. Howard-Hill, 'Crane's 1619 "Promptbook" of *Barnavelt* and Theatrical Processes', *Modern Philology*, 86 (1988), 146–70, p. 147.

45 The Stationers' Register entry of *The Works* on 14 December 1620 attributes the work to 'T.M'. but this is demonstrably incorrect. It does however suggest that Crane knew Middleton by 1620; he may have helped Crane find a publisher for his poem.

from this era have not survived at all, and he may have done work on other plays that the circumstances of printing do not allow us to identify. A broad chronology is this. He completed *Barnavelt* by August 1619. Another play around this date associated with Crane is Fletcher and Massinger's *The False One* which is dated '*c.* 1619 or 1620' (Bentley 3: 340) mainly from its inclusion in a list of plays apparently being considered by the Master of Revels for performance at court. However, because it lacks distinctive signs of adaptation for staging, it is likely that this Crane transcript comes from a later phase of his scribal activity (see p. 128).[46] On 14 December, 1620 his *The Works of Mercy* was entered in the Stationers' Register. There Crane wrote that '*some imployment hath my vsefull Pen | Had 'mongst*' (A6r) the King's Men. The perfective aspect of the verb suggests that the service had not ceased; the whole poem is a retrospective biography in the past tense and this was its last episode. The reference is frustratingly vague and does not claim very much. If we take 'some' and ''mongst' literally, he was a casual employee brought in for specific scribal tasks, an intermediary between (and for) playwrights and the company, as *Barnavelt* indicates. It is significant perhaps that many of the 'theatrical' (as distinguished from 'authorial' or 'literary') transcripts with which he is associated are of collaborative works: Fletcher and Massinger's *Barnavelt*, *The Prophetess*, *The Spanish Curate*, and Fletcher and Rowley's *The Maid in the Mill*. These are also the texts which testify to his direct association with the theatre.

Some time in 1621, if the usual dating and attribution of Middleton's *Women Beware Women* to the King's Men is correct, Crane worked on that play. J. R. Mulryne notes a number of distinctive stage-directions that suggest that the printer's copy for Humphrey Moseley's 1657 edition 'may have been lightly marked by a theatre-official',[47] providing a manuscript similar to Crane's transcript of *Barnavelt* in its theatrical features. Crane's influence on the edition is indicated by the high

frequency of parentheses by comparison with other Middleton plays Thomas Newcomb printed for Moseley, some distinctive spellings, and other details of arrangement and typography (Mulryne, p. xxvi). Nothing in the edition suggests that it was set up from a later transcript prepared for readers; the little evidence of the theatrical provenance that exists places *Women Beware Women* around 1621 in Crane's chronology – if, indeed, he had anything to do with it.

Around the beginning of February 1622, the printing of the First Folio began. Most if not all of the transcripts Crane made for the Folio

---

46 R. C. Bald (*Bibliographical Studies in the Beaumont & Fletcher Folio of 1647* [Oxford, 1938]) includes *The False One* in a list of plays 'in which it has not been possible to find any directions which suggest, even remotely, the specific influence of the prompter' (pp. 109–10). Even had Crane made a fair copy of the play because it was a collaborative work, it is difficult to see either that it would not have been used in the theatre or would have escaped unmarked. Cyrus Hoy ('The Shares of Fletcher and his Collaborators in the Beaumont and Fletcher Canon, IV', *Studies in Bibliography*, 12 [1959], 91–116, pp. 97–8) attributes copy for Fletcher and Field's *Four Plays in One* (1612?) and Fletcher, Massinger and Field's *The Knight of Malta* (*c.* 1616–18) to Crane solely on the evidence of vocative parentheses. In 'Ralph Crane's Parentheses', *Notes & Queries*, 210 (1965), 334–40, I argued that the attributions are not supported by the frequency and distribution of parentheses in those texts, especially as the influence of the Beaumont and Fletcher Folio compositors was not examined. Besides, the high frequency of *non*-vocative parentheses is a surer indication of possible Crane transcription. In any event, *Four Plays* is too early for Crane to have encountered it in the theatre; the company which presented it is not known. *The Knight of Malta* bears signs of preparation for the stage but again is probably too early for Crane to have written the transcript for use in the theatre. There is no need to include these two plays here as even if their copy was written by Crane, their inclusion in the chronology merely amplifies the conclusions that may be reached from securer evidence rather than supports fresh conclusions. I have found no conclusive and few suggestive signs of Crane in them.

47 *Women Beware Women: Thomas Middleton*, ed. J. R. Mulryne. The Revels Plays (Manchester, 1975), pp. xxiv–xxvi.

must have been completed before then, probably by the end of 1621. Later in April he wrote out a short invention for Edward Barkham's mayoral banquet, *A Song in Several Parts*, for Middleton: this was a private commission having no connection with the company. Then Crane seems to have undertaken a series of transcripts of collaborative plays, all of which bear stage-directions apparently added by the King's book-keeper (Bald, pp. 104–9). They are Fletcher and Massinger's *The Prophetess*, licensed for acting on 14 May 1622, their *The Spanish Curate*, acted on 24 October, and Fletcher and Rowley's *The Maid in the Mill*, licensed on 29 August 1623. According to Hinman the printing of the First Folio was completed early in November 1623.[48] This date probably marks the furthest limit of Crane's connection with the company, distinct from the individual playwrights who wrote for it. None of his later work has the distinguishing characteristics of *Barnavelt*, for instance, or indicates a necessary connection with the company as the transcripts he made for the Folio do.

His next transcript was, like his Folio manuscripts, specifically commissioned for publication. Webster's *The Duchess of Malfi* (1614), published in 1623 and apparently lying between the Folio and the transcripts of Middleton's *Game* already examined, gives the first clear witness of how Crane went about his task when he knew that his work would have a general readership. Middleton contributed a commendatory poem to the first edition of Webster's revised play and it was possibly through Middleton's introduction that Crane was commissioned to prepare the printer's copy. Besides the common signs of Crane's influence (punctuation, parentheses, hyphenation, use of italics), the quarto has an unexampled number of sentences distinguished by the use of italic type or introductory speech marks (instances on N1r and N4r have both) in fifteen places. In Webster's edition also is the exceptional manifestation of the influence of the Jonson Folio on both scribe and playwright, the 'massed entries'

ostensibly constructed in imitation of the classical form of scene division Jonson had adopted in 1616. The mystery of Crane's 'massed entries' and, particularly, exposition of the variations of his practice, is a large topic that requires separate discussion. Nevertheless, one observation needs emphasis. The adoption of any style of classical scene division, whether Jonson's adaptation of the system of the Latin comedians or Crane's hybrid synthesis of the classical and native conventions, is essentially non-theatrical. The listing of characters who are to appear in a scene together in the initial entrance stage-direction, with the omission of internal entrances and exits and other descriptive stage-directions, produces a text which could not be used in a theatre as a script for the direction of performances. It is difficult to conceive that a playwright would allow a play to be presented even to readers in so unilluminating a garb, yet, from the instance of Jonson and the fact that Webster appears to have added stage-directions in proof to *The Duchess of Malfi*, without altering the basic structure of the initial entries, it appears that playwrights with literary ambitions admitted the concept of classical decorum in the arrangement of dramatic works presented to readers.[49]

The significance of *The Duchess of Malfi* for Crane's participation in the editing of the First Folio is evident. Crane employed 'massed entrances' for three of his Shakespearian transcripts: *The Two Gentlemen of Verona*, *The Merry Wives of Windsor*, and *The Winter's Tale*. The last of these, according to Hinman, was

---

[48] Charlton Hinman, *The Printing and Proof-Reading of the First Folio of Shakespeare*, 2 vols. (Oxford, 1963), vol. 1, p. 362.

[49] J. R. Brown, 'The Printing of John Webster's Plays (III): *The Duchess of Malfi*', *Studies in Bibliography*, 16 (1962), 57–69, pp. 64–7. However, the internal entrances and descriptive stage-directions that Webster added, according to Brown, do indicate that Webster thought that Crane's austere 'classical' method left the reader substantially at a loss to determine what happened within scenes.

printed in December 1622. Even though Webster's quarto was dated 1623, it could have been printed earlier and post-dated to anticipate the new year, and so its copy written a little earlier. It is possible, then, that the copy for *The Duchess of Malfi* and Crane's Shakespearian texts with 'massed entrances' were prepared within a fairly short span, i.e. from before the Folio printing began in February 1622 to around December 1623. Indeed, when we consider that *The Winter's Tale* was delayed in printing (Hinman I: 357), it is possible to conjecture that Crane wrote out copy for that play *after* he had finished Webster's. We can be certain about none of this, of course. Nevertheless, it seems quite clear that Crane's transcripts of Webster's and Shakespeare's plays are closely connected. In fact, in the light of present knowledge of his activities, the earliest of the First Folio transcripts was Crane's first play prepared for publication. These texts were literary by design not accident. Crane had been commissioned to get the copy for the Folio together, transcribing from copies whenever necessary.[50] With publication in mind, he wrote his copies on the best literary model available to him, Jonson's 1616 Folio.

CRANE'S LATER CAREER

But something went wrong. In 1624 Crane was working for Middleton not the King's Men. His connection with the company appears to have been severed during the printing of the Folio in 1623. All of his transcripts that can be identified are in the comedies section.[51] Possibly he was too old and slow to keep pace with the printer's need for copy. In any event, in 1624–5 he worked on *The Witch* and *A Game at Chess* for Middleton, his client of longest standing. The scene darkened in March 1625 with James's death, the closing of the theatres, and a virulent outbreak of the plague which carried away another client, John Fletcher, at the end of August. Within a short time (on 27 November) Crane had – for the first time – appropriated a

literary work for his own benefit: Fletcher's *Demetrius and Enanthe* bears his, not the playwright's, dedication to a patron.[52] Thenceforth, he copied no plays, but wrote poetical and prose manuscripts for presentation to patrons

---

[50] *The Tempest* and *Measure for Measure* may lack the literary 'massed entries' simply because Crane had earlier made transcripts of these plays for the theatre.

[51] E. S. Donno, ed., *Twelfth Night or What you Will*, New Cambridge Shakespeare (Cambridge, 1985) finds many of Crane's characteristics in *TN*, whereas Gary Taylor (*A Textual Companion*, p. 604) assigns the copy for Folio *Cymbeline* to his pen. These attributions, like those of the Fletcher plays, need more detailed examination. I have made only two tests. In proportion of sets of parentheses to Folio lines, a rough but consistent measure, *TN* with parentheses every 85.97 lines is even less heavily parenthesized than *Cor.* (66.17) (which is definitely not a Crane text) and twice as less heavily parenthesized than the nearest Crane text, *MM* (40.25). *Cym.*'s proportion at 24.79, however, is close to that of *Tmp.* (23.88) and the *Game* Archdall manuscript (21.21). It is also worth noting in the general context that the Folio texts with the highest proportion of parentheses to lines are the rigorously edited texts with 'massed entrances', *WT* (4.78), *Wiv.* (12.57) and *TGV* (18.24). The second test examined the frequency of hyphenated-prefixes in words beginning with 'a, ante, be, de, dis, en, enter, for(e), in, ore, ont, over, re, un, under, up', a good indication of Crane's influence. The results arranged his *Game* manuscripts in order of transcription. The proportion of hyphenated-prefixes to Folio lines in the Crane-copy Folio texts and *Cym.*, *TN*, *Cor.* and *Ant.* places *Cym.* third (i.e. amongst the Crane-copy comedies); *TN* has the least proportion by a significant margin.

Either to include or exclude *Cym.* and *TN* in the chronology does not greatly affect the argument. For *Cym.* however, we could remark that its late printing sheds no light on when Crane could have written the copy, since *Cym.* was apparently always to be reserved for the 'Tragedies' section of the Folio; the copy may have been written as early as 1621.

[52] Fletcher and Massinger's *The False One*, which Bald (p. 110) includes amongst plays apparently printed from private transcripts, must belong to this stage of Crane's career, together with any other of the Fletcherian transcripts that are not clearly theatrical manuscripts. Notwithstanding, it is not clear how Crane could have got access to playwrights' manuscripts to copy for his own use.

(or sale, which amounted to the same thing) until age overtook him around 1632.

Setting aside the repetitive 'humble petitions' to patrons prefixed to some of his collections of poetry, the best source of information about Crane's biography is the enlarged edition of *The Works of Mercy* (1621), revised and printed, perhaps late in 1625 under the title *The Pilgrim's New Year's Gift* (*STC* 5987). Here Crane repeats the earlier acknowledgement of his employment amongst the King's Players. However, although in the revised edition he expanded his tributes to those who had helped him during his pilgrimage 'Through *City, Countrie, Court, Church, Law*' (p. 11), he adds not a word about his work for the stage. He does, however, elsewhere describe his condition in 1625–6. Amplifying his earlier contention that his 'one blest gift (*a ready writers pen*' was not extinguished, despite his age, he goes on:

'Tis not extinct indeed: But yet (alas)
It's a cas'd Instrument, no sound it has:
Time hath worne out (with Teares I strike this
    straine)
Beliefe of what I can: now *young ones* raigne,
Whil'st I (too old to cry about the street
Worke for a Writer) no *Imployement* meet,
But all dismayed, and dis-ioyfull sit
As one had neither *Pen*, nor *Hand*, nor *Wit*:   (p. 3)

He says clearly that increasing age had cast doubt on his ability to meet the obligations of employment so that he can no longer find work for his pen. The addition of these lines in 1625 suggests that the association with the King's Men he had recorded in 1621 had come to an end, on account of his age. In short, the stage was the last way-station in Crane's life's pilgrimage, in 1625 as in 1621.

During the eight years Crane wrote for the stage (1617–25) his function altered from that of a simple amanuensis to that of a responsible servant of the players. He became entrusted with the preparation of copy for the company's great monument to their craft, lost that employment and, by then an experienced literary scribe, for a time undertook commissions for individual playwrights. Finally, when even commissions had fallen off, he wrote solely for his own gain, at first dramatic works, later poetry and prose, works self-consciously prepared for readers according to the editorial principles of the period. No part of his activity is so important for us as his involvement with *Mr William Shakespeare's Comedies Histories, and Tragedies*, one of the greatest editions of dramatic works ever assembled. When we regret how much evidence of the stage was lost from Crane's transcripts as he prepared them for printing, we must also recognize his assiduity in supplying, according to good models, the best texts for the best readers. Fully to identify the effects of his ministrations, many of which are unalterable, requires close and patient study. This paper was not intended to reveal the full extent of Crane's influence on the transmission of Shakespeare's text but rather to give some new information of his practices when he prepared reading texts. Nevertheless, we should recognize that his involvement with the First Folio was so extensive and of such a kind that it is Ralph Crane rather than the playwright Nicholas Rowe whom we should acknowledge as the first person to confront the problems of translating Shakespeare's plays from the stage to the study: Shakespeare's earliest editor.

SHAKESPEARE'S FALCONRY

MAURICE POPE

Talking of hawking – nothing else, my lord.
2 Henry VI 2.1.49

There are two questions I shall try to answer. One is the nature of Shakespeare's knowledge of falconry and whether it can be shown to be based on personal experience. The other is the interpretation of a passage about the haggard falcon in *Twelfth Night* that seems to have been misunderstood by all editors and commentators from Dr Johnson onwards.

First the general topic.[1] It is the common opinion of the few people who have a good knowledge of both falconry and Shakespeare that Shakespeare spoke on the subject from experience, probably picked up in his youth.[2] But for the most part this opinion is presented as a matter of feeling not of demonstration. It is therefore sterile. Nothing can be built on it and it does not offer any technique or method for solving similar problems. But if there were a way of proving it or even of finding objective criteria of assessment, then it would clearly become much more valuable.

Let us begin with the most undebatable point – the frequency with which Shakespeare refers to hawking in comparison with his contemporaries. In Shakespeare there are over fifty mentions. In Kyd, Greene, Marlowe, and Fletcher (except for his sequel to *The Taming of the Shrew*) there are practically none.[3] The same is true of Sidney. Even Herbert who was presumably born to the sport and Ben Jonson who had decided views on it mention hawks and

hawking on only a handful of occasions. This is in itself rather surprising when there is so much about it that is so dramatic – the soaring of the falcon, the idea of a man in command of a bird circling (or 'towering') anything up to five hundred feet over his head, the sudden stoop that can reach a speed of over 200 mph, and the knock-out blow that it delivers with its talons.[4]

---

[1] The basic books for Shakespeare's knowledge of birds and of field sports remain those by James Edward Harting, *The Ornithology of Shakespeare* (London, 1871) and D. H. Madden, *The Diary of Master William Silence: A Study of Shakespeare and of Elizabethan Sport* (London, 1897). G. Lascelles, *Falconry* (London, 1892) and T. R. Henn, *The Living Image: Shakespearian Essays* (London, 1972) discuss many of the falconry passages. The most up-to-date and authoritative English book on falconry in general is by Phillip Glasier, *Falconry and Hawking* (London, 1978, 1986); on the peregrine falcon itself by Derek Ratcliffe, *The Peregrine Falcon* (Calton, 1980). Stephen Bodio, *A Rage for Falcons* (New York, 1984) gives a lively picture of modern American falconry emancipated from the historical traditions which in his view constrain the sport in Britain.

[2] For instance D. H. Madden, *A Chapter of Medieval History: The Fathers of the Literature of Field Sport and Horses* (London, 1924), p. 220; Henn, pp. 5 and 21.

[3] The closest Marlowe comes to a falconry allusion is in *Edward II* 873–4 where Edward threatens his nobles 'soar ye ne'er so high / I have the gesses that will pull you down'. But it does not quite qualify. The nobles are being compared to eagles, not hawks, and the picture of them taking off from tree-tops while still on their creances is an impossible one.

[4] Falcons generally kill by stooping from a height and knocking out the quarry with their talons, though on occasion they may seize it instead and kill it with a bite in

Yet the only other English poet of the period who makes much use of falcons is Spenser. He refers to them in some twenty-five passages, which since his *oeuvre* is about half the length of Shakespeare's means that he gives them the same degree of prominence.

But this is where the similarity ends. The romantic enthusiasm of Spenser's descriptions is quite unlike Shakespeare, and so is the limited number of rôles that his hawks play. They are mainly mentioned for their performance in flight, especially for the stoop, though the most stunning example concerns an eagle, not a hawk:

> As when Jove's harnesse-bearing Bird from hie
> Stoupes at a flying heron with proud disdaine,
> The stone-dead quarrey fals so forciblie,
> That it rebounds against the lowly plaine,
> A second fall redoubling back againe.
>
> (*Faerie Queene* 2.11.43.1–5)

The bouncing of the heron is the point of the simile, but whether it was taken from an incident that Spenser had seen for himself or from a falconer's story we cannot tell.

Another simile compares the elation felt by the Red Cross Knight when he wakes up magically refreshed for his next bout with the Dragon to the first flight of a young hawk:

> Like Eyas hauke up mounts unto the skies
> His newly budded pineons to assay.
> And marveiles at himselfe, still as he flies:
> So now this new-borne knight to battell new
>   did rise.   (1.11.34.6–9)

In an equally vigorous simile the point is moral as well as visual. Arthur, having been forced to give ground, returns to the attack

>   as a Faulcon faire
> That once hath failed of her souse full neare
> Remounts againe into the open aire,
> And unto better fortune doth her selfe prepare.
>
>   (2.11.36.6–9)

Not only are Spenser's hawks nearly always flying but they are nearly always long-winged hawks, that is to say the kind that like to stoop rather than fly at quarry direct from the fist. In fact the only hawk of the short-winged variety that he mentions is the goshawk, and both references – there are only two – are unflattering. They describe how she drops her prey when spied by an eagle.[5]

The plight of the quarry occasionally attracts Spenser's attention, but he does not usually show much sympathy for it. The fowl may be fearful and go into hiding or it may be too vain even to look after its own 'silly life'. On the other hand the heron, being the noblest of quarry, may defend itself successfully, and a haggard, being (for Spenser) an ignoble hawk may lose against a 'hardy fowle'.[6]

The only thing apart from their skills in flying and fighting that Spenser mentions hawks for is their superior position in the hierarchy of nature. For instance when Calidore strayed into a utopian 'wood of matchless hight' inferior birds were singing in the lower branches of the trees

> And in their tops the soring hauke did towre,
> Sitting like King of Fowles in maiesty and powre.
>
>   (6.10.6.8–9)

In the 'antique age' the dove is said to have 'sat by the Faulcon's side' just as the lamb lay down with the lion. Equally expressive of the falcon's innate superiority is a simile where Artegall is compared to 'a gentle Faulcon sitting on a hill' suffering from a damaged wing that has been seen by a puttock (that is to say a kite). It is described as being irritatingly though vainly harried by the 'foolish' bird led by its 'licentious will'.[7]

---

the nape of the neck. Speeds of 170 mph are said to have been measured in a stoop of 30°, and of 220 mph in stoops of 45°. In a vertical stoop they will presumably travel even faster. Flying level a peregrine's normal maximum is 60 mph. See Glasier, p. 20; Ratcliffe, pp. 153–4.

[5] *Faerie Queene* 3.7.39.1; 5.4.42.4.

[6] *Faerie Queene* 1.11.19.5; 2.3.36.2; 3.8.33.4; 5.2.54.1; 6.7.9.1ff.

[7] *Faerie Queene* 5.5.15.2.

In fact it is Spenser's unvarying assumption that the hawk is a king among birds, so much so that its study (along with that of the chase) is *par excellence* fit for kings. Tristram, an exiled prince, claims not to have wasted his youth because he had employed the time in this way (6.2.32.1–4). What is more, its social standing is such that no bad character, witch or dragon, is ever compared to one (never, that is to say to a 'falcon gentle', though once, in *Faerie Queene* 1.11.19.5, such a comparison is made to a haggard).[8]

But for all their honourable status and aerobatic powers Spenser's falcons live an exceedingly narrow life. He never shows them mating, building nests, or laying eggs. Though he describes them as wearing bells and jesses, he never shows them being caught or trained, coming to fist or being flown at quarry. We never hear a falconer's hallo. In fact Spenser never mentions falconers at all and seems to have had no interest in the human side of hawking.

With Ben Jonson it is the opposite. His concern is with the social institution, with the people not the hawks. In a poem paraphrasing Horace (*Underwood* 44.70ff.) he makes a party of young aristocrats say

> What need we know
> More than to praise a Dog? or Horse? or speake
> The Hawking language?

Every Man in his Humour opens with the scene of a young heir buying a falcon and looking for a book to tell him what to do next because unless a man can hawk 'he is no gentleman's company'. Writing in his own person to Sir Henry Goodyere (*Epigram* 85), who had taken him out for a day's hawking, Jonson compares the falcon swooping down on its quarry to a philosopher who has detected a fallacy, draws, as Spenser had done, the moral of 'try, try again' from the way in which the falcon if it misses the first time immediately regains height in order to make a second attack, and declares that he can at last understand why gentlemen

spend so much time on what had previously appeared to him a profitless pursuit.[9]

It is clear from what we have been saying that there was no current orthodoxy about hawking. Ben Jonson and Spenser reacted quite differently from each other and quite differently from the silent majority of literary men who virtually ignored the subject.

And when we turn to Shakespeare we find that he is as different again. His attitudes to the social side of falconry, in so far as he displays any, are in marked contrast with those of Ben Jonson. He certainly knew it as a sport for gentlemen – in *Sonnet* 91 hawks, hounds and horse are listed alongside birth, skill, wealth, strength, and fine clothes, in *Henry VI* Warwick brackets hawks with other concerns of the nobility like dogs, swords, and horses (*1 Henry VI* 2.4.11–14) – but his hawks transcend class barriers. Quite lowly characters possess them and talk about them. In *The Merry Wives of Windsor* Page has 'a fine hawk for the bush' and Ford accompanies him 'a-birding', while Mrs Ford affectionately calls Robin her 'eyas-musket' (fledgling sparrowhawk).[10] In *Hamlet*

---

8 The Lady in *Faerie Queene* 3.4.49.6 who flees like 'fearful dove' from 'tassel gent' is an exception which spotlights the rule. For the Lady had made a mistake. Her pursuer was not, as she had supposed, the wicked Archimage, but the noble Timias who was coming to rescue her.

9 The point is confirmed by a modern falconer who quotes neither Jonson nor Spenser and who may therefore pass for an unbiased witness in the matter. Phillip Glasier says of the peregrine that 'one of her most valuable traits is undoubtedly her persistence' and records of one of his that she 'once chased a gull for over nineteen minutes' giving 'an aerobatic display of the highest order' even though at the end failing to catch the quarry. Glasier, p. 24. But Ratcliffe (p. 159) thinks that falcons, in the wild at least, often give chase to other birds for play or practice.

10 *Merry Wives* 3.3.221; 3.5.43; 3.3.19. Mrs Ford's term of endearment is perfectly apt. According to Glasier, (p. 113), it is desirable for the eyas of the sparrowhawk to be imprinted on its owner because the bird is highly temperamental and imprinting will help the process of manning. And the screaming, unlike the screaming of the eyas falcon (see n. 14), does not matter because sparrowhawks have tiny voices.

the players, who are ordinary people, neither rich nor noble, are urged by Hamlet to be 'like French falconers' and 'fly at anything we see'. And when Hamlet says he can tell a hawk from a heron he is obviously choosing the example as a street-level proof of sanity.[11]

We cannot of course know to what extent the audience understood the technical terms (which can be quite recondite, for example 'imp out our drooping country's broken wing'[12]). What is certain is that Shakespeare used them with familiarity.

Between Spenser's hawks and Shakespeare's there is, as we might expect, some overlap. Shakespeare is equally impressed by the dramatic nature of the falcon's flight:

KING HENRY
    But what a point, my lord, your falcon made,
    And what a pitch she flew above the rest!
    To see how God in all his creatures works!
    Yea, man and birds are fain of climbing high.
SUFFOLK
    No marvel, an it like your majesty,
    My Lord Protector's hawks do tow'r so well;
    They know their master loves to be aloft,
    And bears his thoughts above his falcon's pitch.
GLOUCESTER
    My lord, 'tis but a base ignoble mind
    That mounts no higher than a bird can soar.
CARDINAL BEAUFORT
    I thought as much; he would be above the
        clouds.   (2 Henry VI 2.1.5–15)

Like Spenser too Shakespeare is aware of the falcon's alleged nobility. But he hardly ever exploits it in a positive manner. Instead he uses it, as Spenser had also done, to illustrate an upset in the natural order of the world. Spenser strikes a macabre note by placing the screech-owl where once the lordly falcon towered (Ruins of Time 128). In Shakespeare the corruption of nature is indicated when

    A falcon, tow'ring in her pride of place,
    Was by a mousing owl hawked at and killed.
                (Macbeth 2.4.12–13)

Shakespeare can also, like Spenser, spare a thought for the quarry, though he shows more

sympathy for it than Spenser did. Angelo 'Nips youth i' th' head and follies doth enmew / As falcon doth the fowl' (Measure for Measure 3.1.89–90).[13] Warwick's boast that neither of his opponents 'Dares stir a wing if Warwick shakes his bells' (3 Henry VI 1.1.47), pictures them as prey, bells being as distinctive of a falcon as a curb is of a horse or his desires are of a man (As You Like It 3.3.71–2). Still more sinister, Tarquin, after threatening to murder Lucretia and blacken her name unless she consents to him,

    . . . shakes aloft his Roman blade,
    Which like a falcon tow'ring in the skies,
    Coucheth the fowl below with his wings' shade
    Whose crooked beak threats, if he mount he dies.
    So under his insulting falchion lies
    Harmless Lucretia, marking what he tells
    With trembling fear, as fowl hear falcons' bells.
                            (Lucrece 505–11)

But whereas all Spenser's allusions to hawking are variations on these three or four themes – the nobility of the falcon, its magnificent flight and breathtaking stoop, the fate of its victim – Shakespeare talks about it from every kind of angle. We hear from Pandarus of the enthusiasm with which the female makes love (Troilus and Cressida 3.2.51–2), Hamlet refers to the rowdiness of the little eyases in the eyrie (Hamlet 2.2.339),[14] Juliet shows that she under-

---

[11] Hamlet 2.2.431–2; 2.2.379. The hawk and handsaw is discussed by Madden, Diary of Master William, pp. 214–15, and by Henn, pp. 32–4. According to Madden (Diary of Master William, p. 146). Hamlet's somewhat contemptuous remark about French falconers is to be explained by the fact that they made a speciality of flying short-winged hawks, that is to say goshawks and sparrowhawks, which naturally take smaller quarry.

[12] Richard II 2.1.294. 'Imp' (from imponere) means to fix another feather in the place of a broken one.

[13] Madden (Diary of Master William, p. 202 n. 2) argues stoutly for the Folio reading 'enmew' against what he sees as the over-clever conjecture 'enew'.

[14] Hamlet is right to say that eyasses in the eyrie are extremely noisy. They are programmed by instinct to scream for food at the sight of their parents. See Glasier, p. 112; Bodio, pp. 55–7).

stands the uses of the hood (and two other falconry terms) when she asks night to hood her 'unmann'd' blood that was 'bating' in her cheeks (Romeo and Juliet 3.2.14). Petruchio explains in detail how he is training his wife as one would a haggard, that is to say a captured adult hawk (The Taming of the Shrew 4.1.176–9). In King Henry VI Part II 1.2 we join a hawking party in the St Albans countryside with falconers halloing. In The Winter's Tale we glimpse a young man out for the day for his own pleasure when Florizel tells Perdita 'I bless the time / When my good falcon made her flight across / Thy father's ground' (Winter's Tale 4.4.14–16). Juliet sighs after her departing Romeo and prays 'for a falconer's voice / To lure this tassel-gentle back again' (Romeo and Juliet 2.1.203–4).[15]

We may now consider what is distinctive about Shakespeare's allusions to falconry. The most salient feature is that in contrast to Spenser his characters always talk about trained hawks and the procedures of falconry, not about hawks in the wild.[16] The next is that Shakespeare never makes mistakes, or at any rate never mistakes of the kind that are irredeemable. Contrast the writers (among them Tennyson and Scott) who hymn the praises of the falcon as if she were male or who (like Kingsley) make a peregrine 'shoot out of the reeds like an arrow' as if she were a short-winged hawk.[17] Spenser indeed can be suspected of a similar confusion. When he makes Mercury 'stoop like an arrow from a bow' (Mother Hubbard 1262) it is not clear which of the two kinds of hawk, short-winged or long-winged, he has in mind. And in the lines quoted on page 132b he seems to use 'tower' wrongly to mean 'dominate' when it should mean 'circle' (from the French tour). That Shakespeare never errs like this could in theory be explained by saying that he did his homework thoroughly. The easier explanation is that it was home territory.

In any case book-learning can be ruled out. Knowledge acquired from books will in-

evitably be expressed in the language of those books, and this will be particularly clear in the case of hawking which prided itself on its special terminology. But if we compare the snobbish-sounding lists of dos and don'ts given in, say, Gryndall's edition of the Book of St Albans in 1596, 'You are to understand that Hawkes do eyre and not breed in Woods', say 'cal' not 'cawke' for making love, and so forth with Shakespeare's own vocabulary we shall find that though he uses a great many technical hawking terms they do not belong to this class of words that are different for the sake of being different. For the most part indeed the terms he uses are still in use today, and it is a fair presumption that they were the terms actually employed by the practising falconers of Shakespeare's time as opposed to the artificially archaic language of the manuals.

But the most striking thing about Shakespeare's knowledge of falconry (as is also true of his knowledge in certain other fields)[18] is the casual vividness with which he applies it to a vast variety of situations, very rarely to the same one twice. Indeed this is one of the secrets of his greatness, and the romantic explanation for it has always been that Shakespeare somehow had a magic gift for copying direct from

---

[15] And according to Dover Wilson's very plausible conjecture Romeo on returning whispers up to her 'my nyas'. (Or perhaps 'mine eyas' is still more likely, this being the form of the word Shakespeare uses elsewhere.)

[16] There are only two passages where the context allows of a wild hawk being meant – when Bolingbroke says in Richard II 1.3.61–2 'As confident as is the falcon's flight / Against a bird, do I with Mowbray fight', and when Isabella in Measure 3.1.87–90 describes Angelo as enmewing the follies of youth 'as falcon doth the fowl'. But the weight of his normal usage makes it likely that Shakespeare was thinking of a trained bird here too, as does the choice of the term falcon.

[17] See Madden, Medieval History, p. 232; Diary of Master William, p. 228.

[18] Witnesses to this abound in the literature on Shakespeare. I have myself testified to it in the matter of the physiology of the blood. See 'Shakespeare's Medical Imagination', Shakespeare Survey 38 (1985), 175–86.

nature.[19] Yet however seductive this may be as a picture of genius, as an explanation it is nonsense – for the birds, or rather not even for them.

This will be obvious if we look for a moment at what Shakespeare wrote about birds other than hawks. It is sometimes true to nature, sometimes not. For example pelicans get three mentions, and all three times it is because of the notion that young pelicans feed on their parents by sucking their blood.[20] This is not a fact observed from nature but a fallacy derived from books. Nor did Shakespeare observe for himself what he said about the nightingale – that the female sings, that she never sings in daytime, that no other bird sings at night, and that during her performance she accentuates her sense of pain by leaning against a thorn.[21]

These notions are all borrowed, and we can detect the fact with confidence not just because they occur in earlier authors but also because they are false. Otherwise it is less easy. Martlets (that is to say house-martins) really do build their nests on walls, lapwings really do run away from their nests to decoy marauders, and whether or not cormorants are really gluttonous the idea could certainly suggest itself to different observers independently. So when Shakespeare talks about martlets, lapwings, and cormorants in these contexts he is not necessarily speaking at second hand.[22] Nevertheless it is likely. This is because they are never introduced in any other connection. A genuinely independent observer watching, say, a cormorant could be expected to notice several different things about it, such as its appearance, its dive, and how long it stayed underwater. Moreover in this particular case there happens to be the evidence of literary precedent: cormorants are gluttonous, and never anything else, in both Chaucer and Spenser.

The fact that a bird has one or more stereotyped images attached to it does not prevent it from being the subject of personal observation too. Swans are an example. Juno's two swans and Jupiter as a swan seducing Leda are evidently second-hand since they are fictions of ancient mythology. So are the swans that sing before their death. Shakespeare mentions this as a habit of theirs on six occasions.[23] But he is wrong. Swansongs do not exist in nature and he could never have heard one. On the other hand there were plenty of swans in England in Shakespeare's time, they are eye-catching birds, and it is perfectly possible that he had seen for himself a swan breasting the current and assumed that it was trying in vain to swim against it, that he had noted the swan's black legs, that he had admired a swan sheltering its young beneath its wings, and that he had been struck by the isolation of a swan's nest surrounded by water.[24] There can be no proof, but what makes it likely is the variety of topics, the rather striking way in which they are men-

---

[19] This goes back to Alexander Pope, who in his *Imitations from Horace* chose the labels 'wit' for Cowley, 'art' for Ben Jonson, and 'nature' for Shakespeare. It was carried to effusive lengths by Matthew Arnold in the sonnet beginning 'Others abide our question' with the claim that Shakespeare, 'self-schooled, self-scanned, self-honoured, self-secure' somehow 'knew the stars and sunbeams' and that any attempt to probe his genius that 'out-topped knowledge' was akin to blasphemy.

[20] *Richard II* 2.1.127; *Hamlet* 4.5.147; *Lear* F 3.4.70–1. Belief in the parental virtues of the pelican can be traced back through the Christian fathers to Graeco-Roman Egypt. See D'Arcy Thompson, *A Glossary of Greek Birds*, p. 233. It would be interesting to know if Shakespeare, through the mouth of Lear, was being original when he turned the moral on its head and condemned the pelican's children as bloodsuckers.

[21] *P.P.* 20.8; *Lucrece* 1079, 1135; *Merchant* 5.1.104; *Two Gentlemen* 3.1.179; 5.4.5.

[22] Martlet: *Merchant* 2.9.27; *Macbeth* 1.6.4. (On the identification of the bird see Kenneth Muir's note in the Arden edition.) Lapwing: *Comedy of Errors* 4.2.27; *Measure* 1.4.31; *Much Ado* 3.1.24; *Hamlet* 5.2.146. Cormorants: *Love's Labour's Lost* 1.1.4; *Richard II* 2.1.38; *Troilus* 2.2.6; *Coriolanus* 1.1.118.

[23] *As You Like It* 1.3.74; *Phoenix and Turtle* 15; *Merchant* 3.2.44; *Merry Wives* 5.5.6; *King John* 5.7.21–2; *Othello* 5.2.254.

[24] *1 Henry VI* 1.4.19; *Titus* 4.2.101–2; *3 Henry VI* 5.3.56; *Cymbeline* 3.4.140.

tioned, and the fact that one cannot readily quote parallels from other writers. When these marks of individuality are absent, when for example Romeo's friends challenge him to come to Capulet's party by saying that there will be girls at it who will make his own Rosaline look like a crow to a swan, or when Troilus says that Cressida's hand is softer than cygnet's down, we are in a different territory, the ground of common experience that lies between cliché and first-hand knowledge.[25]

From classical antiquity until after the Reformation birds, along with other creatures, were commonly supposed to exemplify for the benefit of mankind various moral qualities. This creates another problem for us when we want to assess how direct Shakespeare's experience of nature was. Take for example doves or pigeons. He knows that they may be kept in dove-cots, that they are an article of food, that they can be trained to carry letters, that they have no gall-bladder, and that they feed their young by regurgitation: also that they can be gloriously white. But at the same time he considers them symbols of love, fidelity, innocence, peace, modesty, patience, and timidity (though with the capacity to rouse themselves in self-defence). Clearly the former are observable facts about the pigeon (whether or not Shakespeare actually observed them). Equally clearly the latter are not. In a sense therefore they must be second-hand. But it would be absurd so say that they were individually borrowed. We cannot imagine him searching through an emblem book whenever he was at a loss for the right symbol. Rather he must have shared the view of his time that every creature had a meaning, but felt free to make his own observations and reflections within the general limits imposed by that view. What emerges will not be transmitted stereotype. Nor will it be the result of experience, let alone truthful copying of nature. It will be something different. We can call it personal belief.

Before we finally decide about Shakespeare's falconry and into which of these categories it

fits best, we must take a look at his treatment of eagles. This is quite different from the way he treats hawks even though the eagle can be trained and was traditionally supposed to be the best bird to fly. In the *Book of St Albans* of 1486, the first printed English falconry manual, and in the many editions derived from it, the eagle is said to be rightfully reserved for emperors, just as the gerfalcon is for kings, the peregrine for earls, and so on down the list till one gets to a mere hobby for an untitled young man. In fact however eagles have never been seriously used in England. They are slow compared to hawks and only satisfactory for being flown at four-footed prey, not at game-birds.[26] In this discord between tradition and reality Shakespeare stands in a midway position. He never shows us eagles being caught or trained or flown for sport. He occasionally lets us glimpse them in the wild (which he never does for hawks), as in *Henry V* 1.2.169–71 where the Earl of Westmoreland expresses the fear that if 'the eagle England' goes to France 'in prey' she will have to leave her nest unguarded so that 'the weasel Scot' may 'come sneaking and so suck her princely eggs'. But for the most part the eagle in Shakespeare stands for superiority. It is her place at the top of the hierarchy that we are invited to admire. The analogy suits kings, for the monarch 'like an eagle o'er his eyrie towers / To souse annoyance'.[27] Indeed its superiority, its power, and its aggressiveness account for thirty-two out of the forty mentions it gets. The only other attribute of the eagle that Shakespeare dwells on is its eyes, and this not just because they are 'so green', 'so quick', and 'so fair' as the Nurse says to Juliet, but because they can gaze unharmed at the sun – an idea that does not come from observation but from Pliny.[28]

In fact there is nothing in Shakespeare about

---

25 *Romeo* 1.2.89; *Troilus* 1.1.58.
26 On this see Harting, p. 37; Henn, p. 35.
27 *King John* 5.2.149–50.
28 *Romeo* 3.5.220; Pliny *Natural History* 10.3.10.

eagles to make us suppose that he need ever have actually seen one any more than he need have seen a lion or a wolf for all the many mentions he gives them.

Thus Shakespeare's treatment of the eagle, even more than his treatment of other birds, highlights the fact that with his hawks we are in a different sphere. There is no repetition of wrong stereotypes, indeed there are no repeated stereotypes at all unless one counts four references to the 'towering' (viz. circling) of the falcon and two to the 'disdainful' nature of the untrained haggard. There is not even any set of what we have called 'personal beliefs', that is to say consistently held but unverifiable assumptions, relating to hawks. Instead a great variety of different aspects of hawking is described with accuracy. Nor is this done in set-pieces elaborated for their own sake. The allusions are always apt to the context and for the most part extremely brief. Our comparative study of other poets and dramatists has shown that this easy mastery was not automatically conferred by the zeitgeist. What we have seen of Shakespeare's eagles and cormorants and other birds has shown that he was not infallible. We have also seen reason to suppose that his hawking language was not learned from books. The combination of these factors does not amount to proof. Nevertheless the arguments are objective, not just personal impressions, and they are therefore available for public use.

The most ambitious such use would be by investigating other subjects in this way so as to build up a kind of biographical portrait. For though a dramatist may, and indeed a successful dramatist must, give his character opinions and attitudes not his own so that he becomes invisible behind the mask, what he cannot do is to make them knowledgeable about things he knows nothing about. And what one knows and what one doesn't know about make up between them an important part of personality.

Another possible use of our conclusion, pointed out long ago by Madden (1897, 318–62), is in attribution. It could for example

be used against the Baconians if they were amenable to argument. Bacon's known works, which are many and reasonably varied in content, show no interest in or knowledge of hawking whatsoever. This makes it highly unlikely that he should have written the plays and poems attributed to Shakespeare – and the more topics of which the same can be said (like hunting and other field sports) the less likely it becomes. One may add that this argument, unlike arguments from the minutiae of style, is one that can be applied with equal validity to works in verse or prose, in English or in Latin.

A rather more modest use for our conclusion is to help solve individual questions of interpretation. It is to one such that I now turn.

The passage is Viola's speech in *Twelfth Night* where she reflects on the qualities demanded of a fool by his occupation:

> This fellow is wise enough to play the fool,
> And to do that well craves a kind of wit.
> He must observe their mood on whom he jests,
> The quality of persons, and the time,
> And, like the haggard, check at every feather
> That comes before his eye. This is a practice
> As full of labour as a wise man's art,
> For folly that he wisely shows is fit,
> But wise men, folly-fall'n, quite taint their wit.
>
> (*Twelfth Night*, 3.1.59–67)

The stumbling block is the hawking metaphor at line 63. Does Viola mean that a Fool must be for ever on the attack and pounce whenever he sees the chance of a joke? Or does she mean that he must be circumspect and ply his trade without giving offence? Dr Johnson thought the text required the former meaning, the context the opposite. 'The meaning may be that he must catch every opportunity as the wild hawk strikes every bird. But perhaps it might be read more properly "*Not* like the haggard". He must choose persons and times and observe tempers; he must fly at proper game, like the trained hawk, and not fly at large like the unreclaimed haggard, to seize all that comes in his way.' Subsequent editors like Dyce, with less respect for the laws of evidence than Johnson, printed his proposal in the text. More recently there have been second thoughts and the original reading is generally restored. But though honesty has triumphed one cannot say the same for logic. For editors have tried to champion the two meanings simultaneously, that of the text and that of the discarded conjecture. Thus Quiller-Couch paraphrased 'Swoop upon every occasion for a jest and yet be tactful and wary at the same time', and the Arden edition has followed him: 'be continually on the look-out for jests and be discreet in uttering them'. Neither of them explains how the haggard's behaviour delivers a message of tact and discretion.

It is clear where the root of the trouble lies. There is a contradiction between the cautious phrases 'observe their mood on whom he jests' and 'a wise man's art' and the allegedly aggressive hawking language of the simile. The most obvious question therefore is whether the hawking language has been rightly understood. Now the first rule of criticism is to interpret an author by his own usage. If we follow the rule and examine the three terms of substance in the line, 'haggard', 'check at' and 'feather', we shall find that the commentators from Dr Johnson on have misled us, and that the words as used by Shakespeare do not mean what we have been told. Furthermore once we give them their right meanings the contradiction between the simile and its context vanishes.

The most important of the three terms for the basic meaning of the line is 'check at'. We are told that this was a falconer's phrase for 'attack indiscriminately'. But this is not true. The word for 'attack indiscriminately' was 'check', and 'check' is as different from 'check at' as 'stop' is from 'stop at' or 'live' from 'live at'. Furthermore, although 'check' (meaning 'inferior prey') and the rather rare derived verb 'checking' ('pursuing inferior prey') are good falconry terms of the time, neither of them occurs in Shakespeare. The simple word 'check' is therefore a red herring.

What is found in the line is the prepositional phrase 'check at'. Whether or not this is to be recognized as a special falconry term I do not know: but it was a phrase used by falconers, or at any rate by one falconer. In the second part of Symon Latham's *Falconry* of 1618 a well-trained hawk is said 'never to understand what it is to check at the fist' but will prove 'a certaine and bolde comer'.[29] The sense has nothing to do with 'inferior prey': it is quite simply 'shy at' or 'refuse'.

This Latham passage is the only example of the phrase I have found in the technical literature, but it makes three appearances in Shakespeare. The most clear-cut is in *Hamlet*. Claudius, learning of Hamlet's re-appearance in Denmark when he ought to have been on board ship for England, speculates 'If he be now returned, / As checking at his voyage ...' 4.7.60–1. No commentator supposes that Hamlet has abandoned his proper quarry, gone off at a tangent, and attacked his voyage. What he has done is taken fright at it. The sense is exactly as in Latham. Hamlet, like an uncooperative hawk, is refusing to come to the fist.

The second instance is in *Twelfth Night*. Malvolio, reading a false billet doux that has been laid for him as a trap, is stopped by the mysterious letters M A O I, repeats them, and starts wondering if they have a secret meaning. 'What dish o' poison hath she dressed him!' exclaims Fabian aside. 'And with what wing the staniel checks at it!' adds Sir Toby Belch.[30] Here it is true that a meaning like 'has gone off at a tangent and attacked an inferior problem' would make sense in itself. But it would not fit

---

29 Symon Latham, *Falconry* (London, 1618) bk. 2 ch. 11 p. 37. 'Check at' is not (as far as I can find) in George Turbervile, *The Booke of Falconrie* (London, 1575), in W. G. Gryndall, *Hawking, Hunting, Fowling, and Fishing* (Faulkener, London, 1596), or in Edmund Bert, *An Approved Treatise of Hawkes and Hawking* (London, 1619). Nor is it in Latham in the sense of 'fly at'. No instance is cited in *OED* (s.v. 'check' 6b) except an erroneous use by Scott in *Marmion*.

30 *Twelfth Night* 2.5.111. 'Staniel' [= kestrel] is Hanmer's plausible emendation of Folio's 'stallion'.

the context. Malvolio is not being indiscriminate. The puzzle has been set for him by his tormentors. What he has done is to stop and worry at it.

These are the only other instances of 'check at' in Shakespeare. They offer no evidence that in Viola's speech it can mean 'attack inferior prey'. The meaning indicated is 'stop at through fear or suspicion', 'shy at'.

Next 'every feather'. We are always told that this means 'any bird'. But once again there is no evidence. 'Feather' occurs in twenty-four Shakespeare passages. In none of them does it mean 'bird'. Three times it is in the phrase 'of a feather', meaning similar. Five times it is simply the physical object, a bird's feather. Five times it has the connotation, like 'plumage', of adornment or glory. But its most frequent association (ten times other than our present passage) is lightness. And this makes excellent sense – a man in the fool's position must be suspicious of everything however trivial-seeming. The closest parallels are 'Anon he starts at stirring of a feather' (*Venus and Adonis* 302) and 'You boggle shrewdly; every feather starts you.' (*All's Well* 5.2.236). But of course in Viola's speech the falconry metaphor makes the mention of feather particularly appropriate.[31]

But the point of chief interest is why the position of a fool should be compared to that of a haggard and why this should be done in a flattering or at least in a non-pejorative way. For in previous literature the haggard was always cast in an unfavourable light. In a poem published in 1567 George Turbervile compared a girl who had deserted him to a trained hawk that had reverted to the wild.

> You sometime were a gentle hawk,
> And woont to feede on fist . . .
> But now you are become so wylde
> And rammage to be seene
> As though you were a haggard hawke;
> Your manners altred clean,
> You now refuse to come to fist,
> You shun my wonted call . . .
>   (*Epigraph* 15, 29–30; 37–42)

The same in Spenser. We have seen that Spenser's falcons are always noble, and that in the similes of the *Faerie Queene* they always figure on the side of the virtuous lady or the gentle knight, never on that of a witch or dragon. But for the haggard this distinction is reversed. The only time one is mentioned, it is the dragon which is compared to the haggard hawk: the Red Cross Knight is the 'hardy fowle' in its talons.[32]

Yet despite their contrasting images the haggard hawk and the falcon were the same bird. The difference lay in their educational history. A haggard was a wild hawk, caught when adult and then manned, as opposed to a falcon gentle which had come under the falconer's care as a nestling or eyas (originally 'nyas' from Latin *nidiacem*) and had never had to forage for itself.[33] As for which of the two was preferable, opinions differed. The falcon gentle appealed to the prejudices of chivalry, being of known parentage and therefore having a hint of breeding about it. Furthermore the bird's training

---

[31] The use of a feather in the early training of haggards is recommended by Latham. He says to the new owner that on the first day you should 'easily take her upon your fist gently, and cease not to carry her the whole day continually, using a feather instead of your hand to touche and strouke her withall, and when you find her gentle and willing to be touched without starting . . .' It is not impossible that the picture in Shakespeare's mind was of this initial training feather.

[32] *Faerie Queene* 1.11.19.5.

[33] Falcons, though comparatively frequent in Britain, were traditionally caught on their migration. Hence the words passage-hawk and peregrine (Latin *peregrinus*). But they would not be called falcons until they were manned. In their wild state or if training was unsuccessful they were called haggards. After 1771 when under the Linnaean system peregrine became part of the official species name, *falco peregrinus*, the term haggard was restricted to mean an adult hawk captured after its first moult.

Intermediate between an eyas and a haggard was a rammage hawk or brauncher. This was a hawk that was not taken under the falconer's care until able to go from branch to branch. Its merits were praised by Bert (*An Approved Treatise*) but it is not mentioned in Shakespeare.

was comparatively easy as regarded getting her to recognize her keeper's voice, come to fist, and so on. The difficulty was on the other side, getting her to be aggressive and attack game. The haggard, naturally enough, had the opposite qualities. Being accustomed to fend for herself she was ready enough to show her mettle. The difficulty was in tempting her to the lure and in accustoming her to the fist.

Now the earlier falconry books give pride of place to the falcon gentle. The *Book of St Albans* rates her as the nobler bird, fit for a prince, and George Turbervile in 1575 recommends her 'for hir noblesse and hardy courage, and withall the frankness of hir mettel', saying that she is 'valiant, ventrous, strong, good to brooke both heate and cold, and to whom there commeth no weather amisse at any time'. This is evidently the tradition that Spenser (Turbervile's friend) followed. But Turbervile goes on to say, in partial contradiction to the view of these things that he had expressed eight years before,[34] that second comes the haggard falcon ('otherwise termed the Peregrine') which is an 'excellent good bird' for despite what the Italian and French authorities (whom he is translating) say about her being 'very choyce and tender to endure hard weather' she should in theory be hardier than the falcon gentle since she comes from a frozen part of the world and is accustomed to living in the wild.

This shift of sentiment in favour of the haggard is carried further by Symon Latham in 1615. He argues that Turbervile was wrong to make a distinction in kind between the gentle and the haggard since 'the Tassell Gentle is the male and makes unto them both',[35] and wrong too to prefer the gentle since the haggard having had experience of life in the wild will be far superior once she is properly trained. The main purpose of his book is therefore to lay down the proper procedures for training a bird which, he claims 'in these daies most men do covet and desire to prepare'.

Latham's date of birth is not known, but when he wrote his book in 1615 he claimed it as the fruit of long experience. So the haggard may have already been popular for some time. Indeed her star may have been already rising in 1575 for Turbervile to have had the courage to dissent from his original authors in her favour. However the traditional view was not extinct. In *Honor, Military and Civil*, W. Segar, Norroy King-at-Arms, wrote (bk. 4, ch. 15, p. 225) 'as we see Birds even of one *Espece* or kind, some prove noble and some ignoble, as of Falcons, some are Gentle and some Haggard. Likewise of four-footed beasts, some are Noble, as the Lyon; some ignoble as the Wolfe.' The date of this firm pronouncement is 1602, the year after the first performance of *Twelfth Night*.

The fact that the comparative virtues of the haggard and the falcon gentle were a debatable subject gives our question a certain edge. Was Shakespeare on the side of traditionalism with its views of a hierarchic natural order? Or was he on the side of modernism and merit?

There are only four other mentions of the haggard in Shakespeare. In *Othello* it is used for a captured hawk whose training has been unsuccessful: Iago has suggested that Desdemona's wifely devotion is not as single-minded as it ought to be and proposed a way to test the matter. Othello reflects on how he will react in the event of a negative result:

> If I do prove her haggard,
> Though that her jesses were my dear heart-strings
> I'd whistle her off and let her down the wind
> To prey at fortune. (*Othello* 3.3.264–7)

Twice haggards are called 'disdainful'. At the beginning of the third act of *Much Ado About*

---

[34] Turbervile, *Booke of Falconrie*, p. 35, contrasted with the poem in Turbervile, *Epigraphes, Epigrams, Songs and Sonnets* (London, 1567), cited above p. 140.

[35] Latham is right of course on this. What would have surprised him though is the modern discovery, due to the techniques of artificial insemination, that *all* long-winged hawks from the mighty gerfalcon to the small merlin are cross-fertile and breed fertile offspring. See Bodio, p. 81; also Glasier, p. 315 who is decidedly less enthusiastic about the practice.

Nothing Hero stages a conversation for Beatrice to overhear. Beatrice, she tells Ursula, one of her attendants,

> is too disdainful.
> I know her spirits are as coy and wild
> As haggards of the rock. (*Much Ado* 3.1.34–6)

At the end of the conversation, when they are safely out of earshot, Ursula says to Hero, 'She's limed, I warrant you. We have caught her, madam' as if Beatrice was in fact a haggard hawk being trapped. And finally Beatrice, soliloquizing on what she has overheard, tacitly accepts the comparison, saying that she will now 'tame her wild heart' to Benedick's 'loving hand'.

The other occasion is similar. Bianca, Kate's studious sister in *The Taming of the Shrew*, has long resisted her suitors, and one of them, Hortensio, describes her as 'a proud disdainful haggard'.[36]

The most detailed reference to the haggard is also in *The Taming of the Shrew*. Indeed it forms one of the most noteworthy of Shakespeare's falconry passages. It is where Petruchio explains the training programme he proposes to follow in disciplining his new wife. It is entirely modelled on the procedure for training a newly caught haggard:

> My falcon now is sharp and passing empty,
> And till she stoop she must not be full-gorged,
> For then she never looks upon her lure.
> Another way I have to man my haggard,
> To make her come to know her keeper's call, –
> That is, to watch her, as we watch those kites
> That bate and beat, and never are obedient.
> She ate no meat today, nor none shall eat.
> (*Shrew* 4.1.176–85[37])

In none of these passages does Shakespeare condemn the haggard for flying after inferior prey.[38] Its fault is unruliness, the cure training. Once manned and trained it is no longer haggard and Shakespeare does not seem to distinguish the resulting falcon from the 'falcon gentle' that had begun life as an eyas.

To come back now to Viola's speech. The point of comparison between the haggard and the fool is that they are both outsiders. The haggard is wild, unaccustomed to humans, and thoroughly nervous.[39] The fool is wild too, or at least uncultivated: he has not been bred in the educated society he is now expected to entertain, and he has to find out for himself the dangers and the opportunities it offers. Viola does not say that this necessarily makes the clown better than the wise man in the way that Latham claims that the haggard 'hath evermore deserved the most', but she allows him at least the possibility of equal merit.

The simile is a minor detail in a minor speech, but any correction of detail affects the whole picture. Modern falconers were saying that the haggard hawk could be trained to equal the falcon gentle, and Viola is being equally modern when she puts forward the idea that as far as human wisdom is concerned merit need

---

[36] *Shrew* 4.2.39.

[37] Shakespeare took the hawking comparison from his 1594 predecessor (Scene 9, 45–7), but in taking it over he much improved the detail and the appositeness. See Madden, *Diary of Master William*, p. 337. However the hawks in the induction (2.43) are added by Shakespeare. *The Taming of a Shrew* has only the hunting dogs (Scene 2, 21–2).

[38] Shakespeare is orthodox in this. Turbervile in the poem where he accuses his former lady-love of having lost status and ceased to be a falcon gentle limits the haggard's fault to being self-willed and in not coming to the lure: birds which 'fly at check' are said to be 'far worser'. And in his prose treatise on falconry (Turbervile, *Booke of Falconrie*, p. 37) flying at check is explicitly described as a fault to which the falcon gentle is prone and not the haggard. Nor is it said to be a specific failing of haggards to fly at non-game birds in any other textbook on falconry of Shakespeare's day that I have read.

[39] The most sympathetic evocation of the haggard's nervousness is in Ben Jonson: 'He starts away from hand, so, and all the touches, or soft strokes of reason, you can applie! No colt is so unbroken! or hawke yet halfe so haggard or unmann'd!' *Sad Shepherd* 3.3.5–8. It is worth adding that Shakespeare called haggards 'wild', and that 'wild' for him regularly meant 'wilful' or 'unruly', not 'aggressive'.

not be reserved for those who are born in the right place but can be acquired. Her tone is hesitant, and considered as a part of the whole play the suggestion is unobtrusive in the extreme. Nevertheless it is made and as far as it goes it accords with the spirit of the Reformation. This may be to read too much into it, but it seems worth pointing out the possibility.

TELLING THE STORY OF SHAKESPEARE'S PLAYHOUSE WORLD

ROSLYN L. KNUTSON

In Albert Camus's *The Plague* Joseph Grand, a pedantic middle-aged clerk, uses coloured chalk to review the conjugations and declensions of Latin words: blue for variable endings and red for the part that never changes ('*celle qui ne changeait jamais*'). His reclusive neighbour Cottard, attracted by this logic, uses a piece of the red chalk to write a suicide note when he hangs himself ('*Entrez, je suis pendu*'). Though not as desperate or obsessive as Cottard and Grand, we historians of the theatre in Shakespeare's time have seen ourselves traditionally as the keepers of the red chalk. Unlike colleagues in criticism, whose protean theories force them to work in blue, we claim to have maintained the factual part of the discipline, the part that never varies.

We inherit this attitude from nineteenth-century theatre historians who, with historians generally, took up the epistemology and methodology of the scientist. Looking through stationers' records, accounts of Court and civic offices, state papers, parish registers, and the correspondence of courtiers, the historians of Elizabethan drama came to see themselves as dispassionate observers of the natural laws that governed the evolution of the theatre in Shakespeare's time, and they conveyed the data of their investigations in the format of annals and chronicles. Charles W. Wallace epitomized the philosophy and discourse of choice in the field by the language in the title of his essay in 1910, 'Shakespeare and His London Associates as Revealed in Recently Discovered Documents'.

The word 'Revealed' itself reveals the belief that the Truth about the past resides in documents from the past. All the historian has to do to find the Truth is to find and transcribe the documents, down to the last pson and occacōn.

In the last decade, however, we have begun to question the efficacy of the traditional narrative as well as its theoretical foundations. The belief that the past is (or ought to be) one coherent sequence of events with 'a single subject or theme' and characters whose psychology is common to a human nature that transcends historical time seems parochial.[1] Given new information of Shakespeare's playhouse world that does not fit neatly into the old story, we can see that the Truth as formulated by E. K. Chambers is an interpretation based on fragments from already fragmentary clusters of data.[2] That Truth, while insisting on its objective and unrhetorical assembly of facts, is Truth with an agenda. It privileges certain dramatists, players, companies, managerial practices, business activities, and genres of plays. It has a

---

[1] Louis O. Mink, 'Narrative Form as a Cognitive Instrument', *The Writing of History: Literary Form and Historical Understanding*, ed. Robert H. Canary and Henry Kozicki (Madison, 1978), pp. 129–49, p. 137.

[2] I refer here and subsequently to views expressed by Chambers in *The Elizabethan Stage*, 4 vols. (Oxford, 1923), which I cite as necessary in the text as *ES*. Chambers, of course, is only one apologist for the orthodox history, but the most convenient one to use to represent an age and set of attitudes in theatre history.

work ethic, a morality, and an aesthetic. That Truth, in short, is a fiction.

Currently, therefore, theatre historians are reaching for blue chalk with which to construct narratives that challenge old plot lines, introduce new major characters, reassign the rôles of villain and hero, and shift the focus to alternative points of view. To illustrate some of these changes, I would like to choose a few dates of such familiarity in the chronology of the Elizabethan theatre that they call up substantial units of the old story and to discuss permutations that are developing as we open the Shakespeare-centred narrative to narratives that accommodate the greater theatrical and cultural worlds of Shakespeare's time.

1576: THE BURBAGEAD

The year 1576 in traditional theatre history is marked by the construction of the Theatre, a building James Burbage designed exclusively for playing. The fact that he would conceive such an enterprise has implied to us certain conditions in the theatrical industry at the time. One is the market for daily performances at the same location over weeks, months, even years. Another is the availability of companies that had been transformed from small rag-tag troupes of itinerant players to medium-sized, stable organizations with the security and prestige of patrons at the level of Privy Councillors. Presumably Burbage built the Theatre for the commercial advantage of such a company (initially, Leicester's men (his own)) and leased the stage subsequently to all the best companies (perhaps the Queen's men from 1583; certainly the Admiral's men from 1588 and the Chamberlain's men from 1594). This playhouse, in combination with uninterrupted theatrical seasons .by these companies, supposedly fostered the habit of playgoing among Londoners from the lowly apprentice to the rich and powerful members of the business and titled classes.

The central figure in this narrative is James Burbage. His sons thought of him as 'the first builder of Playhowses',[3] and, expanding on the characterization, old-line theatre historians considered him something of a philanthropist who risked capital for the sake of the playhouse enterprise. Such was the opinion even of Charles W. Wallace, who found and published a set of law suits (1587–97) between Burbage and the widow of John Brayne (*The First London Theatre*, 1913). In that the documents in these cases imply as much, Wallace could have characterized James as a liar, hot-head, and cozener who shamelessly cheated first his brother-in-law and then his childless, widowed sister-in-law out of profits from the operation of the Theatre. But he did not, for he was 'an ardent partisan of the Burbages'.[4] However, Wallace's contemporaries in theatre history were more aware of flaws in the Burbage image. After attention shifted to Philip Henslowe due to W. W. Greg's edition of the diary and papers (1904–8), Burbage was quietly retired and his place as theatrical magnate handed down to his youngest son, Richard. Conveniently, there was not much biographical data about Richard as an adult; he could therefore be idealized convincingly as the moral and professional superior of his father in the rôles of player, property manager, and designer (and keeper) of equitable share-holder agreements.

Over the last decade, the narrative of James Burbage and the building of the first London playhouse in 1576 has been challenged by new information about the Red Lion playhouse. In

---

[3] The 'Sharers' Papers', Malone Society *Collections*, vol. 2, pt. 3, 362–73, pp. 370–1.

[4] Brayne, whose sister had married Burbage in 1559, supplied the money to build the Theatre, and to his mind he never received a fair financial return on his investment. After he died in 1586, his widow, in league subsequently with one of his creditors (Robert Miles), took Burbage to court. Burbage reciprocated with a suit of his own. For details of the Brayne–Burbage suits, I rely on the summary of actions by Herbert Berry, whose phrase I quote here (*Shakespeare's Playhouses* (New York, 1987), pp. 19–44, p. 34).

1983, Janet S. Loengard published a transcription of a plea roll for the Court of King's Bench (Hilary Term, 11 Elizabeth (1569)).[5] According to information in this record, John Brayne, citizen and grocer of London, charged that John Reynolds, carpenter, had not built to specifications the stage and turret for a playhouse called the Red Lion at Mile End in the parish of St Mary Matfellon, 'a mile or so east of the City boundary (at the bars in Whitechapel High Street)'[6] or 'within a thirty- to forty-minute walk from St Paul's, in the district famous for the city musters'.[7] The significant new data are those which establish the Red Lion as a playhouse (not a 'playing-inn' (ES, II, 380)), and its stage as a permanent structure. In addition, the evidence that Brayne was not only the financier but also the architectural supervisor of the project suggests that he was not a naif in building construction – specifically theatrical construction – when he and Burbage became partners in building the playhouse in Shoreditch. Knowing Brayne's rôle, we cannot resist asking with William Ingram where Burbage was in 1567 and whether Leicester's men could have been the company set to lease the Red Lion stage when Reynolds completed the carpentry.[8] If Brayne and Burbage did collaborate in some sense on the Red Lion project in 1567, the language of the Brayne–Burbage law suits takes on another layer of texture – especially that language regarding Burbage's business ethics. Even if they did not, we must none the less reconsider the privileged place of the Theatre in the generic sequence of Elizabethan playhouses and James Burbage's privileged characterization as the person to whom the idea of a permanent playhouse first occurred.

Chambers knew that the first public London playhouse was not the only one for long. He believed that the Curtain was built 'very soon after the Theatre' to the south and east 'near the boundary between Holywell and Moorfields' (ES, II, 401), and that by 1580 there was a playhouse about a mile south of London Bridge in Newington. Each playhouse has participated in the traditional narrative accordingly as Shakespeare's company performed there: ten days in June 1594 for Newington; a goodly portion of 1596–9 for the Curtain. Otherwise, each is known by its shortcomings: the Curtain was small and old; the Newington playhouse was too far from London and unavailable for performances 'on working days' (qtd in ES, II, 405).

Yet there has been more information about both the Curtain and the playhouse at Newington in London archives, especially about their owners. With the assistance of such material, William Ingram conjectures that James Burbage purchased the Curtain from Henry Lanman in 1589[9] and that 'the playhouse at Newington Butts was built by the actor Jerome Savage, shortly after he procured the patronage of the Earl of Warwick for his company in 1575'.[10] These discoveries enlarge the histories of the Curtain and Newington playhouse considerably, and as impetus for revisions in the story of the early years of Elizabethan theatre, the information is additionally interesting as it directs us to consider the number and variety of entrepreneurial concepts available to the men who were later to invest in playhouses. The

---

[5] 'An Elizabethan Lawsuit: John Brayne, his Carpenter, and the Building of the Red Lion Theatre', *Shakespeare Quarterly*, 34 (1983), 298–310.

[6] Herbert Berry, 'The First Public Playhouses, Especially the Red Lion', *Shakespeare Quarterly*, 40 (1989), 133–48, p. 136.

[7] John H. Astington, 'The Red Lion Playhouse: Two Notes', *Shakespeare Quarterly*, 36 (1985), 456–7, p. 456; Astington adds that the 'site cannot have been far from the modern Whitechapel tube station'.

[8] 'The Early Career of James Burbage', *The Elizabethan Theatre X*, ed. C. E. McGee (Port Credit, 1988), pp. 18–36, pp. 30, 33–5.

[9] 'Henry Lanman's Curtain Playhouse as an "Easer" to the Theatre, 1585–1592', *The First Public Playhouse: The Theatre at Shoreditch, 1576–1598*, ed. Herbert Berry (Montreal, 1979), pp. 17–28.

[10] 'The Playhouse at Newington Butts: a New Proposal', *Shakespeare Quarterly*, 21 (1970), 385–98, p. 386.

traditional narrative invites us to think in terms of two: the philanthropist model of James Burbage at the Theatre, which his sons democratized for the Globe project by bringing in some of the company sharers; and the capitalist model of Philip Henslowe at the Rose, which the churlish Francis Langley adopted for the Swan in 1595. But the examples of Lanman, who apparently had no motive in the Curtain except as an investment in a building, and Savage, who apparently had no larger empire in mind than a stage whereon his company could perform 'steadily, profitably, and without major incident',[11] imply that in the early years of theatrical construction there were several reasons why the playhouse was an appealing investment for some men and various corporate structures through which to invest. In this context, the putative opposition of capitalist exploitation at the Rose and a consortium of sharer-housekeepers at the Globe does not seem an inevitable development.

Once accustomed to thinking of greater London in 1576 as a place where several playhouses were being operated, each with the expectation of being a successful commercial enterprise, we realize that at this level of theatrical activity there must have been more companies performing in the area than we have been encouraged to notice. These companies needed players, and the better established of the players could use apprentices. Companies that performed for regular playgoers needed a large and diverse repertory, and this expansion created opportunities for dramatists. Who were these players and dramatists? What were these plays like? We have been allowed not to care, for surely the players would have left a mark if they had been members of a significant company. The dramatists would be remembered if they had been talented enough to write good poetry, and the plays would have been printed if they had been popular. But of course the fact that details of these theatrical operations have been lost does not mean that the players had no rôle in the growth of the industry or that the

dramatists and their plays did not affect popular tastes and the development of dramatic formulas, even if that effect was merely to teach Kyd, Marlowe, and Shakespeare what *not* to do. Unfortunately, though, the loss of the players, dramatists, and texts does mean that we cannot evaluate the nature and extent of their influence.

In conjunction with an awareness of the size and diversity of the theatrical industry in the years following 1576, we are looking again at 'the place of the stage – both its status and locale'.[12] Presumably, Burbage chose the property at Holywell for the site of the Theatre in part because the parish of St Leonard Shoreditch lay outside the jurisdiction of the City, whose annual mayor objected with regularity to the very existence of a playhouse industry. Steven Mullaney reinterprets the social and political implications of this location through the metaphors of margins and liberties. In his view, the geography of the playhouses gave the members of the companies who played there and the dramatists who wrote for them the freedom to associate with both the ceremonies of the establishment and the carnival forms of the City's underclasses, that is, to endorse the social and political order or to subvert it. Given this hypothesis to consider, we may appreciate anew the complexities of the etiquette practised by the players, whether they were playing at the time in one of the liberties or at a City inn (as the Chamberlain's men appear to have been in October 1594). For they had always to consider the effect of their companies' behaviour on their own finances, their personal safety and that of their dramatists, and their standing in regard to the favour of their patron.

1588: NEWS OUT OF PURGATORY

The year 1588 in traditional theatre history is marked by disappointment and death. There

---

11 Ingram, 'The Playhouse at Newington Butts', p. 386.
12 Steven Mullaney, *The Place of the Stage: License, Play, and Power in Renaissance England* (Chicago, 1988), p. 30.

was plague in London that summer, and Richard Tarlton – premier clown of the Elizabethan stage, master fencer, dramatist, and charter member of the Queen's men in 1583 – was buried at St Leonard's, Shoreditch, on 3 September, while the infection in the metropolitan area was at its most virulent. With Tarlton died the paradigm of theatrical success that the Queen's men had seemed since 1583 to be inventing. When Sir Francis Walsingham instructed the Master of the Revels 'To choose out a companie of players for her maiestie' (qtd in *ES*, II, 104), the following perquisites (at least) became theirs: the lion's share of performances at Court during the winter holiday seasons, exemption from restraints against playing in London, the top rate of rewards while playing on tour. And yet they did not flourish in anything like the manner that such hegemony should effect. After Tarlton's death, their membership was in disarray (one of their leading men, William Knell, had died too; his widow married young John Heminges and bore him at least fourteen children from 1590 to 1613). Their share of Court performances dwindled. They appear more frequently in provincial records than at the London playhouses. Although we have texts for some of their plays and the titles of a few more, we do not have enough information on their repertory to draw up lists of their offerings year by year.

What went wrong? Cold-hearted as it may seem, we have been encouraged not to enquire too closely or grieve overmuch, for the Queen's men despite their brilliance were not prologue to the arrival of Shakespeare's company on the London theatrical scene. Indeed, had they fulfilled the promise of their selection by the Crown, the Chamberlain's men might not have become the leading company of their time, and we would have the awkward situation of the greatest of dramatists writing for a second-line outfit.

All the same, the fiction created to explain their fate tells a great deal about how the traditional narrative defines success and failure.

If we bring aspects of the company's dramatic activity into the foreground, we see more reasons than the grim reaper's choosing out of Tarlton. Scott McMillin invites us to consider the acting style of the Queen's men and their ability to adapt to the hottest kinds of plays in 1588. He asks how a company performs an English chronicle play or the latest offerings of Kyd and Marlowe when its dramaturgical skills are those of the 'interlude tradition . . . [with an] assortment of standard gestures, intonations, costumes, wigs, false noses, dialects, postures, gags, songs, and pratfalls'.[13] McMillin suggests that these traditional skills, coupled with the 'blandness of plot in their plays', doomed the Queen's men to be unable to compete with rising companies such as the Admiral's men: '[w]hat was to prove a new opportunity for the younger companies was for them [the Queen's men] a dead end' (p. 15).

Touring is also blamed for the company's failure. From the archival work of J. O. Halliwell-Phillipps and J. T. Murray, Chambers knew that numerous companies travelled in the provinces throughout the sixteenth and early seventeenth centuries, but he could not imagine that they would prefer such a life to settlement at the Theatre, or that they could 'saue ther carges' if they should be so foolish as to go on tour or so unfortunate as to have to.[14] He assumed that any company without a London playhouse for an extended period of time must either be an insignificant troupe in the patronage of an insignificant lord, a troupe

---

13 'The Queen's Men and the London Theatre of 1583', *The Elizabethan Theatre X*, ed. C. E. McGee (Port Credit, 1988), pp. 1–17, p. 14. A subsequent citation is noted in the text.

14 The phrase here occurs in a letter dated 28 September 1593 from Philip Henslowe to his son-in-law, Edward Alleyn, who was on tour with Strange's men at the time; it refers to Pembroke's men, who had been on tour also and who (as the phrase implies) had been unable since early August to make enough money to pay their expenses (*Henslowe's Diary*, ed. R. A. Foakes and R. T. Rickert (Cambridge, 1961), p. 280).

with inferior dramatic skills and bad quartos, or a once-competitive organization now irremediably in decline. In plague time, of course, all of the London companies went on tour, for the Privy Council issued restraints that forced closure of the playhouses. Given their London base, these companies could survive for a few summer months, but if the restraints persisted, as they did in 1592–4, 1603–4, and 1608–9, then touring put them too at financial risk.

However, new evidence of theatrical activity in the provinces tells the story of touring differently. Even editors of volumes in the series known as Records of Early English Drama (familiarly, REED) are responding with scholarly whistles of surprise to the number of companies on tour throughout England and Scotland in the 1500s and early 1600s, at the quality of those companies implicit in their longevity, and at the order and consistency of their circuits.[15] Moreover, there is evidence that going on tour was not automatically a prelude to bankruptcy. Simon Jewell, a player with a travelling company prior to his death in August 1592, was not a poor man by the financial standards of ordinary working men of the time. As Jewell cast up accounts in his will, he reckoned that he had invested over £33 in a company share, necessities for playing on tour, and a loan to a fellow player; that he owed a little more than £19 10s, mostly to people from whom he had borrowed cash; and that his estate was therefore in the black by £13 10s. These figures, both in ready money and a line of credit, suggest that he was doing much better financially than breaking even. If Jewell, about whom we have known nothing all these years, was making a respectable living with a touring company (possibly, even, with the putatively moribund Queen's men),[16] we should perhaps assume that players in (for example) Strange's men in 1593, Pembroke's men in 1598–9, and Chandos's men in the 1590s were able to support themselves reasonably well by playing in the provinces. These attitudes toward the life and activity of companies on the road enable us

to approach some peculiar events in the history of the London companies that we have preferred to ignore: for example, why Robert Browne would take his company of Derby's men into the provinces in 1601–2 and sublet the nearly new Boar's Head playhouse in Whitechapel to Worcester's men, and why the Chamberlain's men would leave the London area in the summer of 1594 to give a performance at Marlborough in August.

Furthermore, with the encouragement of historicists to view theatrical activity in a political context, we are reconsidering the scene in a provincial town when news arrived that travelling players were near. We used to assume that the townspeople welcomed the troupe but that civic authorities did not. But perhaps they did – under certain circumstances. If, for example, those players were servants of the lord whose nearby estate represented employment and preferment to citizens of the town, the mayor and town council would welcome the players regardless of the quality of their playing. If those players were the Queen's or King's men, the local politicians would welcome them as an

---

15 At the annual meeting of the Shakespeare Association of America, Philadelphia, 1990, in a session entitled 'Horses, a Wagon, and Apparel New Bought', these issues were addressed by J. A. B. Somerset and Sally-Beth MacLean, respectively; the costs of touring were discussed by William Ingram and touring texts by Paul Werstine. This session represents a small portion of the revisionary work being done on the conditions of touring. There is in fact so much being published that even REED-affiliated scholars cannot keep up. As John Wasson points out, new data coming into print, plus the arguments constructed from the data, cause us to revise and update theories of provincial touring that were constructed just a year or two ago ('Elizabethan and Jacobean Touring Companies', *Theatre Notebook*, 42 (1988), 51–5).

16 Mary Edmond, who published Jewell's will, suggests that his company was Pembroke's men ('Pembroke's Men', *Review of English Studies*, n.s. 25 (1974), 129–36). Scott McMillin identifies several of the names in Jewell's will with members of the Queen's men ('Simon Jewell and the Queen's Men', *Review of English Studies*, n.s. 27 (1976), 174–7).

act of loyalty to the Crown. Peter Greenfield offers yet another motive in the welcome of players: as a means of consolidating power. By allowing the players to play, by inviting the townspeople to attend the performance as guests, but by limiting the number of the company's performances while in town, the mayor and councillors could 'liberate potentially subversive discontent' among the citizenry aroused by the players' satire yet contain that energy in a public ritual that reaffirmed 'the community of the giver [civic authorities] and the receiver [townspeople] . . . in a space that itself symbolizes authority: . . . the town hall'.[17]

1597: WAR WITHOUT BLOWS

The year 1597 was a busy time in the London playhouse world. From the exclusive perspective of Shakespeare's company, a chronicle of important events would begin with its sweep of the Court calendar over the Revels season of 1596–7 and Queen Elizabeth's request to see a play of Falstaff in love. In February, James Burbage died, and the ground-lease on the Theatre expired in the spring. On 28 July the Privy Council ordered that playing be suspended until Allhallows and that the playhouses be 'plucked downe' (qtd in *ES*, IV, 322). The order was not carried out, but the Chamberlain's men were displaced for a few months, touring in Kent and the Midlands (August and September) and opening late in the fall season (October). At some time during the year, three of Shakespeare's plays appeared in quarto with an advertisement of the company on the title-page.

In July, an event occurred in the playhouse world that does not appear to have disrupted the business of Shakespeare's company to any great extent. What happened was that Pembroke's men performed a play called *The Isle of Dogs* at the Swan. Some Privy Councillors, who heard that the play was offensive, sent out orders under which a few of the players and one

of the dramatists were arrested. In October after they were released, the players joined other of their fellows now under contract with the Admiral's men and together they sued Francis Langley, the owner of the Swan, to recover their playing gear. Even though *The Isle of Dogs* affair does not immediately concern the Chamberlain's men, it is significant to them as a unit in the story of their success, for it shows how theatre historians have understood competition among the London companies. This competition is usually portrayed as a war between the rival companies of the Admiral's men and the Chamberlain's men, from which the latter emerged victorious to become the King's men.[18] The plot ingredients in the *Isle of Dogs* affair – troublesome playtexts, fragmentation of companies, indentured service to a company for playing and playwriting, im-

---

[17] Greenfield discusses these issues in terms of an action by the Corporation Common Council in Gloucester, November 1580 ('"Some restreinte ageinst commen Players": Provincial Playing and the New Historicism', seminar paper, 'Essays in Theatre History: What Do Facts Mean', Alan Nelson, leader, Shakespeare Association of America, Philadelphia, 1990). Not all scholars are comfortable with the reception of the REED project in the academic community. Theresa Coletti questions the sanction of 'fact and objectivity' that she sees in the conception of the project and the 'noninterventionist mentality' of its editorial policy ('Reading REED: History and the Records of Early English Drama', *Literary Practice and Social Change in Britain, 1380–1530*, ed. Lee Patterson (Berkeley, 1990), pp. 248–84, p. 249).

[18] In this putative rivalry, the Admiral's men supposedly had the upper hand in 1594 because Edward Alleyn was a more experienced and better-known player than Richard Burbage. But the balance shifted over the years; and when the Chamberlain's men invaded the territory of the Admiral's men in Southwark by building the Globe across from the Rose, the Admiral's men fled to a distant northern suburb. Wallace discovered depositions by John Alleyn in the Brayne–Burbage suits that seemed to introduce a personal hostility between the Alleyns and the Burbages. Greg and Chambers assumed that the enmity persisted between Edward and Richard. By 1935, R. B. Sharpe could speak of the 'Burbage–Alleyn feud' as fact (*The Real War of the Theaters, 1594–1603* (Boston, 1935), p. 4).

prisonment by the Privy Council, litigation between former colleagues – come together in a rhetoric of denigration that justifies the subordination and marginalization of the dramatists and corporate structures of 'other' companies, i.e. those in competition with the Chamberlain's men.

Numerous scholars have challenged the part of this rhetorical construct that relies on a negative characterization of Philip Henslowe and the management practices in his *Diary*. The characterization does not originate with Edmond Malone, who first published material from Henslowe's papers, but with J. P. Collier, who edited the book of accounts in 1845. Collier praised the diary for illuminating the operations of a theatrical business, but he called Henslowe 'an ignorant man' with 'a bad hand' and the accounts 'disorderly', 'negligent', and 'confused'.[19] F. G. Fleay completed the characterization by referring to the Henslowe papers as 'the old, pawnbroking, stage-managing, bear-baiting usurer's MS'.[20] Moreover, Fleay made Henslowe out to be an unscrupulous capitalist who kept players subservient and dramatists in debt. Against this machiavellian portrait, Fleay set the house-keeper-sharers of the Chamberlain's men 'whose interest was that of the whole company' (p. 118). Even though Greg decided that Henslowe's rôle was more as accountant and banker than company manager, he believed that Fleay's contrast of business practices at the Rose and Theatre was 'in the main a true one'.[21]

In 1962 Bernard Beckerman challenged the dogma that business practices at the Rose differed from those at the Globe by insisting that *Henslowe's Diary* preserves the practices and commercial strategies of an Elizabethan repertory system used as well by the Chamberlain's men (*Shakespeare at the Globe, 1599–1609*); in 1971 he reversed the character of 'usurious tyrant' by the audacious claim that Henslowe made interest-free loans to players and dramatists with the benefit to him of ensuring 'the continuous use of his play-

house'.[22] In 1985 S. P. Cerasano published substantial biographical information that places him in the wider context of his many businesses and his rôle as family benefactor.[23] But Henslowe has been hard to rehabilitate. Carol Rutter defends him further in *Documents of the Rose Playhouse* (1984). In a fresh attempt to confront Henslowe's rôle with the company, particularly the implication of his territorial phrasing ('my company', 'to searve me', 'bownd him sealfe vnto me'), Neil Carson concludes that 'Henslowe obviously knew, but tended to forget, that while the theatre belonged to him, the Company did not.'[24] Still, some phrasing in current essays on theatre history appears to equate Henslowe with the Admiral's men: for example, 'Henslowe's company', 'Henslowe's players', the 'Henslowe repertory', 'written for Henslowe', and 'Henslowe company patrons'.[25]

In addition to the belief that Henslowe's business practices contributed to the defeat of the Admiral's men, theatre historians used to agree that the Chamberlain's men triumphed because they had the best plays – because, that is, they had Shakespeare's plays. In 1935 Robert B. Sharpe appeared to grant non-Shakespearian plays value as commodities by discussing the nature of competition in the playhouse industry from 1594 to 1603 with, on the one hand, *all* plays performed by the Admiral's men, and, on the other hand, *all* the plays performed by the

19 *The Diary of Philip Henslowe* (London, 1845), p. xv.
20 *A Chronicle History of the London Stage 1559–1642* (London, 1890; rpt. New York, 1964), p. 94; a subsequent citation is noted in the text.
21 *Henslowe's Diary*, 2 vols. (London, 1904, 1908), vol. 2, p. 113.
22 'Philip Henslowe', *The Theatrical Manager in England and America*, ed. Joseph W. Donohue, Jr (Princeton, 1971), pp. 19–62, p. 43.
23 'Revising Philip Henslowe's Biography', *Notes and Queries*, n.s. 32 (1985), 66–71.
24 *A Companion to Henslowe's Diary* (Cambridge, 1988), p. 33.
25 These are Andrew Gurr's phrases ('Intertextuality at Windsor', *Shakespeare Quarterly*, 38 (1987), 189–200).

Chamberlain's men. Sharpe mentioned plays at other playhouses, but he felt comfortable excluding the companies that performed them because he had been conditioned (as we have been) to assume that companies without a playhouse of their own over the better part of this ten-year span were not a commercial threat.

But of course there *was* theatrical activity at playhouses and inns throughout the London area. The Curtain was still in business after the Chamberlain's men left in 1597, for Thomas Platter went there in 1599 as well as to the Globe, and he had more to say about the play at the Curtain, though he did not name it or the company. The Swan was in business from early summer 1595;[26] Pembroke's men, as we have seen, were there by February 1597; and it continued in use after 1603, for Lady Elizabeth's men played Thomas Middleton's *A Chaste Maid in Cheapside* there (according to an advertisement on the title-page of the quarto in 1611). There were also companies at the Bell, Cross Keys, Bull, and Bel Savage inns in the 1590s. At the Boar's Head inn, as Herbert Berry makes clear, there was a new, permanent stage and galleries in 1598, and companies leased the stage continuously to 1605 or 1606 and sporadically thereafter to 1616.[27]

Sharpe knew that plays influenced one another in story and genre, but he was convinced that texts judged to be good by the literary standards of the early 1900s were responsible for the success of the Chamberlain's men and the plays so judged to be bad were responsible for the defeat of the Admiral's men. It helped his argument enormously that Henslowe's accounts showed how many of the Admiral's plays were the product of collaboration, for scholars readily agreed that plays by two, three, four, much less five men were inferior to plays written by one. It helped that most of the Admiral's plays were lost and that most of the anonymous plays in the Chamberlain's repertories were lost not only in text but also in title. It helped that scholars generally assumed that good and/or popular plays some-

how found their way into print.[28] The 'real war' of repertories, therefore, came down to a competition between old plays in the Admiral's repertories by Marlowe and Kyd plus a few new ones by Chapman and new plays in the Chamberlain's by Shakespeare and Jonson.

However, if we define the competition among the London companies in terms of these few privileged texts, we will not notice a principle of commerce that gave value to the majority of plays in each company's repertory year after year. This is a principle of duplication by which companies acquired sequels (*1, 2 Tamburlaine*; *1, 2 Hercules*; *Love's Labour's Lost, Love's Labour's Won*), extended a popular story in serial form (*1, 2, 3 Civil War of France*, plus the *Introduction*; *1, 2, 3 Henry VI*), and combined sequels and serials with spin-offs (*The Blind Beggar of Bednal Green, 2 Blind Beggar, Tom Strowd*; *1, 2 Henry IV, Henry V, The Merry Wives of Windsor*). Further, they capitalized on material in other companies' repertories *not* by stealing the text or buying it from a bookstall but by getting a dramatist or consortium of dramatists to write a similar play for them (*The Famous Victories of Henry V, Henry V*; *1 and 2 Henry IV*; *The True Tragedy of Richard the Third, Richard III, Richard Crookback*; *King Leir, King Lear*).

None of the companies could afford 'fillers' in the repertory, not even a company with six or eight plays by Shakespeare among its annual

---

[26] William Ingram, *A London Life in the Brazen Age* (Cambridge, Mass., 1978), p. 109.

[27] *The Boar's Head Playhouse* (Washington, DC, 1986).

[28] By theories of the companies' relationships to the stationers that date back to the work of A. W. Pollard, we have believed that companies tried to keep their best plays *out of* publication, as evidenced by orders to 'stay' the printing. Peter Blayney, in a talk delivered at the Folger Shakespeare Library in 1987, severs the connection between staying orders and the company's desire to protect texts by showing that the order applied to texts without the proper approval of stationers' licensers. It had nothing to do with the stationers' acquisition of the text, and it did not signal that the acquisition was a piracy.

offerings. Certainly there were plays each year that did not fulfil the company's commercial expectations, but they none the less mattered to the overall make-up of the offerings in popular subject matter, old and new genres, and multipart plays. The point, really, is that the quality of a play by literary standards of early twentieth-century criticism was not a factor in the company's purchase of a text from a dramatist or team of dramatists. The ways in which a play reflected a broad spectrum of theatrical tastes was. One strain of new narratives in Elizabethan theatre history thus addresses the interests of playgoers for whom the plays were written. In the many circumstances in which these interests were the political, economic, and social conditions in London and England, the plays move out beyond strategies of marketing to situate themselves in the debates about cultural issues among the young swells who cruised Paul's Walk or the revolutionaries who gathered at Essex House.

AFTER 1603: 'TIS GOOD SLEEPING IN A WHOLE SKIN

In comparison with the discord of the playhouse wars, the years after 1603 in the traditional narrative are marked by calm. Shakespeare's company, due to its excellence, was chosen by King James to be his servants, and the rest of the companies fell in place at the rear. The Admiral's men, now the company of Prince Henry, remained at the Fortune in Middlesex; Worcester's men, now the company of Queen Anne, remained at the Boar's Head in Whitechapel for a few years until they moved into the new Red Bull in Clerkenwell. Supposedly, both companies adjusted quietly to the turn in their commerce down market (a position that had always been a fair measure of the dramatic talent on which they relied). The boys' companies lost their novelty and therefore much of their clientèle; the company at Blackfriars was censured for the performance of offensive plays. The King's men moved to

consolidate their control by frequent appearances at Court, the lease of the playhouse at Blackfriars, and the acquisition of plays by a new and successful team of dramatists.

But even this unit of the old story is vulnerable. Leeds Barroll challenges the assumption that the King's men had 'a special relationship to the state or to the person of the monarch'.[29] He reviews features of the political scene of 1603–4 and finds no evidence that the King 'chose' Shakespeare's company to be his servants. He questions the 'honour' received by the King's men in being a mere twelve among the hundreds of royal servants in the coronation procession (May 1604) and the welcome party for the Constable of Castile (August 1604). As for the expanded Court calendar, Barroll notes that James himself attended few of the plays (he seems to have preferred hunting). And as for their two playhouses, repeated outbreaks of plague from March 1603 through 1611 abbreviated each playing year; for much of the time, the King's men did not play at either the Globe or Blackfriars.

Furthermore, the commercial operations of the King's men after 1603 do not show an unusual refinement in all areas. There are texts in the repertory that would be called potboilers if they were owned by Prince Henry's men or Queen Anne's: for example, *The Spanish Maze*, *Robin Goodfellow*, *The Fair Maid of Bristow*, *The London Prodigal*, *Gowrie*, *The Miseries of Enforced Marriage*, *The Devil's Charter*, *A Yorkshire Tragedy*, *Richard the 2* (so called by Simon Forman), *The Knot of Fools*, and *A Bad Beginning Makes a Good Ending*. One of these plays, *Gowrie*, attracted the wrong kind of attention at Court. John Chamberlain, who wrote of the event to Ralph Winwood on 18 December 1604, said that the tragedy was likely to 'be forbidden', even

---

[29] 'A New History for Shakespeare and His Time', *Shakespeare Quarterly*, 39 (1988), 441–64, p. 461. Barroll makes this and subsequent arguments in this paragraph in *Politics, Plague and Shakespeare's Theatre*, (Ithaca, 1991).

though it had been given only twice, because 'some great Councellors' had objected to it.[30] Another of the company's plays, *The Miseries of Enforced Marriage*, was written by a man whose criminal activity would have outraged Chambers, if he had known of it, more than the behaviour of 'the extremely out-at-elbows men of letters' in Henslowe's employ (*ES*, II, 162). This man was George Wilkins, who claimed in 1612 to know both of the principals in the Belott-Mountjoy suit and who may have collaborated with Shakespeare on *Pericles*. According to Roger Prior, Wilkins was repeatedly called before the Sessions in Middlesex on charges for an assortment of unsavoury actions over a period from 1610 to 1618 (at least).[31] These actions include harbouring women at his tavern who were wanted for theft and kicking a pregnant woman in the belly.

Shakespeare's company did have an advantage in terms of the repertory due to the accession of King James, and it was an important economic one, but it was available as well to the other London companies. The advantage was the revival of plays from their Elizabethan repertories. The new monarchs had not seen their old plays, and the companies could use them to fill out their offerings at Court. An account from the Office of the Revels survives for the holiday period in 1604–5, and the titles attributed to the King's men show that over two-thirds of their performances were of plays in revival: *The Merry Wives of Windsor*, *The Comedy of Errors*, *Love's Labour's Lost*, *Henry V*, *Every Man in His Humour*, *Every Man Out of his Humour*, and *The Merchant of Venice*. A letter by Walter Cope to Robert Cecil dated 1604 makes the same point. Cope quotes Richard Burbage as saying that 'there is no new playe that the quene hath not seene, but they have revyved an olde one, cawled *Loves Labore Lost*, which for wytt and mirthe he sayes will please her excedingly'.[32] These revivals were an economic advantage to the companies because as a rule old plays cost less to produce than new ones. The years after 1603, being repeatedly and suddenly interrupted by plague, were hard on the budget of even the best financed company. Plays that were relatively inexpensive to stage and that could be used at Court as well as at the commercial playhouse – and that could also be taken on tour – were newly valuable as commodities.

In the traditional narrative, the Chamberlain's–King's men enjoy a position of privilege for many reasons, including their fortunate connection with the Burbages, benevolent corporate structure, superior repertory, and royal sanction. In recent tellings of the company's history, however, scholars find more similarities than differences among the adult London companies in management practices, acquisition and marketing of the repertory, touring, and patronage. Future discourse in theatre history is likely to continue to offer alternatives to the traditional narrative on the Elizabethan playhouse world, perhaps even contradictory alternatives. Although this new theatre history

---

[30] E. Sawyer, ed., *Memorials of Affairs of State in the Reigns of Queen Elizabeth and King James I*, 3 vols. (London, 1725), vol. 2, p. 41. Chamberlain offers two reasons for the offence: that the play required an impersonation of the reigning monarch (the theatre had long respected a protocol that forbade such impersonations), and that 'the matter or manner be not well handled'. By the latter, Chamberlain might be implying that the dramatization of the Gowrie brothers' conspiracy had not been skilful, giving playgoers who questioned James's rôle in the incident the opportunity to mock the official explanation of the plot. In that official story, the twenty-one-year old Earl of Gowrie and his eighteen year-old brother lured James from a hunting party to their manor house where they attacked him. They were killed in the rescue. Their corpses were put on trial, found guilty of treason, and dismembered at the Cross of Edinburgh. For the public reaction to the official version of the Gowrie plot, see F. Arbuckle, 'The "Gowrie Conspiracy" (part 2)', *The Scottish Historical Review*, 36 (1957), 89–110.

[31] 'The Life of George Wilkins', *Shakespeare Survey 25* (1972), 137–52, p. 142.

[32] *The Third Report of the Royal Commission on Historical Manuscripts* (London, 1872), vol. 3, pt. 3, p. 148.

will not be easy to digest into 'overviews' for editions of the plays, coffee-table books, and reference anthologies, it will have the merit of accommodating the larger theatrical and cultural worlds in which the companies operated.

This discourse, like the traditional narrative, will praise the achievement of Shakespeare, but its praise will not be expressed in hollow, exclusionary rhetoric.

SHAKESPEARE PERFORMANCES IN ENGLAND, 1989–90

PETER HOLLAND

In 1959, in his book on acting, *Mask or Face*, Sir Michael Redgrave had this to say about Shakespeare in Stratford:

audiences drawn . . . from all over the world come to see Shakespeare's plays at Stratford-on-Avon with an extra sense of expecting something more (or rather, something else) than they can get at even the most exciting production in other theatres. Some of them come with a sense of dedication. Quite a few, I am sure, come with a feeling of penance. As a gentleman was heard to remark leaving the theatre one night after one or other of the 'tragedies': 'Every bloody play I come to now seems to last more than three hours.' . . . It sometimes astonishes me that the genius of Shakespeare and the combined skill of the director and actors should succeed in keeping such members of the audience quiet, let alone satisfying them. For really, a number of them have so little idea of what is in store for them that I can well believe the story which was told me by members of the Sadler's Wells Ballet Company who were performing at that theatre for a fortnight before Peggy Ashcroft and I opened there in *The Merchant of Venice*. Two ladies were reading their programme for the ballet *Coppelia*, and one said to the other: 'Oh dear! We've picked the wrong day. Peggy Ashcroft and Michael Redgrave aren't dancing.'   (pp. 103–4)

I have never envied the task of the Royal Shakespeare Company nor indeed of the National Theatre. Audiences have not changed that much in thirty years. For all those who arrive with the sense of dedication, more now arrive with a feeling of penance; indeed I have felt, over this year's stint of reviewing both in Stratford and in London, even more strongly

than Redgrave's gentleman, that 'every bloody play I come to now seems to last more than *four* hours' as productions of *King Lear* seemed to be trying to rival *Götterdämmerung*. Yet audiences are kept quiet and do leave the theatre satisfied. Some of this year's productions seem more deliberately aimed at one or other segment of Redgrave's audience but a production which aims to do little more than keep its audience quiet may do so by working *against* what Redgrave calls 'the genius of Shakespeare' and it may turn into much more of a penance than a four-hour tragedy.

Of all the emotions Redgrave describes the one I distrust most is the audience arriving with a sense of 'dedication', not least because it is the audience with a memory and the audience that weighs down the company with a sense of imposed responsibility. It is this segment of the audience that has only too clear a notion of what is 'in store' for them or rather an idealized notion of what ought to be in store, coming with an inbuilt refusal to let the production work, demanding instead that it accommodate itself to their own version of the text. This audience is also the one that mutters wisely in the interval that this production isn't as good as the one they saw five or ten or twenty years ago and then feels that the RSC has somehow let them down, failed in its duty. Shakespeare scholars make up a significant proportion of this audience but we have no right to demand of the RSC or the National Theatre that productions in Stratford and London consistently give us that 'extra sense' Redgrave pinpoints of 'expecting something more (or rather, something else) than [we] can get at even the most exciting production in other theatres'. Fortinbras claims, with little justification other than military might, 'rights of memory' in the kingdom of Denmark and audiences have even less justification, fewer rights of memory, to demand that this year's RSC production of a Shakespeare play be better or even as good as the magnificent one seen years ago.

When we do that we tend to forget the other awful productions we may have seen elsewhere in between. There is no space in this article for detailed comment on other Shakespeare productions I have seen outside the work of the RSC and the NT but let me emphasize that none of the things that I shall suggest were poor or disappointing in either company's Shakespeare productions last year were a quarter as poor as the execrable productions of *The Taming of the Shrew* and *Romeo and Juliet* which toured the country in the summer of 1990 with well-respected professional touring companies.

In 1989 the Royal Shakespeare Company decided to split its Stratford season in two. The productions from the early part of the year (reviewed last year in *Shakespeare Survey* by Stanley Wells) moved to London in the autumn and the London company moved to Stratford. There were three new Shakespeare productions in the Memorial Theatre and one in the Swan. The experiment of the split-season was not a success: administratively, indeed, it proved a complete nightmare. A device designed to alter the rhythm of the company's work over many years proved largely inefficacious on stage for the new work of the autumn was largely disappointing, as if the company had run out of ideas and energy: directorial clichés and excesses substituted for real reinvestigation of the texts; glib concepts dominated without offering illuminating rediscoveries. Only in David Thacker's *Pericles* in the Swan, his first production for the company,

was there the fresh inventiveness that the company is usually capable of generating.

No one could accuse Barry Kyle's production of *All's Well That Ends Well* of being short of ideas. Three separate concepts vied for dominance in the production; the problem was their inadequacy and mutual incompatibility. Any one of them might, conceivably, have permitted a view of the play to develop, though each had its own particular limitations. But the cumulative effect was of directorial inventiveness unable to reach a decision about the play or even to demonstrate a legitimate inconclusiveness. Instead the play by turns vanished under the concepts or was simplified to a point of banal unrecognizability, leaving a few actors to fight back on the play's behalf through their awareness of what could have been achieved.

Hanging over the stage as the audience entered the theatre were two banners representing James I and Elizabeth I. As a gesture towards the play's date that might be unexceptionable but, though they were whisked away before the action began, they were strangely brought back for the final scene. By this time, the King of France had acquired a plaid doublet, making him some sort of representation of King James, while the Countess was placed on stage and costumed to echo the hanging showing Elizabeth. There is no reason why directors should feel obliged to play up the Frenchness of the play's France but that is not the same as translating it to an exactly defined moment of English history. Any equivalence was, in any case, blurred by such devices as giving Patricia Kerrigan's Helen a gentle Scots accent and giving Lavatch (Geoffrey Freshwater) a much stronger and at times impenetrable one, thereby moving Roussillon to Scotland and conjuring up, in the relationship of the Countess and Lavatch, bizarre echoes of Queen Victoria and John Brown. The illogicality of the connections was only heightened the more one considered this impossible effect. A gesture towards historical meaning was being offered in such a way that the historical sense was denied. It is, I suppose, conceivable that the King of France could still be read as a compliment to or attack on James, depending on one's view of the character's intelligence and perceptiveness, but that does not help to place the Countess as some historicized figure, least of all as Elizabeth. Elementary historical knowledge, so often a problem for such typological reading, produced a bizarre effect of meaninglessness.

Once the banners had gone, the audience was presented with a full-scale rustic festival complete with upstage violinist leading a rustic dance, a table adequately laden with bread and fruit and an actor carrying a corn-sheaf. As productions of *The Winter's Tale* regularly prove, actors are not adept at seasonal exuberances – they were no better here. Rusticity and the cycle of the seasons became key points of departure for numerous scenes, often providing a literalist source for a character's comments. In Act 4 Scene 5, for instance, the stage was set for autumn, with estate workers sweeping up leaves and a bonfire burning in a tidy incinerator. The Countess's despair over Bertram's actions was neatly fixed by her casting his toy soldiers and a bundle of his letters into the fire, while Lavatch's chilling image of hell (4.5.47–55) was simplistically justified by having him stoking 'a good fire' (4.5.48). At other moments, such literalism infected other scenes in an embarrassingly obvious way: Helen's promise to cure the King in two days ('Ere twice the horses of the sun shall bring / Their fiery coacher his diurnal ring' 2.1.161–2) was underlined by her running twice round the stage, just in case the audience might not have got the point.

But, while the seasonal cycle has obvious connections with the play's rhythm, such ideas need to be followed through, not left as dangling possibilities. In 1.3 Lavatch was accompanied by an onstage Isbel, clearly hoping he'll do the decent thing by her, but Lavatch's comments on sowing and ploughing ('He that

ears my land spares my team, and gives me leave to in the crop' 1.3.44–5) have a curiously ironic effect if the Countess is sowing corn in the same scene. Sometimes the agricultural hints seemed purely tangential to the scene. In 3.2, for instance, a rectangular patch of ground with bean-poles was carefully dragged onto the stage but its only purpose appeared to have been its convenient provision of a bunch of sticks for actors to hurl at each other at the end: as Helen's soliloquy left her exhausted and prone, a bunch of French Lords rushed whooping onto the stage dressed as *Boys' Own* images of Red Indians, complete with face-paint, turning the set into an adventure playground of ropes and slides and treating the bean-poles as spears to stick into the large rocking horse left upstage.

Throughout the production the strongest and most effective idea was this treatment of the world of the war as a bunch of schoolboys playing out fantasy playground games. The night-time manoeuvres became nothing more than a boy scouts' wide game, a jolly prank. Much given to hurrahing, practising their sword drill with preening self-regard or posing in front of a line of mirrors, the lords of the French court seemed apt companions for a very young and boyish Bertram, a nice lad who has barely stopped playing with toy soldiers when he discovers that this is apparently a perfectly acceptable gentlemanly and chivalric way of living in the wider world beyond Roussillon. The war may be, as the Second Lord Dumaine suggests, 'A nursery to our gentry' (1.2.16) but that does not mean that it takes place in some Edwardian nursery. Indeed Paris became very visibly a nursery with its dominant rocking-horse and a king costumed like a children's book illustration of an ermine-cloaked monarch. It was appropriate here that the king should wait for Helen curled up on the floor like a small child clutching a pillow in 2.1, that the triumphant Bertram of 3.3 (the opening scene of the second half) should be mounted on the toy horse and that the discomfited Parolles

1   *All's Well That Ends Well* 2.3, RSC, 1989: The King of France (Hugh Ross) gives Helen (Patricia Kerrigan) to Bertram
(Paul Venables) in a court of mirrors

should end up in 4.3 with a toy drum round his
neck.

Set against the naïvety and outright childish-
ness of this male world the production offered
Helen, Diana and the Widow a sisterhood
support group: the four people playing Florentine citizens in 3.5 were all women, with Ma-
riana clutching a baby, another excessively
literal explanation for a character's statement in
its exact definition of the cause of her stringent
warnings about the consequences of 'the wreck
of maidenhood' (3.5.22). These women accompanied Helen to the Widow's house, reappeared
again in 4.4, having apparently agreed to act as

travelling companions to the Widow (who
seemed to be journeying in a cart borrowed
from Brecht's Mother Courage), but vanished
thereafter.

If, again, this was a thought not followed
through then it was more than compensated for
by the single outstanding performance in the
production, Suzan Sylvester's Diana. I shall
have more to say of her work when considering
Pericles but here her arrival was like an immense
burst of energy and joy. There was an infectious delight in her, an excitement in the games
of sexual desire and a happiness in virtue.
Montaigne's description of virtue as 'a pleasant

and buxom quality' could have been coined for such a Diana. There was no doubt about her chastity – she fully lived up to her name – but there was nothing cold about it either. Teasing the court with the riddle of Helen showed her radiant with a spirit of fun, the pleasures of paradox, but also immensely enjoying being at court, making her infinitely preferable to the rather dour pregnant Helen, dressed in bridal white under her pilgrim's cloak: Bertram might reasonably have complained that his second thoughts were far more sensible. This Diana expressed the straightforward joy of goodness and knowledge.

There was little to set beside this. Paul Venables's Bertram was simply over-parted. Gwen Watford's Countess was dignified in her sadness but uncomfortable in her isolation from the rest of the cast. Patricia Kerrigan was at her best in registering the screaming hurt that Bertram's letter causes her. Bruce Alexander's Parolles, much given to 'yer' for 'you' and 'meself' for 'myself', found laughs throughout but no resilience in the transformations of the end of 4.3. Only in his bedraggled desperate appeals to Lafeu for employment in 5.2 and in Lafeu's mocking but finally benign acceptance of the humiliated figure he has become did some glimmerings of the problems posed for the play by Parolles become visible. But so much else was simply flattened. I never thought to see again an *All's Well* in which Bertram and Helen (and, in this case, the Countess) embrace at the end of the play in a full reconciliation, as if nothing very much has happened and all will live happily after. I suppose that in this production nothing very much had happened and in the tradition of good children's stories everything could be glibly resolved. But that is only a small fragment of the play.

After the huge popular success of John Caird's production of *A Midsummer Night's Dream* earlier in the split season the RSC must have felt confident of repeating it with his production of *As You Like It*. Stanley Wells's comments last year suggested that the brilliance of the comic invention, the frenetic cleverness of the production of *Dream* 'held the play at arm's length' (p. 201). This incipient problem is hugely exacerbated when the comic invention dries up, the energy stops flowing creatively and the freneticism is unsupported by the play. Gags and comic business are no adequate substitute when they are vainly trying to cover up a lack of intelligent thinking about the play itself and they are positively embarrassing when they become a succession of cheap theatrical clichés. *As You Like It* was an object lesson in this respect, a banal series of tired ideas desperately trying to invest the production with excitement and popular appeal.

As usual, the wrestling scene revealed much. Audiences have grown accustomed now to seeing the contest blown up into a farrago with all the theatrical showiness of the television form. This time was no exception. I should have known what to expect when Duke Ferdinand's entry was accompanied by the playing of a fake national anthem with the audience encouraged to stand respectfully. Most of the audience meekly did what they were told and I was made to feel unduly curmudgeonly for sitting firmly in my place. For the fight itself some of the cast joined the audience in the stalls and shouted encouraging suggestions like 'Give him a good kicking' or 'Go on, Charlie-boy', suggestions designed to encourage not the wrestlers but the audience. I am not in the least averse to adding the odd extra line to Shakespeare but if the wrestling has any weight for the play it has to be marked by not giving it spurious weight in the production. Here the ballast brought the play to a complete halt. Theatricality and dramatic purpose were hopelessly at odds. Afterwards Orlando signed autographs, posed for photographs and received a huge trophy. Any hope that his act of naming his father would push the play back towards any intelligent seriousness was futile: the consequence was a comic mass panic and the sudden appearance of bodyguards drawing pistols, putting on sunglasses and effectively turning Ferdinand into a comic mafioso surrounded by a gang of protective clichéd thugs.

When the lure of the momentary effect takes such extreme precedence over any sense of the place of the moment in the architecture of the play, when the energy of the moment has to be faked up because nothing in the sequence of the play is generating it and when the effects are neither particularly funny nor particularly well done, then everything that might give the play a sense of purpose, a reason for having started and a reason to continue, is excruciatingly difficult to maintain. There is an obviousness here, a repetition of previous ideas simply because they usually work or, when something different is tried, a confusion of novelty with creative originality. 'Novelties' is the word for the bad jokes and plastic trinkets found in Christmas crackers; 'originality' is what is needed for a complex play in a major production. It is time the RSC abandoned such tedious devices as the dreadful camp-gay Scots Le Beau, slapping Touchstone's wrists for bad jokes or a bunch of actors on the side of the stage in the forest of Arden (3.3) making rustic noises. There is nothing wrong with deciding how to pronounce Jaques's name: Amiens managed to offer a French Jacques, jakwez and jakes. It may be difficult to show the social and economic status of Phoebe and Silvius and, indeed, a production might with good reason choose not to explore the social organization of the dwellers in Arden; but nothing is gained by having them dressed instead as peasants in their underwear, Silvius in vest and y-fronts wearing a garland and carrying a green chiffon scarf. Britain may have had a 'red nose day' that year but Touchstone's liberal distribution of red noses throughout the play did not provide a definition of the spread of his ideas, his view of the comic world of the play; it is one thing to encumber Joanna Mays's large and ungainly Audrey with one, a mark of possession and connection, a fair indication of her touching pride in him, but when everyone ends up with one the production seems only to have failed to understand that Touchstone's image of the world is not shared by the play as a whole.

This endless, meaningless elaboration in production was echoed by the elaboration of the set. Duke Ferdinand's court was set on a foreshortened stage with steps down to the audience, a design of thirties wood reflecting the decoration of the Stratford auditorium and dominated in the middle of the back wall with a large clock working in real time, a heavy warning to those who knew the play that there was to be no clock in the forest and an easy way for those who were bored to calculate exactly how long the play had been running. The transition to Arden took most of Act 2 (and there was to be no hint of Ardennes, though the ministrations of a dialect coach had not stopped the Warwickshire accents sounding totally unconvincing). Duke Senior and his 'co-mates and brothers in exile' arrived from the cellarage by breaking up the stage floor and spending a disproportionate length of time stacking it on the side of the stage, revealing rough concrete underneath. Rosalind at 2.4.13 opened the massive central doors at the back of the set to reveal the magical world of the forest only to show an open, bleak, gloomy and echoing space. While the forest acquired a few token flowers in the second half, this was an almost unmitigatedly wintry landscape in which the second verse of 'Blow, blow, thou winter wind' was bound to produce an answering flurry of falling snow.

Few actors could survive such competition. Sophie Thompson's Rosalind was gamely gamine. Gillian Bevan's Celia, once she had discarded the tiara and hostess manners of the opening scene, demonstrated a powerful sense of isolation and loneliness, finding nothing in Arden for her. Only Hugh Ross's Jaques, very much the actor in black coat with astrakhan collar, fedora, flower in his buttonhole and cane, offered something substantial, unrecognizable from the coarseness of his Le Beau – the production used numerous doubles between the two courts including the Dukes themselves

(Clifford Rose). The whole world seemed a show put on for his benefit; indeed, at times he took a seat in the front of the stalls to watch the parade of folly, leaping back onto the stage at, for instance, 3.3.65 to help Touchstone get married. The bitterness of his out-of-place dignity turned his report on Touchstone into a brutal language that this Touchstone would not have used: there was no ambiguity here in the transition from 'from hour to hour we ripe and ripe' to 'And then from whore to whore we rot and rot' (2.7.26–7). 'Seven ages', marred only by the need to turn it even more explicitly into a party piece with an exit on 'They have their exits' and a prolonged pause before a re-entrance on 'and their entrances'(2.7.141), was painful in its acerbity. His final comments to Touchstone (5.4.189–90) were inordinately vicious, provoking a response of genuine distress from Touchstone himself. But his final exit, on a darkened stage through a lighted door suggesting a close encounter of the third kind, was meaningless, yet another moment of characteristic excess, the play's vision of the impossibility of even a temporary Arcadia appealing to all buried under a cheap stagey device.

Watching *Coriolanus* in December 1989 was a strange experience. Though Terry Hands's production (with unspecified help from John Barton) did nothing whatsoever to conjure up the analogy, exercising admirable restraint, the events in Eastern Europe inevitably became a point of comparison. As the citizens of Rome flexed their political muscles in search of food and freedom from oppression, images from the countries of the dissolving Warsaw Pact whirled through my mind. The patrician world is, of course, nothing like a Soviet-supported régime but the exhilaration of the discovery of the power of mass protest and of the possibility of exerting a previously unsuspected control over government was powerfully present.

It was, though, present *only* in my mind as a reaction to the text; little on stage supported such a weighty comparison. For the production neither managed to explore the social context for the plebeian revolt nor established a coherent and significant relationship of antagonism between Coriolanus and the people. But when Sicinius asked 'What is the city but the people?' (3.1.199) there was a sudden moment of arrest in the impetus of the scene, a realization, shocked and excited, of the potential revolutionary power of the crowd, that could have been fed effectively into the rest of the production.

As it was, the crowd suffered from the tension between realism and stylization, a stylistic insecurity that bedevilled the production. Occasionally individualized, the plebeians were more often treated as an undifferentiated mass, arranged formally into groups to fill the stage but never appearing comfortable with each other, as if the actors, not the plebeians, had hardly ever met before. Their black costumes, heavily broken down and marked with additions to represent their trades and work, connoted a uniformity, parallel to their choric responses. As usual, the director(s) had found no way of making sense of speeches by 'All', the most ungainly of all Shakespearian speech-prefixes.

Rome, a consistently brightly lit city, was obviously a place where a great deal of civic work was being done: in 2.1, for instance, after the victory over the Volscians, plebeians were hard at work cleaning the frieze on the bronze monument that dominated the stage and in 4.6, once Coriolanus had been banished, Roman citizens could be seen taking up basket-weaving (a sure sign of peace) while the Tribunes, now dressed in gleaming white, wandered around patting babies, conveniently presented by passing mothers for them to pat. In the latter scene, admittedly, the babies were a part of the production's determination to ridicule the Tribunes at every opportunity (exemplified by casting two comic actors in the rôles) but the basket-weaving looked like a serious gesture at fleshing out the reality of Rome. It was, however, not the presentation of a theatrical context but a continuous distraction, trivializing the play's vision of the city.

It was directly comparable to the representations of the Volscian society in 4.3, a ghastly scene set, it would appear, in some Volscian nightclub with two appalling dancers swaying in a fake Tartar routine upstage, a couple sitting on a bench whom I can only describe as canoodling and four other Volscians seated at a table, indicating, I presume, the depths of Volscian depravity and decadence by playing dice and drinking. As throughout the production, the bright daylight of Rome was contrasted with the Volscian gloom broken by fiery torches. But the play's finely detailed contrasts between the two communities were coarsened and trivialized by such business, providing only a distraction and not a context for the play's politics.

What was much more intriguing was the careful and thoughtful use of the women in the two crowds, Roman and Volscian. In 2.3 it was the women plebeians who provided the switch of mood against Coriolanus with the Third Citizen's speech (2.3.166–73) divided between a group of women. In 5.1 there was a strong emphasis on the men arming for the threat of war and, by the end of the scene, a powerful image of the women left behind, the city unmanned. The tiny scene of the women's triumphant return to Rome (5.5) was handed over to the women as well. The speech by the senator was spoken by Valeria but the scene was dominated by Volumnia who paraded Young Martius, now in full military costume, as the new Coriolanus, receiving his father's sword from Valeria. As the people knelt to this image of patrician authority in triumph, Coriolanus' fall became Volumnia's victory, her power transferred from son to grandson, the matriarchal control still unquestioned. Even more emphatically the voices of the Volscian people in 5.6 shouting against Coriolanus were all women, a female recognition of the costs of Coriolanus' actions by the people who are

'widowed and unchilded' (as Aufidius calls them at 5.6.152). The Volscian women urged their men to attack Coriolanus who was knifed by Aufidius and then mobbed and beaten to death by the crowd. Such moments created exactly the notion of a society, a community of people, against which Coriolanus himself was set.

The publicity for the production was dominated by a photograph of Charles Dance's head with dead-pan staring eyes and two strong scars. The latter were invisible in performance; I presume that either scars are difficult to apply every night or they would have harmed the image of film-star charisma that Dance exudes. What the production revealed consistently was a glaring gap between characters' reactions to Coriolanus and Coriolanus himself. On his first entrance the citizens scurried away terrified as he stalked magisterially onto the stage, cradling an unsheathed sword in his arms, as so often throughout the play; in 3.3 his glowering at Sicinius across a small table (conveniently placed to be hurled across the stage by Coriolanus later) was enough to reduce Sicinius (Geoffrey Freshwater) to a gibbering, quaking jelly whose papers rustled uncontrollably in his hands. Again and again Hands used stagey devices to increase the menace and authority of Dance's performance. At 1.7.21 the entry of 'Martius, bloody' became an entry of a ghostly figure of power coming down an avenue of light, with another spot glancing flashes of light from the blade of the sword he cradled and with his speech (a very strong 'Come I too late?' 1.7.24) backed up by an exaggerated atmospheric echo. Similarly 'There is a world elsewhere' (3.3.139), spoken in operatic tones as he was virtually offstage, was swollen by an even more intense and 'dramatic' echo.

But such devices only served to emphasize all the more strongly that Dance needed such support to cover his own deficiencies of technique and imagination. At his best as the child of Barbara Jefford's superbly overpowering mother, a performance from her of tigerish

2 *Coriolanus* 2.3, RSC, 1989: Coriolanus (Charles Dance) in the gown of humility meets the people

authority and control, Dance found it easy to underline the potential comedy of, say, the struggle between them in 3.2: 'Look, I am going' (134) sounded like nothing so much as 'look, I really am off to tidy my room', instantly made serious by the force of Volumnia's implied threat of giving up on him in 'Do your will' (137). But at too many other moments the lightness and comedy that Dance finds so much easier surfaced inappropriately: the battlefield request 'Have we no wine here?' (1.10.91) is not a dinner-party enquiry about the contents of the cocktail cabinet. The attempts at demonstrating a vitality and frustrated power were unconvincing. Dance spent too much time

pacing the stage as a weak indication of restless energy. Movement and gesture became mechanical and telegraphed, doing nothing to indicate Martius' character and a great deal to indicate the weaknesses of Dance's stage-skills.

Dance played Aufidius to Alan Howard's Coriolanus. His own Aufidius was Malcolm Storry who demonstrated that he should have been cast as Coriolanus. Shaven-headed for his performance in Peter Flannery's *Singer*, Storry effortlessly produced an aura of brutality and viciousness, a social contempt and an arrogant physicality, all of which Dance lacks. Storry was not helped by the torchlight he was always surrounded by nor by a fight with Martius at

Corioli which was far too long and far too carefully choreographed to suggest a rivalry and danger (with Terry Davies's oriental flute music as inappropriate accompaniment). But he switched between the cold excitement of dominance and the horrified shame and disbelief at defeat. The meeting with Coriolanus in 4.5 transformed magically from the cold, hard threat of the repeated question 'what's thy name?' to an exhilaration of recognition, the realization that Coriolanus had come to him. By the end of the play, standing astride Coriolanus' corpse, Storry's Aufidius was both triumphant and yet emptied by the triumph; as the crowd shuffled off and sneaked away, Aufidius and the nobles, left alone on stage with the corpse, picked it up and bore it off with the last one extinguishing the last torch to leave the stage in darkness, a downbeat ending that showed a confidence in the production rarely visible elsewhere.

I cannot leave the production without congratulating Amanda Harris who as Virgilia displayed the remarkable ability in 1.3 of doing her needlework standing up, a skill that neither I nor anyone else I have ever met has managed to master. If Christopher Morley was unwilling to clutter his design by so much as a single chair, Virgilia might have been allowed at least to sit on the floor.

Some productions seem almost deliberately to set out to offer projects for future academic research. Any production of *Pericles* is bound to lure textual scholars like a swarm in search of academic honey. The advance publicity for David Thacker's production in the Swan announced that the rehearsal process had treated the text as a set of open possibilities for experimentation and I duly prepared myself carefully to be able to report on the relative quantities of Shakespeare, Wilkins and Gary Taylor in the final result. It is a clear indication of the brilliance of Thacker's distinguished work that all my careful preparation proved unavailing. It was not that the text was unclear but that the verve and energy of the performance simply stopped me thinking about and noting textual variants. A few changes I shall record below but any graduate student in search of a theatre history project need search no longer.

What the production exuded through every pore was sheer delight in the possibility of telling a story in the theatre. So much of the best of recent small-scale theatre has been a rediscovery of the pleasures of narrative in performance, a development which fed into the RSC's *Nicholas Nickleby*. But the company's Shakespeare work has rarely seemed to be interested in the virtues and delights of a theatre of story-telling. *Pericles* is a play that demands such treatment and it received it in abundance. The tone was set at once by Rudolph Walker's Gower. The description of Gower in *Greene's Vision*, conveniently reprinted in the Oxford *Complete Works* (p. 1168), suggests an odd figure, a man with the 'wan . . . look' of 'they that plyen their book' and with a minutely enumerated costume that justifies a summary of him as 'Quaint attired'; the archaism of the language of Shakespeare's Gower and the rhythms of his verse imply the usefulness of such an image. But Walker's Gower was a genial author–narrator, reading from a book with a comfortable armchair from which to watch the action, a figure closer perhaps to the traditions of television story-telling, as if the stage of the Swan were no different from the set for BBC's *Jackanory* and the audience an avid group of children, eager to know what happened next. In place of Greene's 'visage grave, stern and grim' was a broad grin and for the 'surcoat of a tawny dye / Hung in pleats over his thigh' he wore a smart but comfortable corduroy suit, the epitome of casual style. The actor, who is black, was an almost deliberate inversion of Greene's suggestion of Gower's 'colour pale'.

Thoroughly convincing, he engaged the audience immediately in the pleasures of his tale. Avoiding the beat of couplets like a dangerous infection and minimizing the oddities of lexis to produce a conversational easiness his performance was accessible not mysterious, familiar and charming, not bizarre and distancing, modern not medievalizing. This charm of narrative was shared within the play's own action later, Pericles, for instance, finding a responsive audience from the mariners for his account of his story in Scene 5. But it was also a basis for another transition on which the production harped, the transition from narrative to action. Gower's promise is that 'Your ears unto your eyes I'll reconcile' (18.22) and the production accepted and then justified the transformation promised by his next line: 'See how belief may suffer by foul show' (18.23 – my emphasis). The sentiments indeed were contested by the production which never produced foul show to make belief suffer, whatever may be done to Pericles in that light. The same link of ears and eyes is repeated later when Gower promises 'Where what is done in action, more if might, / Shall be discovered. Please you sit and hark.' (20.23–4). It is crucial that Gower's account is then listened to and seen, the sound always accompanied by sight, the statement proved by the image and the image proved by the narrative, a continuing interchange of narrative and enactment.

With such a start the production promised to be almost too winning, too concerned to please but it proved irresistibly pleasing, unquestionably winning. There was immediately no question that its theatrical inventiveness was to be entirely at the service of the story. In place of the row of heads which the Oxford edition offers as the explanation for 'yon grim looks' (1.40), Thacker showed a line of actors on the gallery at the back of the stage, near-naked corpses which swayed gently as if in a breeze, a perfect theatricalization of the image, defining both the audience's gaze on their bodies as an image, something to be observed, and finding its strength in a mixture of realism and stylization, in the magic of the theatre to create a visual truth from a palpable fiction. Again and again the production offered such striking pictures as accompaniments and symbolic embodiments of the meaning or context of a scene but always with a lightness of touch, a delight in making theatre as the resource for the story's enactment, the progress of the tale. The repeated framing of Pericles at the top of the central stairs from gallery to stage, for instance, served to pinpoint the stages of his journeyings.

Similarly there was a pleasure in filling the stage. The parade of knights (Scene 6) was a delight and one which Simonides shared with a great deal of giggling and clapping, an almost child-like joy in spectacle but one the audience was fully prepared to share. The joust at Simonides' court was an ancient pentathlon of combats, wrestling, spears and swords, all taking place simultaneously, matching the knights in all the possible permutations, a demonstration of Pericles as the ultimate all-round athlete and increasingly isolating him in our attention. The dance of the knights (7.102) also filled the stage but developed the relationship of Pericles and Thaisa, moving from an initial strong eye-contact and a manifestation of her genuine but also embarrassed delight in dancing with him into a close embrace, responding to the orientalized, unpredictable rhythms of the music (by Mark Vibrans), ending finally with a kiss that left the other dancers, now halted in their dance, awkward observers of two so completely wrapped up in each other. Simonides' wry but firm instruction to 'unclasp' (7.110) became a necessary instruction to end the embrace. At such moments the potential of the stage to be both spectacular and personal, general in its movement but focused on individuals, was perfectly in place.

For each demand of the play the production found the theatrical form it needed. The storm in Scene 11, simple but exhilarating, showed a man struggling with the ship's tiller in doing nothing more than trying to keep a piece of wood on the ground with others slipping and sliding, on ropes and ladders around him, accompanied by more music, an extension of the production's already extensive score, but with this active, busy chaos in ideal balance with the figure of Pericles on a platform suspended over the stage. Never interfering with the play's action, the storm action could stop and restart, allowing a moving and quiet stillness for 'A terrible childbed hast thou had' (11.55) and restarting with the urgent haste of the sailors to be rid of the corpse, forcing Pericles to act with a speed he would do anything to resist.

The virtuosity of the production was at its best in the simple effects that movingly ended the first half in the revival of Thaisa. Cerimon, a female proto-Paulina here, created a stage magic of great and delicate beauty, accompanied by onstage assistants making 'still and woeful music' (12.86) from a vibrating bronze bell and other strange sources. Thaisa, reappearing slowly from her coffin arm first, slowly reinvigorated, coming back to life with a wide-eyed and panic-stricken terror, made to read Pericles' letter while still seated in her coffin (Scenes 12 and 14 were run together). The mixture of stylization and realism was never of mutual conflict; instead the style underlined the confusion and dismay of Thaisa, set off, finally, by Pericles, on the gallery, handing over the baby Marina, a real 'inch of nature' (11.34), to Lychorida, Cleon and Dionyza and speaking the last lines of Scene 13 with great simplicity, while Thaisa, Cerimon and the others still occupied the main stage, a silent commentary on Pericles' temporary loss.

What was so remarkable here was the connection between the theatrical discovery of the scene, making a scene important that has never seemed really to work in previous productions I have seen, and the dramatic rediscovery of the play's architecture. For this scene of theatre magic and rebirth was perfectly complemented at the end of the performance by the reunion of Thaisa and Pericles. If there was no attempt to prove a tremendous theatrical power in the *language* of the last scene (Scene 22) – and indeed how could there be after the reunion with Marina? – there was convincing proof of the tremendous theatrical power of its *action*. Diana

(Sally Edwards) was doubled with Thaisa or, rather, Diana became a vision of a transformed Thaisa so that, as she spoke to Pericles (21.225–35) who slept with his head cradled in her lap, the vision anticipated the close family group of the final reunion. The music for the scene recapitulated a version of the music for Thaisa's resurrection and in the strange lighting of desired vision, the wish-fulfilment world of the final moments was complete with an extraordinarily strong sense of the recapturing of a lost family, embracing closely and warmly and comfortingly, with the total assent of the audience; this was everything, indeed, that the final family reunion of Barry Kyle's *All's Well* production was not, a theatrical moment generated by the text and fulfilling its demands, fully recognizing its problems but solving them.

Plays as extravagant and wheeling as *Pericles* place massive demands on design. For the most part the open stage and fluid range of eclectically historical costumes was allowed to flow as the text demanded. Only in the brothel scene did something approximating to a substantial set and firm sense of historical period emerge, with lines of washing mostly in a filthy and rotten carmine colour which dominated the costumes of whores and bawd. The scene was consciously Hogarthian, full of dirty, unkempt and scabby whores vomiting, sleeping, snoring. Helen Blatch's Bawd in huge and wild wig wore a decayed version of the crinoline style. Marina, who alone seemed to be able to attend to her personal hygiene, was transformed from the electric blue of her first costume to a cleaned-up version of the whores' crimson costumes.

As Marina Suzan Sylvester was triumphant. This is not to suggest that there was a bad performance in the entire cast, nor to underrate the serious and powerful work of Nigel Terry (Pericles) or Sally Edwards (Thaisa) or Russell Dixon (Simonides, less successful as Boult), but simply because it was one of the finest Shakespeare performances I have ever seen. Suzan Sylvester has a rare and extremely important

3   *Pericles* 21, RSC, Swan Theatre, 1989: Marina (Suzan Sylvester) is reunited with her father (Nigel Terry)

skill for Shakespeare: she can speak lines as if they have just been thought, turning the verse with a sensitivity to its rhythm and an understanding of its often inordinately complex syntax until the whole becomes clear and fresh and infused with an interaction of thought and feeling. Everything she does flows directly from this perception and this recognition of the emotional power and sensuousness of the language created a Marina with an unusually tactile and sensuous predisposition. Playing with Leonine it seemed only natural for her to jump on his very preoccupied back and then to be dumped unceremoniously on her backside, for her to play physical games with him and

then to caress him as she pleads for her life. Her virtue and innocence are unquestioned but they are manifest in a physicality that is both endearing and, in confrontation with male desire, deeply threatening.

In the brothel scene, for instance, her way of persuading Lysimachus was to be close to him, making the proximity itself a means of enforcing his attention to her words. This was no removed and distant vision of virtue but instead immediate and direct and powerful in its vigour. When he gave her money (19.133) to ease her conscience she held on to his hand to thank him and the gesture made him weep. Brilliantly this proximity was turned on her when Boult, threatening in his proximity to her for the attempted rape, stayed close as he repented, the brutality of his desire (as in Pander's harsh 'Crack the ice of her virginity' 19.167) transformed into an enigmatically disturbing question about what else he might do (19.195–8). Not surprisingly, for the first time, she now pulled away, edging from him during 'Do anything but this thou dost' (199). The scene ended almost affectionately and conspiratorially ('Come your ways', 223).

Challenged by the sight of Pericles, curled up foetally as if asleep, Marina was warmly benign, smiling and joyful. Her warmth found a response in him, an eagerness to hear her story (yet another aspect of the play's and the production's easy emphasis on story-telling). All went smoothly in the progress of the scene until she said 'My name, sir, is Marina' (21.131), a name which provoked him to a frighteningly huge roar and a twisting movement of desired escape. Characteristically she comforted his weeping, keeping close to him as the reunion unfolded.

Throughout her performance Suzan Sylvester found a delight and a warmth that was infectious and a clarity and purpose that was revelatory. It was precisely the humanizing of the character that the play demands. It was the logical centrepiece for David Thacker's richly sensitive production.

The 1990 Stratford season opened with Bill Alexander's production of *Much Ado About Nothing*, inaugurating a season plagued by the extravagances of designers. There are times when I wonder whether designers have ever read the play they are working on. *Much Ado About Nothing* is hardly the most demanding of Shakespeare's plays for a designer. But there are certain things one cannot do without if the production is to have anything approximating to a realist set at all. There must be somewhere that at least suggests a church for Hero and Claudio not to get married in. There must be something approximating to a convincing

monument for Hero not to have been buried in. Finally it is not unreasonable to expect something for both Benedick and Beatrice to hide behind for their respective gulling scenes. In the long hot summer of 1990 Leonato might reasonably have assumed that the weather would have been good enough to have his daughter married in his back garden. However, Claudio ought to have realized Hero could not possibly be dead since Leonato would never have erected such a vulgar funerary urn on the lawn. The RSC's recent disaster with a Benedick trying to hide behind a deckchair ought to have taught them much but this year's production exercised a sexually discriminatory policy that gave Benedick a cypress tree to climb up and fall out of in 2.3 but left Beatrice in 3.1 propped up against the proscenium arch looking unsure whether she was effectively invisible or not – indeed, the lighting, which left her in semi-sepulchral gloom, seemed equally unsure whether she was on stage or not. By this stage the audience felt sorry for the actress, not Beatrice, with no place to hide.

Kit Surrey's permanent garden set of clipped yew hedges with formal chequer-board forestage was not unpromising. The hedges provided a series of entries and spaces for transient observers, allowing Don John, for instance, to flit across the back of the stage towards the end of 2.1. But the hedges were too far upstage for many scenes to make use of them and the need to have the tree flown in and out at erratic intervals combined with awkward transitions to unquestioned interiors (e.g. 3.4) demonstrated the set's limitations.

Beatrice's – or rather Susan Fleetwood's – plight in 3.1 was of a piece with the production's difficulties with Beatrice all through. Things started well with the discovery of her in 1.1 fencing with Leonato and comfortably beating him, even if it was a rather literal analogy to the wit combats to follow. The fencing gloves anticipated the glove that Beatrice and Benedick used to throw down their challenge to each other, its transfer marking the oscillations of power: thrown down by Beatrice on her exit at 1.1.153, for instance, it was returned by Benedick on his exit at 2.1.257. Susan Fleetwood's confident and intelligent handling of the language, mature and effective, was rather helped by being set against a Hero and co. who were all too like characters in *The Mikado* 'full to the brim with girlish glee'. She even survived the fact that the production gave all the best jokes to Benedick, a string of opportunities finely taken by Roger Allam, but the dryness of her gulling scene was simply confusing. After all there was no lack of inventiveness in the Benedick scene; I particularly cherish the way that Don Pedro, getting no answer from Leonato to his question 'How, how, I pray you?' (2.3.112), walked once round the tree with him so that his next words, 'You amaze me', became a faked response to the silent answer. I had thought that it was no accident that Benedick's response to the awful setting of 'Sigh no more, ladies', sinking down with his fingers holding his nose, mimicked so perfectly the audience's private thoughts – until the setting of the hymn at the monument proved to be equally bad. When Ilona Sekacz produces music this poor it suggests that something is seriously wrong with the RSC's composers.

But Beatrice's defencelessness in the face of Hero and Ursula was more than a consequence of the set. Instead the character had lost her comic defences. That is, of course, a perfectly reasonable reading of the sequence but, left alone sentimentally spotlit on a darkening stage for her soliloquy (3.1.107–16), Beatrice was left to reach for a genuine weight and seriousness that the production seemed unwilling to allow her. This problem was all of a piece with the production's argument about the play's attitude towards women, for clearly they were of far less importance than male-bonding and an awareness of social hierarchies. Beatrice's mocking of Don Pedro's offer of marriage was especially disruptive not only because his status was ridiculed, a comic version of the pro-

duction's recurrent fascination with the way language disrupts and transgresses social formalities, but even more because Don Pedro's offer was plainly not far off being serious. His admiration of her seemed to matter because such feelings so rarely surfaced.

This male focus was visible in the church scene (4.1), where the focus of attention was most often on Leonato, not Hero. His distress and fury led him to assume the truth of the accusations and to come close to putting into practice the violence against her that he promises ('These hands shall tear her' 4.1.193). In this context Beatrice's near-hysteria at Benedick's refusal to kill Claudio was a logical response to her powerlessness and her cry 'O that I were a man!' (4.1.304) sounded like a perfectly sensible ambition and one which her vehemence had brought her halfway towards fulfilling. When later Benedick advised her, with great seriousness, 'Serve God, love me, and mend' (5.2.84) he seemed to be offering her the protection of a male world. By the end of this production the relationship of Beatrice and Benedick mattered much less than Claudio and Benedick, a relationship still as venomous after the rebirth of Hero as it had been after her death. Benedick's barely controlled fury at 'my lord Lackbeard' (5.1.188) has not at all abated. Only Beatrice's intervention stopped Benedick continuing the quarrel after Claudio's sneering delivery of his final speech in the play (5.4.111–15) and the play's climax was effectively the reconciliation of the two men with a handshake.

The production's argument, then, seemed perfectly clear and interesting. But the result was disappointingly dull. Too many performances seemed perfunctory. The reconciliations at the end, Benedick and Claudio apart, were too easy, with Leonato wagging an admonitory finger at Margaret (5.4.4). Benedick apart, everyone else in the production seemed locked into a monochrome style, starting blandly and devoid of the accumulated details of individuality that the text so richly provides. Against such a colourless background, Allam's Benedick's transformation across the interval risked appearing extreme, a transformation into an entirely different emotional register as well as a change of costume, the discarding of beauty-spots and the shaving-off of a particularly magnificent moustache. The change was justified as comedy – his struggles with his high-heeled shoes on his exit at 3.2.67 ought to be a collectors' item – but it also developed with a logic and coherence made manifest through Allam's intelligent playing.

So often at present, the RSC's most successful Shakespeare productions seem to be in the Swan: David Thacker's brilliant *Pericles* at the end of the previous season was followed by Sam Mendes's *Troilus and Cressida*. For a director of such youth and comparative inexperience to achieve so much in a production of a play which the RSC has produced so often and so well over its history was a major accomplishment. The production's success was, even more surprisingly and gratifyingly, based less on the imposition of directorial concept than in allowing the play and the actors space in which to work.

As soon as Norman Rodway stepped out as prologue, without being preceded by the sort of grand procession with which so many directors feel obliged to begin a play, the production made clear its confident belief in the virtue of clarity. Rodway fixed a cultured and wryly witty attitude to the Trojan war, pinpointed as he flicked the medal pinned to his blazer to define himself as the 'Prologue armed' (23). The decision to have Pandarus as Prologue was, in itself, a tidy one, economically linking the beginning and the end of the play together, making the diseased Pandarus of the epilogue a distorted image of the dapper figure at the start.

Though this *Troilus and Cressida* was framed by Pandarus and the power of his urbane wit, its Troy was not defined by him. Throughout the production realized the play's multi-vocality, its refusal to hierarchize the competing tonalities. As the Trojans returned from battle in 1.2 Pandarus and Cressida were displaced from the centre of the stage to the side gallery. Instead of the procession of warriors being mediated for the audience by Pandarus' dominance, Pandarus was forced to compete for the audience's attention with the silent entries, a conflict between what is seen and how it is interpreted that epitomized much of the play's method. Pandarus' wit was allowed its full weight of humour but our interest was focused as much on the ritual of washing which the returning soldiers went through centre-stage, using the pool of water in which Pandarus and Cressida had previously been paddling. Even there there were jokes, actions that echoed Pandarus' mockery, Paris slicking his hair back, Helenus nearly forgetting his sword, Troilus slouching in so that even Pandarus could be excused for not recognizing him, but at the same time there were others who, in effect, fought with Pandarus' wit for the right to behave with dignity, to make a ritual of purification into an integral part of the serious fact of their having survived a day's battle, washing the blood from their swords and then washing their faces or drinking. In such a context the ceremony acquired an importance invested in it by the participants, an importance that Pandarus could not really dent.

Nor could he undermine the feelings of the lovers, for here the actors managed to create their own difficulties, the one area of the production in which they seemed to need more help from the director than Mendes had given them. I have always found Amanda Root an opaque actor, by which I mean that I cannot follow her character's thinking. Her Cressida was light-weight and trivialized, unable to suggest the deliberately confusing range of response that Cressida should provoke. She was at her best in 3.2 where her nervous energy, her giggly shyness found focus. The childish pertness of the early scenes was still strongly in place in the Greek camp so that there was no transition, no disjunction, no creative confusion out of which the ambivalences of the character could emerge.

If her last lines to Diomede, 'Ay, come. O Jove, do come' (5.2.107), mean no more than that she is desperately in need of sex then the complexities have been smoothed out in an oddly misogynistic manner.

She was not helped by Ralph Fiennes's Troilus, for Fiennes is unlike any other actor in the company, an actor who is like a strange throwback to an earlier world of classical emotional performance but who expresses that emotion through a degree of separation from the other actors on stage. This Troilus was unable to touch Cressida, either before their love-making or after it, and while there was a full-throated emotional freedom in his violent response to seeing her with Diomede, there was also a sense in which the actor was happier, freed of the need to respond to any other prompting than his own. I was moved by his distress but without any awareness of a love that preceded it. A Troilus who has not made manifest the sexual excitement of the character has nothing on which to build the distress.

If Troy stands or falls on the dignified Hector of David Troughton, the Troy scenes stand or fall on the appearance of Helen. Like the wrestling scene in *As You Like It*, it has become a way of defining productions, evaluating their intelligence. Paris' servant describes Helen as 'the mortal Venus, the heart-blood of beauty, love's visible soul' (3.1.32–3) but his hands pushing out the front of his vest turned the word 'attributes' ('Could not you find that out by her attributes?' (3.1.35–6)) into a substitute for 'tits', registering the play's ambivalence about Paris' 'Nell'; Pandarus' uneasy response to this wit anticipated his self-evident difficulties in dealing with Helen and Paris themselves.

Helen's entrance was another ritual, the slow unveiling of the gold-wrapped figure carried in high on a dish. What was revealed was not a traditional image of blonde beauty but a buxom Hollywood vamp, a scarlet woman – or at least a woman in a garish red dress, wearing a gold collar whose extravagance was perfectly tasteless. Sally Dexter, acting, as

throughout the season, with remarkable selflessness in her willingness to mock her own appearance, seemed a ghastly parody of Elizabeth Taylor. But the scene, characteristically, allowed her a transformation. Left alone with Paris at the end she was genuinely willing to help Hector unarm, ''Twill make us proud to be his servant' (3.1.152), and deeply aware of her own shaming responsibility for the war.

If I have been suggesting the differing responses to and from Norman Rodway's Pandarus served to define Troy, then in the Greek camp all else paled into insignificance beside Simon Russell Beale's Thersites. I have found it easy to ignore Ulysses, Nestor and even Agamemnon, performances without the strong colours necessary to be visible next to this Thersites. Few could survive such competition. Richard Riding managed it: his Ajax, bullish and magnificently stupid, with a huge inflated physique to match his ego, fully deserved Ulysses' barbed praise of his 'spacious and dilated parts' (2.3.245), but retained a threat of violence in his bullying. There was also Ciaran Hinds's supercool bikeman Achilles, all leather, viciousness and designer stubble, a languid cross between poseur and introvert, and Paterson Joseph's excellent Patroclus, a match for Thersites in the 'pageant of Ajax' (3.3.263ff.) but also deeply moving in his love for Achilles as he registered his pain at Achilles' comments on Polyxena. Little else stood out. We might indeed wonder whether it is right for Thersites to have that degree of dominance but his subversion of others' pretensions was nearly absolute.

From Thersites' first entrance as he slowly and deliberately set up Ajax's dinner and then equally slowly and deliberately drooled into the platter, his denial of value, his reduction of everything below the lowest possible worth, was repulsively unquestioned. White-faced with eyes red with rheum, his hands covered in surgical gloves to hide his eczema, and with a hunchback, Beale oozed physical exclusion and emotional resentment. He fed his loathing,

4   *Troilus and Cressida*, RSC, Swan Theatre, 1990: Thersites (Simon Russell Beale)

encouraging Ajax to beat him, even seeming at first to enjoy his schoolboy whipping. Though he proudly announced that he 'serve[s] here voluntary' (2.1.96), he soon turned up at Achilles' tent with his belongings in carrier-bags with a fool's bauble sticking out the top, looking for employment, desperately ingratiating. Displaying the skills of alternative stand-up comic, it was also characteristic that he should carefully pocket Achilles' discarded apple core or that the careful scene-setting for Hector's arrival at Achilles' tent, with Achilles and Patroclus languidly posed on the ladders, should be undercut by the awkwardness of his attempt to hang on to his ladder while holding a ghetto-blaster playing a sensual song. The song's title was itself a deliberate joke, a number called 'Lover man, where can you be?'

Only at one moment was his perception of the world, his containment of human behaviour into his grid of reference, defeated. After the double-watchings of 5.2, Thersites picked up Cressida's discarded scarf. It looked for a moment as though he was going to sniff it like some fetishist fascinated by women's knickers but instead he contemplated it in genuine amazement. The object which had been invested with such value by Cressida and Troilus was simply beyond his comprehension. He could make nothing of their passion.

Mendes both enabled and was helped by such performances in creating a bleakly comic version of the play. There were a few moments of mistake and excess. The contrast of the council scenes between dirty Greeks in mixtures of overcoats and breastplates and the clean, white-uniformed Trojans was too neatly absolute. Achilles' welcome of Hector to his tent did not need the help of black-masked Myrmidons standing round the back of the stalls clicking chinese blocks menacingly. Nothing is gained by dispensing with the Greek in splendid armour and replacing him with a light shining into Hector's eyes, accompanied by a throbbing heartbeat. The unashamedly symbolic power of the anonymous character cannot be transformed so glibly into Hector's 'fate'.

But time and again Mendes worked with remarkable economy. The addition of the moment of the exchange of Antenor for Cressida, for instance, became another ritual, familiar from spy-films perhaps but still powerful, particularly in the warm welcome Antenor received, defining neatly the unimportance of Cressida for the Trojans. The handling of the battle scenes of Act 5 was simple and adroit, quickly creating multiple perspectives. Most of the cast were lined across the stage facing upstage, backlit so that they became a still frieze, with Thersites in top-hat as Master of Ceremonies, compèring the war, but with the whole scene regarded by Ulysses, Agamemnon and Thersites from the upper gallery. As characters were required to fight they turned and moved downstage before re-assuming their position in the line. Throughout there was a refusal to deny the adequacy of the text, an acceptance that the play works best when it is respected. As a debut production it shared the virtues of clarity, simplicity, and pleasure in the narrative of Thacker's *Pericles*.

In *The Conversations with Drummond of Hawthornden*, Ben Jonson talked about his plans for various plays. Drummond records: 'he had ane intention to have made a play like Plaut[us'] Amphtrio but left it of, for that he could never find two so like others that he could persuade the spectators they were one' (*Works* ed. C. Herford and P. and E. Simpson (Oxford, 1925–52) vol. 1, p. 144, lines 420–3). Jonson, never one to place small demands on theatre companies, wanted two pairs of identical twins. When Shakespeare had tackled the problem of twins in *Twelfth Night* he had deliberately based the likeness of Viola and Sebastian on an impossibility: you cannot have identical twins of different genders. In production now Viola and Sebastian rarely look convincingly alike nor, I suspect, could Shakespeare's boy-actor have looked so like the adult actor playing

Sebastian that Antonio's line 'An apple cleft in two is not more twin / Than these two creatures' (5.1.221–2) could have been visibly true. When Orsino describes 'One face, one voice, one habit, and two persons' (5.1.213) we can only fully assent to the similarity of costume. The 'natural perspective, that is and is not' (5.1.214) which he calls it is true in the play's fiction and untrue in the play's performance. But audiences are often rather troubled by the discrepancy.

Modern technology doesn't really help: when, in a television production some time ago, Joan Plowright doubled Viola and Sebastian, the addition of a small moustache only made her Sebastian look ridiculous and the attempt at a gruff male voice would never have fooled anyone. The difficulty of the gender change was simply insurmountable. The twin Antipholuses and the twin Dromios of *The Comedy of Errors* pose no such problems. The BBC Shakespeare series's production of *Errors* used similar techniques to have each pair of twins played by one actor. This year the RSC did the same. But television is not the stage. Desmond Barrit (both Antipholuses) and Graham Turner (both Dromios), fine actors though they are, lack the paranormal skill of bilocation, necessary without cameras and editing.

Since the idea cannot possibly work in the theatre, I shall be wondering what is lost along in the process. But I also want to wonder whether it would be worth doing even if it could be done. One of the great pleasures for the audience watching *Errors* is that we know the answer. We know, because Egeon has told us, that there are two pairs of twins; we know why Antipholus of Syracuse is recognized by the inhabitants of Ephesus and that the reason has nothing to do with Ephesus' reputation for sorcery nor is it a dream.

What we do find, though, is that the overweening confidence with which we begin, knowing the answers, is shaken in the course of the play. I find, every time I watch the play,

that I end up forgetting which Dromio has been sent on which errand by which Antipholus, which one is locked up with Pinch, which one has ended up in the priory. We know how the play will end, in that moment when the Antipholuses and Dromios will all be on stage together, but along the way we end up nearly as confused as the characters. When both Dromios are played by the same actor the audience's ability to be confused, a confusion that, I am suggesting, the play wants us to undergo, is simply evaded, evaded because the audience comes to follow actor, not rôle, Graham Turner not Dromio. The two Dromios were differentiated by the colour of their waistcoats but the audience, rather than trying to remember which Dromio wears the green one, abandons its interest in the confusions, comforted by its recognition of the actor, not the rôle. When, finally, the character has to face his doppelgänger onstage for the last scene, we come to see not two Dromios but two actors, one whom we know and another whom we do not. The history of the characters is replaced by the history of the performance.

It is the emotional force of the ending that is especially harmed. For Shakespeare's ending teeters gloriously on the edge of sentimentality. As brother finds brother at last there is an emotional release for the characters and for the audience. When it works – and it usually does – there is something oddly tearful about the reunions, the reconstitution of the family. Even the inevitably funny rediscovery of the missing mother does not prevent our joy, prefiguring something of the force of the families re-formed at the end of the late plays. By doubling the Antipholuses the force is diluted. The audience watches how the doppelgänger still tries to keep his back to them, following the theatrical technique, the actor's skill, not the play's argument. Even more unfortunately, Ian Judge's production misjudges Shakespeare's carefully downbeat ending. As the stage empties the two Dromios are left alone, their tentative awareness of their equality deliberately low-key yet moving: 'We came into the world like brother and brother, / And now let's go hand in hand, not one before another' (5.1.429–30). The play denies the full-stage ending and ends up with two servants, beaten and mocked throughout the play, now finding a dignity in what they have in common, their brotherhood. Their exit in Judge's production, into the rays of the setting sun, was pure Hollywood schmaltz; it encouraged the audience to find the moment ludicrous, missing completely its simplicity and innocence.

Once past a sombre prison set for the first scene, the design, by Mark Thompson, was unrelentingly excessive, nine garishly coloured doors surrounding a rectangular playing-area. The games played with surrealism, the echoes of Escher and Magritte and the Beatles' *Yellow Submarine*, became in the playing of Pinch a grotesque parody of Dali turned into a cheap stage-conjuror. Dali, the great modern example of artist as showman, would perhaps have been amused. Such work makes no sense of Dr Pinch – productions rarely do – but the magic was a perfect example of the production's obsessive busy-ness. As Dromio was sawn in two and Antipholus vanished from a cabinet skewered with swords Pinch-Dali's aides rushed meaninglessly around the stage in a frenzy of activity not generated by a response to the action.

But the set's bizarre extravagances also transformed Ephesus into the world that the Syracusan twins wrongly perceive it to be. For Ephesus is not a place of irrationality and dream. Antipholus of Syracuse, confronted by the tirade of Adriana, wonders 'What, was I married to her in my dream? / Or sleep I now, and think I hear all this?' (2.2.185–6) but he is not asleep. The play charts the passage of a day, the day that threatens Egeon's execution, but, apart from the inhabitants of Ephesus appearing from behind their front doors to take in the morning milk, there was nothing in the production that recognized that fundamental diurnal rhythm in the text. The play's stage suggests a single place, with houses on a street and, all

the time, the beckoning possibility of that road to the harbour, the route by which the Syracusans might escape the perils of Ephesus. But this set could do nothing with this. Its only gestures to place, large objects hanging over the stage representing the Centaur, the Phoenix and the other places the text refers to, were empty gestures; indeed, on both the occasions I saw the production, I heard bemused members of the audience wondering what the hedgehog was, unable to connect it with any of the play's five references to the Porcupine. The front door to Antipholus' house was a frame without a building.

Against such a setting the actors were driven to unremitting excess. Estelle Kohler screamed her way through Adriana in a grotesque parody of comic acting. Desmond Barrit's preening, largely undifferentiated Antipholuses were an exercise in high camp, only becoming effective in the quiet wooing of Luciana in 3.2, helped by the calm work of Caroline Loncq, a Luciana easily able to forget her kinship to Antipholus. David Killick seemed embarrassed by the leopard-skin drape jacket, tight black leggings and six-inch platform shoes of Dr Pinch – as well he might – and sought to hide behind a Spanish lisp. Only David Waller's Egeon, narrating his history with dignity and drawing helpful diagrams of the distribution of his family on the mast, showed that comedy is not hyperactive.

But the most serious problem with the production was that it simply wasn't funny. Let me take one example. Antipholus of Ephesus, locked out of his house, is confronted by a voice down an entryphone. The device is, of course, a fine solution to the problem of having only one Dromio where two are needed, though I wonder why, with the sophistication of modern sound technology, the lines had to be so muffled as to be incomprehensible. The gag was 'derived' from an earlier RSC production, the brilliant musical version directed by Trevor Nunn. But watching on video Mike Gwilym in that version, sheltering under an umbrella as

5 *The Comedy of Errors*, 5.1, RSC, 1990: Antipholus (Desmond Barrit) and Dromio (Graham Turner) meet their doppelgängers (Ross Harvey, Ian Embleton)

defence against the indoor Dromio's assault, tearing the entryphone off the wall only to find that the damn thing still went on answering him back, I found a comic energy, a theatrical inventiveness and dramatic pace that I missed this time. I do not ask the production to be that good – for even the RSC has rarely been better – but it is sad to see a production borrowing jokes and gags and business and not learning how to copy the energy and style.

The two productions of *King Lear* which opened a few weeks apart, Nicholas Hytner's for the RSC and Deborah Warner's for the National Theatre, could not have been more unlike. Newspaper critics found themselves unable to praise both: those who had admired Hytner's expressed deep disappointment with Warner's; those who damned the RSC seemed to do so in anticipation of their pleasures at the National. Repeatedly in the course of the summer I found myself obliged to defend the RSC *Lear* against angry or dismissive Shakespearians or, though less often, having to explain my dislike of the National *Lear* to Warner's devoted admirers. That it seemed difficult to like both is a direct consequence of the nature of the two productions.

Since in this article I have praised simplicity over directorial excess it may appear perverse now to be praising Hytner's work over Warner's. But I want at this stage to record that, midway through the first half of the Stratford production, I found that I was shaking with fear, panicked and frightened by the action onstage, and that, going to the National full of the highest expectations, I found myself often bored, engaged as often in thinking about the production as watching it, able to stay serenely indifferent to the events on stage even while admiring much of what was being done. Emotional effect is not everything but Warner's method of work ought to leave the action and particularly the actor as a generator of emotional power. When it does not happen – as here for the first time in my experience of her work – the production appears to have failed by its own intents. Hytner's work, as operatically opulent and inventive as ever, succeeded because the invention, fresh and revisionist, cohered, local effects growing into dramatic architecture. The problem is less the intrinsic adequacy of a view of the play than the theatrical adequacy of the representation of the drama. Unlike, say, Ian Judge's *Comedy of Errors*, where theatre substituted for drama, Hytner's *Lear* depended on theatricality, often of baroque extremes, for a dramatic argument.

I must admit to being slightly *parti pris* about the RSC *Lear*, having spent some time working with Hytner while he was developing his ideas before rehearsals as well as helping to prepare the text, but I believe the production to be a great achievement, the finest theatre *Lear* I have seen since Peter Brook's. This *King Lear* was at times deliberately – almost too deliberately – controversial. Of course there were things that did not work. But if the local effects and sustained theatricality seemed to many nothing more than a display of artifice, factitiously overlaying the action, I found them the means to create a force that was genuine and achieved, both emotionally and intellectually. I can only emphasize my sense of being shaken as I have very rarely been in the theatre.

Hytner's productions have always been marked by a fresh re-reading of the play. Nothing is assumed simply through tradition, theatrical rights of memory; nothing can evade sharp rethinking. In this case the rethinking began with the nature of the text. For the first time in England a major production of *Lear* took full account of recent textual scholarship. Hytner wanted to use a Folio text. The text used was essentially the Wells–Taylor Folio, with a few readings restored from Folio. In the event there were a few tiny variant passages and additions from Quarto, lines actors could not quite be persuaded to part with but nothing that substantially affected the logic of the Folio text. The use of the Folio text was entirely convincing, providing, as I had always expected it would, a slightly leaner, more purposive form than the conflated text allows for. The energy of the third quarter of the play never flagged, not only because of the fine authority of Norman Rodway's Gloucester but also because of the clarifying drive of the text itself.

The only major incursion from Quarto was the mock-trial scene. Hytner argued that Folio 3.6 is weak dramatically, the scene seeming to lack shape and purpose. Given the possibility of censorship as the reason for excision, the dramatic and theatrical argument for including Quarto 13.16–51 was convincing. The scene became a pivotal moment of transition and recapitulation. Set in a room full of piles of chairs, effectively the lumber-room of Gloucester's house, the mock-trial set up two stools and two chairs in a deliberate echo of the arrangement of chairs for the daughters and for Lear himself in the love-test of 1.1, with the 'throne' covered in broken-down blue velvet to echo the blue cloth over the throne at the start. Lear's moves and gestures again and again repeated and distorted his actions in 1.1, a nightmarish reworking of the opening. With the placing of the bodies at the end of the play again made carefully to echo the opening scene

6   *King Lear*, 4.5, RSC, 1990: 'I would not take this from report.' Lear (John Wood) and Gloucester (Norman Rodway)
watched by Edgar (Linus Roache)

– why else does Shakespeare bring the corpses of Regan and Goneril onstage? – the mock-trial became a crucial mark of dramatic shaping, the mid-point of the play's journey, a sign of the distance traversed and that yet to come.

There were moments that Hytner's production failed totally to solve. The storm scene, for instance, was notably banal, one of the moments when David Fielding's set proved inordinately constricting. The centrepiece of the set was a giant cube placed upstage and able to revolve. Scene changes were marked by quarter-turns of the cube, presenting alternately a metallic wall or an open space in which furniture could be set. At times, the effect was brilliant: 1.4, for instance, had the cube set with a dinner-table with Goneril's servants laying the table, ending, as the cube turned, with Albany and Goneril settling down for dinner after Lear stormed out; a 180° turn in 5.2 enabled a change from a green, flourishing, optimistic tree to one blackened and blasted by the cataclysm of the defeat of the Cordelia–Lear army. But placing Lear and Fool inside the cube as it turned continually for the storm, backed by a spinning vertical rectangle with storm-clouds projected behind, failed to suggest substantive disorder, even if there was something unnerving about the way that half-turns of the cube always revealed Lear to be facing the audience.

But such rare misjudgements were offset by dozens of other passages cast in a new and justifiable light, physical action redefining the movement of the drama. The banishment of Kent will serve as an example. Kent's interruption is the most extraordinary disruption of the ceremonial formality of Lear's court. As Lear hurls Kent to the floor Lear himself, as well as his courtiers, was appalled by his violence. Unable to admit to himself the destructive effect of disinheriting Cordelia, he can acknowledge what it means to have stooped to a physical assault on a trusted councillor. John Wood's Lear was left beckoning to Kent (David Troughton) to rise, able to mitigate the

brutal decree only by offering Kent five days' respite, stroking Kent's head as he did so. But he reacquired his awesome power as he moved upstage, stepping back into the cube where the throne was placed: 'Away! By Jupiter, / *This* shall not be revoked' (1.1.177–8), the line pointed with great force, making abundantly clear that while Kent may have demanded that Lear should change his mind, on this matter at least there is no possibility of change. In the physical violence of the action and the emotional range discovered in the language, the forms of social behaviour are defined even as they are being overturned.

It is this intensity of local effect by Wood that has, I think, most irritated many of the production's antagonists. Wood's voice is what used to be called 'a magnificent instrument' and he is unashamed to use it. The result is operatic in the extreme. Each speech is so full of detail, so richly filled with the possibilities of vocal colour that the result is for some simply excessive, language being burdened by the actor's attention. At times the colour seems to be there for its own sake, a self-regarding display of technique, more like Pavarotti than Domingo. Wood demands that we are seduced by his performance, depending on our compliance. We can choose whether to be won over by it or whether to find it offensively indulgent. Its most extreme effects, as in the discovery of a new rich bass colouring on 'You do me wrong' (4.6.38), opened new ranges of emotional experience. What Wood cannot allow for are the play's shattering moments of simplicity.

It would be wrong, though, ever to regard the vocal effects as thoughtless. When Wood's Lear puts down the map which he has carried on to the stage in 1.1, seats himself in the throne and then realizes he cannot reach the map, the line 'Give me the map *there*' (1.1.37, Wood's emphasis) becomes comic but it is not over-reading the moment to see his annoyance, as if it is someone else's fault that he cannot reach it rather than his own, as a small but indicative signpost to Lear's nature and the peremptory tone of the demand as the natural language for someone used to having every whim obeyed. The pointing of the line and its relation to stage-business forces our attention onto the line, as if each moment must be distinctive, a sweet to be savoured. But here at least the fragment is earning its keep.

At their best, Wood and Hytner combined to take a familiar line and make it newly central. At Gloucester's castle, for instance, Lear's line to Goneril 'I prithee, daughter, do not make me mad' (2.2.391) became the key to the whole scene, terrifyingly powerful here, the most intense in the whole production. For the threat that Goneril brings with her was fixed visually by the two attendant nurses and the wheelchair she had in her train; she was not so much making him mad as recognizing him as mad and treating him as such, certifying him insane in modern terms. He knew – and the awareness was excruciatingly painful, frightening and humiliating – that she probably was, for all her harshness, right. His earlier cry, 'O, let me not be mad, not mad, sweet heaven' (1.5.45), was uttered by a man who knew that he nearly was mad already, that the plea was already too late. Now the confrontation with his own insanity was extreme, though his statement transferred his own recognition of his insanity to Goneril as her wish. What was unbearable here, both for him and for us, was the cold rationality of her action.

Such moments anticipate Wood's extraordinary playing of the madness later on. This Lear was quite the maddest I have ever seen, carefully charting the stages of discovery of the liberation that madness provides for him. By the time he met Edgar, Wood's Lear was a willing accomplice in Poor Tom's invented world, chasing across the stage to shoo away the imaginary devils.

It may sound odd to say so but Hytner is a literal-minded director. Sometimes the literalism is almost too much: Gloucester no sooner said 'I shall not need spectacles' (1.2.36) than he took a pair out of his pocket and put them on.

Hytner often encourages actors to angle lines in surprising ways but it is rare for him to work against the text. In the blinding of Gloucester, though, he made a small and highly indicative change. The Folio text marks an exit for Gloucester before Regan's line 'How is't my lord?' (3.7.92), making the line clearly addressed to Cornwall. Instead Sally Dexter made the line a moment of concern for Gloucester himself, a tenderness entirely at odds with her brutality seconds earlier. Again it appears to be a bizarre local moment but it is of a piece with the production's whole approach to the sisters.

If we have grown used to seeing Regan and Goneril as fairytale characters out of, say, *Cinderella*, Hytner argued for a different approach. This Goneril and Regan do love their father; they are driven to action against him by what he himself has revealed of his ungovernable rage in the first scene. The protestations of love in 1.1 may be generated by greed, by fear and by fake rhetoric but they were not treated as insincere. Regan's language refers to her father continually; speaking to Gloucester, for instance, she identifies Edgar as 'my father's godson . . . / He whom my father named' before defining him as 'your Edgar' (2.1.90–1). When Gloucester was raised from his bed by the fight between Kent and Oswald she was tenderly solicitous, wrapping his blanket carefully around him, sitting him down while Cornwall (Richard Ridings as fine here as in *Troilus*) dealt with the hubbub. Gloucester was clearly her substitute father, another example of the displaced affect, the excess of a love that cannot be offered to the right object, that need to love that marks the production. The torture of the old man made her scream, releasing the violence of her hatred of her own father. Her bizarre concern for Gloucester in the redirected line represented her attempt to dissociate herself from the scene and her concern for the father in pain. There was a mixture here of fascination and incomprehension and appalled awareness of her own complicity. Everything Regan had done so far and everything that she would go on to do pivoted on this moment.

The finest performances in the production depended on such fresh and complex thinking. But they were not necessarily revisionist. Paterson Joseph's Oswald, a wheedling and ambitious butler, trying to shift class and betrayed by his accent, was a perfect definition of the social shifts possible in this world. Linus Roache's Edgar, a bumbling student dropping a pile of books on his first entry, found much of the inordinate range the rôle demands. The only major mistake was Linda Kerr Scott as Fool. Hytner had worked with her in a production of Sobol's *Ghetto* at the National Theatre a year before and it is easy to see why he was intrigued by her for Fool. Tiny, waiflike, of indeterminate age and gender, she seemed not quite to belong with other characters, separated by her physical appearance from them. But her brief appearance as Cassandra in Mendes's production of *Troilus* indicated the risks. Though her Cassandra was physically disturbing, her voice, with a strong Scots accent and little projection, was by turns inaudible and incomprehensible. Her training as a mime-artist (she was a non-speaking dummy in *Ghetto*) produced fascinating visual effects but Fool is a part for a vocal actor as well as a physical one and she could offer nothing in that line. Left behind in 3.6, gibbering and shivering with exhaustion, Fool vanished from the play without leaving an absence behind.

I complained earlier about designers who seem not to have read the play they are working on. David Fielding clearly had. If the massive revolving cube as an abstract vision of a spinning world was, literally by turns, revelatory and irritating, the detailing of the set was powerfully responsive to the play. For the first time in my experience a designer took Cordelia's description of her landscape as an accurate basis for the set: Lear has been seen 'Crowned with . . . / . . . all the idle weeds that grow / In our sustaining corn' and is to be found in 'the high-grown field' (4.3.3–7). The

sheaves of corn through which Wood's Lear made his way were a bizarre vision of a perfect English summer, an arcadian idyll which made the characters' pain all the more acute. The set's beauty is no consolation, simply a disjunction, an index of the incoherence of the play's world. At moments like these the production's trust in the play to make its meaning plain was richly rewarded.

Deborah Warner's designer at the National, Hildegard Bechtler, created a set whose link to *King Lear* was purely tangential. I have never objected to stripped bare stages but Bechtler's minimalism did not leave the set bare. Instead the canvas hangings, dangling swathes of cloth and strips of floor covering were regularly altered during the production as if the alterations suggested significant change. But their meaning was opaque. At the beginning of 1.2, for instance, Edmund removed a piece of gold drapery but it was never apparent whether this action belonged to the previous scene, arbitrarily carried out by a conveniently available actor, marking the ending of court opulence and formality, or identified the beginning of Edmund's own action.

The only significant advantage the set gave the actors was a narrow gap in the middle of the back wall of the stage, an opening in the dirty canvas which focused attention for entrances and exits. Lear and Cordelia could walk slowly up the centre-line of the stage towards it at the end of 4.6. Lear could enter through it, pushing the dead Cordelia on his wheelchair, her body lying grotesquely upside down with her red hair streaming, an entrance all the more powerful since it was a focus of attention for the audience but unseen by the other characters who were all facing downstage. This entry, indeed, showed the strengths of Deborah Warner's production. Where Wood's Lear howled his 'Howl's starting off stage, Brian Cox, Warner's Lear as he had been her Titus Andronicus, went quietly up to a number of the people onstage, quietly urging them to howl, speaking the word as if in some perplexity as to why they are not howling, offering the sight of Cordelia as one that ought to have incited an automatic response whose absence is incomprehensible to him. Howling was, for him, the most natural action in the world and he looked for the others to participate, like a director who cannot quite see why the actors are not doing what they should obviously be doing. Downbeat and simple, the playing revivified the line, making freshly painful an emotion which one thought one knew how to handle.

Cox, always a wildly dangerous actor, was, as if inverting Wood's work, most effective in such moments of quiet control. The meeting with Gloucester in 4.5 was marred by excess and coarseness, Lear, for instance, coming on with plastic carrier-bags, full of petals, which he put on his feet to demonstrate how one might 'shoe / A troop of horse with felt' (4.5.180–1) or wiping his hand elaborately in his crotch before sniffing it on 'it smells of mortality' (129). But the awkwardnesses here were magnificently transformed by the metamorphosis of the comic wry speaking to Gloucester of 'Ay, every inch a king' (107) into the calm dignity of 'I am a king. / Masters, you know that?' (195–6). Though dressed only in baggy combinations, a king humbled and humiliated, this Lear was still stating a simple fact, a fact painful precisely because true.

But at other times, director and actor combined to produce enfeebled pieces of business. Red noses were back again. It makes good sense for Fool to stick a red nose on Lear in 1.4 as a mark of the transfer of folly. But it is crass for Lear, cradling Cordelia's corpse, to fish around in his pockets, find the same red nose and try it first on himself and then on Cordelia as if somehow to explain his thinking behind 'my poor fool is hanged' (5.3.281). The business simply detracted from the actor's power to create desolate despair, leaving me wondering how the red nose had been transferred through Lear's changes of costume.

The red nose was a spurious attempt to find coherence and connection across the expanse of the play. In the wheelchair, however, Warner

found a linking motif. Where Hytner's Lear was threatened by the wheelchair Goneril brings with her, Warner's Lear entered in one. Careering wildly onto the stage with his daughters laughing around him, Lear was clearly celebrating his birthday, complete with paper-hats and party favours for all the family. Gone was the solemnity of the moment, gone too was any suggestion that the division of the kingdom was a matter of state. Where John Wood's court was quite well populated with formally dressed courtiers who knelt at the entrance of the removed king, Cox's court had two or three people standing around while he indulged in his private party game.

The wheelchair came well equipped with convenient holders for a rolled-up map and the scissors with which he carefully and playfully cut the map in three; three coronets were also hidden in it and strung onto Lear's arm, paraded like prizes at a game of musical chairs. Lear teased his daughters as if they were still children but the teasing had become repellent and even a form of bullying; the game had gone on too long and the transition to the physical violence of the rejection of Cordelia was all too easily made. Always ready to give Regan a kiss and a cuddle, Lear had tried to preserve her childhood too long and Clare Higgins's Regan clearly found the old man's gropings a denial of her maturity. The wheelchair was in 1.1 a sign of age but also of the resistance to being old. There was nothing restrictive about being confined to it; indeed, like the crutches used by Antony Sher as Richard III, the wheelchair seemed to free Cox's Lear from the problems of physical infirmity. Throughout the scene, this Lear had the gleeful irrationality and irresponsibility of age, the only problem being its inappropriateness both for a king and for the father of two dangerous daughters: Susan Engel's Goneril, a natural schoolmistress if ever there was one, clutched her third of the map with terrifyingly triumphant glee.

If Lear in 1.1 seemed to be mocking the implications of the wheelchair, then, as he

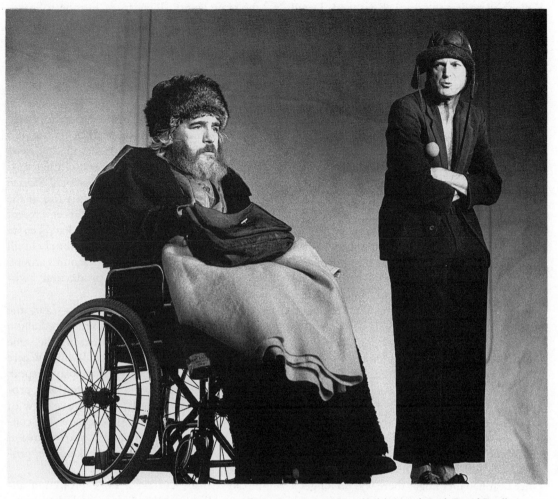

7 *King Lear*, 1.5, National Theatre, 1990: Lear (Brian Cox) waits in his wheelchair with Fool (David Bradley)

waited for his horses at Goneril's palace in 1.5, the demands of the wheelchair had become irrefutable. Bundled up with a rug over his knees, Lear looked old and vulnerable, a geriatric outpatient waiting for the ambulance to take him home. As Lear's world fragmented so too did the chair: in the storm scenes, staged as brilliantly as Hytner's had been disappointing, Lear and Fool sheltered under a cymbal, taken, apparently, from the wheels of the chair, as torchlight shafted across the black stage and two timpanists, visible on either side of the stage, thundered a storm, against which Lear tried to compete, banging on the cymbal with a whip.

All of this must appear very promising but the energy and excitement of such moments were far too intermittent. Warner's commitment to a full conflated text seemed, in any case, after the triumphant justification of Folio by Hytner, to generate diffusion and a lack of energy, magnifying the difficulty of making the production coherent. It was not helped by a series of lacklustre performances. Ian Mc-

Kellen's despairingly loyal Kent and David Bradley's Fool apart, Cox had painfully little support. Peter Jeffrey's Gloucester was little short of embarrassing, revealing how much of the later part of the play depends on Gloucester to carry it through. Any Gloucester who makes the experience of blinding appear little worse than barking one's shins is bound to discourage; Jeffrey offered no range at all, keeping everything within the experience of a retired major from Cheltenham. Once Fool had left the play seemed to fall apart.

Good Fools are dangerous individuals: the brilliance of Sher's Fool destroyed Michael Gambon's chances of success as Lear. David Bradley's Fool posed no such problem, working with great generosity and harmony with Cox. This Fool was clearly an old pro, wearing an old flying helmet and bare-chested under a suit with trousers too short for him. Lean and pinched, he manifested an anger born of frustration at Lear and a self-deprecatory embarrassment born of an awareness of his hackneyed old jokes. But both the anger and the self-dismissiveness were part of his concern for Lear, recognized by his master who could kiss his hand and slap it away immediately after. As Lear moved further and further away from Fool's counsel, Fool became angrier and angrier, doggedly trying to make Lear listen. Once Lear had met Edgar there was no longer a point of contact with Fool. Organizing the mock-trial, Lear, almost without noticing him, casually tipped Fool out of the wheelbarrow in which he was resting. Fool became an unwilling participant, mocking Lear's fantasies with his dry 'I took you for a joint-stool' (Q 13.47). The storm had exhausted him and he was left dying stretched out on the floor, shivering uncontrollably, by the end of the scene, his weak attempts to get up to follow Lear useless. The interval, taken at this point, left the audience with the sight of Fool's corpse alone on stage.

Warner's Lear lasted well over four hours, Hytner's Lear and Nunn's Othello little short of the same length. Reports of European Shakespeare productions lasting six or seven hours have always been received with incredulity in England; now English audiences are expected to have similar stamina. Performances of King Lear should be exhausting experiences – the play demands as much – but it takes sustained energy and drive to justify such a performing length. Warner simply could not. It was not helped by the strong feeling that the Lyttleton stage was too large for her. Though her production of Brecht's The Good Person of Sichuan made outstanding use of the vast spaces of the Olivier stage at the National, Warner's recent Shakespeare work for the RSC has been in small spaces. Actors in Lear moved limply to fill spaces, unwilling to accept the vacuums around them. It seemed a studio production awkwardly metamorphosed.

In tandem with Warner's King Lear, the National mounted Richard Eyre's production of Richard III, performed by exactly the same cast and toured with Lear world-wide. Where Warner's work effectively left the play to speak for itself, Eyre's was a grand operatic production, a complementary alternative view of the requirement to direct Shakespeare. The contrasts between the two were as provocative as anything in contemporary Shakespeare production.

On a black curtain a huge projection announced 'Edward IV'. As it was whisked away, the noise of horses, trumpets and warfare accompanied a thick pall of smoke which cleared as a soldier moved slowly downstage: a First World War officer in full uniform, cap and greatcoat, one arm in his pocket, limping slightly. The voice, when he started speaking, was clipped Sandhurst. The impression, if one didn't listen to what he was saying, was of someone who had returned from the Front with a Blighty wound. The clash of two histories, the authoritative announcement of the projection defining the reign and the scrupulously precise dating of the costumes, recurred throughout the production. The curtain descending for the interval had 'Richard III' projected onto it but the figure caught by the spotlight alone high above the stage was in fascist blackshirt uniform with his arm raised in a disturbing amalgam of a cheery wave and Hitler's version of a Nazi salute.

Eyre's production seemed to have carefully considered and then rejected a number of possible ways of playing. Divorced from the *Henry VI* plays, *Richard III* cannot easily appear the outcome of a long process of early modern history. After Sher, there must have been little to tempt McKellen into a physically virtuosic performance. Instead the production single-mindedly saw in Richard's rise an analogy for a possible alternative history of Britain between the wars, a successful coup by a leader who adroitly perceived and utilized the efficacy of fascist militarism, overthrowing an atrophied aristocracy by the energy of populist thuggery. The production, designed by Bob Crowley, found a consistent argument in the developing use of Nazi iconology. The early images showed the members of Edward IV's court dressed in full white-tie evening dress with sashes and decorations or the normative and – viewed from the later movements of the play – comforting feel of Richard's first appearance in British uniform. As Richard moved towards taking power, the production began to explore the threatening qualities of the new blackshirt uniform: Richard's entry to the council scene (3.4.20) suddenly and startlingly revealed him to have discarded the codes of British costume for his new brutalist style, accompanied by guards from some private army, dressed in the same threatening uniforms. Crowley used the more recent English fascist right's annexation of British nationalism with Richard's triumphant use of armbands and banners, mixing the red cross of St George with a Gloucester-derived boar-motif.

At its best the production turned the insidious takeover of the black costumes into a line marking the movement of Richard's power. The Brackenbury who accompanies Clarence to the Tower in 1.1 was dressed as an English officer; by the time he refused the Queens admittance to the Princes in 4.1 he had taken on the black uniform, defining himself as one of Richard's men. Richard's wooing of Anne (1.2) was played on an almost deserted stage with bored hospital orderlies waiting on the side to find out what to do with the body on the stretcher-trolley. Richard's wooing of Elizabeth for her daughter (4.4.196f.) was played in front of a long line of his soldiers, a grim presentation of his power, silent until Richard's final comment ('Relenting fool, and shallow, changing woman' 4.4.362) elicited a huge guffaw, echoing with male barrack-room mockery of all women.

Careful and controlled use of the armband-motif marked the oscillations and progress of tyranny. Buckingham's realization of his need to escape (4.2.122–5) was pinpointed by his discarding the Richard armband. Stanley, present onstage when Buckingham engineered the assent of the citizens to Richard's coronation (3.7), manifested his reluctance to be there but still wore one of Richard's armbands. The whole scene became a Shakespearian version of a Nuremberg rally (or was it rather more like a piece of Brecht's *Arturo Ui?*) with Buckingham using the technology of thirties propaganda, microphones and all, to converse with Richard who loomed threateningly on the raised platform of an elevating truck (of the kind more normally used to repair street lighting). Richard's acceptance speech (3.7.217–26) was spoken in the rich fruity tones of popular oratory and the crowd's response of 'Amen' (3.7.231) was picked up and turned into an amplified offstage chanting roar with distinct overtones of 'Sieg Heil'.

The line of argument, followed through with powerful dramatic logic in the first half of the production, had the knack of suddenly throwing small segments of the play into prominence through their link to Richard's rise, revealing the logic of their place in the play. The tiny scene of the Scrivener (3.6) details, exactly and disturbingly, the failure of those who can see what is happening to speak out against Richard's cynical manipulation of political process. At the end of the scene the speaking of the speech itself proved to have marked the dangerous transition from seeing 'such ill dealing ... in thought' (3.6.14) to revealing oneself as a target for Richard's men as the Scrivener, the perfect exemplar of the nice, weak middle-class liberal, was hauled away by two of the blackshirt guards. The conversation of citizens in 2.3 became an event in some Whitehall corridor with two civil servants and a gaitered bishop.

The processes of politics in such a world became eerily dangerous. The fall of Hastings (David Bradley), for instance, became a logical and unstoppable process through the simple device of moving away from Hastings's house after the conversation with the Messenger (3.2.1–31). Catesby and Hastings instead conversed at the Council table as Catesby laid out the agenda papers and Hastings worked at a red dispatch box. The conversations with the priest and with Buckingham were held as the meeting assembled. The executions of Rivers, Gray and Vaughan – brutally graphic garottings – were played out downstage in front of the board meeting, specifying what was looming for Hastings. The arrival of the now-blackshirted Richard and his guards left no doubt about the threat to the other Council members if they resisted his will – indeed, the whole story of the withered arm, played as a fabricated excuse, has never appeared more obviously irrelevant to the real reasons for the rapidity of the others' acceptance of Hastings's arrest: Richard's unchallengeable military power. In the bizarre chaos of 3.5, played as a continuation of the previous scene, the board-table was overturned as a makeshift barricade to bemuse the Mayor while the grotesque comedy was completed by the arrival of Catesby (3.5.19) with Hastings's head in a fire-bucket (into which Richard dipped his hand at the end of the scene, presumably to close Hastings's eyes).

Such uses of rituals as contexts within which power-games are played out – here the ritual of the board-room – was simple and sustained. 1.3, for instance, was played as a long formal dinner-table scene with everyone in evening-dress, a scene disrupted by the irruption of Queen Margaret as some kind of religious fanatic, festooned with rosaries and crucifixes (a disappointing performance from Susan Engel). Edward IV's reconciliation of the warring factions (2.1) was defined by the slow setting-up of a group photograph, complete with a flash-gun immediately before Richard disrupted the assembly with the news of Clarence's death (2.1.78), the others previously having failed to notice Richard's black armband.

If the analogy with an imaginary history gave the play a threatening drive it exacted two heavy penalties. The first was that there was little room for a real language of comedy to surround or be generated by this Richard. McKellen is, in any case, not at his best in comedy, even at its most sardonic. His Richard had nothing of the charm of the comic villain, the generic outsider, defining himself instead simply as a wounded soldier. His deformities – hand, leg, merest hint of a hump and a massive piece of facial plastic surgery – always appeared more likely to be the result of active service in the trenches than birth. The adroit way in which he one-handedly extracted a cigarette from his silver cigarette-case and lit it or did up the complicated buckles on his uniform belt suggested a soldier who has had intensive rehabilitation therapy. The drive for power, as a result, seemed generated by the displacement of the soldier in peacetime. With nothing charmingly demonic about him the focus was on the disturbing ease with which he could seize power.

Such a process accounts for the second penalty: a catastrophic loss of direction in the second half. There was, quite simply, nowhere for the production to go once Richard was crowned. The coronation itself was, however, magnificent, with lords in scarlet and ermine,

8 *Richard III*, 3.7, National Theatre, 1990: Blackshirt and Armband: Richard III (Ian McKellen) and the Duke of Buckingham (Brian Cox)

Richard in full medieval costume and the stage backed by a massive example of triumphal fascist art showing marching soldiers, a rearing horse (White Surrey?) and a naked Richard with raised-arm salute, his body healed and perfect as an example of an Aryan ideal. The clash of histories became complete here, a complex intermingling of the two periods: the scene effectively combined the pseudo-medievalism of fascist art and the submerged historicity of Richard's reign.

But Richard's collapse, for all the technical virtuosity of McKellen's trembling, frightened figure as the bad news accumulated or the fighting soldier at Bosworth with his leg twitching in uncontrollable spasms, came from

nowhere and went nowhere. The ghost scene, staged as a series of nightmarish echoes of gestures and moves in earlier scenes, watched over or rather stage-managed by a white-dressed, gold-crowned, beaming Queen Margaret, had an inventiveness that the second half had mostly lacked but it was also excessive, overblown in a way that the first half's tight control had not been. The arrival of Richmond – whom Richard insisted on calling Richemont, to underline xenophobically his non-English background – was heralded by a new backcloth, a chocolate-box saccharine depiction of the English countryside, a rural idyll of everything Richmond is fighting for. I desperately wanted to see this vision as ironic but the

189

production left no space for such a reading. It was hardly Colin Hurley's fault that Richmond appeared dull but the production served only to emphasize his anodyne qualities.

In the mourning of the queens (4.4) another note was heard, their candles making them echoes of Argentinian 'Mothers of the Disappeared', the survivors grieving the victims of the totalitarian state. In the rich dignity of the scene a lamenting estimate of the cost of Richard's rule was defined.

The year's review ends at the National Theatre. I have left over till next year the autumn productions at Stratford, including Terry Hands's final Shakespeare production as artistic director of the RSC. It has been a rich and troubling year, most troubling for the anxiety and lack of confidence that breeds excessive set designs and the desperate search for directorial concept, most rich in the joyful rediscovery of the delights of plot. Even Hands's *Coriolanus*, for all its faults, appeared to enjoy telling the story. The theatre might usefully remember that the Lambs' *Tales from Shakespeare* did give pleasure to generations and might appreciate the message from the Swan Theatre that the story is worth telling.

PROFESSIONAL SHAKESPEARE PRODUCTIONS IN THE BRITISH ISLES JANUARY–DECEMBER 1989

compiled by

NIKY RATHBONE

Information is taken from programmes, supplemented by reviews, held in the Birmingham Shakespeare Library. Details have been verified wherever possible, but the nature of the material prevents corroboration in every case. The list includes a selection of interesting adaptations, but does not attempt to be comprehensive in this area.

ALL'S WELL THAT ENDS WELL

Argonaut Theatre Company, Rheingold Club, London: May 1989
Director: James Barlow
Helena: Anne Roderick
Bertram: Adrian Bull

The RSC at the Royal Shakespeare Theatre, Stratford: 28 Sept. 1989–
Director: Barry Kyle
Designer: Chris Dyer
Music: Jeremy Sams
Helena: Patricia Kerrigan
Bertram: Paul Venables

ANTONY AND CLEOPATRA

The British Actors Theatre Company, Wimbledon Theatre and tour: 11 Oct. 1989–
Directed and designed by the company
Antony: Bernard Lloyd
Cleopatra: Kate O'Mara
Octavius: Peter Woodward
Traditional period costumes and set.

Adaptation

Cleopatra and Antony, adapted from Shakespeare by ATC
Actors Touring Company at the Brewhouse, Taunton and tour: 2 Feb.–3 June 1989
Director: Malcolm Edwards
Designer: Paul Brown
Cleopatra: Pauline Black
Antony: Patrick Wilde
A feminist adaptation exploring the fascination of Cleopatra.

AS YOU LIKE IT

Argonaut Theatre Company, Rheingold Theatre Club, London: 22 Mar.–8 April 1989
Director: Keith Myers
Designer: Rosa Maggiora
Producer: John Greco
Music: Gareth Evans
Rosalind: Rebecca Dines
Elizabethan costuming, no scenery or props.

The Old Vic, London: 18 May 1989–
Director: Tim Albery
Designer: Antony McDonald
Music: Orlando Gough
Rosalind: Fiona Shaw

Spire Productions Ltd, The Rose Theatre Club, London: 31 May–24 June 1989
Director: Paul Jepson
Designer: Liz Thody
Rosalind: Anna Mackmin

Touchstone: David Solomon
Critics praised David Solomon's Touchstone.
Modern dress production.

The Oxford Stage Company at the Rose
Theatre, Oxford and tour, with *King Lear*: 26
July–2 Sept. 1989
Director: John Retallack
Designer: Phil Swift
Music: Howard Goodall
Rosalind: Deborah Findlay
Excellent reviews.

The RSC at the Royal Shakespeare Theatre,
Stratford: 8 Sept. 1989–
Director: John Caird
Designer: Ultz
Rosalind: Sophie Thompson
Celia: Gillian Bevan
Touchstone: Mark Williams
See pp. 161–3.

Second Age at the Tivoli Theatre, Dublin:
Nov. 1989
Directors: Alan Stanford and Ronan Smith
Designers: Caroline Betera and 'Fixers'
Rosalind: Orla Charlton
Touchstone: Derek Chapman
Jaques: Jim Bartley
Modern dress.

THE COMEDY OF ERRORS

Argonaut Theatre Company at the Rheingold
Theatre Club, London: 24 Jan.–25 Feb. 1989
Producer: John Greco
Director: Desmond Maurer
Designer: Mark Maxwell
Music: Ray Daniels

The Octagon Theatre, Bolton: 26 Jan.–18 Feb.
1989
Director: Romy Baskerville
Designers: Mick Bearwish and Katie Wilson
Music: Akintayo Akinbode
Antipholus of Syracuse: Bhasker

Antipholus of Ephesus: Antony Bunsee
A dateless 'eastern' set. The division between
audience and players was deliberately blurred.

Bristol Old Vic, Theatre Royal, Bristol: 16
Feb.–11 Mar. 1989
Director: Phyllida Lloyd
Designer: Anthony Ward
Music: Gary Yershon
Antipholus of Syracuse: Owen Teale
Antipholus of Ephesus: Brian Hickey
Dromio of Syracuse: Colin Hurley
Dromio of Ephesus: Sean Murray
Adriana: Rosie Rowell

Kent Repertory Company at the Lakeside
Theatre, Hever Castle: July–Aug. 1989
Director/Designer: Richard Palmer
Antipholus of Syracuse: Martin Ball
Antipholus of Ephesus: David Bromley
Set in a Turkish bazaar.

CORIOLANUS

Théâtre Plastique at the Bedford, London: 27
Jan. 1989–
Director: Michael Walling
Designer: Mike Pearce

The Young Vic, London: 3–27 May 1989
Director: Jane Howell
Designers: Hayden Griffin, Claudia Mayer,
David Neat
Music: Mark Vibrans
Coriolanus: Corin Redgrave
Edwardian period setting.

The RSC at the Royal Shakespeare Theatre,
Stratford: 30 Nov. 1989–
Directors: Terry Hands and John Barton
Designer: Christopher Morley
Music: Terry Davies
Coriolanus: Charles Dance
Volumnia: Barbara Jefford
Aufidius: Malcolm Storry
See pp. 163–6.

CYMBELINE

Theatre Set Up at Forty Hall, Enfield and tour: 15 June 1989–
Director/Designer: Wendy McPhee and Don Caulfield
Imogen: Stephi Hemelryk
Iachimo/Guiderius: Ben Foster
Posthumus/Cloten: Tony Portacio
The doubling of Posthumus/Cloten made an interesting imaginative link between the two characters.

The RSC at the Royal Shakespeare Theatre, Stratford: 11 July 1989–
Director: Bill Alexander
Designer: Timothy O'Brien
Imogen: Naomi Wirthner
Iachimo: John Carlisle
Music: Ilona Sekacz
Posthumus: David O'Hara
Cloten: David Troughton
The Queen: Linda Spurrier
See *Shakespeare Survey 43*, pp. 189–91.

HAMLET

Compass Theatre Company. Continuation of 1988 tour.
See *Shakespeare Survey 43*, p. 206.

The National Theatre at the Olivier, London: 16 Mar. 1989–
Director: Richard Eyre
Designer: John Gunter
Costumes: Liz da Costa
Music: Dominic Muldowney
Hamlet: Daniel Day Lewis; Jeremy Northam; Ian Charleson
Gertrude: Judi Dench; Sylvia Syms
Polonius: Michael Bryant
Ophelia: Stella Gonet
Also toured Yugoslavia in July.
See *Shakespeare Survey 43*, pp. 194–6.

The Salberg Studio, Salisbury Playhouse: 26 April–13 May 1989

Director: Karl Hibbert
Designer: Bill Crutcher
Hamlet: Colin Hurley
Played concurrently with *Rosencrantz and Guildenstern are Dead* in the main theatre.

Footsquare Theatre Company, Finborough Arms, London: June 1989
Director: Ian Embleton
Hamlet: Nick Carpenter
Set in a black marble mausoleum; modern dress.

The RSC at the Royal Shakespeare Theatre, Stratford: 20 April 1989–
First seen as a RSC/Royal Insurance tour in 1988.
See *Shakespeare Survey 43*, pp. 206, 196–200.

Leicester Haymarket, world tour and Old Vic, London: 14 Sept. 1989–
Director: Yuri Lyubimov
Designer: David Borowsky
Music: Yuri Butsko and James Ford
Hamlet: Daniel Webb
Claudius: Andrew Jarvis
Gertrude: Anne White
The text was radically re-arranged with some interpolations. The main feature of the set was a large, moveable woven curtain.

Northern Classical Theatre, Middleton Hall Theatre, Hull University: 18 Sept. 1989–
Director: Martin Chamberlain
Hamlet: Jack Fortune
A traditional production.

Gateway Theatre, Chester: 10–28 Oct. 1989
Director: Angela Langfield
Designer: Juliet Watkinson
Hamlet: Greg Crutwell

Adaptation

Ophelia Song by Antoine Campo
Mon Oncle D'Amérique/Ang Magnetic at the

Institut Français d'Ecosse, Edinburgh: 14
Aug.–2 Sept. 1989
Choreography: Clara Gibson-Maxwell
Music: Pascal Humbert
Designer: Marc Sonnino
A minimalist opera based on Ophelia's songs
from *Hamlet*.

HENRY V

Best productions at the Black Horse, London:
22 Aug.–10 Sept. 1989

Renaissance Films Plc, 5 Oct. 1989–
Director: Kenneth Branagh
Music: Patrick Doyle
Henry V: Kenneth Branagh
Cast includes Brian Blessed, Richard Briers,
Robbie Coltrane, Judi Dench, Ian Holm,
Derek Jacobi, Geraldine McEwan; Michael
Maloney, Paul Scofield, John Sessions, Robert
Stephens, Emma Thompson, Michael Williams.
Available on video.

JULIUS CAESAR

Rose Theatre Club, London: April 1989
Director: Robin Brockman

Ludlow Festival: 24 June–8 July 1989
Director: Michael Napier Brown
Designer: Ray Lett
Caesar: John Franklyn-Robbins
Mark Antony: Paul Jones
Brutus: Robert Grange

KING JOHN

The RSC at the Barbican Pit. Transferred from
Stratford.
See *Shakespeare Survey 42*, pp. 137–9; 43,
p. 207.

KING LEAR

The Old Vic, London: 23 Mar.–13 May 1989
Director: Jonathan Miller

Designer: Richard Hudson
Lear: Eric Porter
Cordelia: Kim Thomson
Fool: Peter Bayliss
Lear was shown descending into senility. Set:
High, blackened brick walls with blocked up
windows.
See *Shakespeare Survey 43*, pp. 188–9.

ACTER, Riverside Studios, Hammersmith: 26
Mar. 1989 only
Returned from nine-week tour of the USA
Company: Geoffrey Church, Vivien Heilbron,
Bernard Lloyd, Patti Love, Clifford Rose.

The RSC at the Almeida, London: 13 Sept.–28
Oct. 1989
Transfer from TOP, Stratford.
See *Shakespeare Survey 43*, pp. 207–8.

Oxford Stage Company, Theatre Royal, Lin-
coln and tour, with *As You Like It*; 20 Sept.
1989–
Director: John Retallack
Designer: Phil Swift
Lear: Philip Voss
Cordelia: Matilda Ziegler
Goneril: Carla Mendonca
A minimal set and Edwardian costumes.

Northcott Theatre, Exeter: 24 Oct.–18 Nov.
1989
Director: Martin Harvey
Designer: John McMurray
Music: Laurence Roman
Lear: Gareth Thomas
Modern dress.

Adaptations and related work

Seven Lears by Howard Barker
A joint production by the Wrestling School,
the Crucible Theatre, Sheffield and Leicester
Haymarket at the Haymarket Studio and the
Royal Court, London: 1 Nov. 1989–

Director: Kenny Ireland
Designer: Dermot Hayes
Music: Matthew Scott
Lear: Nicholas Le Prevost
Clarissa: Jemma Redgrave
An exploration of Lear's early life.

Lear, an opera by Aribert Reimann
English National Opera at the London Coliseum. British première: 24 Jan. 1989
Music: Aribert Reimann
Libretto: Claus Henneberg, translated by Desmond Clayton
Director: Eike Gramms
Designers: Eberhard Matthies and Renate Schmitzer
Conductor: Paul Daniel
Lear: Monte Jaffe
Goneril: Phyllis Cannan
Edmund: Alan Woodrow
Edgar: Christopher Robson
Fool: Eric Shilling
First performance Munich, 1978.

LOVE'S LABOUR'S LOST

Minerva Studio Theatre, Chichester: 29 Aug.–
22 Sept. 1989
Director: Sam Mendes
Designer: Paul Farnsworth
The King of Navarre: Bille Brown
The Princess of France: Kate Duchene

The Quick Vic Theatre Company, Duke's
Head Theatre Club, London: 17 Oct.–12 Nov.
1989
Director: Pat Miller
Designers: Ginny Borthwick and Anne Le Coz
Set in a symbolic forest glade.

Jerks of Invention at the Bridge Lane Theatre
Club, London: 22 Nov.–9 Dec. 1989
Director: the King of Navarre: John Wadmore
Rosaline: Heather Osborne
Dressed like a Noel Coward musical with the
men in blazers and the girls in white dresses.

MACBETH

The Duke's Head Theatre, Richmond: Jan.–
Feb. 1989
Director: David Gillie
Set in the near future in an atmosphere of brutal
military amorality. The stage was boxed in by
ivy hedges giving a claustrophobic effect.

New Victoria Theatre, Newcastle under Lyme:
1 Feb.–4 Mar. 1989
Director: Chris Martin
Macbeth: Frank Moorey
Lady Macbeth: Shelly Willets
A traditional production.

Pentameters Theatre Club, the Three Horse-
shoes, London: Mar. 1989
Director: Laura Thompson
Macbeth: John Vernon
Lady Macbeth: Lucy Aston
A modern dress production with few props, no
set and stark lighting.

The RSC at the Barbican, London: 27 April
1989–
Macbeth: Miles Anderson
Lady Macbeth: Amanda Root
Transfer from Stratford with some cast
changes.
See *Shakespeare Survey 41*, pp. 170–1.

Beau TIE: The Regent Centre, Christchurch
and tour: 24 May 1989–
Director: Nigel Parkes-Davies
Producer: Glenn Holderness
Macbeth: Steve Whiteley
Lady Macbeth: Lorraine Rowan
Schools tour in the Bournemouth area.

A1 Theatre Company, Jackson's Lane Com-
munity Centre, Hornsey: July 1989
Director: Ivor Benjamin
Designer: Anna Greenhow
Macbeth: Richard Ridings
Lady Macbeth: Catherine Jansen

Argonaut Theatre Company at the Rheingold
Club, London: 25 July–26 Aug. 1989
Producer: John Greco
Director/Macduff: Michael Futcher
Macbeth: Philip Peacock
Designer: Michael Futcher
Lady Macbeth: Helen Howard

British Actors Theatre Company: Theatre
Royal Norwich, Arundel Festival and tour of
Scandinavia: 14 Aug.–2 Sept. 1989
Producers: Kate O'Mara and Peter Woodward
Macbeth: Peter Woodward
Lady Macbeth: Julia Goodman

Promenade production on Inchcolm Island as
part of the Edinburgh Festival: 14–22 Aug.
1989
Producer: Richard Demarco
Director: John Bett
Macbeth: John Cairney
Lady Macbeth: Gerda Stevenson
La Zattera di Babele withdrew and the pro-
duction was re-cast. The audience, wrapped in
grey blankets, became part of the action.
See *Shakespeare Survey 43*, pp. 209.

Livespace Theatre Company, tour in the
Greater London region: autumn 1989

Odyssey Theatre Company, Towngate
Theatre, Basildon and tour: 19 Sept. 1989–13
Jan. 1990
Director: Nigel Jamieson
Designer: Helen Turner
Macbeth: Ian Halcrow
Lady Macbeth: Claire Benedict
The company developed the production in
Bali, and were influenced by Balinese theatrical
traditions. Masks and drums were used very
effectively. Workshops were given on this pro-
duction.

Redgrave Theatre, Farnham: 4–28 Oct. 1989
Director: Graham Watkins
Designer: Clare Southern

Music: David Lancaster
Macbeth: James Bolam
Lady Macbeth: Susan Jameson
A straightforward production, using male
witches.

Citizens' Theatre, Glasgow: 6–28 Oct. 1989
Director: Jon Pope
Designer: Stewart Laing
Macbeth: Simon Tyrrell
Lady Macbeth: Charon Bourke
Modern dress, with the witches in anoraks and
the Scottish lords in overalls and gas masks. A
stainless steel and aluminium set.

Dundee Repertory Theatre: 2–25 Nov. 1989
Director: Cliff Burnett
Designer: Neil Murray
Music: Kevin Murray
Macbeth: Hilton McRae
Lady Macbeth: Leonie Mellinger
The play was set in a modern war-zone, giving
the impression of a society steeped in killing.
The witches were played by a gang of half-
starved, battle-weary children. Schools work-
shops were given on the production.

The Raving Beauties at Battersea Arts Centre:
15 Nov.–3 Dec. 1989
Director: Frances Viner
Macbeth: Greg Hicks
Lady Macbeth/witch: Sue Jones-Davies
A rather bizarre production with actresses in
several male rôles. The intention was apparently to bring out the feminine qualities of the
play.

Full Company, Manchester. Tour of the Manchester area: Nov. 1989–spring 1990
Performed by a company of young itinerant
actors.

Adaptations

From a Jack to a King by Bob Carlton, Belgrade
Theatre, Coventry: 15–21 April 1989
A rock musical based on *Macbeth*.

The Bremer Shakespeare Company at the King's Theatre, Edinburgh: 15–17 Aug. 1989
First performance at the Theater der Stadt, Heidelberg 10 Feb. 1989
Director: Johann Kresnik
Designer: Gottfried Helnwein
Music: Kurt Schwertsik
Macbeth: Joachim Siska
Lady Macbeth: Susana Ibanez
A choreographic adaptation using images drawn from *Macbeth*. The clan violence of medieval Scotland was related to images of blood and fascist Germany.

MEASURE FOR MEASURE

Commonweal at the Theatre Museum, Covent Garden, London: 21 Mar.–18 April 1989
Director: Tony Hegarty
Designer: Rolf Driver
Isabella: Kirsty Fry
Angelo: Malcolm Jones
Duke: David Bateson
Set during the plague of 1604. Workshops were given on this production.

The Young Vic, London and tour: 18 April–May 1989
Director: David Thacker
Designer: Fran Thompson
Isabella: Sarah-Jane Fenton
Angelo: Stephen Jenn
The Duke: Rob Edwards
Modern dress in subdued colours, with Isabella in white. Set in the round on a perspex stage with imaginative use of under-floor lighting.

Not the National Theatre, Sherman Theatre, Cardiff and tour of Wales: 10 April–20 July 1989
Director: Tim Davies
Designer: Janey Gardiner
Isabella/Mistress Overdone: Beverley Foster
Angelo/Abhorson: Derek Hollis
The Duke: Roger Gartland
Victorian period with a minimal set of chairs, a bench and a red curtain. Only ten lines were cut from the text.

The Royal Lyceum Theatre, Edinburgh: 14 July 1989–
Director: Robert J. Carson
Designer: George Souglides
Music: Adrian Johnston
Isabella: Kate Gartside
Angelo: Raad Rawi
The Duke: Gregory Floy
An austere red box set and mid nineteenth-century Italian costuming.

Barebones Theatre, touring the West Country: autumn 1989
Adapted and directed by Tim Clark.

MERCHANT OF VENICE

Phoenix Theatre, London: 1 June 1989–
Director: Peter Hall
Designer: Chris Dyer
Music: Robert Lockhart
Shylock: Dustin Hoffman
Portia: Geraldine James
Antonio: Leigh Lawson
See *Shakespeare Survey 43*, pp. 186–7.

Wolsey Theatre, Ipswich: Mar. 1–18 1989
Directors: Antony Tuckey and Gerry Tebbutt
Designer: David Knapman
Shylock: Brian Ralph
Portia: Nicola Redmond
Antonio: David Beale

Adaptation

Shylock by Arnold Wesker
A rehearsed reading at the Jackson's Lane Community Centre, Highgate, London: 29 Aug.–10 Sept. and the Riverside Studios, Hammersmith 16–22 Oct. 1989
Shylock: Oded Teomi
Oded Teomi is a member of the Cameri Theatre Company, Tel Aviv. *Shylock* was premièred in Sweden in 1976 as *The Merchant*.

In this version Shylock and Antonio are friends and the state law enforces the bond.

A MIDSUMMER NIGHT'S DREAM

The RSC at the Royal Shakespeare Theatre, Stratford: 30 Mar. 1989– and the Tyne Theatre, Newcastle on Tyne
Director: John Caird
Designer: Sue Blane
Music: Ilona Sekacz
Oberon/Theseus: John Carlisle
Titania/Hippolyta: Clare Higgins
Bottom: David Troughton
Puck: Richard McCabe
See *Shakespeare Survey 43*, pp. 200–2.

The New Shakespeare Company at the Open Air Theatre, Regent's Park: 30 May–9 Sept. 1989
Director: Guy Slater
Designer: Simon Dexter
Oberon: Saeed Jaffrey
Titania: Sally Dexter
Bottom: Christopher Benjamin
Puck: Trevor Laird
An evocation of flower power and the 1960s.

CBSO at Birmingham Town Hall: 28 June 1989
Director: Nick Fogg
Oberon/Theseus: Robert Stephens
Titania/Hippolyta: Patricia Brake
Bottom: Leslie Crowther
A reading of the text with a performance of the complete Mendelssohn score.

The Nineteenth Century Actors at Lyme Park Open Air Theatre, Cheshire: 18–22 July 1989
Director: Adrian Lawson
Costumes: Charles Alty
Oberon/Theseus: Stephen Chance
Titania: Kathryn George

Mercury Theatre, Colchester: 13–30 Sept. 1989
Director: Richard Digby Day

Designer: India Smith
Music: Nick Sexton
Oberon/Theseus: Mark Barratt
Titania/Hippolyta: Susan Edmonstone
Set in the nineteenth century. The columns of a marble hall transformed into the trees of the Athenian wood. Small boy fairies were played by local children.

Adaptation

The Lindsay Kemp Company, Sadler's Wells Theatre, London: 10–15 July 1989 and tour
A balletic adaptation directed and devised by Lindsay Kemp
Designers: Lindsay Kemp and Sandy Powell
Music: Carlos Miranda
Oberon/Theseus: David Haughton
Puck: Lindsay Kemp
Bottom: Neil Caplan
Spectacular sets, costumes and lighting effects. First performed at the Teatro Eliseo, Rome, 1979. British première 1983.

MUCH ADO ABOUT NOTHING

The Strand Theatre, London: 11 May–17 June 1989
Director: Elijah Moshinsky
Designer: Mark Thompson
Music: Stephen Oliver
Beatrice: Felicity Kendal
Benedict: Alan Bates
Don Pedro: Nicky Henson
Set on the Mediterranean in the recent past. Felicity Kendal won the *Evening Standard* Best Actress award for her Beatrice.

The Duke's Theatre, Lancaster, promenade production in Williamson Park: 1 June–25 July 1989
Director: Ian Forrest
Designer: Ashley Shairp
Beatrice: Buffy Davis
Benedict: Terence Beesley

OTHELLO

The Duke's Theatre, Lancaster: 25 Jan.–25 Feb. 1989
Director: Ian Forrest
Designer: Paul Kondras
Othello: Wyllie Longmore
Iago: Michael Gunn
Desdemona: Amanda Pointer
Set in the 1960s to Roy Orbison music within a giant picture frame divided into four. Some mime was used in this production.

Greenwich Theatre, London: 10 Mar.–22 April 1989
Directors: Sue Dunderdale and Hugh Quarshie
Designer: Henk Schut
Othello: Clarke Peters
Iago: Paul Barber
Desdemona: Emily Morgan
Set in Cyprus in the 1960s with colour providing an important racial link between a black Othello and brown Iago.

Precious Productions at the Village Theatre, London: April 1989
Director: Michael Halliday
Designer: Stan Johnson
Othello: Michael Skyers
Iago: Ricardo Pinto
Desdemona: Maria Calante
There was no set or properties except the handkerchief. Modern dress.

Wales Actors' Company at Llandaff Bishops' Palace and four-week tour of Wales: 29 June–29 July 1989
Director/Iago: Paul Garnault
Othello: Shiv Grewer
Desdemona: Nickie Rainsford

The RSC at the Other Place, Stratford and the Young Vic, London: 9 Aug. 1989–
Director: Trevor Nunn
Designer: Bob Crowley
Music: Guy Woolfenden
Othello: Willard White
Iago: Ian McKellen
Desdemona: Imogen Stubbs
Emilia: Zoë Wanamaker
Cassio: Sean Baker
Shown on BBC TV on 23 June 1990 and available on video.
See *Shakespeare Survey 43*, pp. 191–4.

Theatr/Clwyd, Mold tour of Wales, London: 22 Sept.–21 Oct. 1989
Director: Toby Robertson
Designer: Simon Higlett
Othello: Hakeem Kae-Kazim
Iago: Oliver Parker
Desdemona: Anna Patrick
Set in the nineteenth century.

The Royal Lyceum, Edinburgh: 27 Oct.–18 Nov. 1989
Director: Ian Wooldridge
Designer: Gregory Smith
Music: John Sampson
Othello: Burt Caesar
Iago: Bill Leadbitter
Desdemona: Gerda Stevenson

PERICLES

The RSC at the Swan Theatre, Stratford: 6 Sept. 1989–
Director: David Thacker
Designer: Fran Thompson
Music: Mark Vibrans
Pericles: Nigel Terry
Thaisa: Sally Edwards
Marina: Suzan Sylvester
See pp. 166–70.

THE PLANTAGENETS

The RSC at the Barbican, London. Transfer from Stratford.
See *Shakespeare Survey 43*, p. 212, pp. 171–81.

RICHARD II

Triumph Theatre Company, touring with Derek Jacobi as Richard II: 23 Nov. 1989
See *Shakespeare Survey 43*, p. 213.

RICHARD III

Triumph Theatre Company at the Phoenix Theatre, London and tour with *Richard II*: 11 Jan. 1989–
Director: Clifford Williams
Designer: Carl Toms
Richard III: Derek Jacobi
A traditional production.

ROMEO AND JULIET

London Shakespeare Group at the Warehouse Theatre, Croydon: 31 Jan.–5 Feb. 1989 and tour of the Middle East
Director: Delana Kidd
Designer: Mariselena Rossi
Romeo: Paul Rattigan
Juliet: Rachel Fielding
Italian Renaissance setting.

The Sherman Theatre, Cardiff: 10 Feb.–4 Mar. 1989 and Welsh tour
Director: Mike James
Designer: John Elvery
Romeo: Christopher Wild
Juliet: Janet Steel
A single set with skulls set into chipped stucco and location changes indicated by the lighting. Mainly black and white costumes.

Stage 65 at the Salberg Theatre, Salisbury Play-house: 17–25 Mar. 1989
Director: Lynn Wyfe
Designer: Kate Derrick
Romeo: Christopher Dickins
Juliet: Clare Humphreys
Played in the round in a modern Italian setting.

The RSC at the Swan Theatre, Stratford: 22 Mar. 1989– and RSC/British Telecom tour Sept. 1989

Director: Terry Hands
Designer: Farrah
Music: Claire Van Kampen
Romeo: Mark Rylance
Juliet: Georgia Slowe
Mercutio: David O'Hara
See *Shakespeare Survey 43*, pp. 184–6.

Nottingham Playhouse: 14 June 1989–
Director: Caroline Smith
Designer: Karen Bartlett
Romeo: John Dougall
Juliet: Jane Arden
Setting: a sun-drenched Italian street façade, of indeterminate period.

Holland Park Open Air Theatre: July 1989
Director: Peter Benedict
Romeo: Andrew Johnson
Juliet: Sarah Reed
A black Romeo and white Juliet in a modern dress production.

Deal Theatre Project, Walmer Castle: 11–26 Aug. 1989
Romeo: Eleanor Edmunds
Juliet: Claire Harrison
Adapted by Luke Dixon and Paul Dart. The Nurse was played by a man and Mercutio by a woman. Some actors were in whiteface, and the costumes were mainly red or white.

Latchmere Theatre, Battersea: 7–25 Nov. 1989
Director: Laura Thompson
Romeo: Pancho Russell
Juliet: Lucinda Galloway
Modern dress in a black box set with minimal props.

New Victoria Theatre, Newcastle on Tyne: 4 Oct. 1989–
Director: Bob Eaton
Designer: Anny Evason
Romeo: Timothy Welton
Juliet: France Fielding
Set in the Edwardian period.

THE TAMING OF THE SHREW

National Heritage Theatre, Guildhall, Windsor: 16 July 1989–
Director: Keith Kendry

Worcester Theatre Company, the Swan Theatre, Worcester: 26 Oct.–11 Nov. 1989
Director: Pat Trueman
Designer: Gayule Friend
Katherine: Tessa Wojtczak
Petruchio: Lennox Greaves
The Christopher Sly scenes were omitted. Period set based on Witley Court, Worcestershire.

THE TEMPEST

Cheek by Jowl, continuation of 1988 tour.
See *Shakespeare Survey 43*, p. 215.
This production visited Prague in March 1989.

RSC at the Barbican, London: 25 May 1989–
See *Shakespeare Survey 42*, pp. 147–8; *43*, p. 215.

Tag and the Dundee Repertory Dance Company at the Tron Theatre, Glasgow and tour of Scotland: 22 Aug. 1989–
Director: Alan Lyddiard
Designer: Neil Murray
Choreography: Tamara McLarg
Prospero: Vincent Friell
Staged within rotating reflecting panels and aimed at young audiences. Prospero was played as a tormented school-masterly character in a crumpled white suit.

Adaptations

Un Re in Ascolto (A King Listens) an opera by Luciano Berio, libretto by Italo Calvino
Covent Garden Opera House, London: British première 5 Feb. 1989
Conductor: Luciano Berio
Producer: Graham Vick

An opera based on *The Tempest* and W. H. Auden's *The Sea and the Mirror* in which different interpretations of the truth are presented to Prospero. World première Salzburg 1984.

Return to the Forbidden Planet, a rock musical by Bob Carlton, Belgrade Theatre, Coventry and Cambridge Theatre, London: 4 April 1989
Director: Bob Carlton
Designer: Rodney Ford
Dr Prospero: Christian Roberts
Cookie: Matthew Devitt
Miranda: Allison Harding
Captain Tempest: John Ashby
Ariel: Kraig Thornber
Science Officer: Nicky Furre
Set on the planet D'Illyria. Matthew Devitt's singing made this a cult musical.

TIMON OF ATHENS

Red Shift at Croydon Warehouse and tour: 3 Feb.–June 1989
Director: Jonathan Holloway
Designer: Charlotte Humpston
Music: Adrian Johnston
Timon: Kate Fenwick
Scenes were re-ordered and new material with a feminist slant added.

TITUS ANDRONICUS

The RSC at the Riverside Studios, Hammersmith and European tour: 7 Mar. 1989–
First performed at the Swan Theatre, Stratford, 1987.
See *Shakespeare Survey 41*, pp. 178–81; *42*, p. 159.

TWELFTH NIGHT

The Everyman Theatre, Cheltenham: 23 Feb.–11 Mar. 1989
Director: John Doyle
Designer: Chris Crosswell
Viola: Polly Irvin

Olivia: Margo Gunn
Malvolio: Stephen Earle
Feste: Barry Killerby
Modern dress. A set with white classical columns and a pool in which the cast took occasional dips.

Hull Truck at Wakefield Theatre Royal and tour: summer 1989
Director: John Godber
Designer: Robert Cheesmond
Music: Richard Stone and Steve Pinnock
Viola: Meriel Scholfield
Malvolio: William Ilkley
Olivia: Andrina Carroll
Feste: Paul Rider
Set on a university campus.

New Shakespeare Company at the Open Air Theatre, Regent's Park: 14 June 1989–
Director: Ian Talbot
Designer: Simon Higlett
Music: John De Prez
Viola: Juliette Grassby
Malvolio: Bernard Bresslaw
Olivia: Sally Dexter
Feste: Teddy Kempner
Regency setting.

Traffic of the Stage at Pentameters Theatre Club, London and tour: 9 Oct.–10 Nov. 1989
Adapted and directed by Tom Leatherbarrow
Viola: Sarah Carpenter
Olivia: Zigi Ellison
Feste: Mandy McIlwaine
Orsino: James Reynard
Set in the world of the movies with Olivia as a star who has temporarily retired from showbiz.

The RSC at the George Wood Theatre, Goldsmith's College, Almeida Theatre, Islington and tour of London colleges: 13 Oct.–1 Nov. 1989
Director: Stephen Rayne
Designer: Emma Ryott
Viola: Penny Downie
Olivia: Geraldine Alexander

Malvolio: Nicholas Woodeson
Feste: Desmond Barrit
Sir Toby Belch: David Calder
Sir Andrew Aguecheek: Mark Hadfield
Orsino: Tony Armatrading
Sebastian: Kevin Doyle
Maria: Jenni George

Birmingham Repertory Theatre: 3–24 Nov. 1989
Director: Pip Broughton
Designer: Jacqueline Gunn
Viola: Jan Ravens
Malvolio: Joseph Charles
Feste: Jim Findlay
Sir Toby Belch: Joseph Marcell
Olivia: Ellen Thomas
Set in the present on a Caribbean island. Viola, Sebastian and Sir Andrew were the only white actors in a production which used colour to differentiate the outsiders from the natives.

Leeds Playhouse: 21 Dec. 1989–20 Jan. 1990
Director: John Harrison
Designer: Simon Higlett
Viola: Alexandra Mathie
Malvolio: David Fleeshman
Feste: David Delve
A bitter-sweet production with a masque-like set, which marked the closing of the old Playhouse. Excellent reviews.

THE TWO GENTLEMEN OF VERONA

First Light Theatre Company at the Theatre Museum, Covent Garden: 8 June–1 July 1989
Director: Graham Mitchell
Proteus: James Powell
Valentine: Adam Roberts
Set in an English summer garden in the 1920s.

THE WARS OF THE ROSES

The English Shakespeare Company at the Old Vic, London: 28 Jan. 1989–
See *Shakespeare Survey* 41, pp. 159–62; *42*, pp. 160–1 for details of this cycle.

THE WINTER'S TALE

The Everyman Theatre, Liverpool: 9 Feb.–18 Mar. 1989
Director: Glen Walford
Designer: Claire Lyth
Music: Paddy Cunneen
Leontes: Neil Boorman
Hermione: Gilian Cally
Perdita: Claire Skinner
Autolycus: Michael Starke
Paulina/Mopsa: Chrissy Roberts
Japanese setting.

Compass Theatre Company (Sheffield) tour continues.
See *Shakespeare Survey 43*, p. 127.

Orchard Theatre Company at the Plough, Torrington and tour: 6 Sept.–18 Nov. 1989
Director: Bill Buffery
Designer: Meg Surrey
Music: Tom Nordon
Leontes/Autolycus: Alan Cody
Hermione: Lucy Maycock
Perdita: Henrietta Bess
Full text production set in an indeterminate period.

SHAKESPEARE APOCRYPHA

The BIRTH OF MERLIN by William Rowley and William Shakespeare
Theatr Clwyd, Mold: 1 June–1 July 1989
Director: Denise Coffey

Designer: Alan Barrett
Music: Stuart Gordon and R. J. Stewart
With Roy Hudd as Bill Rowley, clown.

MISCELLANEOUS

The Complete Works of William Shakespeare (abridged)
Reduced Shakespeare Company, Edinburgh Fringe Festival and tour: 11 Aug. 1989–

A Hard Day's Bard by Roy Wekin
Shakespeare Globe Museum: 29 Oct. 1989
With John Mowat
The adventures of two devotees of Shakespeare.

No Holds Bard by John Christopher Wood
Everyman Theatre, Liverpool: 30 Mar.–6 May 1989
Director: Noreen Kershaw
Michael Starke and Andrew Schofield performing extracts from most of the canon.

Shakespeare's Dark Lady, words and music by Margaret Wolfit
Globe Theatre Museum, London and tour April 1989
A one-woman show.

Shakespeare's Fools
Park Bench Theatre Company, Edinburgh Fringe Festival: 14 Aug. 1989–
Director: Julius Green

THE YEAR'S CONTRIBUTIONS TO SHAKESPEARE STUDIES

1. CRITICAL STUDIES
reviewed by R. S. WHITE

SHAKESPEARE'S RECEPTION

It is arguable that the most original research at the moment is devoted not to the plays themselves but to the ways in which Shakespeare's works have been received and used in different cultural contexts.

The cover of Michael D. Bristol's *Shakespeare's America, America's Shakespeare* (London, Routledge, 1990) is truly ghastly, and would fit more aptly on a hamburger stall than on a scholarly book. This may even be the intention, but is a pity, because the content is significant. Bristol ambitiously takes on the whole field of the reception of Shakespeare into American culture, and his thesis is that this reception has been largely a conservative one that has paradoxically overturned the spirit of the American revolution by allying itself closely with English, traditional assumptions. The hidden political agenda of both 'Institutional Infrastructure' (the Folger Library, tradition, the primacy of editing, the reputation-making function of much criticism) and of particular critics along the way has, Bristol argues, been deeply and uncritically reactionary. He cleverly chooses quotations from some venerated names such as Emerson, Lovejoy, Kittredge, Spencer, Craig, and Mack (whose essay appeared in a journal beside an article supporting America's rôle in Vietnam) to demonstrate their basic social interests which are patrician, paternalistic, white, male and conservative. Even some who would think of themselves as radical come under the lash. The textual 'revisionists' of the last few years are seen as fundamentally allied with their predecessors in still wanting stable texts (just more of them). Stanley Cavell reads from a stance of 'civil privatism' (p. 196) as if individualistic sensibility is threatened by community values, Richard Levin returns us to discredited notions of 'established meanings' and 'consensus' in his struggle against subversive pluralism. Even Stephen Greenblatt, doyen of the new in some quarters, is seen to conclude in 'bleakness and political paralysis' (p. 209) which is an unhealthy response to the burden of his cultural past. In this sorry pageant, only Northrop Frye emerges with some grudging praise as 'egalitarian and ecumenical in spirit' (p. 181), with the heavy qualification that his spirit 'is also evangelical rather than critical'. Bristol's book is intelligent but dispiriting in much the same way that he finds Greenblatt exemplifying a 'political hopelessness that stems from seeing an urgent need for rational political and social change without seeing any credible agency for achieving that purpose' (p. 209). Something like bitterness lurks beneath the surface, as Bristol finds bristling intellectual 'cadres' (a word used so repeatedly as to become stale) massing against any fresh, radical initiative.

A different area of reception (and one largely ignored by Bristol) is mapped out in *Women's Re-Visions of Shakespeare: On the Responses of Dickinson, Woolf, Rich, H. D., George Eliot, and Others* edited by Marianne Novy (Urbana and Chicago, University of Illinois Press, 1990). Both feminist criticism and female readers are the twin subjects. There is a range of responses. Mary Lamb in her *Tales from Shakespear* and particularly in her retelling of some of the stories shows a sensitive consciousness of disadvantages faced by women, Anna Jameson 'anticipates and makes possible later feminist criticism' and 'makes Shakespeare a province for women' (p. 54), Charlotte Brontë in *Shirley* uses *Coriolanus* functionally both in character creation and as a model of class conflict, and George Eliot alludes to and reshapes several Shakespeare plays in her novels. Emily Dickinson who said 'There's nothing wicked in Shakespeare, and if there is I don't want to know' (p. 109) based 'The Orient is in the West' on *Antony and Cleopatra*. There is an essay by Christine Froula on the seminal comments about 'Shakespeare's sister' made by Virginia Woolf in *A Room of One's Own* and the analysis moves on to her novels. Coming up to date, Adrienne Rich is seen to draw on *King Lear* in dealing with father–daughter relations. The volume ends with openly feminist, reader-response accounts of how Shakespeare can be centre for sympathies, aid to maturation, and an obstructive, patriarchal force. The collection as a whole provides an interesting monitor of the subtle and complex state of feminism itself in the early 1990s, while at the same time raising new questions about Shakespeare.

Kiernan Ryan in *Shakespeare* (Hemel Hempstead, Harvester Wheatsheaf, 1989) tries to pave the way for a new kind of reception of Shakespeare. He takes issue with the defeatist pessimism which marks many of the critics on both sides of the Atlantic who would call themselves radical:

The aim of this study is to further the development of fresh readings of Shakespeare's drama: readings designed to activate the revolutionary imaginative vision which invites discovery in his plays today.

(p. 1)

Ryan argues that recent 'progressive' critics who condemn writers such as Tillyard perversely confirm Tillyard's assertion that Shakespeare was a conventional and conservative thinker. Instead, Ryan argues that there are latent but recoverable meanings in Shakespeare which provide an 'oppositional vision' (p.24) in what he sees as 'potentially dissident plays' (p. 27). It is critics who have tried to 'muzzle' the dissident voices and have created a 'conservative' Shakespeare. *Othello* is regarded as socially rather than psychologically determined, a critical representation of racism and misogyny in practice. *King Lear* owes its power not to any transcendental vision but to its depiction of an assault upon traditional structures by a new, competitive individualism – a clash of politics rather than characters. Comedy and romance can, Ryan argues, be read as an education in 'utopian norms and expectations' (p. 75), generated by 'an implicit egalitarian vision' (p. 86). Reading Ryan's book provoked an unexpected response in me. I was predisposed to agree with his argument, but felt provoked into nitpicking opposition and outright disagreement by his tone of assertiveness (rather than argument), his glibness of interpretation when he talks about plays, and the generality of the approaches he adopts. If the book can do this to its potential friends, I am sure its enemies will have sport at its expense. Obviously a book of only 130 pages cannot be expected to deal thoroughly with the whole of Shakespeare, but if just a few, central points had been firmly and memorably substantiated it could have done its job in re-aligning some ways in which new readings can be conducted. As it stands, it is a missed opportunity.

Jonathan Bate returns us to more empirical ground in *Shakespearean Constitutions: Politics, Theatre, Criticism 1730–1830* (Oxford, Clarendon Press, 1989). This book is full of erudition and wit. 'Appropriation' is the word Bate singles out as his key term, and he initially offers some thoughts on the 'afterlife' of writers, and the 'history of reception'. The really solid part of the book (in the scholarly sense) is an examination of the ways in which caricaturists in the early nineteenth century used Shakespeare (and actors such as Kemble and Garrick) to comment on burning issues of contemporary political life. Quotations and immediately recognizable images from Shakespeare were used with ever expanding sophistication and prominence in the public arena by such artists as Cruikshank and Gillray to satirize and parody public figures. The ill-fated Boydell project of the 'Shakespeare library' was also fair game for satirists. The second half of Bate's book is devoted to 'The Example of Hazlitt', who often used Shakespeare to enter the arena of contemporary events. Even his *Political Essays* is laced with Shakespearian quotations. Although Bate's book might at first sight appear to be untheorized, the 'Epilogue' shows that he is very well aware of the wider implications of the 'act of mediation' which is being both studied and exemplified in the book.

Penguin Books seem to be embarking on a welcome rejuvenation of their old and invaluable anthologies of critics on Shakespeare. The first volume is *Samuel Johnson on Shakespeare* edited by H. R. Woudhuysen (Harmondsworth, New Penguin Shakespeare Library, 1989). A completely fresh selection with some inevitable overlaps with Wimsatt's out-of-print volume, this should allow Johnson's criticism to be dusted off. It stands as a helpful adjunct to the revisionist account by C. F. Parker reviewed in these pages last year, and although Parker's book presumably came too late for the editor to consult, they agree on the central proposition that 'this turning away, this not wishing to look at what evidently offends, is necessarily part of Johnson's essentially imaginative response to Shakespeare' (p. 35). 'Imaginative' may not be the word usually used about

Johnson, but the case is made cogently. Woudhuysen begins his Introduction disarmingly by showing the influence of Shakespeare on Johnson's *Dictionary*.

D. F. Bratchell contributes a more sweeping anthology of reception in *Shakespearean Tragedy* (London, Routledge, 1990). The Introduction charts briskly 'The Development of Tragedy', and then the book allows critics down the centuries to speak in their own words on their broad approaches. The section on 'Later Critical Texts' gestures towards the burgeoning of critical method in the 1980s but stops short of analysis.

'WORLDS' AND THEMES

Ideas of 'the world of the play' and 'the world of Shakespeare' had a good run in the 1970s but seemed to die down. They have returned, hardly with a vengeance, in at least the titles of three books.

Those who have read Vivian Thomas's book on the problem plays will know roughly what to expect from *Shakespeare's Roman Worlds* (London and New York, Routledge, 1989). Thomas is particularly interested in what Shakespeare did to his sources, in this case mainly Plutarch. He argues that in each play Shakespeare selects and transforms his material in order to create a 'world' which is marked by the creation and operation of a certain value system which differs from play to play whilst having some common aspects between plays. There is 'an intense sense of a social universe' filled with 'an awareness of the values, attitudes, aspirations, and idiosyncrasies of the different Romes which are portrayed in *Titus Andronicus*, *Julius Caesar*, *Antony and Cleopatra* and *Coriolanus*' (p. 1). Although each world is unique, they share some 'fundamental' values of 'service to the state, fortitude, constancy, valour, friendship, love of family and respect for the gods' (p. 13). One more which is shared by most characters (if not by Shakespeare) is 'contempt for the plebeians' (p. 15). The 'world' of *Titus*, although historically the latest, is consciously 'primitive'. It is a world where the tender touching of bodies is brutally opposed by violence and mutilation. *Julius Caesar* presents the 'bloodbath' which results from opposing political forces. It is a world of dehumanizing images and self-images, notwithstanding the touches of warm affection. The contrasts between Rome and Egypt in *Antony and Cleopatra* give images which show the interplay between realities and imaginings, while *Coriolanus'* world is one of 'sounds, words, gestures and deeds' where the central character is 'a victim of his culture' (p. 214). Thomas reads this play against the critical current as one of tragic power. In his study of the interrelationships between character, political forces and society, Thomas draws on Plutarch for both thematic patterns and small details, concluding that the 'enigmas' in the Roman sources are not avoided but preserved as ambiguities in Shakespeare. The whole enterprise is thorough and useful, but the criticism is unadventurous and tame.

There is nothing tame about the approach of Johannes Fabricius in *Shakespeare's Hidden World: A Study of his Unconscious* (Copenhagen, Munksgaard, 1989). I leave it to others to judge whether it is valuable as a contribution to Jungian psychology. As a book on Shakespeare it has all the subtlety of a person using a hammer and chisel to repair a watch. Drawing mainly upon the work of a Jungian analyst, Margaret Mahler, who observed infants' behaviour towards their mothers during the first few months of life, Fabricius finds the same drama of infantile attempts at individuation in Shakespeare's unconscious mind as it is manifested in the plays. It is a little worrying that the chronologically arranged book stops at *Twelfth Night*, since this raises the alarming possibility of a sequel.

Much better as a contribution to psychological criticism is *Shakespeare's Personality*, a set of essays edited by Norman N. Holland, Sidney Homan and Bernard J. Paris (Berkeley, Los Angeles, London, University of California Press, 1989). Norman Holland in his Introduction readily admits that the subject of the book, the personality of the writer, 'has disappeared' in the sense that criticism and literary theory have written it out of our consciousness. However, the writers in the book do make a convincing case that Shakespeare's works are still ripe for psychoanalytical scrutiny, even if 'The psychoanalyst plays by different rules from the literary historian' (p. 5). Shakespeare emerges, by almost unanimous consent, as somebody who is obsessively interested in aggression, particularly within the family. Intertextualists may say he picked this up from other dramatists, new historicists that he simply observed the politics of his day, reader response critics that it is the reader or viewer who chooses to construct readings based on aggression. But the psychoanalyst is convinced that Shakespeare learned it from his parents' knees. C. L. Barber and Richard P. Wheeler, and also Kirby Farrell, focus on Shakespeare's father's loss of authority within the family because of financial ruin, Sherman Hawkins sees Shakespeare sublimating his familially acquired aggression into the writing of history plays, Holland himself finds a recurrent pattern of the son doing what the father does not or cannot do for himself. Marianne Novy revives and elaborates an older view that William's plays reflect resentment towards his younger brother Gilbert. Carol Neely finds running through the works a disturbing masculinist ideology that women are dangerous, while in contrast Shirley Garner sees Shakespeare maintaining a view that women are divinely forgiving. There are other essays, all tending to similar conclusions that Shakespeare shared the aggressive, masculinist values of his society, but that he could equivocate with the wit and dualities of his mind, effacing himself into many rôles. The book is quite engrossing, but there is still, it must be admitted, a lurking doubt that the writers reveal more of themselves, their own historical positioning and the state of current psychoanalytical theory concerning transference and drives, than of the personality of the playmaker – we shall never know.

Christopher Pye's book, *The Regal Phantasm: Shakespeare and the Politics of Spectacle* (London and New York, Routledge, 1990) is concerned with the ways in which monarchy uses theatre to coerce its subjects. As metaphor and as occasion, spectacle can set up complex relationships between ruler and ruled, all of which serve to maintain absolutist power. Three plays are analysed. In *Henry V* the 'mock' quality of sovereignty is related to Kantorowicz's idea of 'the king's two bodies'. *Richard II* develops the centrality of the gaze, of eyes seeing and of subjects being seen, in the context of *Richard II*. *Macbeth* links monarchy's defeat of treason with 'theatre of rapture' as a political strategy inducing melancholy. In between these Shakespearian sections are chapters which present a wealth of historical exemplifications concerning theatricality, iconology of portraits of Elizabeth, power and the politics of punishment. Throughout, however, there is a sense in which (to quote the author mischievously out of context) the account 'in some instances leaves us uncertain about just what the problem is being described' (p. 119). The quotations may be by turns funny, gory, suggestive, but the analysis maintains such an uncritically solemn distance from them in its stance and its language that the vitality and potential of the material is lost. After quoting how a traitor William Perry 'was sentenced to be drawn through the streets on a hurdle, hung, cut down, and then to have his "private parts cut off and [his] entrals [*sic*] taken out and burnt in [his] sight"', the analysis, however intellectually justifiable, seems oddly irrelevant: 'the very sequence of the punishments suggests an epistemological as much as an affective aim ... Through and beyond his castration and death, the criminal is shown to maintain a political body well in excess of his natural one' (pp. 114–15). Throughout the book, we get the impression of

a writer who has discovered a fertile and fascinating bed of material but is unable to decide just what to do with it.

In contrast, Annabel Patterson's *Shakespeare and the Popular Voice* (Oxford, Basil Blackwell, 1989) is a truly excellent, historically based book on a subject which has in the past been treated with uncritical bias on one side or the other of the question. Patterson shows with statistics that at least ninety-five per cent of the population in 1600 were not peers or gentry, that these 'commons' were excluded by law from any voice in affairs of state, and that Shakespeare and his audience would not assume an automatically élitist attitude. The reading of Shakespeare which makes him into a court apologist, as popular now among new historicists as it used to be among royalists, was initiated by Coleridge as a response to his own times and was rapidly transported to America, apparently never to be radically challenged. Shakespeare's plays are read by Patterson as a series of changing reflections on the structure of English society, through phases of qualified assent to the Elizabethan settlement, intense political scepticism and mature radicalism. *Hamlet* is seen to be crucial and transitional. Popular grievances are raised even in the early comedies, and most potently in *Coriolanus* which with its 'embarrassing frontal political nakedness' (p. 120) raises the disconcerting question '*how* should the voice of the people be heard?' (ibid.) As an aftermath of the Midlands Rising it shows people speaking for themselves when their 'voices' are called for in a specifically political context. By not presupposing Shakespeare's innate conservatism, Patterson provides a comprehensively new account of *Coriolanus* and she even finds in *The Tempest* voices from below proclaiming protest and resistance. Even Prospero is in service to a hungry audience. While speaking of contemporary relevance and topical issues, a mention should be made of an article by A. Stuart Daley, 'Shakespeare's Corin, Almsgiver and Faithful Feeder' in *English Language Notes* 27 (1990), 4–21. By contrasting

Lodge's character Coridon with Shakespeare's Corin, and concentrating on his status as agricultural labourer, Daley shows that even in this apparently most aristocratic and make-believe of comedies there is a quite explicit train of references that draws attention to the plight of the poor, the need for hospitality and almsgiving in the 1590s, the new class of avaricious landlords, and generally speaking the existence of severe social injustice and class tension.

'Theatrical notation' as used by Rudolf Stamm in *Shakespeare's Theatrical Notation: The Early Tragedies* (Bern, A. Francke Verlag, 1989) is a much more precise concept than the general description, 'the relation of gesture and word, of theatre and drama' (p. 7) implies. Stamm really means 'gestic' language whose primary function is to tell us just what is happening on-stage or off. Gertrude's report of Ophelia's death, Ophelia's relation of Hamlet's distracted pose are given as examples, and the simple word 'this' can be notational. Word-scenery is also included. It is quite a specialized, even rarefied subject, but it enhances our respect for Shakespeare's comprehensiveness of imagining. There is a welcome, very full analysis of *Titus Andronicus*, and an interesting comparison of how six German translators deal with certain passages in *Hamlet*. The other two plays dealt with are *Romeo and Juliet* and *Julius Caesar*.

Anne Barton in *The Names of Comedy* (Oxford, Clarendon Press, 1990) raises with a vengeance the question, what's in a name? A long span of the history of comedy, from Aristotle and Plato down to Beckett, is constructed with skill, some would say ingenuity, around the idea of names. The organizing distinction is between Aristophanic 'cratylism', the inextricable linking of name and nature, and the Menandrian 'hermogenean' where names are distanced from the function of the individual and give an effect which is potentially more psychologically complex. Shakespeare, inevitably, uses both approaches from time to time, alternating between limited comic figures and complex human beings. Barton's book has

the unique property of bringing to consciousness a host of forgotten and unnoticed characters like John Naps, Peter Turph and Henry Pimpernell in *The Shrew*, but overall I found it disappointing. The basic distinctions are somehow catalytic in themselves, limiting the range of perceptions available to the initial binary model set up, and although an impressive range of texts is dealt with they do not emerge with distinctiveness. The author tiptoes into poststructuralism, which deals centrally with the indeterminacy of language and by implication naming, as a construction in itself, but gingerly tiptoes away again. A more wholehearted leap could have led to some fundamental and searching questions being raised. As it is, everything is somehow too neat and self-enclosed.

Another book which promises more than it delivers is David Farley-Hills's *Shakespeare and the Rival Playwrights 1600–1606* (London, Routledge, 1990). What is expected is a fresh view of the war of the theatres in the context of the politics of patronage and theatrical factionalism. Such a study would indeed be welcome. What we get is more narrowly literary in its concerns, a set of comparisons between plays evidently related in some way. For instance, *Othello* is read beside *A Woman Killed with Kindness*, *Timon of Athens* and *King Lear* beside King James's *Basilikon Doron*, and although the commentaries are tidy enough they do not illuminate much of what was going on in the more total theatrical and historical context. E. A. J. Honigmann's *Shakespeare's Impact on his Contemporaries* (not cited by Farley-Hills), while brief and even quirky, is much more suggestive and provocative.

The Idea of Conscience in Renaissance Tragedy by John S. Wilks (London, Routledge, 1990) is a sound if rather stodgy survey of how the rival conceptions of conscience fed into Elizabethan drama. Scholasticism built on the thinking of Aquinas saw conscience as rational and related to the Natural Law, but it was replaced at the turn of the seventeenth century by a more authoritarian notion of Divine Law which places conscience as a faculty directly controlled by God rather than reason and nature. Shakespeare is the heir to Thomist humanism and he is in consequence able to create complex characters facing dilemmas of conscience, Marlowe deeply qualifies this medieval approach, while writers like Marston, Webster and Ford show man disobeying or compromised by Divine Law.

Another who deals with Shakespeare's medieval inheritance, specifically in the field of dramatic form and imagery, is Cherrell Guilfoyle in *Shakespeare's Play within Play: Medieval Imagery and Scenic Form in 'Hamlet', 'Othello' and 'King Lear'* (Kalamazoo, Michigan, Medieval Institute Publications, 1990). All but one of the chapters have been published before as articles, the new one being '"Lead to the Sagittary": Victim and Predator in *Othello*' which draws on the *Reynard* fables to examine the plight of the victim, Desdemona, as prey. Each chapter (covering *Hamlet* and *Lear* as well as *Othello*) is elegantly reasoned from solid, detailed scholarship. The book is worthy of a fine scholar of the neglected but important area of links between the Medieval and the Elizabethan stages.

If the early history plays were more often taught at school and university level, Donald C. Watson's *Shakespeare's Early History Plays: Politics at Play on the Elizabethan Stage* (London, Macmillan, 1990) would have a chance of coming into its own as a clear-headed and succinct introduction, not only to the *Henry VI* plays, *Richard III* and *King John*, but to the general field of the historical contextualization of Shakespeare. Watson may not break new ground, but he helpfully defines the relationships between theatricality and politics which allow Shakespeare's England to emerge through plays set in the past:

All the world's a stage. Read forward and backward, the equation discloses the political dimension of Elizabethan theater, especially of drama portraying the English kings, and its potential for promoting or subverting the dominant ideology of its immediate culture. (p. 11)

Kirby Farrell, although he warmly acknowledges the appearance of J. L. Calderwood's *Shakespeare and the Denial of Death* in 1987, must have been just a little worried at how closely that book touches on his own preoccupation in *Play, Death, and Heroism in Shakespeare* (Chapel Hill and London, University of North Carolina Press, 1989). Both seem inspired by Ernest Becker's *The Denial of Death* although Farrell is more primarily influenced by Freud. Farrell's special interest lies in the play-death followed by resurrection as analogue for death and rebirth, self-sacrifice and heroic apotheosis. In plays such as *Antony and Cleopatra* and *Romeo and Juliet* states of dread and exercises in self-effacement lead to fantasies of transcendence which are the stuff of heroism and its related belief in immortality. In plays that deal directly with hero-worship, 'Followers release their own strength through a leader' (p. 59). Farrell argues that the pattern is of service in interpreting all groups of plays, and he concludes with wide-ranging comments about the links between play-death and individuation in psychoanalytical theory. The account is considerably more closely in touch with the Shakespearian material than Fabricius's, although the often elliptical development of the argument does not make it easy to read. Occasionally we get examples of the sort of thing that gets Freudian critics a bad name:

When Pyramus calls for a kiss, his beloved kisses 'the wall's hole' (5.1.201) as her 'cherry lips have often kiss'd [the wall's] stones, / ... stones with lime and hair knit up' (190–1). The obscene joke insinuates the daughter's submissive love for the father: she kisses his arse and also the symbols of his stones/testicles.

(p. 177)

Since we are in the thick of psychoanalytic theory, mention can be made of Horst Breuer's *Historische Literaturpsychologie. Von Shakespeare bis Beckett* (Tubingen, Francke Verlag, 1989), where we find another literary personage described as compulsively anal, namely Robinson Crusoe. The book attempts to set up a new field of criticism, psychohistory, which traces in literature the ways in which emotions and drives have been subject to historical change. Shakespeare does not play a particularly looming rôle in the book, although there are sections on his comedies, on *Timon of Athens*, and on *Hamlet*.

Thomas Kullmann in *Abschied, Reise und Wiedersehen bei Shakespeare: Zu Gestaltung und Funktion epischer und romanhafter Motive im Drama* (Tübingen, Max Niemeyer Verlag, 1989) provides us with a thorough study of departures and greetings as part of the larger themes of travel and journeys in Shakespeare. Particular scenes from plays are examined as stage models which Shakespeare built upon as his work evolved, and larger thematic significances of metaphors of travel, wanderings in the wilderness, sea voyages, and reconciliation are dealt with in the romances. The book is well researched and the argument is elegant in presentation.

Harold Toliver's book, *Transported Styles in Shakespeare and Milton* (University Park and London, The Pennsylvania State University Press, 1989), compares and contrasts Shakespeare and Milton in their respective attitudes to rhetoric and poetry. Shakespeare, working in the medium of drama, sees rhetoric often as a functional aspect of developing plot or as an arm of power, while poetry, in excess of specific dramatic tasks, may be unassimilable, and can take us into a 'second world' of significance where the irrational is explored. The plays examined in some detail are *Antony and Cleopatra*, *Othello*, *King Lear*, and *The Winter's Tale*. In Milton as puritan, the whole debate takes on a more ethical dimension. Both rhetoric and poetry take their colouring from the particular, underlying moral basis of the work. In general, rhetoric is the enemy of reason, while inspired poetry is a medium for figurative truth, and it may be unadorned and plain. While arguing that in Milton the areas of rhetoric and poetry are dialectically presented, Toliver does not oversimplify the terms into crude polarities. The book is a thoughtful one,

with close and detailed textual exegesis as its *forte*.

THEATRICAL APPROACHES

Anthony Brennan in *Onstage and Offstage Worlds in Shakespeare's Plays* (London and New York, Routledge, 1989), a stage-centred commentator, has crossed swords before with 'testy' critics who question his emphasis on plotting and logistics of the plays. As I have mentioned in these pages (testily?) Brennan's tone of beleaguered defensiveness against more closeted critics seems unnecessary, particularly since his own roll-call of acknowledgements includes names of many who are not immediately associated with the stage. He is especially respectful of Francis Berry, whose seminal book *The Shakespeare Inset* is given pride of place. Brennan's approach is interesting whether one is producing the plays in the theatre or (as another writer below says) in the 'mind's eye'. The business of reporting offstage events and the questioning of absences where we would expect the presence of characters are significant for all those who are interested in the potential of the plays which can be released in the theatre. The net is cast widely to include most of Shakespeare's plays. Where once again I part company is over the importance accorded by Brennan to schematization and quantification, with the many tables showing down to half-lines the actual periods of absence of a character from the stage. One can marvel at the sheer amount of statistical computation that lies behind the book, but one surely can with justice rather than testiness ask whether it really explains or conveys the sense of excitement which Brennan would undoubtedly agree is the aim of performance.

Ralph Berry's *On Directing Shakespeare* (London and New York, Hamish Hamilton, 1989) deserves brief notice as a reminder that practitioners in the theatre can help critics by having to think hard about the possibilities and problems of staging plays in the late twentieth century. The book consists of generous interviews with directors such as Jonathan Miller, Peter Brook and Michael Bogdanov about their own theories and practice.

Is Shakespeare Still Our Contemporary? edited by John Elsom (London and New York, Methuen, 1989) records not interviews but discussions between an international array of directors and theatre critics on the occasion of the twenty-fifth anniversary of the publication of Jan Kott's *Shakespeare Our Contemporary*. Kott's book is described as 'the most influential work of Shakespearian criticism of our time' (p. 8), and he was the guest of honour at the meeting. The purpose was to consider 'how far words like "universal" and "contemporary" can be sensibly applied to Shakespeare's plays' (p. 8), not in any theoretical fashion but in a personal and pragmatic spirit. Discussions arise from particular questions such as 'Is Shakespeare sexist?', 'Does Shakespeare's verse send you to sleep?' 'Does Shakespeare write better for television' and (the final session) 'Should Shakespeare be buried or born again?' The precise answers to all these questions are of absolutely no interest, and there is often self-indulgent waffle. But from the likes of Kott, Bogdanov, Moshinsky, Erich Fried and others, there are inevitably many interesting comments, sometimes conspicuously irrelevant to the matter in hand, but full of sporadic insights that experience in the theatre can give.

David Young's *The Action to the Word: Structure and Style in Shakespearean Tragedy* (New Haven and London, Yale University Press, 1990) can without injustice be regarded as a contribution to theatrical approaches, although it is also more than this alone. Young examines the tension between eloquent language and vigorous action, things said and things done, in *Hamlet, Othello, King Lear* and *Macbeth. Hamlet* is seen as playing off linguistic dilation against an action which is economical, even thrifty. The pattern of *Othello* shows the titular hero as one who starts as a grand storyteller and deteri-

orates, while Iago, at first a rough, bad storyteller, improves and gains our complicity, before Othello finally regains his narrative abilities.

COLLECTIONS

Philip Brockbank's weighty contribution to Shakespeare studies over the years has not been adequately reflected in his published work, which has been largely editorial rather than critical. It is, therefore, important to have his final book of essays, *On Shakespeare: Jesus, Shakespeare and Karl Marx, and Other Essays* (Oxford, Basil Blackwell, 1989). Some of the essays have been published before, but they repay re-reading, and there are six which have not been published. Many of them began as lectures in various countries. The breadth of Brockbank's range of reference is indicated not only in the title, but also in his uses of Blake, Bodin, Gramsci, Nietzsche, Wittgenstein and others. Whilst being fully aware of the historical context from which the plays emerged, Brockbank never allowed them to remain of interest for historical or theoretical reasons alone, but instead he found in Shakespeare a fresh relevance for the twentieth century. Shakespeare anticipated 'that nineteenth century prophet Marx' (p. 24). 'Shakespeare's Language of the Unconscious: The Psychogenesis of Terrorism' (first published in an earlier version in the *Journal of the Royal Society of Medicine* of all places) takes its bearings from Freud, Jung and Lacan, and dwells on 'one strain of Shakespeare's interest in the more elusive processes of our thought and language – those that go to the making of the terrorist, from Clifford to Brutus and Macbeth' (p. 152). Nor is the theatre neglected. '*Troilus and Cressida*: Character and Value 1200 BC to AD 1985', brooding upon the rival claims of individualism and community values, reaches towards 'the unperformed play' by considering a specific production in 1985. 'Shakespeare and the Fashion of These Times' offers some justification for interpreting Shakespeare from our own perspective rather than claiming 'timelessness' either for the dramatist or the critic. Brockbank writes with a voice of gravelly ruggedness all his own, and with a manifest moral commitment to values of equality and social justice which clearly he felt deeply.

Le Forme del Teatro: Contributi del Gruppo di ricerca sulla communicazione teatrale in Inghilterra, edited by Viola Papetti (Rome, Edizioni di Storia e Letteratura, 1989) is a richly deserved festschrift for Giorgio Melchiori, whose published works listed in the volume attest to his status as one of the best European scholars of Shakespeare. He contributes a textual (or more precisely pre-textual) study of *Hamlet* and Barbara Melchiori provides an entertaining discussion of 'the idea of Caliban' (p. 61) taking the archetype of the primitive man up to the era of science fiction. Vanna Gentili leads us to *The Comedy of Errors* as a neglected antecedent for *Gli Equivoci* by Lorenzo da Ponte, and Maria Vittoria Tessitore writes eloquently 'On the Part of Juliet'.

Brian Vickers is best known for his work on Shakespeare's prose and for the mammoth undertaking of *The Critical Heritage* volumes on Shakespeare. In the 'autobiographical preface' to *Returning to Shakespeare* (London and New York, Routledge, 1989) he tells us something of the problems in compiling the latter, as well as charting the road towards his winning the coveted Charles Oldham Shakespeare scholarship at Cambridge. The volume collects together some of Vickers's substantial and diverse essays, only one of which has not been published before. This is '"Mutual render": *I* and *Thou* in the *Sonnets*', in which it is argued that the intimacy and complexity of the Sonnets is generated by Shakespeare's use of 'an *I–Thou*, and above all a *We/Us/Our* relationship' to replace the '*I/She*' one used by Sidney and more conventional sonneteers. The long essay '*Coriolanus* and the demons of politics' (previously published as a short book) is probably the strongest argument yet made for the

tragic status of the much disputed figure of Coriolanus, a reading which I find unconvincing.

PLAYS

The Harvester New Critical Introductions to Shakespeare series has produced at least one very fine volume this year. Sheldon P. Zitner's account of *All's Well That Ends Well* (New York and London, Harvester Wheatsheaf, 1989) is far more than introductory in its scope, and it is likely to remain the best sustained criticism of the play for many years. What is impressive is that Zitner is able to historicize the issues (for example, by examining Elizabethan marriage customs, class gradations and medical debates) while also producing close readings that are strikingly original and subtle:

All's Well opens with a social thunderclap which has been muffled by the passage of social history ... What adds to her grief at the loss of her husband is that the Countess is being treated as a non-mother, for purposes of law an un-person, and her son – foolish as she knows him to be – made a kind of artificial orphan. (p. 45)

Seeing the play very much as a 'mingled yarn', Zitner delicately evokes the greyland of emotional states which derive from the questioning of power and status, the treatment of gender and sexuality which is centred on the women characters, and the complex interplay between old and young. A lengthy quotation is deserved, since it implies a whole reading of the play:

There are no villains among the older generation, though with the exception of the Countess they are not quite paragons. The King's high-minded arbitrariness and self-pity are realistically observed. Lafew is a charming rôle, but there is an unpleasantly self-conscious archness about his sexual allusions that suggests the brave face put on declining potency. Nor are there really any deep villains among the young. Parolles is far too cowardly actually to be an Iago and he is driven less by personal ambition than by the demon of his peculiar talent. Of Bertram, as insufferable as he can be, there is a great deal of unlicked cub and sheer fool in him. The differences among the generations are not moral but simply generational. The young are climbing, venturing: the old have arrived. They can look down and with complete sympathy like the Countess see their earlier selves in the climbers, or see themselves only imperfectly and with regrets as does the King, or even with hopefulness as does Lafew . . . It is the old who are concerned with continuity and strive to foster it, the women in the play more effectively and consistently than the men. Their concern provides some of the warmest and, in the King's fifth-act offer to Diana, some of the most ironic moments of the play.

(pp. 145–6)

In such a careful study, the odd oversight can be forgiven: there appears to be no reference for Susan Snyder's article which is admired on page 94, and old Gower unexpectedly strays into *The Winter's Tale* on page 3.

To go from this book to another in the Harvester series, Michael Long's *Macbeth* (London and New York, Harvester Wheatsheaf, 1989) is like moving from the art of the careful miniaturist to that of the broad-brushed oil painter. Both writers dwell on the 'mingled yarn' of Shakespeare's vision, but whereas Zitner recreates complexities of mood and morality, Long sees bold contrast:

The play's very medium . . . embodies a vision of primal solitude in constant competition with bonding, the one dark, brooding and violent, the other clear, bright and gentle. The drama shows how the two coexist in human life, how they come and go in the soul like night and day. (p. 29)

Even allowing for the vivid clashes in *Macbeth*, Long's treatment relies too heavily on evocative metaphor and too lightly on patient explication, and often the result is oversimplification. Duncan is treated with almost reverential respect and the martlets are given far too much work to do. There are undeveloped assertions and the register is sometimes strident. The author may be trying to reproduce the flashes of lightning he finds in *Macbeth* but in criticism the achievement of such an effect requires different techniques. Admittedly, however, the book has an ambitious scope, invoking Wagner, Mozart, Munch and Strindberg to establish the cultural context in which *Macbeth* may be placed.

Shakespeare's Mercutio: His History and Drama by Joseph A. Porter (Chapel Hill and London, University of North Carolina Press, 1988) is more than a contribution to the study of one character in *Romeo and Juliet*. Porter conducts a wide-ranging exploration into the evolution of Mercutio. Shakespeare took the character from an intriguing passage in Arthur Brooke, where Mercutio as a wedding guest grips Juliet's hand, and she discovers his hand to be colder than frozen mountain ice. Porter explores not only what Shakespeare did with the vignette, but raises the question why Shakespeare lavished such attention on the character. His answer is that Mercutio derives from the god Mercury with all his wide cultural reverberations. I cannot know how the book was composed or over how long a period, but it moves in an interesting way through various stages in the development of criticism over the last couple of decades. The early parts give us a study of iconography in Medieval and Renaissance emblem books, and trace the transformations undergone by the figure of Mercury in these contexts, down to the erotic, phallic figure who appears in the moralized Ovids. Iconography study is far from dead, but its heyday is associated with the 1960s under the influence of Panofsky, Wind and Seznec. The book then takes a leap into the 1970s with a shift to the linguistic theories of Speech Acts associated mainly with the work of H. P. Grice and J. R. Searle. This school is a kind of linguistic equivalent to iconography, since it deals with the sign-language of speech and leads into semiotics. We seem to be on more shifting ground here, as a lot of weight is placed on 'liminality' in a study of the speech acts of reporting in *Romeo and Juliet*. Something like new historicism of the 1980s is then invoked to develop the possibility which has been suggested before that in his depiction of Mercutio Shakespeare is performing an elegy for Marlowe, his dead competitor. Stage history comes next, with a close study of representations of Mercutio, aided by promptbooks from 1780 to 1904 and film versions from 1908. The conclusion picks up on the 'margins' again and ponders the present-day 'marginalization' of Shakespeare from the central position he used to hold in cultural studies, a scheme which smacks of recent approaches associated with the social scientist's study of popular culture. The book is probably as multi-focused as it could be, and it ought to add up to a comprehensive coverage of Mercutio's relatively brief appearances in the play. And yet, despite the exhaustive range of reference and critical modes, the argument has a tendency to seem like a set of margins in itself, and the centre constantly slips away. This is not to deter anybody from reading it, however, since the book is genuinely clever.

Hamlet continues to spawn a vast critical progeny. Michael Cohen's *Hamlet in my Mind's Eye* (Athens and London, University of Georgia Press, 1989) is by no means the most pernicious of its offspring. The title of the Epilogue, 'Watching ourselves: What Happens (To the Reader) in Hamlet' tells part of the tale. The book is concerned with the 'multivalence' of the play, asserting that 'there are many Hamlets . . . as *Hamlet* is played on the stages of the mind's eyes' (p. 3). Cohen draws on prompt-books, performances, and film and television records of *Hamlet*, assuming that each of these is a specific realization of an infinite potential offered to the liberated reader. It is certainly not a coercive book, and Cohen is true to his word in holding many possibilities open. It is, however, a fairly bland one, both in its organization (going through the play scene by scene) and its interpretations which are often tentative to the point of tepidness. But it is a book one could safely recommend to students for its full treatment of many points of view, and for its lack of dogma.

Fredson Bowers was known to my gener-ation as the one who cast a long shadow on textual studies, proclaiming that we have no right to say anything about a play until the text is definitively established, a possibility which is still steadily receding into an infinite future. *Hamlet as Minister and Scourge and Other Studies in Shakespeare and Milton* (Charlottesville, University Press of Virginia, 1989) shows him in a more benign light as teacherly guide and critical inspiration. The essays have all been published before, but they are appropriately gathered into a single volume. Bowers is particularly strong on dramatic structure, and so, although most attention gravitates to *Hamlet*, it is useful to have under the same roof essays on structure in *King Lear* and in *King Henry IV, Part 1*. Milton, although he has some exits and some entrances in the body of the book, gets only one chapter to himself, an analysis of justice and recon-ciliation in *Samson Agonistes*.

Although the central subject of *The Renais-sance Drama of Knowledge: Giordano Bruno in England* by Hilary Gatti (London and New York, Routledge, 1989) is not Shakespeare, it contributes to *Hamlet* studies. In its own right it is a fascinating book, and the best so far written on Bruno and his contact in the 1580s with the 'Northumberland group'. What makes it so good is that it resists the mumbo-jumbo of a school of night with its smoky fumes of cabba-lism and black magic which the papacy of the time would have promoted, and instead repre-sents Bruno as a serious philosopher who cour-ageously (and at the cost of his life) pursued Copernican theories in the face of theological opposition. We are reminded that Bruno was also a dramatist. Gatti argues that Bruno stimu-lated a new conception of the rôle of intellectual individualism, and it is here that *Hamlet* comes in. The long, final chapter on *Hamlet* makes the case for Shakespeare's indebtedness to Bruno, in language and images as well as general world-view. Hamlet's love-letter, it is argued, posits the new science, the play deals with concepts of infinity and eternal vicissitude which were ex-plored by Bruno, and Horatio is seen as

Bruno's figure of the Calm Spirit. I find myself still unconvinced of a definite indebtedness by Shakespeare to Bruno, but a good deal less certain than I was before reading this thoroughly researched book. The section on Marlowe's *Doctor Faustus* is very scrupulous.

The casebook format can be stultifying to both editor and reader. Susan Snyder has done her best in collecting *'Othello': Critical Essays* (New York and London, Garland Publishing Inc., 1988), but some would have preferred a new essay (or even a book) from Snyder herself to the roll-call through Coleridge, Bradley, Murry (rather vacuous), Leavis, Gardner, Heilman, and Kernan. I still consider John Bayley's chapter in *The Characters of Love* to be one of the best things published on *Othello*, but anthologizers seem not to agree (it is not even in the Bibliography). Two recent essays, Edward Snow's 'Sexual Anxiety and the Male Order of Things in *Othello*' and Peter Stallybrass's 'Patriarchal Territories: The Body Enclosed' represent the feminist approach which Snyder herself clearly favours, although she is embarrassed by the fact that they are not written by women.

The European Tragedy of Troilus edited by Piero Boitani (Oxford, Clarendon Press, 1989) contains an excellent feminist essay, 'Shakespeare and Chaucer: "What is Criseyde worth?"' by Jill Mann. In its reassessment of Cressida as a woman who is unjustly placed at the mercy of male constructions and estimates of value, and in its striking definition of the separation between a man's world and a woman's in *Troilus and Cressida*, it is timely and strong. The book itself shows a kind of European community of scholars appropriate to the 1990s, tracing the twists and turns of the myth of Troilus and Cressida from antiquity up to Christa Wolf's *Kassandra*, a novel published in Germany in 1983. Apart from Mann's, the two essays which will interest Shakespearians are Agostino Lombardo's 'Fragments and Scraps: Shakespeare's *Troilus and Cressida*' and Sergio Rufini's '"To Make that Maxim Good": Dryden's Shakespeare'.

ARTICLES AND ESSAYS

How better to launch a new journal than with an issue dedicated to Shakespeare? Such happy judgement is shown by the editors of *Critical Survey* 1 (1989), a new journal from Oxford University Press. It is not, however, entirely new, since it was initially a companion publication to *Critical Quarterly* edited by Cox and Dyson between 1962 and 1973. Its intention is 'to encourage a dialogue between those engaged in the fields of literary and cultural studies' (Editorial), with some emphasis on pedagogically constructive contributions. The first issue does not reflect the former aim, since none of the articles reflects developments in cultural studies, but it is early days. Rather, they are either generalist ('Pluralist Shakespeare' by Stanley Wells, 'Are Shakespeare's Tragic Heroes "Fatally Flawed"?' by Graham Holderness), or 'close readings' of plays (Bill Overton on *Richard III*, R. P. Draper on *Richard II*, Peter Hollindale on *Othello*). But some essays do concentrate on teaching Shakespeare, notably Inga-Stina Ewbank's 'Much Ado about Imagination' and David Lindley's 'Some Thoughts on the Relationships of School and University', and a review article by Ann Thompson, 'Which Shakespeare?: A Consumer's Guide to Editions'. The journal also includes original poetry and fiction.

The pages of *Shakespeare Survey 42* (1990) are enlivened by a *tour de force* by Lois Potter, '"Nobody's Perfect": Actors' Memories and Shakespeare's Plays of the 1590s' (pp. 85–98) which elegantly deals with the intriguing question of how actors memorized their lines. Juliet Dusinberre surveys differing approaches to the 'embarrassing women' adopted in stage productions of *King John* in the nineteenth and twentieth centuries, and Charles Edelman gives an interesting analysis of a neglected subject, sword-fighting.

Barbara Hardy contemplates 'Shakespeare's Self-Conscious Art' in the F. E. L. Priestley Lecture Series for the University of Lethbridge

(Lethbridge, Alberta, University of Lethbridge Press, 1988). Self-consciousness is defined in various ways, as self-reminiscence (being reminded of an earlier play by Shakespeare), narrative intrusions, use of the metaphor of theatre, and characters' use of language and metaphors that make reference to the creative process which the dramatist is pursuing. A number of works by Shakespeare are considered, and there is an effortless allusiveness to other writers. The subjects and general perspectives are not new, but Hardy has the capacity to make them the vehicle for many finely sighted details which make suddenly clear a significance in an incident which has gone unnoticed.

An essay by E. A. J. Honigmann, 'Crime, Punishment and Judgement in Shakespeare', is a contribution to *L'Europe de la Renaissance: Cultures et Civilisations: Mélanges offerts à Marie Thérèse Jones-Davies* (Paris, Jean Touzot, 1989, pp. 285–93). It deals with problems of poetic justice raised by plays written by Shakespeare in mid-career. Honigmann argues that Shakespeare's unsettling challenges to the notion of poetic justice are at least as strong as his adherence to it. 'Defeated judgement' lies at the heart of the tragedy of *Hamlet* and *King Lear* equally, while 'the poet of the Sonnets was . . . disinclined to condemn or punish' (p. 292).

Comedy

Articles at the moment abound in references that draw together language and economics, but not necessarily in a Marxist fashion. We shall encounter several of them below. Margaret Maurer in 'Figure, Place and the End of *The Two Gentlemen of Verona*', *Style*, 23 (1989), 405–29, notes that *The Two Gentlemen* is the first of Shakespeare's comedies to emphasize exchange in the economic sense (of goods and words), and she argues that this fact explains the play's narrative inconsistencies and its characters' erratic gestures.

Shakespeare's and Jonson's interventions in the war of the theatres are detected by Henk Gras in '*Twelfth Night, Every Man out of his Humour*, and the Middle Temple Revels of 1597–8', *Modern Language Review* 84 (1989), 545–64. Finding an intertextuality between the plays, so different in kind as they are, Gras suggests that Shakespeare's Ovidian romance and Jonson's satire were part of the debate about contrasting dramaturgical ideas which patrons of the Middle Temple were well placed to appreciate. Gilian West also links up two comedies but with a different emphasis in 'Lost Humour in *The Comedy of Errors* and *Twelfth Night*', *English Studies* 71 (1990), 6–15. She provides a lengthy list of examples where '*because of language change* a woeful number both of ironic ambiguities and the verse of serious-minded characters and of outrageous jokes in the prose of low-life characters are now lost to audiences and readers' (p. 6). The labour of recuperation relies heavily on the Oxford English Dictionary.

Barbara A. Mowat in '"A Local Habitation and a Name": Shakespeare's Text as Construct' in *Style*, 23 (1989), 335–51 emphasizes the ingratitude of Theseus in condemning poets for their fine, inventive frenzy, pointing out that he himself would not exist except for texts, pages and books, repeated and quoted over centuries. Mowat points out that Shakespeare does not create from his seething fantasy but from folios and quartos written by others.

David Lucking compares the casket scene and the trial scene in 'Standing for Sacrifice: The Casket and Trial Scenes in *The Merchant of Venice*', *University of Toronto Quarterly*, 58 (1989), 355–75. He detects similarities in the presentation in each of an 'ethic of sacrificial love' (a phrase borrowed from R. F. Hill). Both Venice and Belmont are marked by quest and sacrifice, although in other ways the realms are opposed in their respective value systems.

'*All's Well That Ends Well* and "The Common Stock of Narrative Tradition"' by G. A. Wilkes, *Leeds Studies in English*, 20 (1989), 207–16 argues that a ballad tradition based on the story of the Nut-Brown Maid is more appropriate than the 'clever wench' story in explaining the indignities visited on Helena in pursuing the high-born Bertram. In particular, it explains her submission and self-abnegation, which are rarely part of a clever wench's makeup. On a quite different tack, Willem Schrickx in '*All's Well That Ends Well* and its Historical Relevance' published in *Multiple Worlds, Multiple Words: Essays in Honour of Irene Simon*, edited by H. Maes-Jelinkek, Pierre Michel and Paulette Michel-Michot (University of Liège, 1988), pp. 257–74 has ransacked contemporary documents to find that the King of France in the play surprisingly represents King James I, and the Duke of Florence represents Maurice of Nassau. According to this hypothesis, the play becomes a commentary on 'the overwhelming Spanish presence in London in 1604' (p. 261).

History

The days of New Historicism may be numbered, since grumbles about the approach are surfacing. Frank Romany in 'Shakespeare and the New Historicism' in *Essays in Criticism*, 39 (1989), 271–87 launches a mild attack. While welcoming the return to cultural studies of historical awareness, Romany finds shortcomings in the work of proclaimed new historicists, in particular Stephen Greenblatt. Greenblatt and his followers, Romany suggests, beg important questions about history, ignore some very obvious historical contexts while searching for the colourfully eccentric, and are limited in their illumination of the plays. Conference-goers around the world cannot fail to notice the increasingly vocal challenges mounted on new historicism. Literary critics are reluctant to yield the high moral ground, and there are some fully fledged historians who say it is bad history. But no doubt the debate is only just beginning.

The influence of new historicism is evident but not predominant in a tricky essay by John Kerrigan, '*Henry IV* and the Death of Old Double', *Essays in Criticism*, 40 (1990), 24–53. Kerrigan builds his argument on the various layers of 'doubling' observed in the *Henry IV* plays, between past and present, two kings, borrowed titles, the recurrent motif of 'counterfeits', and indeed in the doubling inherent in the two-part structure of the juxtaposed plays. Apparently taking a leaf out of Greenblatt's book, Kerrigan plays sportively with an anecdote from Montaigne about a monstrous child, although the obliquity of the story makes it somewhat unnecessary to the argument.

David Womersley emphasizes the topicality in the mid 1590s of *King John* in 'The Politics of *King John*', *Review of English Studies* n.s. 40 (1989), 497–515. The play and the times, he argues, were marked by unease about unclear succession. The studied reversal in the political world anatomized by the Bastard reveals an absence of absolute values. The Bastard adopts a stance of loyalty and submission to order as a rational choice rather than as an automatic reflex, in contrast to those around him.

Russ McDonald examines the place of language as an unstable and potentially duplicitous tool in the hands of politicians, in '*Richard III* and the Tropes of Treachery', *Philological Quarterly*, 68 (1989), 465–83. The linguistic strategies used in the play, often embodying forcible shifts of meaning, are regarded as revealing Shakespeare's increasing scepticism about language itself. Meanwhile, the contractual basis of language is examined by Sandra K. Fischer in '"He means to pay": Value and Metaphor in the Lancastrian Tetralogy', *Shakespeare Quarterly*, 40 (1989), 149–64. Breaking bonds, the non-payment of debts, and the very metaphor of indebtedness are seen to dominate the *Henry IV* plays, and language is based on contract and exchange rather than just ceremony.

This year the history plays seem to be replacing the comedies as the testing ground for theory. Instability of language is a preoccupation of that branch of modern literary theory indebted to Jacques Derrida, and Jonathan Goldberg explicitly acknowledges his debt to

Derrida in 'Rebel Letters: Postal Effects from *Richard II* to *Henry IV*', *Renaissance Drama*, n.s. 19 (1988), 3–25. In his examination of letters and messages, Goldberg suggests that the notion of writing – textuality – as instrument of and complicit with power, is central to the history sequence of plays. But although letters are often allied with power, they are also seen to be devalued by power, and replaced with speaking.

Lacan, another luminary amongst theoretically inclined critics, fuels an essentially feminist reading of the history plays by Valerie Traub, 'Prince Hal's Falstaff: Positioning Psychoanalysis and the Female Reproductive Body', *Shakespeare Quarterly*, 40 (1989), 456–74. Traub argues that fantasies and anxieties about women in the history plays revolve around the figures of the virgin and the madonna.

Barbara Everett writes with characteristic stylishness and dash on 'The Fatness of Falstaff' in *London Review of Books*, 16 August 1990, 18–22. Starting with and returning to the phlegmatic dog Crab in *The Two Gentlemen*, she celebrates the 'heroic physicality' of some characters such as Bottom and especially Falstaff. There are some memorable moments, such as the capturing of the 'ludicrous, deathly beauty, a mildewed richness' (p. 22) of the Gloucestershire scene, but by and large the essay is an eloquent and witty reiteration of contributions such as Michael Goldman's in *The Energies of Drama*. The wit is worth it.

James Shapiro in 'Revisiting *Tamburlaine*: *Henry V* as Shakespeare's Belated Armada Play' in *Criticism: A Quarterly for Literature and the Arts*, 21 (1989), 351–66 gives us 'an historicized conception of influence, one that locates Shakespeare's response to Marlowe – in particular to the two parts of *Tamburlaine* – within the framework of the political climate in London during the spring and summer of 1599' (p. 351). *Henry V* is categorized as 'conqueror drama', reflecting a revival of nationalistic aspirations which accompanied the threat of the Armada in 1599 and recalled the earlier Armada in 1589.

Instead of writing against the Marlovian grain as he had in his earlier writings, Shakespeare now writes over, or through, Marlovian history. But because the political and historical conditions were different, the later play is adjudged more complex.

Tragedy

Titus Andronicus gets more than its usual share of attention in a number of *Shakespeare Quarterly* (40 (1989)). Gillian Murray Kendall in '"Lend me thy hand": Metaphor and Mayhem in *Titus Andronicus*' (pp. 299–316) examines the figurative use of language, and in particular the distortion of metaphor, as a figure for physical mutilation. Douglas E. Greene in 'Interpreting "her martyr'd signs": Gender and Tragedy in *Titus Andronicus*' (pp. 317–26) applies a feminist perspective. Although Lavinia's rôle as victim and Tamora's as avenger threaten to usurp Titus' centrality, in the end, 'just as Elizabeth's gender was submerged' (p. 319), so Shakespeare's women are made to serve the construction of Titus as patriarch, tragic hero and central consciousness.

Another of the Roman plays, *Julius Caesar*, is treated by Mark Rose in 'Conjuring Caesar: Ceremony, History, and Authority in 1599', *English Literary Renaissance*, 19 (1989), pp. 291–304 as 'mobilizing some of the contradictory feelings toward the absolute authority of the crown that were beginning to be felt even as early as 1599' (p. 304). The tribunes are seen as proto-puritans, suspicious of all forms of ceremony, while the play as a whole presents us with mystery and apparently justified superstition.

H. A. Kelly's 'Chaucer and Shakespeare on Tragedy' in *Leeds Studies in English*, n.s. 20 (1989), 191–206 is a general essay arguing that Chaucer's meaning of tragedy as the *de casibus* type, derived from Boethius, was adopted in preference to the Aristotelian type by Shakespeare. Modern theorists have tended to ignore the medieval form, which allowed depiction of the fall of both the innocent and the guilty.

'"So Unsecret to Ourselves": Notorious Identity and the Material Subject in Shakespeare's *Troilus and Cressida*' by Linda Charnes in *Shakespeare Quarterly*, 40 (1989), 413–40 takes as its haunting refrain 'This is and is not' in dealing with characterization. The legendary status of characters in the play is belied by their material representation, and the effect is thickened by the overt theatricalism of the events.

Hamlet has its share of articles as of books. James V. Holleran exhaustively and with massive research investigates 'Maimed Funeral Rites in *Hamlet*' in *English Literary Renaissance* 19 (1989), 75–93. The unfortunate circumstances surrounding Ophelia's disputed and disrupted funeral rites provide just one example amongst many of corrupted ceremonies in Claudius' court. *Hamlet Studies* has established a style blending the provocative and the conservative in equal measures. In volume 11 (1989), David Shelley Berkeley in 'Claudius the Villein King of Denmark' (pp. 9–21) opens a completely new can of worms in the Hamlet familial situation by arguing that Claudius is in fact a bastard child. Carole T. Diffey in '"Such Large Discourse": The Rôle of "Godlike reason" in *Hamlet*' (pp. 22–33) sticks to safer territory in giving evidence that it is Hamlet's reason that leads him to delay, rather than a tendency to procrastinate. Rachel V. Billigheimer in 'Diversity in the Hamlets of the Eighteenth-century Stage in England, France and Germany' (pp. 34–48) shows that from his position in the seventeenth century as a straightforward avenger, he took on several different guises in the succeeding century. In the English-speaking world, Garrick's 'familiar yet forcible style of rant' (p. 40) was as influential as Kemble's dignified and rhetorical approach. France never took to the Prince. In their Enlightenment 'climate of rationalism advocating logic, order and clarity' the French 'regarded the play as distasteful and the character of Hamlet as hardly that of a hero but rather that of a deranged genius fit to amuse an audience of barbarians' (p. 42). Goethe in Germany, indifferent to neo-classicism, saw *Hamlet* in terms of a family tragedy and the Germans 'appreciated an introspective and emotional Hamlet as a piece of poetry' (p. 46). David L. Pollard in 'Belatedness in Hamlet' (pp. 49–59) provides yet another image of Hamlet as Juvenilian scourge, raging with 'bitter wisdom' (p. 57) against a corrupt world.

In dealing with *Macbeth* in '"Hours Dreadful and Things Strange": Inversions of Chronology and Causality in *Macbeth*', *Philological Quarterly*, 68 (1989), 283–94, Brian Richardson reinterprets the play's chronological oddities and discrepancies as central to the play's concerns rather than as flaws in the design. By departing from strictly linear sequence *Macbeth* inverts the order of cause and effect. For example, both the old man and Ross comment on inversions and foreshortening of time, which are precisely what the play draws attention to in its own design. Richardson regards the more flagrant temporal antinomies as daring effects, often mirroring the supernatural at work in a play which enables the future to be seen before it happens.

Michael Neill argues that *Othello* has created a 'fascinated anxiety' in commentators, artists and audiences alike, because it deals with taboos like race and adultery in deeply ambiguous and disturbing ways. In 'Unproper Beds: Race, Adultery, and the Hideous in *Othello*', *Shakespeare Quarterly*, 40 (1989), pp. 383–412, Neill stresses the shocking way in which the marriage bed is opened to public gaze. 'Wrecked in Unknown Fate: Othello's Loss and Recovery of Self' by Fumio Yoshika, published in *Studies in English Literature* (Tokyo, Japan), English number (1990), pp. 3–22, argues that a condition of universal unawareness pervades *Othello*, from its opening in secrecy and ambiguity to its many anecdotes of theft and loss. These aspects of the play's atmosphere and imagery are linked up with a more general theme of losing self-knowledge. Joan Rees also writes thematically on *Othello* in '*Othello* as a

Key Play', *Review of English Studies* n.s. 41 (1990), 185–90. Her chosen themes are trust (in others and in one's sense of self) and betrayal, and these recur in other tragedies (which makes *Othello* a 'key' play). The betrayal of Desdemona points towards the romances.

Barbara C. Millard contributes to the growing body of criticism devoted to Shakespeare's women in 'Virago with a Soft Voice: Cordelia's Tragic Rebellion in *King Lear*', *Philological Quarterly*, 68 (1989), 143–65. She argues that the ambivalent responses stimulated in audiences by Cordelia are a consequence of contradictory functions given to the character. She is supposed to be by turns loving daughter and virago destined to lead an army back to England and to reclaim her father's throne and power. In doing so she is enacting the plight of the royal female child in a patriarchal system. In her redemptive rôle, she anticipates the heroines of the last plays.

Romances

Laurence Wright in 'When does the Tragicomic Disruption Start?: *The Winter's Tale* and Leontes' "Affection"', *English Studies*, 70 (1989), 225–32, re-examines the old chestnut of when Leontes reveals his jealousy, precipitating the main action of the play. He pins the moment down to the line 'Affection? thy Intention stabs the Center', which is seen as a crucial point of transition from rationality to fevered imagination. The argument turns on defining affection as a condition besetting Leontes rather than imputed to Hermione – it is not lust but 'intensity' or 'intentness', which presumably is analogous to Macbeth's raptness, an overwrought psychological state, that convinces Leontes of the reality of his dreams. 'Fevered imagination' might be a rough and ready equivalent. 'The very intensity of his passion convinces Leontes of its basis in reality' argues Wright. Such a reading accredits to Leontes an unusual degree of self-consciousness about his own state of mind.

Peggy Munoz Simonds provides an emblematic study linking the elm and the vine in marriage when considering Posthumus' memorable words 'Hang there like fruit, my soul, / Till the tree die' in 'The Marriage Topos in *Cymbeline*: Shakespeare's Variations on a Classical Theme', *English Literary Renaissance* 19 (1989), 94–117. The elm and the vine symbolize marriage, mutual support and the friendship of equals and, more generally, political unity which is figured in the peace between Britain and Rome.

The Tempest is read as a radical challenge to state power by Curt Breight in '"Treason doth never prosper": *The Tempest* and the Discourse of Treason', *Shakespeare Quarterly*, 41 (1990), 1–28. Breight argues that the play is constructed as a series of conspiracies which take their place in the debates concerning opposition to authority in Elizabethan and Jacobean London. Given its central concentration, the article is inevitably unsympathetic to Prospero. Donna B. Hamilton, in 'Defiguring Virgil in *The Tempest*', *Style*, 23 (1989), 352–73, begins more modestly than Breight in tracing the indebtedness of Shakespeare to Virgil's first six books of the *Aeneid*. Her conclusions, however, lie in the same field of political discourse, when she finds that the language of transcendent absolutism in *The Tempest* is adjusted by the language of limitation and self-abnegation. Shakespeare is seen as remaking the politics of the *Aeneid* for the time of Jamesian absolutism.

Poems

Although it also deals with plays, Robert B. Schwartz's *Shakespeare's Parted Eye: Perception, Knowledge and Meaning in the Sonnets and Plays* (New York, Peter Lang, American University Studies, 1990) is most original in its approach to the Sonnets. Taking as his epigraph Hermia's 'Methinks I see these things with parted eye, When everything seems double', and owing much to Norman Rabkin's notion of 'complementarity', Schwartz cites relativities, subtle antitheses and simultaneous affirmations and denials as problems of both philosophical method and perceptual perspective. Eye and heart, form and substance, truth and falsehood are some of the paradoxical dichotomies dealt with in the levels of awareness present in the Sonnets. There are also accounts of the *Dream*, *As You Like It*, *Twelfth Night*, *Hamlet* and *King Lear*.

Lars Engle in 'Afloat in Thick Deeps: Shakespeare's Sonnets on Certainty', *Publications of the Modern Languages Association* 104 (1989), 832–43 confirms that because 'survival value' is a theme of the Sonnets, so they have a built-in canonical argument for cultural centrality which makes them in self-prophesying fashion, self-conserving. The idea of survival value presented in the Sonnets, Engle argues, is not Platonic as so many critics have asserted, but rather economic and pragmatic. Margreta de Grazia also looks at the *Sonnets* but from the point of view of the implanted autobiography which has dominated criticism from the eighteenth century. In 'The Motive for Interiority: Shakespeare's *Sonnets* and *Hamlet*' in *Style*, 23 (1989), 430–44 she examines the critical history of the respective works and speculates on why psychologized authorship has been posited so often to explain (or avoid) surface problems of ambiguity concerning gender and desire.

For those, like Gary Taylor and the other editors of the present Oxford edition of Shakespeare's works, an ominous note is sounded by Thomas A. Pendleton's 'The Non-Shakespearian Language of "Shall I die?"', *Review of English Studies*, n.s. 40 (1989), 323–51. The article is a detailed examination of internal evidence establishing, at least to its author's satisfaction, that the poem 'Shall I die?' claimed in a seventeenth-century manuscript, and then again in 1985, to be Shakespeare's, is not.

EPILOGUE

I crave the indulgence of an epilogue in the vein of Prospero since, like him, after five years on the magic island of reviewing for *Shakespeare Survey* I should now drown my books deeper than did ever plummet sound. The last five years has seen an unprecedented re-definition of what it means to carry out research and criticism in Shakespeare, as literary scholars learn from philosophers, social scientists, anthropologists, linguists and historians. It is now generally considered essential to examine and justify theoretical procedures and basic assumptions. In 1985 it looked possible that the proliferation of literary theories and practices would marginalize a 'canonical' writer like Shakespeare, but he seems if anything now renewed as the focus for scrutiny, the 'site' of cultural and social debates. In the mid '80s there was also a tendency to see him as an arch-conservative cloaking his anti-populist tendencies in a veneer of liberalism, whereas from the vantage point of the early '90s he seems a much more progressive figure. Avid readers from the past like Marx, Engels, Brecht and Kozintsev would be delighted with this, even as the social and economic structures they sought to implement are apparently being radically modified.

My impressions of the profession of literary studies have deepened through the activity of intensive reviewing. In North America it would seem that the imperatives of tenure will always require prolific publication often derivative of the latest fashionable theory and at the expense of originality of perspective. In Europe the drive is towards thorough study of circumscribed areas, often without theoretical reference. The gap between theory and empiricism remains a great divide. In both cases the result can be the hypnotic power of tedium. In Britain the currents of innovation lap as against a backwater with the exception of a few who strike out into deeper waters. Meanwhile, amongst the doyens of the new, self-definition, the act of labelling, through an -ism or a post-, whether cultural materialism, new historicism, post-structuralism or something else, can lead to overnight fame, followers and fortune, but in the longer term can destine critics to permanent oblivion for boxing themselves in too narrowly, and publishers to series that peter out. Things are changing so quickly that approaches radical in 1985 now look out of date. At least the signs of activity, manifested particularly in a return to the Renaissance doctrine that literature teaches as well as delights, are healthy. Feminism has paved one particular way, and the time may have come more generally for the kind of -ism that sceptically questions all authority whether 'new' or old.

My particular horror is the new mystification of Shakespeare's works. I am convinced that ideas, no matter how subtle or complex, can be expressed clearly, especially in discussions of a writer who has proved such a durably popular force. Conversely, clarity and simplicity of expression are not necessarily signs of banality or lack of originality, as many critics nowadays seem to think. Even as they seek culturally to demystify the texts, some critics are capable of wrapping them in ever deeper fogs of obscure language. This contradiction is not forgivable, since it merely delivers Shakespeare into the hands of a new and arrogant élite, a group of self-appointed high priests who are comprehensible only to each other. Above all, Shakespeare belongs to people who read his works and attend performances of his plays, and they are entitled to enlightened and progressive forms of criticism that pay respect to their central function in the Shakespeare 'industry'.

2. SHAKESPEARE'S LIFE, TIMES, AND STAGE
reviewed by RICHARD DUTTON

Proud in their numbers and secure in soul,
The confident and overlusty conservatives,
    revisionists, feminists etc.
Do the low rated new historicists play at dice . . .

In fact, the battle is well and truly joined. Howard Felperin's *The Uses of the Canon: Elizabethan and Contemporary Theory* (Oxford, 1990) is a more-in-sorrow-than-in-anger attempt to convince the new historicists, and particularly Stephen Greenblatt, that they are fighting the wrong battle at the wrong time, with the wrong weapons: 'The problem of relativism . . . looms large at a moment when the value of the humanities within an increasingly utilitarian and implicitly reactionary culture is in serious question' (p. viii). Felperin describes himself as a deconstructionist and, being on 'the left', believes himself to share some of the ultimate values of those whose approach he finds limited and unsatisfactory, a form of fiddling while the humanities burn. Of Greenblatt's reading of Marlowe in *Renaissance Self-Fashioning* (Chicago, 1980) he argues: 'For all his Renaissance erudition, command of historical detail and local incident, and attentiveness to contemporary texts, it is his own culture Greenblatt broods on and depicts *without realizing it*' (p. 121, my emphasis). This is condescending and misses a key tenet of much new historicist thinking, which is precisely that the 'construction' of history is irreducibly a product of the present and that any contemplation of the past is thus in part also an analysis of that present. His own conviction that these processes are dissoluble is most apparent in an engaging reading of *The Tempest* and *Heart of Darkness* as romances, in which he insists we must not fail to recognize that both are equally 'demystified': 'To do so is at once to underread the past by over-simplifying it and to overread the present by making it the locus of all complexity' (p. 34).

As the book unfolds, its principal concern – focused, in particular, on the recent status of *The Tempest*[1] – becomes the supposed new

---

[1] To his list of 'Marxist' readings of *The Tempest* he might add Curt Breight, '"Treason doth never prosper": *The*

historicist agenda of abolishing not only the present 'canon' of literary texts but the concept of canonicity itself (though others have roundly condemned them precisely because, whatever they profess, they have pointedly failed to do this): 'without a canon and its record of re-inscription, there would be no ground on which literary studies could oppose the state and its strategies of containment by teaching the curriculum against the grain. Nor would there be any basis without it on which to construct the newer historicism some of us might envision' (p. 190). But is 'teaching the curriculum against the grain' the only method of registering opposition, and is a 'canon' really an *essential* weapon for historicists? Some of us find them convenient, but that is not quite the same thing. His case might be stronger if he gave us some idea of what this 'newer histori-cism' he more than once envisions might consist of. My reading of this book is undoubtedly clouded by my memory of Felperin advancing some of its arguments at the MLA Convention in New Orleans in 1988, and being reduced to virtual speechlessness by the clinically hostile responses he received. I rather doubt whether the book will win him friends where he claims to want them either.

Richard Levin, by contrast, shows no sign of wanting to make friends in these quarters, but every sign of wishing to expose cant and muddle wherever he believes he finds it, and for the moment this is mainly among the new historicists and cultural materialists. In two essays he confronts firstly 'Bardicide' and secondly 'New Historicizing' more generally.[2] In the former he argues that the 'rejection of The Author Function is not just a negation, the removal of a constraint, since it creates a herme-neutic vacuum that must be filled by something else that replaces authorial intention as the determinant of meaning. And for these critics ... what fills the vacuum is a universal law — the Law of Concealed-but-Revealed Ideo-logical Contradiction (or, for the neo-Freudians, the Law of the Absent-yet-

Omnipresent Mother) – that dictates what one must look for, and find, in every play' (p. 502). If there is a germ of truth in this parody, may it not be argued that all criticial methodologies are in fact subject to the same propensity to find what they are predisposed to find, however much some of them may seek 'objective' vali-dation for this in the name of 'the author' or 'the text'? In the latter essay Levin clinically dissects a number of representative assertions by new historicists about concepts of the self, 'literature' as a separate high category of writing, the biological determination of gender, and the non-illusionistic nature of Elizabethan theatre: 'There is, however, one idea that I suspect really was unthinkable to [the Elizabethans] – that anyone in the future would seriously maintain that they were unable to think of the relationship of gender to biology, or of a unified and continuous self, or any of the other alleged nonideas-of-the-time presented in these discoveries' (p. 444). Of course, the issue might not be so much what was thinkable as what ideas carried most weight at the time. And if the new historicists *have* sometimes over-stated their cases they might justly claim that they were cases which for many years did not receive a hearing at all.

Tempest and the Discourse of Treason', *Shakespeare Quarterly*, 41 (1990), 1–28, which locates the play in the context of a fiercely repressive government bent on 'domination' rather than a form of consensus.

[2] 'The Poetics and Politics of Bardicide', *PLMA*, 105 (1990), 491–504; 'Unthinkable Thoughts in the New Historicizing of English Renaissance Drama', *New Literary History*, 21 (1990), 433–47. Incidentally, Alan H. Nelson adds support to an earlier argument of Levin's ('Women in the Renaissance Theatre Audience', *Shakespeare Quarterly*, 40 (1989), 165–74, mentioned here in the last issue), about the influence of women in the *audiences* of Renaissance theatres. In Cambridge, at both town and college theatricals, he finds that women 'were a significant although not dominant factor in dramatic performances, particularly in their rôle as audience members but in some minor cases even as performers': 'Women in the Audience of Cambridge Plays', *Shakespeare Quarterly*, 41 (1990), 333–6, p. 336.

Levin's conservative common sense is a useful corrective, but it is not the last word it would like to be – as Catherine Belsey and Jonathan Goldberg confidently demonstrate in their invited responses to the latter argument.[3] Jonathan Dollimore was invited to join in this battle, but chose to fight another one instead, responding to complaints by Carol Thomas Neely, Linda Boose, and others that the 'cult-historicists' have marginalized women.[4] He defends materialist readings of gender difference and of the cultural construction of human nature, but (implicitly answering another charge often levelled against criticism of this persuasion) does not take himself too seriously: he channels his case into imagining a cross-dressed production of *Antony and Cleopatra* that would give all conservatives apoplexy but would (surely?) be fun. Theodore B. Leinwand, meanwhile, wishes to take new historicism through the impasse its adherents may be said to have reached in their debate about 'containment' and 'subversion' models of social energy, suggesting that a 'negotiation-based model of social relations' that 'can account for change or for resistance to change has the significant advantage of recognizing that the lower orders are not limited to a choice between quietism and insurrection'.[5] He applies this notion quite effectively to *Much Ado About Nothing* and *Measure for Measure*.

Wayne A. Rebhorn also demonstrates the freshness of perspective that such approaches can bring in a detailed reading of *Julius Caesar*, noting that it is often read as 'about the killing of a king and expressing real ambivalence on that score, [but] it could be equally productive to see it as depicting a struggle between aristocrats – senators – aimed at preventing one of their number from transcending his place and destroying the system in which they all ruled as a class'.[6] Since the first recorded performance of the play fell in the week before Essex's desperate return from Ireland, this would give urgency to the whole context. Clearly, given the dating, the play cannot be an allegory of what hap-

pened to Essex, but it is possible to read the careers of Caesar and Essex as parallel 'illustrations of aristocratic emulation and factionalism that were played out to their logical, tragic conclusions' (p. 106). In this view Shakespeare is neither a journalist nor a propagandist, but a writer alive to the tensions within the ruling class whose servant he was, to 'the imperial will, which animates the behaviour of the entire class of aristocrats and leads ineluctably to their unintended, collective self-destruction' (p. 109).

Of course, such an apocalyptic reading of the play ('a sick world in the process of stumbling to centralized, absolutist, one man rule', p. 108) depends upon a similar reading of the history of the time, and this is something that academic historians (or, at least, the revisionists among them) increasingly demur over. Maurice Lee Jr's *Great Britain's Solomon*, for example, the culmination of a career largely devoted to the early Stuarts, presents a very different picture of the government of James VI and I from that implied, say, in Jonathan Goldberg's *James VI and the Politics of Literature* (Baltimore, 1983), in Rebhorn's article, or indeed in that of Curt Breight mentioned in my first footnote.[7] Lee points out how unfortunate James has been in his reputation, uncritically contrasted with his predecessor, made guilty by association with his much less able son and successor, and largely consigned to posterity in the accounts of disaffected men with axes to grind. Until quite

3 Catherine Belsey, 'Richard Levin and In-Different Reading', Jonathan Goldberg, 'Making Sense', *New Literary History* 21 (1990), respectively 449–56, 457–62. Levin's 'Reply' (463–70) only continues, and does not conclude, the argument.

4 'Shakespeare, Cultural Materialism, Feminism and Marxist Humanism', *New Literary History*, 21 (1990), 471–93.

5 'Negotiation and New Historicism', *PMLA*, 105 (1990), 477–90.

6 'The Crisis of the Aristocracy in *Julius Caesar*', *Renaissance Quarterly*, 43 (1990), 75–111.

7 Maurice Lee Jr, *Great Britain's Solomon: James VI in His Three Kingdoms* (Urbana and Chicago, 1990).

recently both Whig and Marxist historians had reasons for perpetuating the myths that emerged from this ill-luck, and even the most reliable scholarly biography was written by someone with no real affection for his subject.[8] It is perhaps to be regretted that *this* work is not strictly a biography – there are too many areas it does not cover – but it touches on many of the major issues of James's reigns, including his upbringing, attitudes to kingship, religion and witchcraft, relationships with his parliaments, the nature of his courts, the complexities of having in his maturity to govern three very different kingdoms. In all these areas Lee is patiently and usually convincingly revisionist, arguing that: 'As a king of England James was not a great and imaginative innovator . . . nor was he a man with a mission . . . But by any fair-minded estimate he was a successful one . . . Undeniably he had his faults' (pp. 317–18) but these were 'mostly those of style rather than of substance' (p. 308). From these pages it would be difficult to construct a monarch bent on 'domination' or even 'one-man government'.

Two overlapping accounts of the mythology surrounding his predecessor underline how difficult it has been for James to win a fair hearing. Peter McClure and Robin Headlam Wells conclude: 'While the idea of Astraea may be regarded as the key-stone of Elizabethan state symbolism, it is not its apex. The virgin who returned was celebrated in many guises and by many names; but it was in the shape of a second Virgin Mary that her sacred identity and authority were most profoundly revealed', an emphasis which they note intensified after she was excommunicated by the Pope in 1570.[9] This may not please all feminists, who are inclined to stress Elizabeth's active manipulation of her unusual status rather than the passivity of her iconic construction, but it squares well enough with John N. King's detailed 'diachronic view of contemporary manuscripts, printed books and artistic works' which 'indicates that instead of a continuous and timeless phenomenon, Elizabethan iconography was closely tied to the life history of the monarch and to political events of her reign' – and indeed after her reign, when the dissatisfaction of William Camden, Fulke Greville and others with the Jacobean court coloured the image of Elizabeth transmitted to later eras.[10]

The fact that, in the latter half of the sixteenth century, two women were sovereign queens of England and another was Queen of Scots undoubtedly put strains on the patriarchal basis of early modern political theory. It remains a moot point what effect this had on the status of other women in the era or on the discussion of such matters in its drama. Nancy A. Gutierrez adds to the recent spate of discussions of the blatantly 'transgressive' Joan of Arc in *1 Henry VI*: 'As both battleground and cultural scapegoat, a *medium* by which men gain power and a touchstone by which gender stereotypes are reinforced, the theatrical representation of Joan demonstrates how the masculine mindset transforms what it perceives as a female challenge into a reinforcement of the patriarchate', while Theodora A. Jankowski suggests that '*The Duchess of Malfi* is an unusual play not only because it explores questions of rulership as they relate to a female sovereign, but also because it explores these questions as regards the sovereign's marriage'.[11] A recurrent intangible in the theatrical representation of women is the practice of using boys for those parts. Michael Shapiro draws attention to 'two unnoticed metaphoric allusions to acting' by boys in Lady Mary Wroth's *Urania*, one in the 1621 published text, the other in its unpublished

---

[8] D. H. Willson, *James VI and I* (London, 1956).

[9] 'Elizabeth I as a Second Virgin Mary', *Renaissance Studies*, 4 (1990), 38–70, p. 70.

[10] 'Queen Elizabeth I: Representations of the Virgin Queen', *Renaissance Quarterly*, 43 (1990), 30–74, p. 32.

[11] 'Gender and Value in *1 Henry VI*', *Theatre Journal*, 42 (1990), 183–93, p. 193; 'Defining/Confining the Duchess: Negotiating the Female Body in John Webster's *The Duchess of Malfi*', *Studies in Philology*, 87 (1990), 221–45, p. 222.

sequel.[12] Since both emphasize a self-conscious attention to the art of acting, they 'might at first seem like persuasive evidence for the theory that acting on the English Renaissance stage was "formal"' (p. 190). But Shapiro argues that they actually make it possible to go beyond the 'formal/natural dichotomy', in which the debate about Elizabethan acting has long been stalemated, and appreciate that 'some of the richest moments of the drama of the period result from ... an interplay between the audience's perception of character and actor, its sense of mimetic illusion and theatrical reality, its awareness of representational effect and presentational means' (p. 192) – a delicate compromise with many interesting possibilities, but one that may not suit some entrenched interests.

Steve Brown openly confronts the possible homoerotic implications of the employment of boy actors, but questions modern categorizations not only of gender (long a feminist issue) but also of sexual behaviour itself, looking at the concept of 'boyhood' from a variety of Renaissance perspectives, including those of the boy as a social and economic dependant as well as the boy as object of desire.[13] This might usefully be set alongside Alan Bray's careful and critical exploration of the relationship between 'the image of the masculine friend' and 'the figure called the sodomite' in Elizabethan England, in which he observes that 'the one was universally admired, the other execrated and feared: and yet in their uncompromising symmetry they paralleled each other in an uncanny way'.[14] He casts particular light on *Edward II*, suggesting that Gaveston's transgressions in getting so close to the king are more explicitly social than they are sexual; Bray's approach might very usefully be brought to bear on Shakespeare's Sonnets and such relationships as that between Antonio and Bassanio in *The Merchant of Venice*, not to mention the question of James I's attachment to his favourites. Douglas Brewster also reminds us of the close relationship between social and gender stereo-

typing in a reconsideration of the constant concomitant of Elizabethan comedy, the cuckold's horns; linking the issue to the disturbing growth of the metropolis, he argues that 'London's drama seized upon the cuckold myth as a dialectical metaphor capable of reconciling – however uneasily – evolving tensions between country and city, production and reproduction, male and female ... [it] came to form an indispensable part of the London theater's rhetoric of social and economic relationships, a cultural grammar'.[15]

Katharine Hodgkin's analysis of the autobiographical writing of the sixteenth-century musician, Thomas Whythorne, echoes some of this as it focuses in particular on his fixation with the *difference* of women from himself as he works towards a definition of his own 'mastery' in the unstable medium of language: 'Whythorne's book negotiates his obsessions: with words, which reveal and conceal at once; with dissemblers, those who seem to be what they aren't; with women, who are what he is not; with time in its manifold changes.' Alison Wall approaches the question of theory and practice in Elizabethan female behaviour from a different angle, contrasting the realities of female activity in an aristocratic household (Longleat) with the models and advice prescribed to women in sermons and conduct books – one of them, notably, *A Brief and Pleasant Discourse of Duties in Marriage* (1568, also known as *The Flower of Friendship*), which was written by Edmond Tilney, later to

[12] 'Lady Mary Wroth Describes a "Boy Actress"', *Medieval and Renaissance Drama in England*, 4 (1989), 187–94, p. 187.

[13] 'The Boyhood of Shakespeare's Heroines: Notes on Gender Ambiguity in the Sixteenth Century', *Studies in English Literature*, 30 (1990), 243–60.

[14] 'Homosexuality and the Signs of Male Friendship in Elizabethan England', *History Workshop*, 29 (1990), 1–19, p. 1.

[15] 'The Horn of Plenty: Cuckoldry and Capital in the Drama of the Age of Shakespeare', *Studies in English Literature*, 30 (1990), 195–211, pp. 210–11.

become the principal censor of Shakespeare's plays as Master of the Revels.[16]

Such matters were low in his priorities as a theatrical censor, however, as we can see from Janet Clare's '*Art Made tongue-tied by authority': Elizabethan and Jacobean Censorship*, the first book-length study of the subject for more than eighty years.[17] I should declare an interest here, since my own study of this subject is currently in proof and will be in print before this review. Inevitably what we have to say overlaps to a degree, but our approaches are very different: hers is a meticulous study of a wide range of texts where official interference is demonstrable or may be inferred: I have concentrated on the political and patronage context of the post of Master of the Revels and the likely influence of it on the nature of the control he exerted over the theatre of the day. Where, for example, she concludes 'that all the plays of the period were written in the shadow of the censor and that no dramatist could unchain his thoughts from the agent of that most arbitrary and punitive instrument of state control' (p. 215) I would argue that the very existence of the Master of the Revels and his unique court-based authority gave the actors and their dramatists a degree of security and confidence which they would not otherwise have enjoyed, and that this contributed to a *relative* freedom of expression in the plays they staged. We should not forget (though Dr Clare makes nothing of this) that the City of London authorities did their level best to displace or buy Tilney off in the 1590s: it is difficult to believe that the actors would have flourished as they did had they succeeded. Other broad areas where we differ include the supposed censorship of *Richard II* and the question of whether George Buc served as Tilney's 'deputy' after 1603 – an unsubstantiated notion which seems to me to introduce a degree of coherence into the regulation of early Jacobean theatre belied by the incoherence (and indeed outright contradictions) in the evidence. I am most surprised, however, that she makes nothing of Henry Herbert's change of heart

over his refusal to license Massinger's *Believe as You List*. Although it lies outside her period, we are so dependent on what has survived of Herbert's papers for our understanding of the other Masters' operations that it seems odd to ignore the way that he gave a licence to a play he had earlier turned down as too politically sensitive, apparently on the grounds that the author had – merely by relocating the action in antiquity – provided an acceptable fictional/historical veil to subject matter that would otherwise be proscribed. The implications of this for how audiences of the period (and the censors) looked to the actors as the 'abstracts and brief chronicles' of their time seem to me extremely important. Dare I hope that people will read both books to make up their minds?

Such differences of emphasis derive in large part from perceptions of the place of the theatre in the life of the sixteenth-century community: adjunct of the court, proto-capitalist enterprise, marginalized denizen of the 'liberties' (or, more awkwardly, a mixture of all three)? Suzanne R. Westfall's *Patrons and Performance: Early Tudor Household Revels* (Oxford, 1990) makes no pretensions to answer any of these questions and I run the risk of distorting her very proper refusal to make this study 'another "roots of Shakespeare" exercise' (p. 6) by invoking it in this context. But it is precisely because it has no axe to grind here that the evidence it adduces seems to me so compelling. This is an exemplary piece of scholarship which for once gives due weight to the issue of dramatic entertainment within royal and aristocratic households in the early sixteenth century. These contributed very little to what has been regarded as canonical drama in the period, and have so been relegated to the sidelines of literary

---

[16] 'Thomas Whythorne and the Problems of Mastery', *History Workshop*, 29 (1990), 20–41, p. 39; 'Elizabethan Precept and Feminine Practice', *History*, 75 (1990), 23–38.

[17] The Revels Plays Companion Library (Manchester and New York, 1990).

history. But by examining them firmly in their place in the life and expectations of the community, Westfall demonstrates just how significant they were, how integrated in the social patterns of the time. This is extremely valuable in itself, but also surely *does* have implications for the later professional drama which in some ways evolved from these household contexts, not least in respect of relations between noble patrons and the actors who wore their livery. The heads under which Westfall summarizes her main conclusions are themselves (all bar the fifth) highly suggestive: 'First, household entertainments were intended for a known audience and could therefore be specifically geared towards the group's knowledge and interests . . . Second, the presence of a myriad of entertainers within one household created the opportunity for multimedia performances . . . Third, household revels were generally intended to celebrate an occasion . . . Fourth, space within the manors and castles of the aristocracy provided convenient and familiar stages . . . Fifth, household revels were strictly non-profit ventures . . . The sixth quality of great household revels – motivation – grows out of and governs the other five. Noble patrons had several reasons for providing theatre for their retainers: to inform, to educate, to entertain, to communicate, and ultimately to control' (pp. 205–7). Clearly the fact that the fifth consideration ceased to be operative, once the primary motivation of the actors was to make money, distorts all the other considerations. But, against this wealth of meticulous detail, the question remains how much and for how long the other considerations shaped the thinking and practice of Shakespeare and his fellows.

Once outside those noble households, what of the companies they formed, the theatres they used and the men who built them? Mark Eccles, still indefatigably pursuing the lives of the Elizabethans, mainly through the legal records, has uncovered more about Edward Alleyn, particularly in relation to the family in which he grew up.[18] Mary Edmond meanwhile puts together a biographical outline of John Griggs, the man who (though formally a butcher) was employed by Philip Henslowe to build the Rose (where his son-in-law, Alleyn, enjoyed his greatest successes) in 1587 and to effect the principal repairs in 1592; she also tracks down something of the elusive John Cholmeley, who was apparently in partnership with Henslowe at this time.[19] Susan P. Cerasano then demonstrates that it was Alleyn, rather than Henslowe, who was the principal mover behind the construction of a further theatre *c.* 1615–17 in the Blackfriars 'called by the name of Lady Saunders house or otherwise Porters Hall'.[20] For once this astute businessman miscalculated; the Privy Council backed the residents in that well-to-do neighbourhood and the Lord Mayor, in resisting this new theatrical venture, and Alleyn lost out considerably. But, while information flows in, it also flows out: Scott McMillin has deconstructed the tissue of hypothesis and guess-work, now widely taken for gospel, by which W. W. Greg assigned the 'plot' of *2 Seven Deadly Sins* to Richard Tarlton, a date before May 1591 and an amalgamated company of the Admiral's and Strange's Men (in the process of which he allocated a rôle to Alleyn, though he is *not* one of the twenty actors named in the 'plot').[21] In so doing, McMillin demonstrates the danger both of constructing 'narratives' from minimal data and of skewing those narratives to incorporate as many charismatic names as possible – essential reading for anyone working in the half-light of what we think we know about the Elizabethan theatre.

---

[18] 'Edward Alleyn in London Records', *Notes and Queries*, n.s. 37 (1990), pp. 166–8.

[19] 'The Builder of the Rose Theatre', *Theatre Notebook*, 44 (1990), 50–4.

[20] 'Competition for the King's Men? Alleyn's Blackfriars Venture', *Medieval and Renaissance Drama in England*, 4 (1989), 173–86.

[21] 'Greg, Fleay, and the Plot of *2 Seven Deadly Sins*', *Medieval and Renaissance Drama in England*, 4 (1989), 53–62.

Of course, what we think we know about it is already being revised by what is emerging from the unearthing of the Rose and the Globe on the South Bank. Andrew Gurr offers a couple of preliminary glimpses from the front line. One is an examination of some of the more striking discoveries at the Rose site, partly in relation to Henslowe's records and especially its 1592 rebuilding (largely by Griggs) only five years after its original construction; he singles out the steeply-raked, mortar-surfaced yard and the 'shallow stage, with its angled rear walls, and its trapezoidal shape' (p. 34) as distinctive features that will repay further investigation, while warning against over-hasty assumptions about how typical any of this may prove to be. The other piece discusses a stair-turret found on the external north-east side of the Globe site, which may well have been an innovative feature of the original Globe design, replicated in its rebuilding; there is speculation that this system of entry might reflect different priorities in the collection of monies from those that pertained in earlier theatres, but what seems certain is that it left more usable seating space in the galleries.[22]

Information of a kind may also be derived from a very different source, a recently discovered *impresa* in the hand of Sir John Coke, which includes a rough sketch of an Elizabethan public theatre; Hilton Kelliher speculates that it may be based, however loosely, on the Curtain and that the design may relate to the creation of Henry as Prince of Wales in 1610.[23] Basic and unsatisfactory as it palpably is, it is perhaps second only to De Witt's drawing of the Swan as a pictorial record of the interior of an Elizabethan theatre. Turning the deductions to be made from such evidence on their head Andrew Gurr, again, discusses the theatrical thinking behind the building of the new Globe complex in Southwark: the need to replicate original lighting conditions (hence this site and no plastic cover to keep out the rain); the addition of something approximating to the Blackfriars to reproduce conditions of both

summer and winter playing that the King's Men encountered after 1608; the main auditorium only taking half of the original 3,000 capacity, partly because modern physiques are ten per cent larger on average but also because we have what Burbage, Shakespeare and the others to their cost did not – fire regulations.[24]

If archaeology can take us closer to the theatres Shakespeare used, can genealogy take us any closer to the man himself, to the micro-history of his family and professional relationships? David Honneyman's *Closer to Shakespeare* (Braunton, Devon, 1990) is written in the belief that it can, but the results are rather less than satisfactory. He does produce two plausible (though far from proven) candidates for the vacant rôles of Shakespeare's grandmothers, and has some interesting information about his Greene cousins. But the limitations of what is very often only speculation become most apparent when he attempts to further the Shakespeare/Shakeshaft connections with the Houghtons of Lancashire by linking Sir Toby Belch with Toby Houghton, illegitimate half-brother of Alexander and Thomas Houghton (p. 106). What exactly are the allusions he purports to discover meant to prove, and what audience would ever make any sense of them? Our conviction of the reliability of his genealogical information is unlikely to be strengthened by his command of other matters. He repeatedly (pp. 95, 97, 112) ascribes the notion of Shakespeare as a schoolmaster in the country to Jonson, though John Aubrey (admittedly quoting Jonson on 'little Latin and less Greek') does not mention his source for the information, but his papers make it fairly clear that it

---

[22] 'Archaeology and the Elizabethan Playhouses', *Deutsche Shakespeare-Gesellschaft West Jahrbuch* (1990), 24–35; 'A First Doorway Into the Globe', *Shakespeare Quarterly*, 41 (1990), 97–100.

[23] 'Sir John Coke's Theatre-*Impresa*', *Deutsche Shakespeare-Gesellschaft West Jahrbuch* (1990), 36–47.

[24] 'Rebuilding the Globe with the Arts of Compromise', *Deutsche Shakespeare-Gesellschaft West Jahrbuch* (1990), 11–23.

was William Beeston, son of Shakespeare's former colleague, Christopher. When Honneyman further tells us 'Shakespeare of course helped to launch Ben Jonson on his career as a playwright by facilitating the production of his first play *Everyman [sic] in his Humour*' (p. 134), he does nothing to enhance his credentials. This is unfortunate, because some of the speculation here might amount to something, handled more circumspectly. I was particularly struck by the identification of Will Kemp as a younger son of Sir Thomas Kemp of Olantigh in Kent (a hypothesis that all too readily slips into 'fact'). This would make him a scion of the gentry – an interesting angle to his ironic country clown persona – and would relate him to Leonard Digges, who contributed verses to the First Folio, and more distantly to the Earl of Southampton. Intriguing possibilities are also raised about other Shakespeare associates, including Robert Wilson and John Heminge, but this is not a book for the unwary.

The title of Peter Lloyd's *Perspectives and Identities: The Elizabethan Writer's Search to Know His World* (London, 1989) seems to offer us another route to get 'closer to Shakespeare', possibly even a new historicist one, but the reality is far otherwise. It is in fact a *belle-lettrist* survey of writing and thought, mainly in the last quarter of the sixteenth century. By that I mean that it is scholarship handled at the level of polite conversation rather than detailed argument, in the atmosphere of a gentlemen's club rather than of a university library or seminar-room. There is evidence of an acquaintance with more specialist literature, though some of it is a little dated, the footnoting is perfunctory and the bibliography seems something of an afterthought (in which it is not certain if Stephen Greenblatt wrote on Raleigh or Ralegh, or if he published in 1973 or 1975). Slips of this kind are also too frequent for comfort in the text itself: playwrights are 'playwrites' in the early chapters (pp. 34, 37), *Cynthia's Revels* is described as a masque (p. 55), Philip Sidney marries in 1593, seven years after

his death (p. 145), the Prince of Orange is given the Garter in place of Count Casimir of the Palatinate (p. 149), and while Anne Barton has published under a number of names I do not believe 'Miss Richter' is one of them (p. 81 and index). The book is not unlike Patrick Cruttwell's *The Shakespearean Moment* (1954) in its apparent aims, though less impressive in its execution and, where Cruttwell stressed the sceptical strain of thought through Montaigne and Bacon, Lloyd devotes more attention to Sidney, Bruno, and Dee.

The half-lit world of hermetic magic and secret societies continues to attract attention elsewhere too. Ron Heisler seeks to associate Shakespeare with a network of Rosicrucian adherents including Richard Field (publisher of *Venus and Adonis* and *The Rape of Lucrece*), Edward Alleyn, the Digges and Salusbury families, and the Stanleys. As with his brief earlier attempt to detect Rosicrucian elements in *The Two Noble Kinsmen*, he spins some intriguing webs, but the profit and substance of them is at best questionable.[25] Mr Heisler seems to me on rather firmer ground in his attempt to trace freemasonry in the literature of the late sixteenth century, such as the Harvey/Nashe pamphlets, suggesting links with notable figures such as Lord Admiral Howard, Lord Buckhurst and the third Earl of Pembroke. He touches on the significance of gloves as freemason symbols and their wide distribution as presents, a fact of some note in relation to Shakespeare's father's profession. St John the Evangelist's day, 27 December, was the feast-day of the freemasons (as later of the Rosicrucians) and he tries to make something of the choice of plays, including *Love's Labour's Lost* and *Old Fortunatus*, known to have been given at court on that date – intriguing but (like

---

25 'Two Worlds that Converged: Shakespeare and the Ethos of the Rosicrucians', *The Hermetic Journal*, n.s. 1 (1990), 149–62; 'Shakespeare and the Rosicrucians', *The Hermetic Journal*, 33 (1986), 16–19.

Honneyman's genealogy) still inconclusive.[26] Less speculative scholars will find more of substance in Frank L. Borchardt's short survey of Renaissance magic, which emphasizes how many of its key exponents, from Ficino onwards, eventually expressed their dissatisfaction with it – a history which must be of relevance to both Faustus and Prospero.[27]

Marlowe's *Dr Faustus* has now appeared in the Oxford *Complete Works of Christopher Marlowe* edited by Roma Gill (volume 2, Oxford, 1990). The edition as a whole seems to me an expensive duplication of Fredson Bowers' labours (2 vols., London and New York, 1973); scholarship would have been equally well served with a volume of annotation to Bowers's bare text. Furthermore, the principles on which this edition are based seem most eccentric. The first volume (1987) contained all the non-dramatic verse, together with *Dido, Queene of Carthage*, under the elastic grouping of 'Translations'. Now *Dr Faustus* appears on its own, presumably on the grounds that it is the one Marlowe text likely to sell widely; if the original plan is adhered to, this means that all the other plays will be crammed into one bumper volume. Following the new orthodoxy, this *Dr Faustus* is basically an edition of the 1604 'A' text, with major 'adicyones' from the 1616 'B' text relegated to an appendix; it is copiously annotated and usefully reproduces relevant portions of the main source, *The English Faustbook*. Much more questionable, however, are the opinions of the state of the 'A' text itself expressed in the Introduction: 'I suggest that when Marlowe died he left his play on *Dr Faustus* unfinished: it had a beginning and an ending ... but not much more to fill the two hours' traffic of the stage ... Marlowe might have abandoned his play because he was bored or frustrated by the banality of his source' (p. xviii).[28] Given this slim conjecture the editor has to conjure up authors for the middle of the play and comes up with Thomas Nashe and the clown John Adams. These would be interesting speculations at a conference, but

their very existence seems to derive from the unwarrantable view that Marlowe was a great tragic poet but only intermittently a dramatist and certainly not a comic one. The relationship of Nashe and Adams to this text is no more real than that of the spirit summoned by Faustus to the real Helen of Troy. Such matters should not be advanced with so little qualification in a text which is likely to be widely used by students.

The question of Shakespeare's own hand in a variety of texts is also much to the fore. Two articles reach flatly contradictory conclusions about *Pericles*. Karen Csengeri puts together a rather woolly argument for Shakespeare as the sole author, positing a man weary after writing *King Lear* and, initially half-heartedly, picking up this plot to fulfil his commitments to the company, but leaving traces of his authorship in a range of characteristic imagery. She never even mentions one of the prime candidates for part-authorship, George Wilkins, though MacD. P. Jackson produces a far more disciplined case for Wilkins's hand in the first two acts of the play.[29] Jackson also uses a similar methodology, based on a computer-aided analysis of key words, spelling, and style to question Eric Rasmussen's ascription to Shakespeare of the pasted-in additions to *The*

---

26 'The Impact of Freemasonry on Elizabethan Literature', *The Hermetic Journal*, n.s. 1 (1990), 37–55.

27 'The Magus as Renaissance Man', *The Sixteenth Century*, 21 (1990), 57–67.

28 More scholarly substance to the argument that *Dr Faustus* was first performed posthumously is given in Eric Rasmussen's suggestion that the reference in T. M.'s *The Black Book* (1604) to the 'Divells in Dr Faustus when the old Theater crackt' is to a passage in *The Second Report of Dr John Faustus* (1594, the so-called 'English Wagner Book') rather than to some event at Burbage's Theatre, which led W. W. Greg and others to suppose that there must have been performances there prior to the ones that Henslowe recorded at the Rose from 1594 onwards: '*The Black Book* and the Date of *Dr Faustus*', *Notes and Queries*, n.s. 37 (1990), 166–8.

29 'William Shakespeare, Sole Author of *Pericles*', *English Studies*, 71 (1990), 230–43; '*Pericles*, Acts I and II: New Evidence for George Wilkins', *Notes and Queries*, n.s. 37 (1990), 192–6.

Second Maiden's Tragedy, concluding that Middleton – the presumed author of the main body of the play – is more likely.[30] But there is still room to believe that Shakespeare and Middleton collaborated on occasions: Roger Holdsworth adduces new biblical allusions in *Timon of Athens*, which have counterparts in the works of Middleton, to further the case for him as a part-author of that play.[31]

Mention of the Bible inevitably opens up the Reformation and Counter-Reformation tensions in which the status of that work and its translations was such a fraught issue. G. W. Bernard surveys recent thinking on the Church of England from its inception under Henry VIII to the time of the Civil War, arguing that at the heart of the 'monarchical view of the church' propounded by Henry and Elizabeth 'lay a desire that was essentially political, but which could be expressed without insincerity in more idealized language: a desire for comprehensiveness, for a church that would embrace all their subjects', and that the major developments in the early seventeenth century are only to be understood in relation to those sixteenth-century foundations.[32] One widely misunderstood aspect of religious developments under Elizabeth is the presence of puritan voices within her own Privy Council; Simon Adams, who is engaged on a major biography of Leicester, suggests both that his puritanism was sincerely held and that 'the support Leicester and his colleagues gave to moderate puritanism and the "Calvinist consensus" may have done much to provide her government with the broad base of support that was so distinctly lacking in the succeeding reigns'.[33] Two examples of how these tensions surface in Shakespeare's writing are the rôle of the 'precisian' Malvolio and the religious polarities in *Measure for Measure*. Winfried Schleiner examines the 'exorcism' scene in *Twelfth Night* in the light of the notorious Darrell–Summers case and the rhetorical theatricality that runs through contemporary discussions of such matters, including Samuel Harsnett's *Discovery of the Fraudulent Practices of John Darrell* (1599) and *Declaration of Egregious Popish Impostures* (1603). Margaret Hotine furthers the case for *Measure for Measure* being written in 1604, against growing Puritan *and* Roman Catholic expectations in the new reign, including a revival of the custom of women entering convents.[34]

As to the Bible itself, David Daniell has made good a major omission in making available one of the key texts in the Englishing of that contentious work, Tyndale's 1534 translation of the *New Testament* (New Haven and London, 1989). Daniell's vigorous introduction to this handsomely produced modern-spelling text outlines what we know about Tyndale, demonstrates his influence on most English Bibles in the following century (including the Geneva version with which Shakespeare was most familiar), and explains why, given his death as a heretic, this influence was so rarely acknowledged at the time. The most striking omission in this regard relates to the Authorized Version of 1611, whose transcendent prose has attained a canonical status in our culture parallel to that of Shakespeare; as Daniell demonstrates, many of the linguistic virtues of that work derive directly from Tyndale while, since it was originally designed for use in the pulpit rather

---

30 Rasmussen's argument was put forward in 'Shakespeare's Hand in *The Second Maiden's Tragedy*', *Shakespeare Quarterly*, 40 (1989), 1–26. Jackson questions it in 'The Additions to *The Second Maiden's Tragedy*; Shakespeare or Middleton?', *Shakespeare Quarterly*, 41 (1990), 402–5. Rasmussen stands his ground in a reply, pp. 406–7.

31 'Biblical Allusions in *Timon of Athens* and Thomas Middleton', *Notes and Queries*, n.s. 37 (1990), pp. 188–92.

32 'The Church of England, c. 1529–1642', *History*, 75 (1990), 183–206, p. 187.

33 'A Godly Peer? Leicester and the Puritans', *History Today*, 40 (January 1990), 14–19, p. 19.

34 'The Feste-Malvolio Scene in *Twelfth Night* Against the Background of Renaissance Ideas About Madness and Possession', *Deutsche Shakespeare-Gesellschaft West Jahrbuch* (1990), 48–57; '*Measure for Measure*: Further Contemporary Notes', *Notes and Queries*, n.s. 37 (1990), 184–6.

than private reading or discussion, its influence in its own time was less than is commonly supposed today. Daniell rehearses many of the same arguments in a section on the Authorized Version in *The Seventeenth Century*, the fourth volume of *The Cambridge Guide to the Arts in Britain*, edited by Boris Ford (Cambridge, 1989). The editor assures us that 'these volumes do not consist of a sequence of mini-surveys, packed with facts and dates. Rather they are designed to help readers find their bearings in relation to the arts and culture of an age, identifying major landmarks and lines of strength, analysing changes of taste and fashion and critical assumptions' (p. x). So in 350 heavily illustrated pages we have a cultural and political overview of the century, and chapters of varying length on the Bible, architecture, masques and pageants, literature and drama, London, music, Belton House (Grantham), painting, sculpture, and the decorative and applied arts. These are all written by distinguished authorities in their field and are invariably illuminating, though for the most part they lack the charge of a polemical view or a thesis to argue. The result is a handsome collection of vignettes which, despite exhortations to use the index (and a very useful appendix of further reading), never falls into a coherent or challenging picture. Boris Ford is inescapably associated with the Pelican Guide to English Literature, in its time a brave and largely successful attempt to bridge the gap between the academy and the general reader. This is in a similar vein, but at a time when attitudes to 'culture' are so much more sharply divided and the concept of the 'general reader' is so much more problematic, an attempt to provide an informed but dispassionate overview of such a large topic is a more questionable undertaking.

There is never space here to address all the work being done on Shakespeare's literary contemporaries, but some of it is of such concern to Shakespearians that we cannot ignore it altogether. In *Shakespeare Survey 41*, when I reviewed Rosalind Miles's solid but rather pedestrian *Ben Jonson: His Life and Work* (London, 1986), I warned readers that another major biography of Jonson was on the way from the States. David Riggs's *Ben Jonson: A Life* (Cambridge, Mass. and London, 1989) is that work, all 399 pages of it. Length, of course, is not the only criterion of substance, but here we have a biography as big and as complex as the man himself. The title's 'A Life' is actually rather misleading, since what we get is at least two lives, as Riggs foreshadows in explaining his approach: 'When he is acting like a professional artist making practical choices, I adopt the outlook of a social historian . . . When Jonson's behavior resists this kind of explanation, I seek out a psychological one' (p. 2). The lack of an articulated bridge between the arguably incompatible methodologies of social history and (broadly Freudian) psychology may be seen by some as a flaw, though I have come myself to appreciate it as an honest reflection of the contradictions, if not necessarily within Jonson himself, at least in our perception of him from this distance. Even at this length there are matters one would have liked to see pursued further: we get a good deal on Jonson's difficult relations with women but, perhaps surprisingly, no follow up of Dekker's hints in *Satiromastix* that Jonson was 'hermaphrodite' or bisexual (a possibility, of course, that also dogs Shakespeare); Riggs does not even air the possibility that Jonson's release from prison over *Eastward Ho*, his sighting in the company of the Gunpowder Plotters and his employment by Salisbury in the aftermath of the Plot amount to a *prima facie* case for his being a government double agent; nor does he mention Jonson's apparent attachment to Gresham College around 1623. But these are minor quibbles about a book of many felicities, constantly perceptive and challenging, never the slave of the quantities of information it assembles, but always opening up new perspectives on them.

Jonson is a focal point where so many themes of the day intersect. We know, for example, that his personal emblem was compasses with a broken foot, the unfinished circle and the motto 'deest quod duceret orbem'; we know that Shakespeare wrote the motto for, and Richard Burbage painted, an impresa for the Earl of Rutland. But until recently (see the last issue of this review) we have paid little real attention to such devices and what they tell us of the arts of the age. John Manning has furthered the case for emblems belonging to particular historical moments and causes, rather than being repositories of universal truths; he shows how Whitney's *Choice of Emblemes* was specifically addressed to Leicester as an ideal reader and was published in conjunction with his military campaign in the Low Countries.[35] Of more immediate concern to readers of plays will be John Dixon Hunt's incisive analysis of the relationship between emblems as a formal genre and emblem-like devices in Shakespearian drama, which focuses on *Timon of Athens*, a play rich in such material: 'Comparison with an earlier Roman tragedy, like *Titus Andronicus*, where emblematic devices and intentions are striking, is instructive; it reveals the extent to which Shakespeare was then dependent upon the vocabulary and syntax of the emblem book. Yet even at this early stage in his career, I would suggest that Shakespeare explored the theatrical potential of possible tensions, rivalries, or *paragone* between the conventional emblem's words and images' (p. 168). This provides a very constructive model for further exploration of this field.[36]

Jonson is also a central figure in the evolution of the play-script from the functional tool of the actors to the printed document in which an author might address a readership beyond the playhouse audience. T. H. Howard-Hill has examined this process, the nature of the 'transcriptions' involved, and their implications for our understanding of early dramatic texts, in some detail.[37] He emphasizes how 'the transmission of Renaissance plays, and especially the function of their scribes, can hardly be understood without reference to the mixed traditions that eventually determined the form of the modern play texts' (p. 112), these being the 'native tradition' derived from European liturgical drama (e.g. the mss of morality and Corpus Christi guild plays) and the classical method used in the printing of Terence, Plautus and Seneca, and adopted by scholarly writers like Jonson in the late sixteenth century. From the macro- to the micro-scale of editorial practice, I must also mention Homer Swander's sobering account of how the tiniest of slips in Rowe's transmission of the text of *A Midsummer Night's Dream* – a stop for a comma – has written Titania's bower into generations of stage directions and staging practice, when it seems likely that Shakespeare intended it to be a 'reserved mystery', alluded to but not seen.[38]

To take Jonson as one last point of intersection/departure, he is a writer particularly concerned with narcissism, images of the self and their relationship to social structures. This is the theme of Robert Wiltenburg's *Ben Jonson and Self-Love: The Subtlest Maze of All* (Columbia, Missouri, 1990), a careful and rewarding study in a traditional humanistic manner. It follows Jonson's absorption in these matters in *Cynthia's Revels*, *Volpone*, and his two most structured verse-selections, *Epigrams* and *The Forest*. This narrow focus makes for a coherent argument, which refines and sharpens our sense of the issues rather than dramatically recasting it, but it does rather constrict Jonson to the prim rôle of classical scholar-poet; one of the strengths of Riggs's biography is to demonstrate that this is only one facet of such a complex man, only one of the responses he made to the contradictions and tensions of the

---

[35] 'Whitney's *Choice of Emblemes*: A Reassessment', *Renaissance Studies*, 4 (1990), 155–200.

[36] 'Pictura, Scriptura and Theatrum: Shakespeare and the Emblem', *Poetics Today*, 10 (1989), 155–71.

[37] 'The Evolution of the Form of Plays in English During the Renaissance', *Renaissance Quarterly*, 43 (1990), 112–45.

[38] 'Editors vs. A Text: The Scripted Geography of *A Midsummer Night's Dream*', *Studies in Philology*, 87 (1990) 83–108.

literary profession he was helping to shape. Charles R. Forker ranges much more widely in seeing incest as a form of narcissism, and both as recurrent themes in a period when dramatists 'were composing in an intellectual, cultural, and political milieu that not only raised the subject of incest to unusual prominence but also nurtured contrary and discrepant attitudes towards it'.[39] Forker almost mischievously refuses to reduce the examples he draws from his 'desultory reading' (p. 14) of sixty plays in the period to any sociological or anthropological explanation, but notes classical and biblical precedents and surveys the problems of consanguinity raised by Henry VIII's multiple marriages as factors which may have had a bearing on the themes' recurrent fascination.

A play in which a sub-textual exploration of incestuous longing is often suspected, and has been the focus of some feminist criticism, is *The Duchess of Malfi*. But such concerns are a long way removed from Christina Luckyj's very traditional concentration on the formal construction and tragic vision of Webster's plays.[40] Her focus is announced in a sentence which betrays the book's origin in a doctoral dissertation: 'Although the frequency of repetition in Webster's plays has often been noted, little critical attention has been devoted to its contribution to the plays' rhythm and overall dramatic structure, or to its rôle as a powerful unifying force on the stage' (p. xxiii). She makes good this omission with attention both to Renaissance rhetorical theory about repetition and to modern performances of the tragedies. The book furthers the case for Webster as a consummate dramatic artist, further laying to rest the ghosts of the Tussaud laureate and of the author of gem-like but incoherent fragments. I would have said that these have both been exorcized more comprehensively than she is prepared to concede, but perhaps Andrea Henderson's article on *The Duchess of Malfi* sees the latter walk again in a new guise, in the debate about Webster's place in the transition from performance to print culture: 'this play, for all its spectacular qualities is in fact anti-theatrical and reflects a movement towards a literary culture which privileges private reading.'[41]

Henderson's contentious conclusion is at least based on an imaginative and engaged reading of the all-important death scenes in Webster's play. They figure too in Michael Cameron Andrews's extended consideration of such scenes in a wide variety of plays, *This Action of our Death: The Performance of Death in English Renaissance Drama* (Newark, Delaware, 1989). Yet, despite the intensely emotive nature of the subject and some clear sensitivity to dramatic situations, this seems to me a strangely bloodless piece of writing. Although there are extensive early quotations from Stephen Greenblatt's account of the death of Ralegh in *Renaissance Self-Fashioning*, Andrews himself makes very little of the cultural placement of death, or the complexities of the representation of identity, or indeed considerations of staging. He basically divides the dramatists' depiction of the moment of death into two categories: those that ring the changes on what he calls 'the rhetoric of death' where, following Seneca's *Hercules Oetaeus*, the dying report the effect of what is killing them on their bodies; and 'those who, like Shakespeare, focused instead on the way the dying see themselves and the world they leave' (p. 175). The former he sees as unimaginative and uninspiring, save only for exceptionally wrought examples, such as we find in Ford's *The Broken Heart*; the latter he takes to be inherently more memorable and dramatic. And, for large stretches, the book reads as a catalogue of assorted sheep and goats. Although the material is handled broadly

---

39 '"A Little More Than Kin, and Less than Kind": Incest, Intimacy, Narcissism and Identity in Elizabethan and Stuart Drama', *Medieval and Renaissance Drama in England*, 4 (1989), 13–51, pp. 30–1.

40 *A Winter's Snake: Dramatic Form in the Tragedies of John Webster* (Athens, Georgia, 1989).

41 'Death on the Stage, Death of the Stage: The Antitheatricality of *The Duchess of Malfi*', *Theatre Journal*, 42 (1990), 194–207, p. 206.

chronologically, there is no suggestion of historical or generic development; the 'rhetoric of death' persists well into the Caroline era, while Shakespeare (as ever) emerges as the example *par excellence* of the writer who grasps, if not more naturalistic possibilities, more imaginative and individualized ones. It is striking that, when Andrews does acknowledge recent criticism that has made something of this theme, he relegates it to the notes, as if unwilling to disturb the simple lines of his argument.[42] The result is a more mechanical and less taxing book than it might have been, which might be contrasted with Karen Cunningham's modish but stylish consideration of death on the Marlovian stage: 'when Marlowe translates violence from the executioner's to the theater's scaffold, he exaggerates ... the profound ambiguity of artifice, thereby undermining the persuasiveness of the moralizing that accompanies spectacles of torture and transforming a theater of pain into a drama of subversion'.[43]

Like Lear's doctors, let us use music to revive ourselves. *The Well Enchanting Skill: Music, Poetry, and Drama in the Culture of the Renaissance*, edited by John Caldwell, Edward Olleson, and Susan Wollenberg (Oxford, 1990), is that awkward camel of the academic world, a *festschrift*, here in honour of F. W. Sternfeld – a camel in the sense of being put together by a committee rather than with a unified design. There are pieces here on Italian madrigals, opera and sacred music, on poetry from Henryson to Milton, on drama from Campion to Rochester, and perhaps only Frederick Sternfeld himself will read them all with equal engagement. But Shakespearians should certainly seek out David Lindley's 'Shakespeare's Provoking Music' (pp. 79–90), in which he addresses the old equation between music and social or personal harmony in the plays. While conceding the neoplatonic commonplaces about music being a reflection of the divine, he emphasizes that it also stirs emotions painfully and unpredictably, in ways that the texts reflect: 'Music may be an emblem of order and an

instrument of power, but the individual expression it allows and the unspecificity of its effects mean that the dramatist, like Prospero, can only watch in disappointment as Ariel eludes command. Therein lies the potency of Shakespeare's provoking music' (p. 90). David Greer's 'Five Variations on "Farewell dear love"' (pp. 213–29) considers aspects of the popularity and performance of the air by Robert Jones that Sir Toby and Feste speak and sing between them in *Twelfth Night*. Christopher R. Wilson's 'Aspects of Campion's Masques' (pp. 91–105) adds to the thin literature on this subject, considering in particular the implications of Campion being the only practising musician to have a leading rôle in the devising of masques at the Jacobean court. John Stevens is, as ever, illuminating in 'Sir Philip Sidney and "Versified Music". Melodies for Courtly Songs' (pp. 153–69), demonstrating that the implications of Sidney's famous formula, 'words set in delightful proportion, either accompanied with, or prepared for, the well enchanting skill of music' are not as straightforward as is usually assumed; he shows how 'the courtly poet, exercised as Sidney was with the problems of proper verbal "music" *of* poetry and the proper music *for* poetry, had a wide and diverse repertoire of melody to draw upon' (p. 165).

Sidney inevitably figures centrally (albeit uncomfortably) in Sukanta Chaudhuri's *Renaissance Pastoral and Its English Developments* (Oxford, 1989), a painstaking and comprehensive survey of English Renaissance pastoral, which will be found especially useful for the way it traces the roots of the form in Virgil and the classical past and fills in the picture as

---

[42] For example, Derek Cohen, 'The Rite of Violence in *1 Henry IV*', *Shakespeare Survey 38* (1985), 77–84; Claire Saunders, '"Death in His Bed": Shakespeare's Staging of the Death of the Duke of Gloucester in *2 Henry VI*', *Review of English Studies*, n.s. 35 ((1984), 19–34.

[43] 'Renaissance Execution and Marlovian Elocution: The Drama of Death', *PMLA*, 105 (1990), 209–22.

regards parallel contemporary forms in neo-Latin, French, and Italian models of the genre. But its focus on pastoral as a generic form with an almost Platonic essence, effectively transcending the uses to which it is put by particular poets in particular historical contexts, leads to oddly imbalanced judgements on particular works. Of Sidney's *Arcadia* Chaudhuri grudgingly observes that 'the work approximates to the pastoral from several angles, none of them affording much scope for genuine development of the mode. We are soon lost in a maze of non-pastoral and anti-pastoral concerns' (p. 303); and he seems genuinely surprised by the anti-Puritan strain in Jonson's *The Sad Shepherd*: 'Jonson is taking pains, almost gratuitously, to link his pastoral to contemporary reality – especially no doubt to the Puritan opposition to the theatre, which lends an unexpected touch of allegory to the fable' (p. 380). In fact I think it had very little to do with opposition to the theatre and far more to do with those elements of English country life which might be said to embody the spirit of pastoral and which the Puritans were bent on disrupting. Such remarks demonstrate how basically *unhistorical* Chaudhuri's approach is, something we find again in his treatment of Shakespearian pastoral, especially in relation to *A Midsummer Night's Dream*, *As You Like It*, and *The Winter's Tale*; there is no suggestion, for example, that the state of things in Arden might relate, however obliquely, to the actual conditions of rural workers or the effects of early enclosures. In this he is at odds with recent work by David Norbrook, Louis Montrose, and Alan Sinfield, who have seen in pastoral less a self-sufficient genre than a set of literary conventions within which the Renaissance aristocracy and their adherents could explore their rôle in the early modern state. From this perspective the link with 'contemporary reality', like the readiness to sacrifice purity of form to immediate concerns, was anything but surprising or gratuitous: it was what motivated the key exponents of the form and is likely to be of most interest to modern readers.

Chaudhuri very reasonably takes Spenser's *The Shepheardes Calender* to be a key text in the development of English pastoral and devotes a whole chapter to it. If I am only lukewarm about the book as a whole, because in one sense it seems to me to miss the point of its subject, I recognize and respect its scholarship and its appreciation of the literary conventions involved. And in that context I would be very happy to recommend the chapter on *The Shepheardes Calender* as a sensible foot-hill to take in before tackling the mountain of J. M. Richardson's *Astrological Symbolism in Spenser's 'The Shepheardes Calender': The Cultural Background of a Literary Text* (Lampeter, 1989). At enormous length (pp. 563), this relates Spenser's poem to Renaissance astrological lore, as popularized by the French almanac, *The Kalender of Sheephardes* (translated 1503), hypothesizing that the eclogues were devised in relation to the astrologically ascribed motifs, destinies, and character-types associated with each month. It is admirable in its erudition, but the spotlight is precariously narrow, and while it may provide *a* cultural background, Chaudhuri's book is a useful reminder that astrology was far from being the only influence on a form like pastoral that drew on so many disparate traditions.

A much more convincing model for discussions of 'cultural background' is offered by Louise George Clubb's admirable *Italian Drama in Shakespeare's Time* (New Haven and London, 1989). Comparative studies of Elizabethan drama with its Continental European counterparts are still often conducted at the level of tracing specific sources, allusions, and influences. In as much as a wider picture is invoked, it is usually one that Clubb succinctly characterizes: 'Most polarizations divide European theater into regular, "Aristotelian", theoretical Italian and French on one hand and irregular, pragmatic Spanish and English on the other, whether the antipodal concepts are labeled classical and romantic, or have been further dehistoricized as learned and spontaneous, or artificial and natural, or evolved politically into conservative and progressive or élite and popular' (p. 3). This mature and wide-ranging book transcends these intellectual horizons to place Shakespeare historically in the context of mixed theatrical practices in both Italy and England that were to a degree responses to specific local conditions (including those explored in Suzanne Westfall's book, reviewed above) but also part of wider European developments. In so doing it offers illuminating generic perspectives on the comedies (notably *The Comedy of Errors*, *Measure for Measure*, and *All's Well That Ends Well*), the tragedies (especially *Hamlet*), and the tragi-comedies (especially *The Winter's Tale*). Like their counterparts in Italy, these plays were the products of 'comici, sellers of theater' (p. 280), and the points of similarity between them are more pervasive and revealing than positivistic notions of 'influence' can hope to demonstrate.

James M. Vest is similarly chary about questions of influence and tradition in his engaging exploration of *The French Face of Ophelia from Belleforest to Baudelaire* (Lanham, Maryland, and London, 1989). His focus is on the female figure we know as Ophelia, who had a specifically French manifestation in Belleforest's *Histoires tragiques* before she was transformed by Shakespeare and then reintroduced into French culture as generations of writers and artists (perhaps most notably the Romantics, including Hugo and Delacroix) appropriated *Hamlet* for their own purposes. On the vexed question of how much Belleforest may have influenced Shakespeare, Vest carefully observes that 'one of Belleforest's most distinctive narratological contributions was his introduction of an embryonic amatory relationship, potentially reciprocated, that included an ambiguous rapport between Amleth and the lovely girl. In these and other points where Belleforest's text differed from Saxo's, the French version specifically anticipated Shakespeare's' (p. 23). But the central issue here is less specific borrow-

ings than of successive appropriations and adaptations of a figure who has achieved iconic status in her own right. This is not a feminist reading as such, but its sympathies are not very far removed from Sandra K. Fischer's account of what Shakespeare makes of the Ophelia figure: 'Hearing Ophelia . . . greatly enriches one's appreciation of the structural aesthetic of the play. The textual politics of Ophelia's rhetoric offer a feminine counterpoint to Hamlet's tragedy as well as a devastating commentary on it.'[44] Of course, a sympathetic reading of Ophelia's situation cannot but reflect badly on her father and that in turn must reflect badly on much of the established thinking of the day if we concede Alan Fisher's argument that Polonius is 'a recognisable version of the kind of man that a humanist training was supposed to produce', full of false confidence in a *Hamlet* where 'the confident minds are mediocre and . . . their mediocrity is a function of their confidence'.[45]

The status of women in the Renaissance, their education and influence, are all central issues in Margaret P. Hannay's major study of *Philip's Phoenix: Mary Sidney, Countess of Pembroke* (New York and Oxford, 1990). This is not the first biography of that remarkable lady, but must now I think be an essential starting point for future study of her life and reputation. The thesis of this meticulously documented book (the end-matter comprises one-third of its 300 pages) is reiterated in its closing words, which look forward to the fifth Earl of Pembroke, Mary's grandson, who 'continued the Protestant alliance conceived by Northumberland, established by Leicester, ennobled by Sir Philip Sidney, carried on by William, Earl of Pembroke, and made legendary through the

---

[44] 'Hearing Ophelia: Gender and Tragic Discourse in *Hamlet*', *Renaissance and Reformation*, n.s. 14 (1990), 1–10, p. 9.
[45] 'Shakespeare's Last Humanist', *Renaissance and Reformation*, n.s. 14 (1990), 33–47, pp. 37, 46.

works and patronage of Mary Sidney, Countess of Pembroke' (p. 213). That is, Mary's identity in her life and writings is subsumed into a programme to enhance the reputation of her family, not just narrowly her immediate relations (though Philip inevitably looms larger than most) but more generally the network of political and religious alliances to which the Sidneys and Herberts were central. Paradoxically, that subsumption amounted not to passivity or self-effacement but to the creation of an independent identity, one that empowered her in her own right, in defiance of many of the disabling pressures faced by her sex in that society. For some tastes the picture that emerges may smack too much of the feminist paragon, not least where Hannay seems to go out of her way to shield Mary Sidney from improper associations. For example, John Aubrey's suggestions of an incestuous relationship between her and Philip are only obliquely touched upon in the text (p. 149) and dismissed rather abruptly as 'preposterous' in the notes (p. 259, n. 41). His report of her supposed interest in the sight of horses mating is not mentioned at all, though it may well be a distortion of a genuine interest in selective breeding methods, matters which certainly attracted the attention of her sons, the third and fourth Earls of Pembroke, who were notably hard-headed agricultural 'improvers'. Either way, Aubrey's salacious tittle-tattle is surely evidence of a kind of how threatening feminine independence such as that achieved by Mary Sidney could be to a conservative old bachelor. Surely it would have been better to confront such matters directly rather than dismiss them as unthinkable or leave them unspoken to undermine confidence in what is in so many ways an excellent and compelling study.

The mother of 'the incomparable pair of brethren' to whom the First Folio was dedicated takes us, naturally enough, into Shakespeare's legacy and what we have made of it; even more naturally she takes us into the question of what *women* have made of it, a question which – despite current interest in the subject – has not often been considered in a historical perspective. *Women's Re-Visions of Shakespeare*, edited by Marianne Novy (Urbana and Chicago, 1990) brings, as the editor observes, 'two usually discrete concerns – feminist criticisms of Shakespeare and feminist criticism of women readers and writers – together for a conversation' (p. 1). In doing so it reveals a range and complexity of women's responses to Shakespeare through, in the main, the last two centuries that most traditional histories of reception conspicuously ignore: feminist reading did *not* begin with Virginia Woolf! The various essays consider readings, appropriations and adaptions by four novelists (Charlotte Brontë in debt to *Coriolanus* in *Shirley*, George Eliot linking Gwendolen with Rosalind in *Daniel Deronda*, Woolf as Shakespeare's sister, Margaret Laurence's use of *Tempest* analogues in *The Diviners*), by three poets (Emily Dickinson drawing on *Antony and Cleopatra*, H. D.'s 'remembrance' of Shakespeare in *By Avon River*, Adrienne Rich's sustained 're-visioning' of him), one dramatist (Charlotte Barnes's adaptation of *The Tempest* in *The Forest Princess*), one popularizer (Mary Lamb's *Tales of Shakespear* as influenced by the radical feminism of the Romantics), and a critic (Anna Jameson, shamefully neglected in most accounts of nineteenth-century criticism). There are also three deliberately 'personal' essays about the effect of reading Shakespeare on the authors' private lives and professional careers. Carol Thomas Neely remarks in an epilogue upon the 'convergence' in these ostensibly disparate essays, the extent 'to which these women's responses to Shakespeare galvanize their critique of patriarchal society's subordination of women and energize their capacity to fight this subordination' in a series of appropriations of his rôle as an artist (p. 242).

A rather different form of subordination is a sub-text in a number of pieces about the reception of Shakespeare away from Anglo-American shores, notably Sándor Maller's enthusiastic survey of his reputation in Hungary.[46] That reputation is high, despite some uncomplimentary references to the country in the works themselves (for instance, Pistol calling Bardolph a 'base Hungarian wight' in *The Merry Wives of Windsor*). Although this account was probably written before the dramatic events in Eastern Europe and makes no reference to recent political pressures, something emerges of how Shakespeare's status as a transcendent genius (ironically the subject of attack in the English-speaking world) has been exploited by democratic – and even more so nationalist – movements in that part of the world. Rather less of this is apparent in Brigitte Schultze's more narrowly focused account of Polish dramatists' adaptation of *Hamlet*.[47] Even less is apparent (though the potential is surely there) in Mahmoud F. Al-Shetawi's stab at Shakespeare in Arabic, which only scratches the surface of a long and complex subject, much more crossed by nationalist and cultural tensions than he begins to suggest.[48]

The stage-history of Shakespeare in England continues to be a fruitful source of study. Nancy A. Mace demonstrates that *The Merry Wives of Windsor*, though phenomenally successful when James Quin played Falstaff between 1720 and 1751, was much less popular otherwise, contradicting modern misreadings of the evidence which have concluded that it was uniformly successful on stage throughout the eighteenth century: the player, not the play, was the thing.[49] David George traces the (mis)-fortunes of *Coriolanus* on the London stage in the early nineteenth century; Edmund Kean and William Macready both applied their considerable, if contrasting, talents to the title rôle on a number of occasions and both creditably used something close to the Shakespearian text, but John Philip Kemble's *Coriolanus; Or The Roman Matron* based on Shakespeare and another play by James Thomson, had more popular success, even in the hands of lesser actors.[50] David Barrett makes a modestly successful attempt to rescue the reputation of

Frederick Balsir Chatterton, who largely ran the Drury Lane Theatre from 1864–78, distancing him from the famous assertion that 'Shakespeare spelt ruin and Byron bankruptcy' and suggesting that, if he was not an idealistic proponent of the Bard, he was prepared to give the plays a serious chance, with good (but not *star*) actors, who sometimes attracted reasonable audiences but never enough to cover the enormous overheads; he was rapidly overshadowed by Irving and made to look dated, but on this showing does not deserve the scorn he often receives.[51] Coming right up to date, Andrew Jarvis has been interviewed about his playing in various English Shakespeare Company productions of the histories, including such rôles as a punk Gadshill in *1 Henry IV*, an unusually powerful, almost psychopathetic Dauphin in *Henry V*, and a gangster-style Richard III almost prophetic of the current Hollywood vogue for the genre.

The last of these came too late to be considered in Hugh M. Richmond's analysis of the stage history of *Richard III* in the 'Shakespeare in Performance' series (Manchester and New York, 1989). This is no simple roll-call of performances, facts and figures, but a book with a strong view of its subject. The villain that stalks it is not Shakespeare's crook-backed king but Colley Cibber's deformed version of the play that held the stage for so long, its

---

[46] 'The Shakespeare-Heritage in Hungary', *American University Studies*, Series 29 General Literature, 25 (1990), 215–32.

[47] '"The Time is Out of Joint": the Reception of Shakespeare's *Hamlet* in Polish Plays', *New Comparison*, 8 (1989), 99–113.

[48] 'Shakespeare in Arabic: An Overview', *New Comparison*, 8 (1989), 114–26.

[49] 'Falstaff, Quin and the Popularity of *The Merry Wives of Windsor* in the Eighteenth Century', *Theatre Survey*, 31 (1990), 55–66.

[50] 'Restoring Shakespeare's *Coriolanus*: Kean Versus Macready', *Theatre Notebook*, 44 (1990), 101–18.

[51] '"Shakespeare Spelt Ruin and Byron Bankruptcy": Shakespeare at Chatterton's Drury Lane, 1864–1878', *Theatre Survey*, 29 (1988), 153–74.

influence persisting into Laurence Olivier's 1944 performance in the title rôle and his 1955 filming of the play. So, while acknowledging the film as 'an important document recording a distinctive stage interpretation', Richmond deplores the fact that 'Olivier's high impact has . . . merely updated Cibber's conviction that Shakespeare's archaic script must be recast to survive' (p. 63). The hero, meanwhile, is a somewhat idealized version of the-play-as-Shakespeare-wrote-it, which to an extent Richmond invents in a reconstruction of how Burbage might have played it and into which he reads rather a lot: 'Far from a simple celebration of his own language skills, Shakespeare's *oeuvre* investigates their potentiality for deception and evil as much as for good . . . The author's ultimate goal appears to be the emancipation of the audience from the hypnotic power of language whenever (as too often) it is used against humane values' (p. 143). Cibber and Olivier are not alone in obscuring or corrupting this aim; Antony Sher's celebrated performance is also castigated as 'picturesque and startling, provocatively perverse, but the overall interpretation remains ultimately facile politically, intellectually, and even morally' (p. 123). If the word were in his vocabulary, Richmond would have condemned it as 'postmodern'. But, while some reputations suffer in this crusade, other less celebrated performances – notably those at Stratford of Marius Goring and Christopher Plummer in 1953 and 1961 respectively – are commended for the integrity of their interpretation of (Richmond's view of) the Shakespearian text. Incidentally, while we never can know exactly how Burbage played Richard III, or any of his other major rôles, Martha Tuck Rozett has been exploring how verbal cues in the texts themselves (especially *Hamlet* and *Macbeth*) provide signals both to actors and to audiences that contribute to the characterization process and, in relation to otherworldly phenomena, 'summon up visions in the mind of the spectator, creating images that no stagecraft . . . could equal'.[52]

I draw to a close with two very different books on the stage/page debate that has dogged Shakespeare for the past thirty years. The great puzzles about *Staging Shakespeare: Seminars on Production Problems*, edited by Glenn Loney (New York, 1990) are why it has been published at all, in the form it has, and why it has been published now. It consists of edited transcripts of the proceedings of a conference at Brooklyn College, and these do not all sit comfortably on the printed page: conversations ramble, the transitions are stagey, too many people are either feyly deferential or set on airing their own egos. That being so, some of the contributions here are less than riveting and a nagging question (never directly answered) came to dominate this reader's attention: when exactly did this conference take place? Three of the four contributors to the section on 'Shakespeare: Playwright and/or Poet' (Alfred Harbage, John Houseman, Bernard Beckerman) are now dead, as are at least two other contributors to the conference, Richmond Crinkley and Virgil Thomson. One of the more fruitful sections of the book is devoted to John Barton's celebrated production of *Richard II*, at Stratford in 1973/4, but apparently being staged at the Brooklyn Academy of Music while the conference was going on: this perhaps puts us in the mid-1970s. An editorial note seems to confirm this when we are told, in 'A Stage for Shakespeare', that 'Professor Nagler was speaking well over a decade before the discovery of the Rose and Globe foundations [i.e. 1989]' (p. 171). Why have we waited so long for it to see print? That discussion also involved such authorities as Richard Hosley, C. Walter Hodges, and Glynne Wickham, and was obviously up-to-the-minute when it took place. But most of what is said there has long since emerged in print elsewhere, and much has been superseded by subsequent scholarship. Had the

---

52 '"How now Horatio, you tremble and look pale": Verbal Cues and the Supernatural in Shakespeare's Tragedies', *Theatre Survey*, 29 (1988), 127–38, p. 127.

book been published immediately after the conference, the currency of ideas and values it represents would have excused much of the awkwardness of its format. As it is, and despite some felicities, it is at best a curiosity and at worst a cynical cashing in on Shakespeare's capacity for opening library purse-strings.

By contrast Harry Berger Jr's *Imaginary Audition: Shakespeare on Stage and Page* (Berkeley, 1989) is a timely and thoughtful contribution to the stage/page debate. The first part of the book is an attack on what Berger mischievously dubs the New Histrionicism, the advocacy of theatre- or performance-centred study of the plays, represented pre-eminently by Richard Levin in *New Readings v. Old Plays* (Chicago, 1979) and Gary Taylor in *Moment by Moment by Shakespeare* (London, 1985). In the second half of the book Berger confirms himself as an 'arm-chair critic', but a far from complacent one, in that he attempts 'to reconstruct text-centered reading in a way that incorporates the perspectives of imaginary audition and playgoing . . . to put into play an approach that remains text-centered but focuses on the interlocutory politics and theatrical features of performed drama so as to make them impinge at every point on the most suspicious and antitheatrical of readings' (p. xiv). This is all done in the context of a detailed close reading of the second scene of Act 3 of *Richard II*, offered as a prologue to a full-scale study in this mode of *The Henriad*, which will be truly monumental if sustained with anything like this close focus. Many of us pay lip-service to keeping performance in mind when we analyse the plays, but few of us do it with this scrupulosity. This is a lively, controversial, and stimulating book, required reading for anyone who perceives the distance between page and stage to be at all problematic.

Let me conclude by paying tribute to John Cavanagh's labours in producing an indispensable reference-tool, *British Theatre: A Bibliography, 1901–1985*, The Motley Bibliographies: One (Mottisfont, 1989). Taking as its remit all monographs on British theatrical subjects published between those dates, it is bound to be a starting-point for much scholarship to come. Of course, we can regret that Cavanagh was not, for reasons of length, able to include articles published in periodicals and had to exclude more purely literary or critical studies (especially in the period up to 1970, where his efforts would duplicate those of the *New Cambridge Bibliography of English Literature*), but what remains is a formidable accumulation of information, clearly and helpfully arranged under logical and comprehensible headings, minimally but perceptively annotated. We are further promised supplements to J. F. Arnott and J. W. Robinson's *English Theatrical Literature, 1559–1900* (1970), of which this volume is a continuation of sorts, and to this volume itself, rectifying omissions (which I suspect will be fewer than the compiler modestly allows for) and bringing the cut-off point up to 1990. More power to his word processor!

3. EDITIONS AND TEXTUAL STUDIES
reviewed by H. R. WOUDHUYSEN

New editions of three of Shakespeare's plays from Oxford (*Macbẹth*, *The Merry Wives of Windsor*, and *Love's Labour's Lost*) and four from Cambridge (*2 Henry IV*, *Henry VIII*, *1 Henry VI*, and *King John*), of the narrative poems from Penguin and of a new venture in photo-facsimile publishing, amounting in all to well over two thousand pages, present a daunting prospect to the neophyte reviewer. All of these editions contain valuable and useful material, which Shakespeare scholars cannot afford to ignore: they all deserve close attention, but they are of rather varying quality.

The single-volume Oxford and Cambridge

editions go their different ways, the one rather grand and austere, the other from time to time quite lively. As a whole the introductions to these editions are disappointing. Only Brooke's to *Macbeth* rises above the discussion of character and narrative and, while the other editors have interesting things to say about the plays, they are surprisingly lacking in ideas about them as dramatic fictions. Too often (especially with this group of plays), editors resort to an appeal to the theatre of the 'This may not be Shakespeare's best or most interesting play, but it works on the stage' kind. Most of the editors of the Oxford and Cambridge volumes feel that the way to show how the play works in the theatre is to go through its plot but, with the exception of Beaurline's *King John* (heavily indebted to Emrys Jones), they make little use of scenic analysis and rarely point out Shakespeare's self-borrowing beyond the purely verbal level. Few editors draw on the work of Shakespeare's contemporaries outside the theatre to set his achievements in the context of Renaissance poetry or prose; there is little here to suggest how he might be responding to the works of other writers.

Modern editions of Shakespeare either follow the traditional practice of relying on the *OED* for their annotations, or simply supply one-word glosses of a kind which can mislead. Outside their introductions, editors are reluctant to explain what Shakespeare does with words and how he creates an individual and distinctive dramatic language in his plays. Of all the newer editorial aids R. W. Dent's *Shakespeare's Proverbial Language: An Index* (1981) has proved its worth by being the most widely used: it appears in the tables of abbreviated references of all the plays apart from *Henry VIII*. Developments in literary theory leave the editors largely untouched; if the 'new historicism' has a practical application in editing Shakespeare, it cannot be found in these volumes.

With respect to textual matters it is fairly clear that the influence of the Oxford Shakespeare project is not as great as might have been anticipated.[1] This is partly because its apparent availability to and use by the New Cambridge editors is so far very patchy (they also have their own hobby-horses to ride), but also because the single-play Oxford editors tend to be rather conservative and a little sceptical about the parent project's methods and conclusions. The revolution in editing Shakespeare that the original Oxford editors promised has not yet, as far as one can see, come about. Theories about the nature of the underlying copy from which plays were printed may become more elaborate, or may be put more assertively, but their implications are rarely thought through or acted upon. Ideas about modernizing texts, especially proper names, and rewriting stage directions, may have changed – not always for the better – but when it comes to altering the early printed texts, the rage for emendation cools. On the other hand, editors seem willing to accept, and to expect their readers to accept, some of Oxford's most controversial ideas, not least about authorship, even when these are based on material which is still unpublished.

There is no doubt that in a sense Oxford has contributed to making editorial work on Shakespeare more 'professional'. In the Cambridge series the innovative textual work is all too often marred by simple errors, at least on the evidence of the volumes under review here. Oxford and Cambridge are now in full flood; New Penguin is drawing to a close; a new Arden series is about to begin. The different series may think of themselves as boldly innovative, but the editor's dull duty, of making sure that the text and its apparatus are correct, remains.

What will probably be the most widely used of these volumes, Nicholas Brooke's *Macbeth*, is textually cautious and conservative.[2] On the

---

[1] There is a long and important review of the *Complete Works* and the *Textual Companion* by Brian Vickers in *The Review of English Studies*, 40 (1989), 402–11.

[2] *Macbeth*, ed. Nicholas Brooke (Oxford, Clarendon Press, 1990), in the Oxford Shakespeare series. Passages

fifteen or so occasions outside the Hecate scenes where he rejects a reading from the one-volume Oxford edition it is usually to do so in favour of F. As well as a fuller stage direction to get Lady Macduff's son off stage at the end of 4.2, he proposes two entirely new readings. At 4.1.108 he explains his reasons for adopting 'Dunsinan' instead of the traditional 'Dunsinane', Rowe's regularization (the Ordnance Survey, he reports, has 'Dunsinnan'). In the play the name is stressed on both the second and third syllables.[3] His other emendation seeks to sort out the crux in Ross's speech in 4.2.22, by printing 'Each way and move'. Here, he argues, 'move' is a noun meaning 'motion' or 'movement'. Most editors from Johnson onwards have assumed that Ross never completes what he intends to say and separate 'Each way and move' from 'I take my leave of you' by a dash. Brooke has both the full-stop and a dash and acknowledges that the 'move' 'finally suggests departure'. The reading is a possible one (although historically quite unsupported by the evidence of *OED* concerning 'move' as a noun), and does little violence to the text.

The emendation draws attention to Brooke's exceptionally heavy reliance on the dash. At the end of the comparable speech 'If it were done when 'tis done' in 1.7.28 where Macbeth seems unwilling to say any more, Brooke rejects F's and Oxford's stop and ends 'And falls on th' other –'. He resorts to the dash on just under two hundred occasions in a play of slightly over two thousand lines. Yet, while the language of *Macbeth* is often curt and elliptical, Brooke's reworking of so much of F's punctuation (particularly its colons) into dashes produces a surprising sense of editorial heavy-handedness, as though the play needed some sort of telegraphic orchestration. At times Brooke's text becomes clogged and less rather than more dramatic, as with Banquo in 2.1.5–6: 'Hold, take my sword. – There's husbandry in Heaven, / Their candles are all out. – Take thee that too. – / A heavy summons lies like lead upon me . . .' F prints this as 'Hold, take my

Sword: / There's Husbandry in Heauen, / Their Candles are all out: take thee that too. / A heauie Summons lyes like Lead vpon me . . .' which is tense and understated, but quite clear.

The problem with this example is the lineation to which the Oxford editors all pay close attention: Brooke newly aligns some twelve passages. He believes that F was set from a copy of the prompt-book with some theatrical cuts. The work of setting the manuscript was evenly divided between Compositors A and B and all but two of the twelve reassigned passages occur during A's stint. Brooke discusses A's inability to set prose and verse correctly, and the solutions he proposes generally read well. Unfortunately, like the other Oxford editors, Brooke ignores some relined passages and tends to provide slightly inaccurate and confusing references for others.[4] Brooke perhaps does not give compositor B sufficient credit for his care with lineation.[5]

Brooke's text is accurate. He stumbles over the stage direction at 2.1.0 where he prints

---

and words in this and subsequent editions are located by each edition's own line-numbering. Thomas Wheeler's *Macbeth: An Annotated Bibliography* (New York and London, Garland Publishing, 1990), lists and summarizes just under 2,700 items relating to the play.

[3] At 1.3.32 he justifies his modernization to 'Weïrd' of F's 'weyward' and 'weyard'.

[4] 2.3.64–6 is not discussed in Appendix A (as promised in the note on the passage), nor is 3.5.69. There are some confusing errors in his cross-references for line numbers between his commentary and Appendix A (see, for example, 1.2.32–5, 2.3.46–52, 3.3.15.1 (correctly 19.1), 16–18 (correctly 20–2) and 21–2 (correctly 25–6).

[5] 4.3.102–3 where B set 'Natiõ' is not, as Brooke claims, the first instance of his 'compressing the type' to keep to the line (p. 224), for he had already set 'ỹ' in TLN 1852 (4.3.33). He repeated this at TLN 2279 (5.3.55), and used another tylde in 2391 (5.6.9). But he also drew heavily on the ampersand. Where A used it twice, but only once to save the line (at TLN 873 (2.3.110); he also drew on the tylde once at TLN 648 (2.2.1)), B resorted to it eleven times, omitting a full stop at the end of a speech, TLN 2019 (4.3.179), and necessary marks of punctuation at the end of two lines (TLN 1266 where Brooke (3.4.9) prints a full stop and TLN 1396 (3.4.118) where he prints a comma).

'Fleance with a torch before him', saying that he has retained Folio's punctuation: but Folio has a comma after 'Fleance' which, as Brooke allows, would mean that 'torch' was a torchbearer and 'him' referred to Banquo. On p. 126 he cites readings from Chambers whose edition is not specified in the table of abbreviations.

The difficulties associated with the Hecate scenes (3.5 and 4.1) and the 'brilliantly written' but unsatisfactory exchange between Lennox and a Lord (3.6) lead him to argue that 'the material available for these three scenes consisted of working sheets of a revision not finally tidied up for performance' (p. 52). Hence the Hecate scenes are revised versions of ones originally written without her. Following the modern view, he attributes the revisions to Middleton and assumes 'that Shakespeare accepted the Hecate material even if he did not write it' (p. 55). Although he argues firmly against the idea that *Macbeth* was performed before James I on 7 August 1606 during the visit of King Christian of Denmark, Brooke dates the original version of the play to the second half of 1606 (p. 64) and argues that it was revised by Middleton in 1609–10 (p. 66). He dates *The Witch* to 1615 and argues that Middleton reused the songs that he added to *Macbeth* in his later play. His evidence for this is strong, but vitiated in part by two slips. Firstly, the dedication to the manuscript of *The Witch* is not autograph (p. 64), so that it may not be a reliable witness to the play's history; secondly, Brooke makes Middleton say in the dedication that the play has rested in 'an impassioned obscurity' where the manuscript actually has the more pregnant phrase 'imprisoned obscurity'.

For Brooke, *Macbeth* displays Shakespeare's ability 'to sustain at once credulous amazement and rational intelligence' (p. 32). He contrasts the naturalism of the Macbeths' relationship with the use made of dramatic illusions (p. 23) and approaches the play through a lengthy comparison with the Baroque art of Cara-vaggio and Bernini (pp. 24–34). This does not take the pressure of contemporary politics out of the play, but makes it much less of a Stuart party-piece (pp. 71–6). Not a great deal of this gets into the commentary (but there are important notes on 1.5.40, 2.1.16–20, 2.3.93–8 and one artistic reprise from the Introduction at 5.7.83.1).

In the case of *2 Henry IV* some facts are quite clear, but others seem beyond certain resolution.[6] There is no doubt that the play was written about 1597–8; that the quarto of 1600 was set by one compositor from Shakespeare's foul papers and that the F text was purged of profanities. Beyond all this few editors and scholars agree about either its origins or its relationship with *1 Henry IV*. Just as controversially, there is little common ground among those who have examined the reasons for the omission of 3.1.1–106 in the first issue of the quarto (Qa) and its replacement by a cancel (Qb), and for the omission of eight passages in F amounting to about 160 lines. The New Cambridge Shakespeare has assigned the first part to Herbert Weil and the second to Giorgio Melchiori. His edition is predicated on the supposition that Shakespeare wrote the first part of the play without a second in mind. Melchiori's edition is dense and complex, richly annotated in an allusive and sometimes speculative way (see, for example, his notes to 1.3.41–62 and 3.2.220). It is full of interesting ideas and the fruit of close observation, but it is also marred by a large number of errors in the text and its apparatus.

To explain the origins of Shakespeare's play, Melchiori would start with the old two-part play in which Tarlton acted (he died in 1588). A version of the play is preserved in a memorial reconstruction, *The Famous Victories of Henry the Fifth*, printed in 1598. Shakespeare, Melchiori argues (p. 9), 'was an expert at remakes

---

[6] *The Second Part of King Henry IV*, ed. Giorgio Melchiori (Cambridge University Press, 1989), in the New Cambridge Shakespeare series.

of old plays' and used the original of *The Famous Victories* to write two separate history plays about Henry IV and his son. What is now substantially *1 Henry IV* was completed in 1596 with the character of Sir John Oldcastle in it. This 'ur-*Henry IV*' was withdrawn under pressure from the Lord Chamberlain, William Brooke, Lord Cobham, at some time between his assumption of the office in August 1596 and his death in March 1597. Instead of cutting the offensive comic rôle of Sir John Oldcastle, Shakespeare renamed the knight Falstaff and expanded the whole comic part. *1 Henry IV* was written in 1597 and the second part, still drawing on the 'ur-*Henry IV*', soon after.

Several levels of composition and revision are visible in Part Two (see, for example, notes on 3.2.211–13, 5.2.33, 5.5.84 and the Epilogue). These levels can be detected, Melchiori argues, by narrative and dramatic discontinuities, but also by a close examination of the textual difficulties of the play in its two substantive versions. Q was set from Shakespeare's foul papers, but those papers had already, before they went to the printer's, been the subject of revision. Of the eight passages present in F but not Q, four were cancelled in the foul papers to avoid problems with the Master of the Revels and the other four were cut for theatrical purposes caused by the need to double some parts. The reviser who cut these passages was not Shakespeare himself, but he had to accept the cuts 'as a matter of theatrical expediency' (p. 198). While Qb was being printed, Shakespeare decided to add the passage 3.1.1–106 which he already had to hand since like at least two other passages in Q (1.2.74–135, containing the speech prefix 'Old.' at 1.2.96, and 2.2.1–52 which has '*sir Iohn Russel*' in the initial stage direction), it belonged to the 'ur-*Henry IV*'.

Following Eleanor Prosser's lead, Melchiori believes that F was set from a scribal transcript made from Qa and from Shakespeare's foul papers. Unfortunately, the 'misleadingly pedantic scribe' (p. 202) had 'a literary turn of mind' (p. 191) and improved and regularized

the text at will; his errors were compounded by 'an undistinguished compositor [*sic*]' (p. 202). If Melchiori's textual theories are rather elaborate in places, they have the great merit, especially in relation to Q and the disturbance evident in the text around some of the cuts, of stimulating thought about the problems compositors faced in setting from foul papers. Jowett's and Taylor's work on *2 Henry IV* as a play revised by Shakespeare is largely ignored, but Melchiori's account of the text is often persuasive, although one sided – it would have been useful to have a sharper discrimination between scribal sophistication and compositorial expediency in F.

The result of his theories allows Melchiori to print the scene 3.1 which was omitted in Qa and the eight passages only in F with a clear editorial conscience. His text is based on Q which he attempts to follow as often as he can (see for example 2.4.271–2, 4.2.276–8 and 289–91). Most of his emendations affect stage directions, speech headings, punctuation and lineation. He regularizes Pistol's Italian at 2.4.145 and 5.5.89, and offers 'whet' for Q's 'wet' and F's 'write' at 4.2.104 where Fortune will 'whet her fair words still in foulest terms', setting a bitter edge on them ('fortune' is not personified at 5.3.107, but 'Time and Spite' are at 1.1.151).

All this would be well enough if Melchiori's text were accurate, but it is spoilt by a long run of minor and irritating errors.[7] There are also errors in the textual apparatus: 2.2.14 both Q and F read 'thy', 2.4.225–6 Q reads 'come it

---

[7] 1.1.4 'worship' for 'Lordship', 1.1.67 'fight' for 'fright', 1.1.73 'had' for 'was', 1.1.89 'for' for 'as', 1.2.103 'shall' for 'should', 1.3.21 'have' for 'had' (an F only passage), 1.3.73 'infirm' for 'unfirm', 2.1.144 'at' for 'to', 2.2.3 'so high a' for 'so high', 2.2.13 'pairs' for 'pair', 2.2.14 'the' for 'thy', 2.4.225 'a growes' for 'it growes', 3.2.11 'at' for 'of', 4.1.135 'at' for 'of' (an F only passage), 4.1.208 'the' for 'an', 4.1.222 'reunited' for 'united', 4.2.126 'folks' for 'folk', 4.2.225 'the' for 'thy', 5.1.30 'your' for 'thy', 5.1.48 'Master Shallow' for 'Master Robert Shallow', 5.2.112 'hands' for 'hand', 5.3.9 'a good varlet, Sir John' for 'a very good varlet, Sir John', 5.5.31 'hands' for 'hand', Epilogue 12 'promise infinitely' for 'promise you infinitely'.

growes ... weele', 3.1.107 the SD is in Qb, 3.2.22 F agrees with Qa against Qb. A few editorial changes are not noted in the apparatus: the SD at 4.2.178 follows line 177 in both Q and F, in Westmoreland's speech 4.1.30–1 are set as one line in Q and the Justice's speech at 5.5.87–8 is set in prose in Q. These slips (there are more in the apparatus's readings from F), detract from what is a genuinely innovative and lively edition, which will probably be used a good deal.

There are 'more tricks with Falstaff' in T. W. Craik's edition of *The Merry Wives of Windsor*.[8] Craik's unpretentious introduction firmly associates the play with a first performance at the Garter Feast celebrated on 23 April 1597 when George Carey, second Baron Hunsdon, was installed. Craik feels that it was a 'strong probability' (p. 5) that Hunsdon commissioned the play, which also draws on the *in absentia* election to the Order of Count Mömpelgard, later Duke of Württemberg. Other topical allusions which have been found in the play (to William Gardiner, to Lord Compton, and to Lord Cobham) are examined and rejected. Rumours of Hunsdon's appointment as Lord Chamberlain had been in circulation since mid-February 1597 and, Craik believes, 'he would have enough time to commission an appropriate play from Shakespeare, to be performed on St George's Day' (p. 3). Shakespeare must have worked quite fast to meet his deadline but, as Craik argues (pp. 12–13), he was already in the swing of work on *2 Henry IV*. In 3.2 of that play, Shallow seems to live in the East Midlands, but by 4.2 his house is in Gloucestershire. Between writing these scenes, Shakespeare broke off work to execute his commission and decided when he resumed work on *2 Henry IV* to move Shallow's home nearer to the Windsor setting.

Craik seeks to simplify the account of the play's textual history put forward by John Jowett in the *Textual Companion* to the Oxford Shakespeare. There is no disputing that the quarto of 1602 is a reported text, probably assembled by the actor who played the Host,

and that F was set from a transcript made by Ralph Crane. Q, Craik argues, was not based on a revised version of the play performed in 1597 (p. 51), nor was it 'intended to provide a script for acting troupes to perform' (p. 52); instead he thinks that it 'was compiled for sale to readers' (p. 53). The evidence that Crane's copy-text was Shakespeare's own foul papers is supplied from inconsistencies within the play (pp. 54–5). But there are difficulties with this theory, not the least of which is that Slender, having taken the fairy 'in green', does not get Anne at the end of the play; Mistress Page explains he should have taken the fairy 'in white', but then Caius complains that he did not get Anne although he took the fairy 'in white'. Craik concludes that this error 'can hardly derive from Shakespeare's manuscript' (p. 55).

There are further difficulties with Ford's false name – Brook in Q and Broom in F, although the text clearly calls for a pun on ford/brook. F's error leads Craik into arguing (pp. 57–8) that to avoid trouble with the Cobham family, Broom was substituted for Brook at the court performance. Given the pressure under which Shakespeare and the company were working there was no time to make a separate prompt book and Shakespeare's manuscript had to serve. The change was made in the manuscript (but Falstaff's pun on the name in 2.2.143–4 was allowed by an oversight to stand). Craik raises the question of whether it was Crane himself or a reviser who purged Shakespeare's foul papers of profanities for inclusion in F (pp. 58–61), but drops the issue without coming to any conclusion. His theories about the origins of F's text might well strike some readers as a little tenuous.

Craik defends the play against its detractors and those who would use it for ideological purposes by appealing to its success in the

---

[8] *The Merry Wives of Windsor*, ed. T. W. Craik (Oxford, Clarendon Press, 1989), in the Oxford Shakespeare series.

theatre: 'Nothing makes some critics more uneasy than a thoroughly happy ending, especially in our irony-obsessed modern age' (pp. 46–7). One consequence of this view is that if the play's action is to be as coherent as possible an editor must regularize and complete what Shakespeare left in a rough and unfinished form. The vast majority of Craik's emendations are concerned with stage directions, which might strike some readers, and perhaps actors, as a little fussy. Given his views on the origins of the text, Craik allows himself a free editorial hand. Even though it is largely set in prose, he has little to say about the rôle of compositors in the production of F. He knows well that using Q to emend F is a hazardous business (see the discussions of the cruces at 1.3.88 and 4.4.40). The apparatus prints some dozen of his own conjectures, several of which are attractive.

In emending 'the fatuity uttered by Shakespeare's scatterbrains' (see the note to the famous crux 1.1.19–20), Craik treads a wary path with new verbal readings at 1.2.8, 1.4.81, 2.1.143–4 where Mistress Page now asks her husband to 'come home to dinner' rather than simply 'come to dinner', 3.3.60–1 where the 'not' is removed from F's 'if Fortune thy foe, were not Nature thy friend', 3.3.190–1 where, with some prompting from Q, a 'not' is added to the end of F's 'You vse me well, M.*Ford*? Do you?', 4.1.65 where Evans's habit of adding a final s to words makes his 'foolish Christian creatures' a singular and so in need of 'a' after 'foolish', 4.2.23, 4.2.179 adopting Q's 'espied' to F's 'spie' to read 'spied', 4.6.49 'marriage' for 'marrying', 5.2.2, and 5.2.2–3. On more than one occasion he defends the F reading which has usually been emended: 1.4.20, 2.1.5, 3.1.89, 3.4.87, 3.5.8, 3.5.111 and 4.5.51.

Craik's text is almost free from error ('the' has slipped out of 'for the which' at 2.2.77–8 and the indentation of 5.5.61–2 needs adjustment). There are a few minor errors in the readings reported from Q in the apparatus; 3.5.24–5 are divided in F after 'mercy' not

'marry' (p. 230) and in F (2.1.12, TLN 565) 'By me' is printed as part of Falstaff's rhyme at the end of his letter to Mistress Page. In a play rich in difficult language and expressions, his commentary is most helpful and makes good use of quotations from other authors to explain the sense or record a usage. In particular he draws on Nashe's works (the index does not list all the occasions on which he is cited) and suggests that Falstaff's speech at the opening of 5.5 is derived from Lyly's *Euphues*. Among the matters which still await some sort of explanation are the choice of the name Caius for the French physician (1.2.1), the meaning of Falstaff's 'French thrift' (1.3.80), the Host's 'Cried game' (2.3.82), why Ford calls Robin a 'pretty weathercock' (3.2.15), the meaning of the Host's asseveration ''tis in his buttons' (3.2.62), and Mistress Quickly's line 'You orphan heirs of fixèd destiny' (5.5.38). In the scene where William's grammar is tested (4.1) there is no explanation as to why Craik thinks Shakespeare probably refers to the 1577 edition of Lily's and Colet's *A Short Introduction*. The explanation that Evans's 'Got's lords and ladies' (1.1.216) is unintentionally bawdy and refers to the flower known as 'cuckoo-pint' is convincing.

The divisions of opinion on *King Henry VIII* make it an awkward play to edit.[9] Is it all of Shakespeare's work or is it his and Fletcher's? Should it be called *King Henry VIII* or *All is True*? Is it an occasional play, or not? Is it one of Shakespeare's late masterpieces (as, among others, Richard Wagner thought), or was his attention less than fully engaged? To these questions might be added difficulties about the nature of F's copy – a scribal, or an authorial, transcript of foul papers – and an analysis of the work of its compositors, A and J. It is a pity for enthusiasts of the play that John Margeson's edition in the New Cambridge series does not

---

[9] *King Henry VIII*, ed. John Margeson (Cambridge University Press, 1990), in the New Cambridge Shakespeare series.

really deal with these issues satisfactorily. His introduction tends to brush them aside and instead suggests that closer attention to the play itself is more rewarding. Unfortunately, what he says about it is rather staid and lacking in intellectual energy. His account of the play's text is very brief.

Nothing that has been published after 1986, including the Oxford Shakespeare project, appears in Margeson's edition. It is heavily indebted to Foakes and Maxwell and there is little else genuinely new in it, much of the annotation being very thin and some consisting merely of single-word glosses. Sometimes he follows F closely where other editors abandon it (2.1.86 and 3.2.339), rather more often he follows later emendations (1.1.172, 3.2.171, 3.2.343 and 5.2.159–60). Editors have been happy to emend F in the interests of historical accuracy, so that F's 'Michaell' Hopkins in 1.1.221 becomes the historical 'Nicholas' and in the stage direction beginning 2.4 Canterbury is raised from a bishopric to an archbishopric and so on. Modernizing elsewhere in the play poses more difficult problems. Margeson leaves modern Kimbolton Castle in 4.1.34 as 'Kimmalton', but silently emends F's 'Stokeley' to Holinshed's 'Stokesley' at 4.1.101. The 'Parish Garden' is allowed to stand at 5.3.2, 'covent' for 'convent' at 4.2.19, and 'chamblet' for 'camlet' at 5.3.81 because these spellings were current or common, but F's 'Powles' is modernized to 'Paul's' at 5.3.13 and 'Strond' to 'Strand' at 5.3.47. There is no explanation for the form of the name 'Capuchius'.

This edition cannot be said to be marked by particularly close attention to detail. Departures from F's lineation are not recorded in the textual apparatus at 2.2.82–3, 2.4.9, 2.4.66–8, 3.1.80, 4.1.59–60, 5.1.174–5 and 5.3.29 (unusually, Margeson sets the preceding lines 26–7 in verse). Johnson's stage direction at 5.1.108 is also omitted from the apparatus, and the relocation of Lovell's entry from 1.3.16 to 1.3.15 is unnoted. At 5.3.3 the apparatus records that F's 'M.' has been expanded to 'master', but this has

not been done again at line 25 or 26 where F's 'M.Puppy' is rendered as 'master puppy' without comment. The verbal errors are not extensive, but include the serious omission of the second half of the line 2.2.60 where Norfolk responds to the Lord Chamberlain.[10] Altogether, Margeson's edition seems rather thin and will disappoint those who want a full and imaginatively charged account of the play's place and importance in the canon.

It is perhaps premature to judge Michael Hattaway's New Cambridge edition of the *Henry VI* plays only on the basis of Part One, but this first instalment promises that it will meet high expectations.[11] Like Margeson he realizes that the authorial and textual problems of the first part cannot finally be solved. But unlike Margeson, his account of the text is thorough and clear, while his well-written and convincing introduction explains why the play is worth serious attention. Hattaway believes that the sequence, written if not performed before 1592, was composed in the order of the narrative it unfolds. He is willing to push *1 Henry VI*'s date as far back as 1589 (p. 35) and following Honigmann's lead – rather unquestioningly (see the note on 4.7.61–70) – is ready to associate it with Lord Strange's company (p. 39).

The treatment of the text shows a close attention to its meaning and stage realization. There are a few minor slips – at 2.1.31 'that' for 'the', 2.2.45 'into' for 'unto' and 3.1.91 'you' for 'ye' – but also evidence of a good deal of careful thought. Rejecting theories that F was set from a scribal copy of foul papers, or from foul

---

[10] The following errors also occur: 1.1.60 'not' for 'nor', 1.1.120 'venom-mouthed' for 'venom'd-mouth'd' (this may be a silent modernization), 1.4.36 'gentlemen' for gentleman', 1.4.48 ''tis such' for ''tis to such', 3.2.5 'more' for 'moe', 4.1.104 'great lover' for 'great good lover' (a mistake Maxwell also made) and 4.2.82.4 'palms' for 'palm'.

[11] *The First Part of King Henry VI*, ed. Michael Hattaway (Cambridge University Press, 1990), in the New Cambridge Shakespeare series.

papers annotated by the book-holder, Hattaway convincingly argues that compositorial
error was responsible for most of the play's
serious anomalies – the stage directions at 2.1.7,
3.2.35 and 4.1.181, as well as F's treatment of act
and scene divisions. He is particularly aware of
the problems caused by dittography (p. 189),
that some mislineation is present in F's text (see
notes to 3.3.45–8 and 5.4.109–10), and that a
line may be lost (2.5.10–12).

Hattaway's text sticks closely to F and he
rejects previous emendations and several new
Oxford readings at 1.3.19, 36 etc., 1.4.65,
3.1.51–5, 4.2.29, 4.4.16 and the related passage
5.3.11. He admits few new emendations of his
own (one at 1.5.3 'men' for 'them' is actually in
Oxford and 2.4.57 'law' for 'you' is not entirely
new) apart from ones affecting stage directions
and speech headings. Instead of 'centre', which
can be supported by Spenser's usage, he proposes 'cincture' at 2.2.6, but does not refer to
the similar crux in King John 4.3.156. Cauti-
ously, he relegates several good conjectures
(including the stage direction at 2.1.7) to his
apparatus: at 2.4.13 'shows' for 'bears' was
caught, he suggests, from the next line, and
'yea, for' instead of 'and for' at 5.3.136 makes
better sense. At 4.1.170, 4.2.7 he proposes his
own changes, and at 5.3.68 accepts Oxford's
emendation, to regularize the metre. This is a
recurrent problem in the play and one which
causes him to turn frequently to Cercignani.

His commentary is generally very good. It
pays much attention to problems of staging in
the Elizabethan theatre and, unusually, seeks
out a good number of parallels from The Faerie
Queene and biblical allusions: one of these leads
him, probably correctly, to restore F's 'Yet'
instead of 'Let' to 3.2.117. He also does much to
place 1 Henry VI in its time, with frequent
reference to Marlowe's works and contemporary drama. He draws an interesting analogy
between the play's opening scene and Thomas
Lant's engravings of Sidney's funeral, and between the quarrelling bishops of 1.3 and the
Marprelate controversy (p. 13 n. 3 and note to

1.3.35). At 5.4.74 ('Alençon, that notorious
Machiavel?') he notes that Innocent Gentillet's
Contre-Machiavel was dedicated to François,
Duc d'Alençon, but wrongly says that he,
rather than his brother, went on to become
Henri III. This is an impressive debut. Hattaway does not make claims for 1 Henry VI
which the experience of reading or watching
the play cannot justify: his achievement really
lies in giving it the sort of intelligent critical and
editorial attention which it deserves.

Many of the virtues of Hattaway's approach
are shared by L. A. Beaurline's edition of King
John.[12] The introduction reads well, although it
devotes perhaps a little too much attention to
the play's history in the theatre. His notes are
full, possibly too full (there are over twelve
pages of densely printed supplementary notes),
but make some good points, especially about
the play's use of emblems. Beaurline is interesting about the political aspects of the play in its
contemporary setting and shows how it fits in
with some of the pamphlet debates of the 1580s.
His attention also focuses on its dramatic construction. Comparing Shakespeare's treatment
of his sources with their treatment in The
Troublesome Reign he argues that John is the
earlier play, written certainly before 1591. His
appendix on the relationship between the two
plays is persuasive, as far as it goes, but it largely
confines itself to considering the evidence
which supports his theory.

There is also another difficulty. Beaurline
follows John Jowett in believing that the F text
of King John was set by compositors B and C
from a transcript of foul papers made by two
scribes whose work divides somewhere between 4.2.171 and 260. The absence of profanities and the presence of Act divisions point to a
date after 1609. There is therefore a considerable gap between the possible dates of the play's
composition and the preparation of the copy
used in F. Beaurline mentions the snag at the

---

12 King John, ed. L. A. Beaurline (Cambridge University
Press, 1990), in the New Cambridge Shakespeare series.

end of his account of the relationship between the two plays (p. 210 n. 3): 'It is also possible that *TR* has adapted Shakespeare's play from a lost early version or a scenario of it, but since we know nothing of that hypothetical script, speculation is fruitless.'[13] It may well be 'fruitless' but it should encourage a greater degree of scepticism as to whether a relationship between the two plays as they survive can be constructed.

Until Jowett's and Taylor's evidence for the work of the two scribes is published in full, Beaurline's reliance on it, despite a few additional pointers of his own, seems a little worrying. Indeed, Beaurline's use of the Oxford edition suggests it came too late to be of great use to him (there is no mention of Braunmuller's edition of the play). The *Textual Companion* is referred to in his analysis of the text (p. 185 n. 3), yet his apparatus draws only on the modern-spelling edition of 1986. His use of this leads him to restore the profanities throughout the play, attributing all but two (3.1.155 and 5.7.60) to Oxford in the apparatus; but his reasons for doing this are only explained in the 'Textual analysis' (p. 186 n. 1). The only other new reading he takes from Oxford is an aside at 5.1.78. His treatment of stage directions is extremely erratic, with nearly thirty editorial additions being introduced into the text, but although they are inserted within square brackets (except at 3.2.4), their editorial provenance is not recorded in the apparatus. Similarly, the apparatus is rather capricious in recording variant spellings in F.[14] Some relineation at 2.1.133 is not noted; the correct placing of a stage direction in F is not recorded in the apparatus at 3.2.4 and the direction in the apparatus at 4.2.66 should refer to 4.2.68.

Beaurline's text is reasonably accurate.[15] Despite his belief in the scribal origins of the copy for F, he is cautious about emending his text. He prints some interesting new readings – at 1.1.170 'above' for 'about', at 3.4.44 he follows Maxwell's conjecture to regularize the line by reading 'too holy', and he makes good sense of

the punctuation at 1.1.236–7. Less happy are 'consorted' at 3.4.2 and 'privity' at 4.3.16. He follows F convincingly at 2.1.335 'roam', 3.3.66 'My Lord' and 4.2.117 'care', but less so at 5.2.104 'banked'. His reasons for printing 'ear' at 3.3.39 and 'insensible' at 5.7.16 and for reassigning the speeches at the beginning of 5.6 are not quite persuasive. On the other hand, his explanation on textual grounds for the doubling but separate identities of the Citizen and Hubert in 2.1 and 3.3 is attractive.

King John is a play which editors like to discuss and annotate at length: Beaurline's contribution to the debate about it is very full and valuable. He shows that the play has interesting textual problems and important implications in the development of Shakespeare's career, but he also knows that it has real dramatic power.

Some of the same things might be said about G. R. Hibbard's edition of *Love's Labour's Lost* which is stronger textually than critically.[16] His ample introduction concentrates on the play's success in the theatre, its theatrical and linguistic patterning and their deliberate artificiality, which together produce a serious comedy. He deals briskly with its background in French history and rejects theories about contemporary literary allusions and the 'school of night': he compares Biron, interestingly, with the young John Donne (p. 40). While he accepts that Marcadé derives from Robert Wilson's *The*

---

13 He believes the author of *TR* had got hold of Shakespeare's plot of the play.

14 The edition's adoption of 'grandam' as against F's 'grandame' at 2.1.133 is recorded, but similar instances at 2.1.159 and 3.3.3, as well as F's 'fearefull bloudy' at 1.1.38 and 'faire-play' at 5.2.118 are not.

15 At 2.1.356 he prints 'those' for 'these', at 2.1.554 'With' for 'Some', at 3.1.63 'to' for 'or', at 3.1.102 'spill' for 'spill mine', at 3.3.43 'make' for 'made', at 3.3.51 'sounds' for 'sound', at 4.3.48 'vildest' for 'vilest' (as in the apparatus), at 5.7.34 'So' for 'Do', and at 5.7.43 'ungrateful' for 'ingrateful'.

16 *Love's Labour's Lost*, ed. G. R. Hibbard (Oxford, Clarendon Press, 1990), in the Oxford Shakespeare series.

Cobbler's Prophecy, Hibbard has no time for Glynne Wickham's theory that the play is indebted to the court entertainment of 1581 *The Four Foster Children of Desire* (pp. 47–8). Despite all this, it is hard to feel that Hibbard's critical introduction has a great deal more to offer than John Kerrigan's to the New Penguin edition (1982) in explaining the play's oddity and its distinctive intellectual toughness.

Hibbard adopts some of Kerrigan's solutions to the play's problems in his long and very clear account of its text. Essentially, he follows Werstine in believing that Q is a reprint of a lost good quarto set from foul papers. Q was set by three compositors who introduced a large number of errors. Shakespeare did not revise the play (pp. 76–7), but F was set by three compositors from Q with reference to 'a better text' (p. 81), which tends to validate the authenticity of F's final sentence. F tried to correct some of Q's mistakes, yet if it had access to a further witness, it is unfortunate that it made no attempt to clear up the false starts in 4.3 and 5.2 and that when it tried to sort out the speech headings in 2.1.114–25 it failed.

Hibbard explains the problems of speech prefixes in 2.1 by arguing that Shakespeare was 'dithering' (p. 61) or 'havering' (p. 63) over the names for Rosaline and Katherine. The wrong names in 4.2 are explained, perhaps, by Shakespeare's writing the scene in two different places where he was unable to refer to what he had already set down (p. 64). Hibbard relegates both the false starts after 4.3.292 and 5.2.804 to an appendix but prints 5.2.130–1 in his text. Another appendix is devoted to arguing that Armado's page should be called 'Moth' not (as in Kerrigan and the Oxford Shakespeare) 'Mote': the argument hinges on Costard's calling him a 'most pathetical nit' (4.1.147), where a 'nit' is an insect like a moth and a living not an inanimate creature. Both spellings have points in their favour and were apparently pronounced in the same way.

There are a few errors in Hibbard's textual apparatus, which is a little selective in some of the Q/F readings it records. He frequently rejects the emendations and conjectures proposed in the Oxford *Textual Companion*. Yet he follows Oxford's adoption of Rowse's conjecture at 4.2.12 and 20 of 'a "auld grey doe"' for QF's 'a *haud credo*' and adopts some other Oxford readings emending Latin at 4.2.126, omitting most of Jaquenetta's line at 4.2.128, sorting out the masquers at 5.1.115–16 and introducing slight changes at 5.2.46 and 273. Hibbard's own verbal emendations at 1.1.251, 2.1.227 are fairly minor; at 5.2.67 for the crux 'perttaunt like' he offers 'fortune-like', which is not very well supported by the parallel examples he cites, and his solution of 'mad man' at 5.2.338 for which he proposes 'map o' man' is ingenious; his change of Holofernes' final line in 5.1 to 'Most dull Dull' is not so happy. In annotating the play, Hibbard notes much of its linguistic ingenuity and is happy to acknowledge his own uncertainty over some matters (see 1.2.129, 3.1.48–52, 3.1.131 ('incony'), 4.2.157 and 5.2.323). For some reason the Oxford editors, especially in this play, do not record their changes to the plays' functional indentation.

The late Maurice Evans's *The Narrative Poems* for the New Penguin Shakespeare appears in a field with little competition.[17] It is a useful volume to have, with sound and unpretentious introductions and serviceable annotation which draws helpfully on the editor's knowledge of Spenser and Sidney. But there is a slight uncertainty of purpose about the volume which puts it at a disadvantage when compared with John Kerrigan's edition of the *Sonnets* in the same series. One difficulty is that the New Penguin Shakespeare has already issued a separate *Lucrece* edited by J. W. Lever (1971). Evans evidently took his text from this edition, reproducing several of its errors ('Upon' for 'Unto' in line 427, 'bank' for 'banks' in line 1119 and 'Then' for 'The' in line

---

17 *The Narrative Poems*, ed. Maurice Evans (Harmondsworth, 1990) in the New Penguin Shakespeare series.

1793), but also adding at least one of his own ('the' for 'that' in line 8) as well as a few typographical errors (see lines 271 and 552). In his commentary he is more aware of problems of modernization than Lever was, with notes on several passages which Lever ignores (456, 598, 812, 1338, 1436, 1444, 1648 and 1652), but not on others which deserve attention, in particular those at 352 and 950.

The editions of both *Lucrece* and *Venus and Adonis* ignore Oxford's work on the texts of the poems, although its readings are implicitly rejected on a number of occasions where Evans goes his own way. For example, he prefers 'morning' to 'morning's' in *Lucrece* line 24, 'blow' to 'blows' in line 550, 'Thy' to 'Thine' in line 1475 and more importantly 'wretched' to 'wreathed' in line 1662. But Oxford's presence can be strongly felt in the other poems which Evans includes. As well as 'The Phoenix and Turtle' and poems from *The Passionate Pilgrim*, Evans prints 'Shall I Die?' and other poems ascribed to Shakespeare under the heading 'The Epitaphs' – an unsatisfactory heading for the poem on James I, first printed in 1616. Yet Evans's inclusion of the last two groups of poems is, at best, half-hearted. Of Gary Taylor's claim for Shakespeare's authorship of 'Shall I Die?', he writes (pp. 63–4) 'I would think that overall, the weight of the evidence is against' it, adding 'In my own opinion it is possibly, though not probably, by Shakespeare ... My own largely subjective judgement of the poem is that it is not good enough for Shakespeare.' His text of the poem differs in several details from Oxford's, rejecting its readings in lines 10, 52, 61, 70 and 77. Evans chides the Oxford editors for not mentioning in the modern-spelling edition that its ascription to Shakespeare is 'at best doubtful' and points out scholarly scepticism about his authorship of the 'Epitaphs' (p. 67) and yet he himself does not relegate these poems to an appendix.

The last of the editions under review is the most innovative and the most sumptuously produced. Michael Warren's *The Parallel King Lear 1608–1623* forms a self-contained volume, well within the range of most scholars' purses.[18] Essentially it consists of photographic facsimiles of QI and F arranged in parallel columns on the left and right-hand sides of the inner margins of each two-page opening. In the outer margin Warren reproduces the corrected states of Q and F. Each speech, act and scene number in F and, where they begin a new line, stage direction has been cut out and mounted separately and the two texts of the play have been arranged to allow instant comparison between Q and F. By the use of shading, the texts reproduced are remarkably clear; the only minor and unavoidable awkwardness occurs where speeches have to be joined from one column or page to another, leaving a slight dislocation to the flow of the text (new pages are marked in Q and F, but columns in F are not). Both plays are supplied with Through Line Numbers.

Warren's intention is clear: he wants to provide 'as direct access as possible to the raw data crucial to any conception, discussion, edition, or performance of the play' (p. xxxvii). The only additional material he includes in this part of the project is a brief description of both quartos and F, followed by a general survey of the history of the treatment of the text (pp. xiv–xxi) and an annotated bibliography of studies in the textual history of the play (pp. xxiii–xxxiii). Throughout, Warren seeks to be impartial in his summaries.

The second part of his project is more ambitious and very much more expensive. The purchaser of *The Complete King Lear 1608–1623* is supplied with a folder containing photographic facsimiles of both the quartos and of the F text of the play as well as a soft-bound version of *The Parallel King Lear*.[19] The facsimiles of the

---

[18] *The Parallel King Lear 1608–1623*, prepared by Michael Warren (Berkeley, Los Angeles and London, University of California Press, 1989).

[19] *The Complete King Lear 1608–1623*, prepared by Michael Warren (Berkeley, Los Angeles and London, University of California Press, 1989).

texts reproduce, firstly, an ideal copy of the formes in invariant and corrected states and, secondly, formes in uncorrected states, the corrections being marked in the margins outside the text by asterisks.[20] Both sets of facsimiles are reproduced on unbound leaves, with the uncorrected states printed on only one side of the paper to facilitate comparison. Each text is accompanied by a booklet listing and discussing variants and obscured readings, as well as in the case of QI and F a table of the copies used, and lists of manuscript corrections in a copy of QI in the British Library (C.34.k.17) and of the corrections on the two known proof pages of F.

There can be no doubt of the importance of Warren's work or of the value of the full and lavish form in which it is presented to the reader. The materials appear to be scrupulously presented with the minimum of editorial interference.[21] Where he does comment as in his discussions of 'genuine' against 'doubtful' variants, Warren is careful and judicious. With his wife's help, Warren has selected, cut up and reproduced thousands of photographs to make his books. In doing this he is well aware that his work is in its own way created by just one more of those 'historically and socially conditioned yet idiosyncratic intelligences' which composed the original texts (pp. xx–xxi). *The Complete* and *The Parallel King Lear* show what photo-facsimiles on a grand scale can reproduce. At the same time they pose interesting questions about the nature of editing texts and above all about the rôle of the editor.

The scope and constraints of this year's survey have not allowed more than a brief mention of the following items: *Collections Volume XIV* of the Malone Society's publications, edited by Suzanne Gossett, Thomas L. Berger, H. R. Woudhuysen and John Pitcher contains seven short Jacobean academic plays from two manuscripts in the Folger Shakespeare Library; *The Queen of Corsica* by Francis Jaques, prepared by Henry D. Janzen, H. R. Woudhuysen, Lois Potter and John Pitcher for the Malone Society (1989): the unique manuscript of the play in the British Library is dated 1642; the Smock Alley prompt-book of *A Midsummer Night's Dream*, edited by G. Blakemore Evans for the Bibliographical Society of the University of Virginia (1989) is reproduced in facsimile and its two sets of revisions (the earlier of which may belong to between 1664 and 1692) are collated. Giorgio Melchiori's first instalment of Shakespeare's complete plays published by Arnoldo Mondadori (1990) in parallel English and Italian texts (the translations are by several hands), consists of *Le Commedie Eufuistiche: Shrew, Errors, Two Gentlemen, Love's Labour's* and *Dream*. There are a few textual notes on the page, some annotation at the end of each play and brief introductions to them, which include interesting tabular summaries 'delle strutture spazio-temporali', altogether forming an imaginative and attractively produced edition. A further Garland Shakespeare Bibliography (other than that mentioned in note 2 above) has appeared: *Coriolanus* compiled by Alexander Leggatt and Lois Norem (New York and London, Garland Publishing, 1989). The third of Kristian Smidt's five-part investigation of 'unconformities' in Shakespeare is devoted to *Unconformities in Shakespeare's Tragedies* (London, Macmillan, 1989).

---

[20] Q2 is simply reproduced from a Huntington copy and its variant forme from a British Library copy; this allows the blank pages in Q2 to be reproduced from an actual copy, whereas since QI is reproduced from an ideal copy Warren has omitted the blanks.

[21] Warren is a little unforthcoming about the question of tolerances in enlargement and/or reduction in his photo-facsimiles.

The coverage of periodical articles published towards the end of 1989 and during 1990 and of some books published in that year has had to be held over to next year.

BOOKS RECEIVED

This list includes all books received between 1 September 1989 and 31 August 1990 which are not reviewed in this volume of *Shakespeare Survey*. The appearance of a book in this list does not preclude its review in a subsequent volume.

Bratton, J. S., ed. *King Lear. Plays in Performance*. Bristol Classical Press, 1989 (paperback).

Fox, Hugh. *The Mythological Foundations of the Epic Genre: The Solar Voyage and the Hero's Journey*, Studies in Epic and Romantic Literature 1. Edwin Mellen Press, 1989.

Greetham, D. D., and W. Speed Hill, eds. *Text: Transactions of the Society for Textual Scholarship*, Volume 4. New York, AMS Press, 1989.

Hankey, Julie, ed. *Othello. Plays in Performance*. Bristol Classical Press, 1989 (paperback).

Kimberley, Michael. *Lord Ronald Gower's Monument to Shakespeare*, Stratford-upon-Avon Papers, 3. The Stratford-upon-Avon Society, 1989.

Nag, Ramendra Narayan. *Towards Hamlet*. Calcutta City Press,, 1990.

Rubinstein, Frankie, ed. *A Dictionary of Shakespeare's Sexual Puns and their Significance*, Second Edition. Macmillan, 1989 (paperback).

Seary, Peter. *Lewis Theobald and the Editing of Shakespeare*. Clarendon Press, Oxford, 1990.

Stock, R. D. *The Flutes of Dionysus. Daemonic Enthrallment in Literature*. University of Nebraska Press, 1989.

INDEX

INDEX

INDEX

INDEX

INDEX